MW01199373

THEATRES OF VIOLENCE

War and Genocide

General Editors: Omer Bartov, Brown University; A. Dirk Moses, European University Institute, Florence, Italy/University of Sydney

There has been a growing interest in the study of war and genocide, not from a traditional military history perspective, but within the framework of social and cultural history. This series offers a forum for scholarly works that reflect these new approaches.

"The Berghahn series Studies on War and Genocide *has immeasurably enriched the English-language scholarship available to scholars and students of genocide and, in particular, the Holocaust."*—**Totalitarian Movements and Political Religions**

For a full volume listing, please see back matter

THEATRES OF VIOLENCE
Massacre, Mass Killing and Atrocity throughout History

Edited by

Philip G. Dwyer and Lyndall Ryan

berghahn
NEW YORK · OXFORD
www.berghahnbooks.com

First published in 2012 by
Berghahn Books
www.berghahnbooks.com

©2012, 2015 Philip G. Dwyer and Lyndall Ryan
First paperback edition published in 2015.

All rights reserved.
Except for the quotation of short passages for the purposes
of criticism and review, no part of this book may be reproduced in any form
or by any means, electronic or mechanical, including photocopying, recording,
or any information storage and retrieval system now known or to be invented,
without written permission of the publisher.

Library of Congress Cataloging-in-Publication Data

Theatres of violence : massacre, mass killing, and atrocity throughout history /
edited by Philip G. Dwyer and Lyndall Ryan.
    p. cm. -- (Studies on war and genocide ; v. 11)
  Papers from an international interdisciplinary symposium held at Newcastle,
Australia, September 2008. Includes bibliographical references and index.
  ISBN 978-0-85745-299-3 (hardback. : alk. paper) -- ISBN 978-1-78238-922-4
(paperback : alk. paper) -- ISBN 978-0-85745-300-6 (ebook)
  1. Massacres--History--Congresses. 2. Mass murder--History--Congresses.
3. Atrocities--History--Congresses. I. Dwyer, Philip G. II. Ryan, Lyndall, 1943-
  D24.T54 2012
  303.609--dc23   2011032765

British Library Cataloguing in Publication Data

A catalogue record for this book is available from the British Library.

Printed on acid-free paper.

ISBN: 978-0-85745-299-3 hardback
ISBN: 978-1-78238-922-4 paperback
ISBN: 978-0-85745-300-6 ebook

PART III.   CONTESTED NARRATIVES: MEMORY,
            ATROCITY AND MASSACRE

PART IV.   THE DYNAMICS OF MODERN MASSACRE
           AND MASS KILLINGS

CONTENTS

₰₰₰

LIST OF TABLES, ILLUSTRATIONS AND MAPS

Tables

Illustrations

Maps

ACKNOWLEDGEMENTS

Unlike the claims made for genocide and the Holocaust, there is nothing unique about massacre. It is part and parcel of the evolution of humanity and has been a constant theme throughout recorded history. The papers in this volume are based on an international interdisciplinary symposium on the massacre in history organized by Philip Dwyer and Lyndall Ryan at Newcastle, Australia, in September 2008. A number of the essays published here were presented at the conference but have been reworked, revised and expanded in the light of discussions that took place during and after the conference. In addition to the contributors we would particularly like to thank Paul Bartrop, David Cahill, Robert Cribb and Piotr Kosicki whose presence and participation made the discussions at the symposium so worthwhile. Moreover, we solicited a number of other essays in order to fill lacunas and offer a more complete picture of mass killings throughout history. They shed different light on some well known massacres, as well as massacres that are less well known, touching on issues of gender, race, religion and empire. Longer versions of three of the chapters have been published elsewhere: Harper's chapter in *The William and Mary Quarterly*, 64:3 (2007); Dwyer's piece in *War in History,* 16:4 (2009); and Ryan's chapter in *Journal of Australian Studies*, 34:3 (2010). The authors would like to thank the publishers for permission to use revised and updated versions of that material.

The maps have been prepared by Robert Anders, School of Geography & Environmental Studies, University of Tasmania. The maps of the Americas incorporate data sourced from Environmental Systems Research Institute's (ESRI®) sample data disks, ESRI® Data & Maps 9.3, distributed under license agreement with ESRI's ArcGIS® software. Permission has been granted for use in map production by the data vendors who have supplied data on the sample data disks, which are protected under copyright laws. The vendors acknowledged and thanked for the provision of their data include DMTI Spatial Inc., USGS, ArcWorld™ Supplement, US Census, ArcUSA™ 1:25M, and Tele Atlas. The Australian maps are based on source data provided by Geoscience Australia.

The project could not have got off the ground without the support of the School of Humanities and Social Science at the University of Newcastle. We would also like to thank the anonymous readers at Berghahn for their suggestions. This book is part of an ongoing research programme encompassing aspects of the history of violence in the modern world. It is our hope that his volume will not only be used in the classroom but stimulate further debate and reflection about the nature of mass killing in the modern world.

INTRODUCTION

THE MASSACRE AND HISTORY

Philip G. Dwyer and Lyndall Ryan

Massacres have occurred throughout recorded history and are even known to have existed in pre-recorded times. Archaeologists have found, for example, evidence of a Neolithic massacre in Talheim, Germany, which is believed to have taken place over seven thousand years ago. The remains of thirty-four victims, male and female and ranging in age from two to sixty, were unearthed during digs in 1983 and 1984. They were bound and most killed by a blow to the left temple before being thrown into a pit.[1] There is more than enough evidence to suggest that as agricultural societies expanded in Neolithic times, so too did disputes over territory resulting in an increase in the frequency of massacres.[2] In recorded times, one of the earliest known reports of a massacre is to be found in the Bible, which details how, around 1350 BC, Joshua and the Israelites, after laying siege to Jericho, 'utterly destroyed all that was in the city, both man and woman, young and old, and ox, and sheep, and ass, with the edge of the sword... And they burnt the city with fire and all that was therein'.[3] It is a scene that has been played out countless times, almost as though it were part and parcel of warfare, although until quite recently scholars have paid scant attention to and failed to explain the dynamics and indeed the psychology of massacre.

Much of the scholarship surrounding mass killings has come out of genocide studies.[4] Indeed, the words 'massacre' and 'genocide' are still often used interchangeably, especially in genocide research where mass killings of innocent civilians come under scrutiny. Scholars have only recently turned their attention to the study of massacre as a separate phenomenon. Although the two approaches – genocide on one hand and massacre on the other – began along parallel paths of development, massacre research has been overshadowed by genocide studies to the point where few scholars outside the field of massacre studies differentiate between massacre, mass killing and genocide.

A number of scholars have nevertheless set themselves apart in the field of massacre studies. Brenda K. Uekert, a sociologist, investigated and analysed ten cases of government massacres in both authoritarian and democratic states across five global regions between 1987 and 1989.[5] She identified two types of government sponsored massacre: the 'politicidal massacre', designed to maintain the balance of power, and which occurred when the state, often authoritarian, felt threatened; and the 'genocidal massacre', designed to manipulate the balance of power, and which was used to promote or exacerbate ethnic tensions. Massacre in these instances was an act of state terror whose purpose was either to instil fear into the population or eradicate a particular group.

A few years later, Mark Levene and Penny Roberts attempted to establish a framework within which massacre could be examined seriously from a number of different perspectives.[6] Levene then attempted to set an agenda for the study of massacre in part by posing a number of simple but essential questions such as whether 'man's inhumanity to man' was the result of our evolution, whether one could proffer an overarching explanation, or whether massacre was simply an aberration that did not normally happen in 'civilized' societies.[7] It is of course impossible to answer these questions with any certainty – perhaps they are too broad – but they did prompt the other leading scholar in massacre studies, also a sociologist, Jacques Semelin, to argue that rather than dismissing massacre as an aberration, outside of rational discourse, it should be studied as a rational act with its own internal logic and therefore within the structures of social science. This is what he has attempted to do in a series of articles and books that have provided historians in particular with an interpretive framework to study the 'event of massacre', which include discussion of its function and characteristics, as well as a definition and methods to investigate it.[8] The act of massacre, Semelin has argued, is not so much an expression of power by a strong regime but a sign of its weakness. The preconditions suggest a state under siege from within in which 'the weight of fear and of the imaginary seem to be ever present'.[9] Massacre can therefore be initiated from 'above', by leading military and political and religious leaders, but it can also be initiated from 'below' by local militias or settlers on the colonial frontier, for example. Massacre is, in other words, a dynamic process which can easily get out of hand.

Notes for an Anatomy of Massacre

This collection sets out to differentiate even further the processes involved in massacre, mass killings and what often accompanies the sort of personalized killing that is dealt with here, atrocities committed against the bodies of the victims. Along with Jacques Semelin, massacre, we would like to underline, is an entirely separate phenomenon from genocide.[10] Genocide cannot occur without massacre, but massacres do occur without genocidal intent. As with the term 'genocide', so too is there little consensus over what actually constitutes a 'massacre' or indeed a 'mass killing'. Jacques Semelin defines massacre as 'a form of action that is most often collective and aimed at destroying non-combatants'.[11] As a general rule, this is true, but this neither takes into account the frequent occurrence of armed civilians killing other unarmed civilians or combatants in times of war, of oppressed peoples rising up against their oppressors,[12] or of the numbers of deaths that must occur. In a case study of 'rage and murder' that took place in an isolated French village in 1870, for example, Alain Corbin referred to the killing of one man by a group of local villagers as a 'massacre'.[13] In a sense, it was. The manner in which the killing took place, which involved torture committed against the victim by a number of members of the community, fits within the traditional, literary usage of the word and can legitimately be referred to as a 'massacre' because of the brutal nature of the act. It is not uncommon, in other words, for historians to refer to the killing of one or two people as massacre. We think it preferable, however, to see this kind of killing as murder or as lynching,[14] in part because the individual identity of the victim, unlike in the case of massacres, is entirely relevant.[15] In this respect, we would suggest, as has the Guatemala Human Rights Commission in the United States, that a minimum of three people must be killed, collectively, in order for the murders to make up a massacre.[16] On the other hand, a massacre must occur for a mass killing to take place, although mass killings are not, generally speaking, geographically or temporally limited, that is, they usually occur over a longer period of time and involve greater numbers of people than a massacre. Where mass killings occur, there is no intention to eliminate entirely the victim group in question. It is not genocide, although it may be a step along that path.

A distinction should in effect be made between a legal and an historical working definition of massacre. There is no legal definition of massacre (as there is for genocide). The International Criminal Court and the *International* Criminal *Tribunal* for the Former Yugoslavia do not use a definition of massacre in their proceedings against war criminals but instead rely on definitions of crimes against humanity. One of the articles – 7(1)(b), 'Crime against humanity of extermination' – refers to perpetrators killing 'one or more persons, including by inflicting conditions of life calculated to bring about the destruction of part of a population', and 'a mass killing of members of a civilian population'.[17] Individual homicide and mass killings are thus confounded. Amnesty International has defined massacre as the 'unlawful and deliberate killings of persons by reason of their real or imputed political beliefs or activities, religion, other conscientiously held beliefs, ethnic origin, sex, color or language, carried out by order of the government or with its complicity'.[18] For the historian, however, these definitions are too restrictive. They presuppose armed conflicts in which civilians are the target and do not, for example, take into account massacres committed by armed civilians against unarmed civilians or indeed unarmed combatants.

Levene and Roberts have rightly pointed out that massacres are one sided and that they thus demonstrate an 'unequal relationship of power'.[19] A massacre occurs then when 'a group of animals or people lacking in self-defence, at least at a given moment, are killed – usually by another group who have the physical means, the power, with which to undertake the killing without physical danger to themselves. A massacre is unquestionably a one-sided affair and those slaughtered are usually thus perceived of as victims; even as innocents'.[20] Levene considered that this definition took account of military massacres, as occurred, for example, after Culloden, when the remnants of a defeated army were cut down in flight; a Saint Valentine's Day massacre when one group of gangsters liquidates another; or a series of communal massacres, such as the killing of thousands of Ibos in Northern Nigeria in 1965.

Jacques Semelin has found that the key types of massacre were in a dichotomous relationship. For example, local massacres, such as face to face encounters where the perpetrators and victims probably knew each other, were the reverse of long-range massacres, such as aerial bombings, where neither the perpetrators nor the victims knew each other. Bilateral massacres which took place in civil wars were the reverse of unilateral massacres, which the state carried out against its people. Finally, what Semelin describes as 'mass massacres', as in Indonesia in 1965 or Rwanda in 1994 where between 500,000 and 800,000 were killed in a few weeks, were the reverse of the smaller scale 'mass massacres' as in Algeria and Columbia where large groups of people were killed in mass demonstrations in operation.[21]

More recently, David El Kenz, in a bid to further distinguish between violence, mass killings and what has been termed 'genocidal massacres', proposed a new term – massacrology – and outlined three problems common to the study of massacre. First, there is what he dubs the instrumentalization of the massacre event itself, that is, the concealment of the massacre among the perpetrators and the demand for recognition among the victims. This will often lead to different historical treatments of the event and, indeed, debates and controversies surrounding the histories of a region or country. That is why there is a debate about the nature of violence in the colonial frontier in Australia and North America. Second, if massacre remains a recurring theme throughout history, then recourse to an historical anthropology appears necessary, as long as it is contextualized. Third, sources are at the centre of any massacre study, and will reveal attitudes and constructions around the meaning of massacres that are significant to particular periods.

* * *

There is little possibility of there ever being a widely held consensus on what constitutes massacre, so varied are the circumstances in which they have occurred throughout history. What we hope to provide here is an 'overarching explanatory framework' that will throw light on both individual cases of massacre, mass killing and atrocity, as well as providing a mechanism for understanding the phenomenon across time and space.[22] We would thus describe massacre as the killing by one group of people by another group of people, regardless of whether the victims are armed or not, regardless of age or sex, race, religion and language, and regardless of political, cultural, racial, religious or economic motives for the killing. The killing can be either driven by official state policy or can occur as a result of the state's lack of control over those groups or collectives on the ground. Massacres, in other words, can occur with or without official state sanctions although the state, especially in the colonial context, often turns a blind eye to the killing of indigenous peoples by groups of settler-colonizers that are geographically removed from the centre of power and over which it has little or no control.[23] The massacre is limited in time, that is, it takes place over hours or days, not months and years, and is generally confined in geographical space.[24]

Some Common Features

Semelin distinguishes between massacres committed close up (person to person); those committed at a distance (such as bombings); bilateral massacres (committed during civil wars); unilateral massacres (committed by the state against its people); and 'mass massacres' which aim at eradicating a particular group (but which are not genocide).[25] One other category can be added to this. In her chapter in this collection, Inga Jones points to massacres taking place during the Wars of the Three Kingdoms occurring either in the heat of the moment, when for example a town was stormed after a siege – referred to as hot-blooded killing – and massacres that were planned – referred to as cold-blooded killing – such as the killing of Irish prisoners and the drowning of female and children camp-followers after the battle of Philiphaugh in 1645.

Massacres are, fundamentally, a masculine enterprise. They are often a brutal but short event, aimed at intimidating the survivors. Military massacres, especially those following battles or campaigns, are common to most periods of war from ancient times to the present. Massacres are rarely if ever spontaneous or irrational, even if the atrocities which often accompany the killings appear to verge on the unhinged.[26] A distinction can also be made between mass killings conducted from afar, as with the aerial bombing of civilians that occur as a result of advances in warfare and that are consequently distant and removed, and massacres that take place on the ground and which are therefore up-close and personal. The decision to exclude aerial bombings from a definition of massacre and to describe them as mass killings will no doubt irk some people. Some of the contributors to this volume see bombings as massacre. And since we have defined massacre as limited in time and space, the killing of large numbers of people over extended periods of time (weeks, months and even years) – such as the murder of hundreds of thousands in Russia during the Stalinist purges, or the man-made famines, or the killings that took place in Indonesia under Suharto in 1965 – are better categorized as mass killings, although massacres can occur within that time frame.

We would also argue that in order for massacre to occur the perpetrators have to be present at the killing site and that the act of killing has to involve the direct physical intervention of the perpetrator. This more narrow description does not necessarily exclude massacres committed by lone gunmen suffering from psychological problems of one kind or another and with which we have become all too familiar in recent times, from Columbine in the United States to Port Arthur in Australia. Most perpetrators of massacres, however, are sane and have clear intent, that is, they are 'normal' and are part of a wider community set on eliminating another group or community.

All of this leaves out a fundamental question surrounding the dynamics of massacre, namely, why groups kill other groups in the first place. Every massacre is surrounded by a particular set of circumstances, and the perpetrators are driven by different reasons that have to do with the place and timing of the killings. This is true even when there is a consistent pattern for the circumstances of massacre, as on the colonial frontiers in Tasmania and Victoria in Australia, and in California, Montana and Old North West in the United States. On the frontier, as the chapters by Rob Harper, Lyndall Ryan, Ben Madley, and Blanca Tovías de Plaisted show, the consistency in pre-conditions is extraordinary, namely, the alleged destruction of valuable property and/or the alleged killing of a colonist coupled with the over-riding belief that the Indigenous people have no right to the land. In these cases, massacre is a well-planned reprisal, usually in the form of an armed dawn attack on a camp of sleeping men, women and children.

Circumstances

Given the enormous variation in circumstances that can occur over time and place, it becomes problematic when trying to formulate a general theory of massacre. Mark Levene questioned whether massacre is a function of grass-roots 'fears, anxieties or even violent impulses which find their focus, or alternatively are projected into a convenient out-group'.[27] One can go even further and postulate, given the monotonous regularity with which massacres have occurred throughout the ages, whether there is not some kind of natural disposition in people that drive them to eliminate groups they see as a threat to their own survival, even though scholars tend to shy away from this kind of biological pre-determinism. John Docker has not. He suggests that the explanation for massacre might be found in our primate origins.[20] When that happens, he points out, the perpetrator can give himself up to an orgy of killing that can only be described as pleasurable.

This type of observation is, however, a statement of fact; it is not an explanation. Common to all types of killing is the distinction between groups. Once a group is perceived as the Other, 'a shifting and uncertain category' as Docker points out, even if they had lived in close proximity and cooperation up till that time, then the desire on the part of one group to eliminate the other group comes to the fore. Massacres and mass killings occur when a group of people or a community wishes to subjugate, eradicate, exact revenge on, or impose power and control over another population, or when it sees another group as a threat to its own survival. It is sometimes done to recover lost prestige, and sometimes done to change the existing political order. Religion and race undeniably play a role, but all massacres and mass killings, regardless of the circumstances, are 'political' in the broadest sense of the term. Scholars of massacre, however, would do well to delve a little deeper in order to go beyond the most obvious motives. Rob Harper makes the point in his case study of the massacre of 100 Moravian Indian converts in 1782. Each massacre, argues Harper, has to be placed in its social and political context. In doing so, and in moving beyond motive-centred interpretations, we can come to a better understanding of why and when massacres occur, why the perpetrators are so bent on the physical elimination of the Other, and why, more often than not, bystanders are prepared to look the other way.

The Perpetrators and the Victims

Local grievances can often begin the process towards massacre, but they invariably require a higher authority to either approve or to turn a blind eye to the killings.[29] This is certainly the case for the examples provided here on the Australian and US colonial frontiers, but similar scenarios occurred in other theatres, even if, once again, the circumstances surrounding this particular factor can vary. We can assume that in the case of the Khoisan people on the Eastern Cape frontier of South Africa, for example, that Dutch settlers who sent out raiding parties to kill Khoisan did so without the knowledge of any central authority, but with the complicit approval of the local Dutch communities.[30] In My Lai in Vietnam, the massacre was perpetrated by men who took the law into their own hands, relinquishing responsibility to a higher authority, and believing that they would either escape arrest or conviction.[31] While the perpetrators of genocide act on orders from the state, a massacre can be either ordered from above or it can be driven from below.

The targets of massacre are invariably groups of people who are defined as an unwanted Other – 'enemies of the Revolution' for example – or who, in the case of the colonial frontier, are in the possession of a resource desired by the colonists. The victims are consequently 'dehumanized', a necessary precondition in order for massacres to occur. The rhetoric of extermination, regardless of ideology or the degree of state control, is often therefore a prerequisite for the massacres to be carried out. They do not have to belong to a racial or religious Other – in the case of the civil war in the Vendée during the French Revolution, for example, or again during the English Civil War, victims were targeted because of their supposed political affiliations – but it generally is the case. The perpetrators, on the other hand, are more often than not young men,[32] although there are rare instances in which women also take part in massacres and mass killings.

Massacre and Atrocity as Performance

One of the distinguishing features of the My Lai massacre was that many of the victims were first tortured and mutilated, then killed, or mutilated after being killed. The study of atrocities, loosely defined as exactions committed by perpetrators against the body of a victim, living or dead, such as rape and torture or the removal of body parts, but which can also include instances of cannibalism, has not received much attention from scholars, although some sociological studies exist.[33] Massacres, and to an even greater extent atrocities, can be interpreted on one level as public, performative acts in which the body serves as a kind of stage on which suffering is inflicted. The victim thus becomes part of a perverse morality play, of sorts, in which the mutilated body serves as a warning to others. In Spain during the Napoleonic wars, for example, the mutilated body served as a warning to those who collaborated with the French as well as to those who opposed them. This can also occur in the modern urban context, as both Annie Pohlman has demonstrated for Indonesia, and Hélène Jaccomard for Paris in 1961, when a number of Algerians were found 'hanging from trees in the Boulogne woods, and others, disfigured and mutilated, floating on the Seine'.

When killers mutilate the body of their victims, either before or after the killing takes place, the type of mutilation carried out can often contain a symbolic dimension. As Natalie Zemon Davis has pointed out for the early modern period in Europe, mutilation often involved religious symbolism so that the removal of an offending body part – a hand, the tongue – was seen as a symbolic purging of the (social) body.[34] One can find the same potential symbolic value in mutilation in the modern era. Tutsi men were literally cut down to size by Hutus during the Rwandan crisis.[35] In Indonesia, the mutilated body of Communists, as Annie Pohlman shows in her chapter, served a similar function. Mutilation could also be a means of affirming the killers' identity upon the victims' bodies in which they transgress their own cultural taboos. 'It is another means of destroying the victims before killing them' but it could also mean that the killers gain pleasure from the act.[36]

* * *

Patterns of violence exist then across cultures and across the ages; the same atrocities are to be found in seventeenth-century England as in twentieth-century France or Indonesia. To understand them, however, they have to be placed in context. It is only once that has been done that we can hope to draw some preliminary overarching conclusions about massacre, mass killing and atrocity. From the studies in this collection, therefore, we can assert that:

* The perpetrators often (but not always) know the victims and have often (but not always) lived in close proximity to them for many years before the massacres and atrocities occur. This was the case, for example, in the Indonesian massacres of 1965–66. This was also the case for the settler-Aboriginal massacres on the Australian frontier; the perpetrators knew the victims well. In other instances, however, such as the Japanese sack of Nanking, or the Katyn massacres, the killing was often a calculated attack on unknown innocent people.

* The tendency to cover up a massacre or mass killing is a relatively recent phenomenon. Attitudes towards killing and massacre have distinctly evolved over time. In the ancient world, as is aptly pointed out by Jane Bellemore, the Romans not only widely practiced massacre, and boasted about it, as did Caesar in his semi-autobiographical work, the *Gallic Wars*, but they even exhibited it on monuments, such as Trajan's column. For the ancients, massacre was the right of the victor, and was practiced against those who were outside of civilization. In the sixteenth century, hostages were regularly taken from hostile communities and often consequently executed.[37] The denial of massacre therefore almost never occurred before the end of the eighteenth and the beginning of the nineteenth centuries. In the modern era, on the contrary, massacres are often reported as a 'battle' or military engagement. Various other code words exist, especially in the colonizers' lexicon, to describe what in effect is a massacre – 'dispersal', 'clash', 'collision', and 'rencontre' to name but a few. This seems to have been common on the Australian colonial frontier, where settlers, soldiers, Native Police and Military Police were the perpetrators. The corollary to that is the realization that the act of killing innocents is morally reprehensible, hence the desire to cover it up.

* In order for a massacre to be uncovered, it is either the sheer size of the killings that makes it impossible for them to remain ignored, such as at Srebrenica in July 1995 when more than eight thousand Bosnian men and boys were killed by Serbian troops, or when individuals, perpetrators or survivors speak out about their experiences. In many other instances, however, scholars only come to know of massacres and mass killings if they are later revealed in memoirs, letters, journals, oral accounts, more often than not long after the incident. Within these accounts, there is a tendency to provide minimal detail of the massacre in which the witness come perpetrator may have been involved, and a great deal more detail of massacres perpetrated by others. Writing in these instances can often act as a catharsis for both the perpetrators as well as those who managed to survive (although these are rare). Indeed, perpetrators sometimes assume the voice of the victims, describing the horrors they witnessed and experienced.

* Massacres can thus be 'discovered'. This was the case, for example, with the sites of mass killings during the Terror in Stalin's Russia in the 1930s, or indeed of the discovery of the Katyn graves in Poland in 1942. On that occasion, as Claudia Weber shows in her chapter, the discovery can be used by the perpetrators to cast doubt on their own responsibility, effectively laying the blame on others. On occasions when massacres occurred openly, on the other hand, they were meant to be public statements, examples that everyone knew of. On occasions when they were covered up and conducted in secret, it becomes much more difficult for succeeding generations to determine when and where those massacres may have occurred and who was implicated in them, either as victims and perpetrators. As François-Xavier Nérard demonstrates, the Soviet State was so secretive about its state-sponsored mass killings that even the executioners were later executed. Even when massacres are later discovered, not always evident given that perpetrators generally attempt to hide the traces of their actions and deny any involvement in them, some in the public, unable or unwilling to confront their own nation's dark past, will not believe that what occurred was a massacre at all.[38]

* Discovery raises questions about who will be believed, who are the witnesses, and how they can speak out. Witnesses can rarely speak out at the time, so formal investigations usually begin long after the event, when witnesses find the courage to speak out.[39] When that happens, however, perpetrators are sometimes already immune from conviction. Particular massacres, moreover, can often traumatize entire communities either because they were complicit in them or because they had lost so many of their own people. The act of investigation in war crimes trials or political mediation does not always bring reconciliation. In any event, the witness, who may not speak out until long after the event, is critical to understanding how historians can investigate massacre. Rather than relying on the evidence closest in time to the incident, the

historian may have to rely on the evidence furthest in time. In taking this approach to interpreting the evidence, the historian needs a coherent methodology.[40]

Understanding the Perpetrators

Descriptions of particular massacres are not enough to capture the processes behind the mass killings. In general, the focus of case studies or theoretical works which attempt to explain the dynamics of massacre focus on the victims. Little attention is paid to the perpetrators of massacre, their motives, and the psychological processes involved, except in the broadest of terms. Massacres are generally explained away by racial, political or religious hatreds. That only goes part way to explaining the dynamics of killing. Important too is understanding the cultural and social contexts which enable what are very often people inexperienced in the act of killing to now commit the most barbarous acts. In short, what enables an individual to take part in a massacre, what are the inner workings of the perpetrators, their logic, their thought processes, and actions? How does an ordinary person become a mass murderer?

In the search for answers to these questions, massacre studies can learn much from the mechanics of killing and the Holocaust. Barbarity is not a biological predisposition – it is learned, cultivated and taught and is the end product of interaction with others.[41] It is, in one sense, within the reach of any individual who might be subjected to the processes of transformation. As we see time and again in these pages, ordinary people, in the right circumstances, can commit extraordinary acts of barbarity.

Nor do we know much about the psychological impact of mass murder on the perpetrators. Dwyer's essay is one of the few that dwells on the horror relived many years later by men who either witnessed or carried out atrocities and who brought themselves to write about it, in this case, veterans of the Napoleonic wars. The men (and women) who commit massacres are not sadists and do not do so for pleasure. They are often traumatized by what they have done or seen for many years after. While the acts they are involved in might be barbaric, the people committing them are not: they come from all walks of life.

The Future of Massacre Studies

The studies in this collection show the potential for massacre within all societies throughout the ages to the point where, it could be argued, 'civilization' and 'massacre' go hand in hand. Violence, mass killings, and atrocities have always existed; this should as such be seen as key to understanding how, when and why massacres occur. The question, however, should not be whether they occur as a result of 'rational' processes or whether they should be regarded as fundamentally 'irrational' or 'barbaric'. The question should be about the conjunction of how rationalized society and violent passions' erupt at particular points in time to produce massacres and mass killings.[42] Jacques Semelin has argued for the importance of studying massacres not only as isolated incidents, and as the most dramatic and tragic form of an overall process of destruction, but also as an organized process of civilian destruction, targeting both people and their property. These one-sided acts of destruction, aimed at individuals and groups who are not in a position to defend themselves, involve 'a totally dissymmetrical relationship between aggressor and victim' and could involve at some point a role reversal where the victims in turn become murderers.[43]

There is a need for a coherent method of approach to the study of massacre in all its ramifications. In 2005, Jacques Semelin cautioned researchers about the pitfalls of comparison of massacres in relation to equivalence or uniqueness. He argued that each sequence of massacres had their own uniqueness that needed to be explored in historical context. None could transcend history. Above all it was critical for the massacre researcher to be free from ideological and normative approaches. The fact that most modern massacres are carried out in secret suggests that a forensic approach is the best way to proceed, one which covers the following: an identification and profile of the perpetrators and victims according to age, sex, social origin, motive and benefit; constructing the figure of the enemy; the modus operandi; the historical time frame; and the political and media effects and 'aftermath narratives'.[44]

Massacre studies perform a critical role in the protection of human rights. The modern conception of the state is that it holds a monopoly over violence and that, when necessary, it will use its armed forces – the army, the police – to suppress dissent and rebellion. With regard to massacres, however, the question is much more complex. While it is a truism that the state can impose itself on a people through the use of extreme violence, repressed and abused peoples can also rise in revolt against the state, resorting to often extreme measures of violence against its representatives or supporters. The appearance of Mark Levine and Penny Robert's seminal work, *The Massacre in History*, in 1999, was one of the first attempts to draw attention to the phenomenon in a systematic way. Since then, the field of massacre studies has moved onto new ground. Although there is much about the dynamics of massacre that remains to be understood, historians are also interested in how massacres are remembered and recalled, and just as importantly, how they are represented and made use of in history. The increased attention to the history of violence has shed light on mass killings and atrocities in more general terms, to the point where we now better understand specific massacres and mass killings. It is now obvious, in the light of recent work on memory and massacre, that how the ways these events are recalled and celebrated is tremendously important for our understanding of their impact on the societies in which they took place.

Massacre is never an aberration. It is an integral part of human history. The twenty essays in this collection range in chronological time, from prehistory (Docker) to the Greek and Roman periods (Bosworth, Baynham, Bellemore), across the Medieval and Early Modern periods (Marvin, Jones), to the Napoleonic era (Dwyer), nineteenth-century colonial settler societies (Harper, Ryan, Madley, Tovías de Plaisted, Schlunke), to twentieth-century imperialist societies (Finaldi, Weber, Nérard) and their responses to colonial resistance (Jacommard, Pohlman, Laderman, Baines) to incidents in the late twentieth-century postcolonial societies (Pohlman, Baines), and the early twenty-first-century war in Afghanistan (Rockel). The collection, deliberately, does not contain essays about the Holocaust and genocide. Rather, the purpose is to explore the varieties of massacre across a long period of historical time (*la longue durée*), and how each is remembered, as a way of drawing out the differences and similarities. We trust that the collection will encourage further research on other instances of massacre and further inform this emerging and increasingly important field of study.

Notes

1. T. Douglas Price, Joachim Wahl and R. Alexander Bentley, 'Isotopic Evidence for Mobility and Group Organization among Neolithic Farmers at Talheim, Germany, 5000 BC', *European Journal of Archaeology*, 9 (2006), 259–84.
2. Alain Beyneix, 'Aux origines de la guerre: actes de violence et massacres dans la néolithique européenne', *Revue des études anciennes*, 103 (2001), 329–42.
3. Cited in Geoffrey Parker, 'The Etiquette of Atrocity', in idem., *Success is Never Final. Empire, War, and Faith in Early Modern Europe* (New York, 2002), 151.
4. See, for example, Robert Gellately and Ben Kiernan (eds), *The Specter of Genocide: Mass Murder in Historical Perspective* (New York, 2003).
5. Brenda Uekert, *Rivers of Blood: A Comparative Study of Government Massacres* (Westport, Conn., 1995), 16, 21.
6. Mark Levene and Penny Roberts (eds), *The Massacre in History* (Oxford, 1999).
7. Mark Levene, 'Introduction', in Levene and Roberts (eds), *The Massacre in History*, 2.
8. Jacques Semelin, 'In Consideration of 'Massacre', *Journal of Genocide Research*, 3 (2001), 378.
9. Semelin, 'In Consideration of 'Massacre', 384.
10. Jacques Semelin, 'Analysis of a Mass-Crime. Ethnic Cleansing in the Former Yugoslavia, 1991-1999', in Gellately and Kiernan (eds), *The Specter of Genocide*, 354, differentiates between 'mass crime',' 'genocide' and 'massacre'.
11. Jacques Semelin, *Purify and Destroy: The Political Uses of Massacre and Genocide* (New York, 2007), 4.
12. As happened, for example, in Peru (David Cahill, 'Genocide from Below: The Great Rebellion of 1780–82 in the Southern Andes', in A Dirk. Moses (ed.), *Empire, Colony, Genocide: Conquest, Occupation, and Subaltern Resistance in World History* (New York, 2008), 403–23; and in Haiti in the 1800s (Philippe R. Girard, 'Caribbean Genocide: Racial War in Haiti, 1802–4',' *Patterns of Prejudice*, 39 (2005), 138–61). See also the studies in Nicholas A. Robins and Adam Jones (eds), *Genocides by the Oppressed: Subaltern Genocide in Theory and Practice* (Bloomington, 2009).

13. Alain Corbin, *The Village of Cannibals: Rage and Murder in France, 1870* (Cambridge, Mass., 1992).

14. On lynchings and their dynamics in the United States see, for example, Christine Harold and Kevin Michael DeLuca, 'Behold the Corpse: Violent Images and the Case of Emmet Till', *Rhetoric & Public Affairs*, 8 (2005), 263–86; and Kirk W. Fuoss, 'Lynching Performances, Theatres of Violence', *Text and Performance Quarterly*, 19 (1999), 1–27.

15. Tzvetan Todorov, *The Conquest of America: The Question of the Other* (New York, 1992).

16. Guatemala Human Rights Commission/USA, *Information Bulletin*, 7 (October/November 1989), 1.

17. The Official Journal, International Criminal Court, http://www.icc-cpi.int/Menus/ICC/Legal+Texts+and+Tools/Official+Journal/Elements+of+Crimes.htm

18. Amnesty International Report, 1983, 5.

19. Levene, 'Introduction', in Levene and Roberts (eds), *The Massacre in History*, 1, 4.

20. Levene, 'Introduction', in Levene and Roberts (eds), *The Massacre in History*, 5.

21. Jacques Semelin, 'From Massacre to the Genocidal 'Process', *I nternational Social Science Journal*, 174 (2002), 435.

22. The term is from Dan Stone, *History, Memory and Mass Atrocity: Essays on the Holocaust and Genocide* (London, 2006), vii.

23. See, for example, Tony Roberts, *Frontier Justice: A History of the Gulf Country to 1900 (*St Lucia, Qld., 2005).

24. Levene, 'Introduction', in Levene and Roberts (eds), *The Massacre in History*, 6.

25. Semelin, 'From Massacre to the Genocidal 'Process', 435, 436.

26. Semelin, *Purify and Destroy.*

27. Levene, 'Introduction', in Levene and Roberts (eds), *The Massacre in History*, 6.

28. On the other hand, Robert Gellately and Ben Kiernan, 'The Study of Mass Murder and Genocide', in idem. (eds), *The Specter of Genocide: Mass Murder in Historical Perspective* (Cambridge, 2003), 10, think there is little to be gained from the notion that human nature 'explains' the collective drive to kill.

29. Levene, 'Introduction', in Levene and Roberts (eds), *The Massacre in History*, 15.

30. See Nigel Penn, *Forgotten Frontier: Colonist and Khoisan on the Capes Northern Frontier in the 18th Century* (Athens, 2005).

31. See Kendrick Oliver, *The My Lai Massacre in American History and Memory* (Manchester, 2006).

32. Levene, 'Introduction', in Levene and Roberts (eds), *The Massacre in History*, 18; Gellately and Kiernan, 'The Study of Mass Murder', 13.

33. See, for example, Michael Humphrey, *The Politics of Atrocity and Reconciliation. From Terror to Trauma* (London, 2002). On legal attitudes towards rape in France at the end of the eighteenth century see, Georges Vigarello, *A History of Rape: Sexual Violence in France from the 16th to the 20th Century* (Malden, Mass., 2001), 87–102. On rape and warfare in the modern context, see Joanna Bourke, *Rape: A History From 1860 to the Present Day* (London, 2007), 357–86.

34. Natalie Zemon Davis, 'The Rites of Violence: Religious Riot in Sixteenth-Century France', *Past and Present*, 59 (1973), 57–65.

35. Christopher C. Taylor, *Sacrifice as Terror: The Rwandan Genocide of 1994* (Oxford, 1999), 99–106, 127–42.

36. Jacques Semelin, 'Towards a Vocabulary of Massacre and 'Genocide', *Journal of Genocide Research*, 5 (2003), 207–208.

37. Parker, 'The Etiquette of Atrocity', in idem., *Success is Never Final*, 145.

38. This was the case for some in the American public who believed My Lai was concocted by Viet Cong sympathizers (Oliver, *The My Lai Massacre*, 53).

39. Semelin, 'In Consideration of 'Massacre', 388.

40. Semelin, 'Towards a Vocabulary of Massacre and 'Genocide', 200.

41. Henri Zukier, 'The Twisted Road to Genocide: On the Psychological Development of Evil during the Holocaust', *Social Research*, 61 (1994), 444.

42. The same question is asked of the Holocaust by Stone, *History, Memory and Mass Atrocity*, 12.

43. Semelin, 'From Massacre to the Genocidal 'Process', 436.

44. Semelin, *Purify and Destroy*, 376–78.

PART I

*MASSACRE AND ATROCITY IN THE
ANCIENT AND PRE-MODERN ERAS*

CHAPTER 1

THE ORIGINS OF MASSACRES

John Docker

Extreme violence, as in war, massacre and often in genocide, raises disturbing questions about us as a species. Extreme violence haunts our sense of the fundamental nature of humanity, of history as progress, of the ethical bases of societies, of the honour of nations, of ethnic and cultural identity, of intellectual life itself, which is intricately entwined with all these questions. Massacre and genocide studies, separate yet closely related fields, are moved by an anxiety that genocide and massacre possess features that may be impossible to explain. For example, why do groups suddenly turn on their neighbours with whom there may have been friendly relations for many years, why do massacres occur at certain times and not others, in what ways do massacres involve or not involve state authorities, or are massacres coldly calculated or inspired by passion and fantasy? Why do massacres often involve the most appalling atrocities, as in mutilation, disembowelling, cannibalism, the drowning of or setting fire to victims? Are certain kinds of societies, like democracies or totalitarian or authoritarian regimes, less or more propitious to massacres happening? How implicated historically is religion across the world?

Massacre scholars like Jacques Semelin emphasize that such dreadful happenings constitute enigma and mystery.[1] We might say that the genre of massacre studies, in its epistemological uneasiness, finds itself drawn to the baroque and Gothic, genres of disorientation and derangement. A methodological premise of massacre studies – we can see it in Mark Levene's work as well as that of Semelin – is that massacres are characteristically so gruesome that in trying to comprehend them no single discipline in the humanities and social sciences will necessarily suffice; we need all our scholarly resources, from anthropology to history to sociology to psychology to the study of literature and art.[2] We must, says Semelin, always be 'multi-factoral'.[3] Even then, as Mark Levene and Semelin stress, caution is always required in our attempts to establish general patterns or characteristics; in the rhetoric of massacre studies there is a fondness for terms like 'however' or 'yet' or 'that said', as soon as a general proposition is advanced.

In genocide and massacre studies, methodology must be both cautious and daring. Dan Stone urges those who study extreme violence and destruction to be as imaginative and innovative as possible in seeking explanations,[4] and suggests that historians draw on other disciplines like anthropology and cultural theory.[5] Stone proposes that modern genocides and massacres, such as in Cambodia and Rwanda, the Rape of Nanjing and My Lai, share, in anthropological terms, a transgressive violence: the enjoyment of violence, including killing and anticipation of killing, and the theatre of violence itself.[6] The perpetrators enjoy the acts of violence to a degree that can be called orgiastic, and together, in the act of killing, the perpetrators form temporary ecstatic communities, experiencing a heightened sense of belonging to their own group in the act of performing violence, which may also be erotically charged: a collective effervescence in belonging. Like Levene and Semelin, Stone believes that extreme violence and destructiveness dissolve the opposition between the civilized and barbarous, referring to George Bataille's contention that the same peoples can be alternately barbarous and civilized in their attitudes and actions; so called ordinary or normal people, says Stone, commit genocide and massacres.[7] Indeed, we might reflect that in history the very distinction between the civilized and barbarous so favoured in European and Western history is a major cause of violence, including extreme violence, upon those considered uncivilized or less civilized.

As fields, genocide studies and massacre studies overlap but can also follow different paths. Although genocide as a mode of inter-group violence frequently involves massacre, massacres can be a distinct and more diffuse phenomenon, involving for example the actions of a single individual. Thus violence against groups can encompass the killing of twenty-nine Palestinian Muslim worshippers by Baruch Goldstein in Israeli-occupied Hebron in February 1994, or the lone gunman who in March 1996 walked into a school in the Scottish town of Dunblane and fatally shot sixteen little children and their teacher.[8]

Concepts were often once metaphors, or concealed metaphors within them; concepts carry a history of such metaphoric traces like a palimpsest, creating ambivalence and layered shifting meanings.[9] In France in the sixteenth century, the term 'massacre' was thus once used for a butcher's chopping block. In 1545, the judges of the sovereign court of Provence undertook a campaign that has been referred to as religious cleansing, attacking Protestant heretics, such as the Waldensians, involving assaults on their communities as part of a larger pattern of campaigns to extirpate the growing Protestant heresy. A pamphlet around this time referred to the campaign against the Waldensians as 'un massacre', and the name stuck. In its palimpsestial history as a concept then, massacre suggests, in the metaphor of the butcher's chopping block, a swift and terrible action. But from the beginning massacre could also be recognized as part of a longer term process, in this particular instance involving the decades long campaign against Protestant heretics that would culminate in the spectacular St Bartholomew massacre of August 1572. From France, the term then entered the English political vocabulary.[10] The term massacre then encompasses within itself the possibility of both event and process or sequence.

Raphaël Lemkin Defines Genocide

The original definition of genocide so eloquently proposed by Raphaël Lemkin, the brilliant Polish-Jewish and then American jurist in his 1944 book *Axis Rule in Occupied Europe*, is far more wide-ranging than definitions proffered in the decades that followed, especially those of North American sociologists, influenced by recognition of the Holocaust from the 1970s to the 1990s, which reduced genocide to clearly intentional state-directed mass death.[11] Lemkin suggested that his new concept was derived from the Latin *cide* and the Greek word *genos* (tribe, race). Genocide, then, shares with terms like tyrannicide, homicide, fratricide a notion of sudden sharp action, a terrible event or episode. However, in insisting on genocide as wide-ranging, in both his published writings and in his manuscript book on the worldwide history of genocide which remained unfinished and unpublished when he died in 1959, Lemkin was suggesting that genocide could thereby include long-term and incremental processes as well as catastrophic events, acts or episodes.

According to Lemkin, genocide is to be regarded as composite and manifold; it signifies a coordinated plan of different actions aiming at the destruction of the essential foundations of life of a group. Such actions can but do not necessarily involve mass killing. They involve considerations that are cultural, political, social, legal, intellectual, spiritual, economic, biological, physiological, religious, and moral.[12] Genocide can encompass long-term processes like settler colonialism that may include destructive acts, episodes or events:

> Genocide has two phases: one, destruction of the national pattern of the oppressed group; the other, the imposition of the national pattern of the oppressor. This imposition, in turn, may be made upon the oppressed population which is allowed to remain, or upon the territory alone, after removal of the population and the colonization of the area by the oppressor's own nationals.[13]

Lemkin's definition of genocide here as a two-fold process of destruction and replacement, a process that entwines genocide and colonization, has explosive implications, and proved a major inspiration for the New Genocide Studies which has flourished since the 1990s.[14] In the unfinished manuscript book, Lemkin develops a sophisticated methodology that permits the possibility of intricate and subtle analyses of genocide. He points out that the relationship between oppressor and victim in history is always unstable, and that in world history there are many examples of genocidal victims transforming into genocidists, the formerly persecuted into the persecutors of others. He highlights recurring features in historical genocides: mass mutilations; deportations under harsh conditions often involving forced marches; attacks on family life, with separation of men and women and the removal of the opportunity of procreation; removal and transfer of children; destruction of political leadership; death from illness, hunger, and disease through overcrowding on reserves and in concentration camps.[15] Is it necessary to observe how similar such phenomena of genocide are to at least some features of massacre?

The Origins of Violence

Discussions of genocide, colonialism and empire often focus too narrowly on modernity, as if that is sufficient to illuminate all we need to know about the questions we ask. The notion of genocide, however, can indeed go back a long way, and has attracted the attention of key theorists in primatology and world history such as Jane Goodall and Jared Diamond. Goodall's premise is that since humans and chimpanzees once diverged from common stock, behaviour patterns that exist in modern humans and modern chimpanzees were probably present in that common ancestor, and therefore in early humanity as well.[16] Part of her study is devoted to the aggression and violence that occurred when a group from the Kasakela community of chimpanzees split away and began to live in a different valley. In the 1970s, Goodall and her fellow field workers recorded the assaults on and dispersal of the breakaway Kahama Valley community by the Kasakela group, their relatives and with whom they had had affectionate relationships. It was in 1972 that Goodall's observers recognized that the new community, the Kahama group, had come into existence at Gombe, but it was to last for only five years. In 1974 the Kasakela males initiated a southward movement of violent aggression that culminated in 1977 in the complete destruction of the Kahama community and annexation of the Kahama community range. Goodall describes in detail the 'consistently brutal and protracted' attacks on members of the Kahama group. In 1978 the Kasakela community began to sleep as well as feed in what had been Kahama territory.[17]

Goodall speculates on the evolutionary issues raised by this genocidal episode for chimpanzees and early humans alike. For one thing, she finds the term 'xenophobia' inadequate for what she and her fellow field observers witnessed and recorded. Goodall ponders that the members of what became the Kahama community had, before the division into two groups, enjoyed close and friendly relations with those who would become their aggressors. However, by seceding, Goodall reflects, the Kahama chimpanzees lost their right to be regarded as group members, and were instead now treated as strangers. The category of stranger is a shifting and uncertain one.[18] Once they were no longer recognized as belonging to the Kasakela group, the Kahama could now be considered as though they were no longer fellow chimpanzees or, as Goodall wryly puts it, they were *dechimpized*.[19] They could now be treated as if they were prey animals, to be hunted and slain. In her reflections on such aggression for human evolution, Goodall conjectures that since warfare involves conflict between groups, rather than between individuals, warfare has, through the genocide that occurs during war, played a major role in group selection.[20]

What interests Jared Diamond in Goodall's evocation of the chimpanzee genocide is that, lacking weapons, the Gombe chimpanzees are largely inefficient in their killing compared to humans. Diamond refers to how by contrast Australia's settlers, who were highly armed, 'often succeeded in eliminating a band of Aborigines in a single dawn attack'.[21] Diamond defines genocide much as we might define massacre in certain of its manifestations, as 'collective killing'. Diamond argues that genocide among human groups probably began millions of years ago, when the human species was just another big mammal. Human group living, he suggests, probably came about as a way of defence against other human groups. In history, the main danger to human life has come from other humans.[22] He believes that perhaps the commonest motive for 'collective killing' in history occurs in disputes over *Lebensraum*, when a 'militarily stronger people attempt to occupy the land of a weaker people, who resist'.[23]

This fits with Diamond's view of agriculture as a 'two-edged sword'. He questions the conventional 'progressivist' view that situates agriculture, from its origins in the Near East around 8000 BC, as a sacred milestone in humanity's march towards civilization. On the contrary, says Diamond, we should return a mixed report card on the introduction of agricultural society into history, with some gains and many losses for humanity,[24] not least its introduction of what he refers to as 'crowd epidemics' like cholera, measles, tuberculosis, leprosy, smallpox, and bubonic plague, diseases that could not survive and persist in small, scattered bands of hunters and gatherers who often shifted camp, but could thrive in sedentary living and cities.[25]

Farming, and the storage of food which accompanies it, also introduced, Diamond believes, more curses for humanity, breaking with the patterns of egalitarianism that generally characterize hunter-gatherer societies. Who can appropriate stored food and who can control it led to class divisions in farming societies. The specialization afforded by agricultural societies also introduced 'standing armies of professional killers'. Agricultural societies, says Diamond, have brought humanity 'starvation, warfare, and tyranny'.[26] Diamond concludes his reflections by suggesting that at the end of the Ice Age, the choice by some hunter-gatherer groups to adopt agriculture, even if they were in no position to anticipate the 'evils of farming', led to a new global force for destruction. Huntergatherers were forced out of all areas of the world that farmers wanted, and persist now only in the Arctic, deserts, and some rainforests.[27]

What we can draw from world history works like those of Diamond or Hugh Brody's powerful book *The Other Side of Eden* (2000), on huntergatherers in the High Arctic of Canada, is that in history, inter-group violence and massacre were immensely and disastrously intensified with the coming of agricultural societies, driven by a metaphysical imperative to spread across the globe, and to keep spreading whatever the consequences. Such has been the world we have lived in for the past eight thousand years.

Pericles, Thucydides, and the Idea of Europe

In both Herodotus' *Histories* and Thucydides' *History of the Peloponnesian War* there are stories of protest at and criticism of the inter-group violence involved in war, colonizing and empire. Thucydides' *History*, for example, is harshly critical of the Athenian desire for war and the ethical deterioration in Athenian society to which this desire led, including attitudes to war, empire and subject peoples of the statesman Pericles. One can feel confident in making this assertion because of recent historiography in classical studies concerning ancient Athenian democracy and war. David Pritchard, for example, has drawn attention to Athens' enthusiasm for war, while Sophie Mills evokes an Athenian self-image that saw war as admirable and beneficent, contrasting it to Thucydides' highly critical stance.[28]

The misery of war, civil war, colonization, and attempted extensions of empire are features of Thucydides' *History*, with egregious examples of genocide, population transfer or ethnic cleansing, and massacre, examples so appalling in their implications that Thucydides' *History* has forever since shadowed the claims of democracies to be superior in history. In Thucydides' *History*, we witness Pericles as foremost among those, Athenian or Spartan, who incited the war of nearly thirty years. A brilliant orator in the Sophist tradition, in his speeches to the assemblies Pericles tells his fellow citizens how Athens acquired its greatness: 'the reason why Athens has the greatest name in all the world is because she ... has spent more life and labor in warfare than any other state, thus winning the greatest power that has ever existed in history, such a power that will be remembered for ever by posterity'.[29] Athens, Pericles insists, had become a great city because of the warfare practiced by their forebears that established their empire. Whatever the feelings of the peoples of the subject states, the empire was the means of making Athens great, to be remembered for all time for its civilized achievements: democracy, equality before the law, advancement by merit, relaxed freedom and tolerance in private life, laws protecting the oppressed, the beauty and good taste of Athenian homes, excellent education system, and Athens as an open city (2.35–42).

Pericles' speeches reveal the kind of nationalist and ethnocentric values and imperial hauteur and arrogance that increasingly alarmed the other Hellenic nations, including Athens' own allies and subject states, who more and more tried to revolt and break away. Pericles' long-term concern, it is evident, was with Athens itself, its survival and continuance as an imperial power. In the stress of the plague that almost immediately struck Athens after the war had begun, he urges his fellow Athenians to recall their 'superiority' and 'imperial dignity': they must hold onto their empire even when they know that they have incurred the 'hatred' of its subject peoples in administering it. Pericles even admits that it may have been wrong to have taken the empire in the first place, because it has become a 'tyranny'; but, if the Athenians wish to continue as a great society, they must not let their empire go (2.62–63).

As the war continued, the Athenians' ethical deterioration, an increasing heartlessness, a lack of sympathy and empathy with others subject to Athens or those who should in their view be subject to Athens, is chillingly evident. Such heartlessness is particularly striking in two scenes involving a near massacre and an actual massacre: the Mytilinean Debate and the Melian Dialogue.[30] In the Mytilinean Debate, the demagogue Cleon distinguished himself by declaring to the assembly that to feel pity and compassion for a conquered people like the Mytilineans, who had tried to revolt, was against the interests of an imperial power like Athens, which must accept that it was a tyranny and act accordingly; for Cleon, the rights and wrongs of why Mytilene attempted to revolt were irrelevant (3.37–40). Cleon recommended mass death for the Mytilineans, though this was averted at the last moment (3.49). In the Melian Dialogue, presented in Book 5, the people of the island of Melos, originally a colony of Sparta, wished to preserve their longstanding independence and to stay neutral in the war between Sparta and Athens. Athens refused their offer of neutrality and friendship, and the Melians were destroyed in the subsequent siege.[31]

Thucydides helps us to reflect on how much, in democracies ancient and modern, hubris, with its thirst for power and glory through war, is embodied in recurring figures like the statesman, the demagogue, the parvenu, and the adventurer, figures who take to the political stage with relentless enthusiasm. The *History* decisively explodes the myth that because a society (like ancient Athens) is democratic, it cannot engage in destruction, genocide, massacre, and cruelty. Quite the contrary: democratic nation-states that are also settler-colonial in character or possess a colonizing empire or work through an imperium are especially likely to perpetrate such acts. Classical Athenian culture bequeathed to Europe and the West a dual, uncertain, and ambivalent legacy in relation to war, conquest, empire, and colonization.

On one hand, descending from Pericles there is self-admiration and self-idealization in the idea of European societies engaging in war, conquest, empire and colonization for beneficent and selfless reasons, always with honourable intentions. On the other hand, there is a counter-tradition, evident in Thucydides' cosmopolitanism, anti-ethnocentrism, and internationalism, and in the powerful denunciations of and protests at genocide and massacre, including the slaying of men and deportation and enslavement of women and children, in Euripides' Trojan plays. In this counter-tradition, the human costs of war, conquest, empire and colonization are brought to the fore, as are their consequences in death, misery, trauma and destruction, often to be witnessed in massacres and their aftermath.

Such a legacy of foundationally conflicted thought, of competing perspectives – let us call it the Periclean versus the Thucydidean – has haunted Western history to the present. In the early modern period and in modernity, the tradition justifying conquest, colonization and empire as honourable can be seen working its way forward from the English humanist promoters of colonies in Ireland and North America in the early British empire during the sixteenth and seventeenth centuries, to the values informing the later British empire and the present American imperium. As we can see with the history of the American imperium from the end of the Second World War, the vast massacre of Hiroshima and Nagasaki to the mass death inflicted on Vietnam and the invasion of Iraq, the notion of powerful Western military states always acting with benevolent and honourable intentions has proven a protean force for death and suffering in the world, yet one which is imbued with a kind of self-idealization and claimed purity of motives and intentions that means the desire and justifications for such wars are ever renewed. The counter-tradition can be witnessed in Enlightenment critics of colonialism and empire like Diderot,[32] in the development after the Second World War, inspired by Lemkin, of international law concerned with genocide and crimes against humanity,[33] and in contemporary historiography that sharply questions and brings to the fore the human costs of settler colonialism and empire.[34]

Three Suggestions for Massacre Studies

In Lemkin's unpublished manuscripts, under the heading 'Revised Outline for Genocide Cases', there is a diagram suggesting detailed categories by which to analyse historical genocides. In this proposed analytic method, the history of genocide is to be explored in terms of categories such as historical background; methods and techniques of genocide, physical, biological, and cultural; the attitudes of the genocidists; propaganda, that is to say, the rationalizations of the crime; responses of victim groups, active and passive; responses of outside groups; and the aftermath.[35] There is no suggestion that all of these methodological categories and sub-categories can be simply applied to massacre studies. It is clear, for example, that Lemkin regards massacre as a technique of genocide, whereas massacre studies wishes to explore massacres in their manifold historical existence. There are, however, a number of notions, concepts and terms by which group violence can be explored:

Supersessionism: one of the most destructive beliefs in world history. It is the view that some peoples can be erased, removed or superseded by other peoples and groups, who now see themselves as history's true heirs.

Victimology: a belief that earlier bondage and persecution and suffering justifies later violence, conquest, and destruction in other lands, directed against peoples who had no part in the original bondage and persecutions.[36]

Chosen People: a belief held by a group which claims to be blessed by God or the gods. Yet the view of oneself as chosen is always precarious, because chosenness may be claimed by another group who look to other gods. The notion of a chosen people can be found in the biblical stories, Cicero's *Republic*, Virgil's *Aeneid*, and Tacitus's *Agricola* and *Germania*.[37]

Promised Land: a concept close to and usually overlapping with the notions of a chosen people and victimology. In these influential narratives, a people from elsewhere, perhaps having suffered persecution and the agony of wandering and exile, are divinely assisted by a father god, whether monotheistic or polytheistic, to find final refuge by conquest and colonization in another land. This 'new' land is promised to them by the father god, even if already occupied and inhabited by indigenous or previous peoples.

Culture bringers: this concept is taken from Richard Waswo, who draws attention to the importance in historical conflicts of the notion of culture bringers, those who come from elsewhere as conquerors and colonizers, who see themselves as culture-bearers in possession of what they regard as superior knowledge of agriculture, cities, law and religion. Such culture-bringers, Waswo observes, regard their presence in a place as more worthy of the support of God or the gods than indigenous peoples or people already inhabiting a land whom they subdue by conquest and colonization, death and destruction, displacement and replacement.[38] Culture bringers are closely related to the next category, those who regard themselves as honourable colonizers.

Honourable colonization: in possession of a high moral consciousness, honourable colonizers in effect reassure themselves of their own innocence in history. They are aware of the dangers of colonization, especially in the initial stages, in infringing the rights of the colonized and as a threat to their own morality and standing. For this awareness, they are always to be admired in history, whatever the actual long-term consequences of colonization. Instead of colonization being a catastrophe for those facing destruction, as evoked in Herodotus and Thucydides, or in Greek tragedy concerned with the ruining of Troy, or in aspects of Cicero's *Republic*, Virgil's *Aeneid*, and Tacitus's *Agricola*, colonization becomes a celebration of the complex, ambivalent, and even anguished moral state of the colonizers.[39]

Lastly, massacres may have remarkable effects on intellectual life itself, concerned with fundamental questions of humanity, honour, and violence. My first example is the kind of massacre that colonizers usually perpetrate in their colonies, but which occurred in the metropolis itself. On 17 October 1961, Algerian demonstrators in Paris were massacred by the French police.[40] The Prefect of the Paris police responsible for the massacre was none other than the notorious Maurice Papon, who under the Vichy regime was guilty of deporting some 1,500 Jews from France to Germany.[41] In Simone de Beauvoir's autobiography *Force of Circumstance*, published only two years later, there is a passage concerning this massacre and her anguished response to it. Beauvoir described a visit to her sister who lived in a village near Strasbourg; the next morning Beauvoir rang Claude Lanzmann in Paris, who raged at her about the clubbing by the French police of peaceful Algerian protestors as they emerged from the metro stations. Lanzmann had seen with his own eyes teeth smashed and skulls fractured; later he heard that the hands of those with shattered wrists had to be amputated; corpses were found hanging in the Bois de Boulogne, and others, disfigured and mutilated, in the Seine. Beauvoir likened the behaviour of the French police to that of the French authorities during the Second World War, herding the thousands of Algerians as the Jews had been rounded up and herded in Drancy on their way to the concentration camps. She continued: 'I loathed it all – this country, myself, the whole world.'[42] As John Milfull comments, the massacre not only reopened the wound of French complicity in the Holocaust but also threatened Beauvoir's whole relationship to France, her self-respect, and her belief in humanity.[43]

The horror of a massacre perpetrated by one's own society moved, we might speculate, Beauvoir to become a stranger, an outsider, an inner exile, with a detachment from the world and history that might recall Isaac Deutscher's notion in a famous essay of the 'non-Jewish Jew'.[44] Perhaps she had become, in this moment recorded towards the end of

Force of Circumstance, a non-French French person, a position of alien-ation and self-estrangement yet also productive of perspectives on the whole course of human history. Perhaps, we might say, her perspective is that of Thucydides, who wrote his great history in his long exile from Athens.[45] I am also reminded here of Dirk Moses' argument that many contemporary German intellectuals now wish, because of the Holocaust, to regard themselves as non-German Germans.[46]

The second example concerns the massacre at the Sabra and Shatila refugee camp in Beirut in 1982 by a Phalangist militia acting under the protective umbrella of an invading Israeli army, an event with remarkable consequences for Jewish political and intellectual life. In the introduction to *The Massacre in History*, Mark Levene recalls that news of what had happened precipitated a demonstration of 400,000 Israelis, who recognized that the massacre posed a direct challenge to Israel's cherished self-perception as a nation founded on victimhood.[47] The repercussions quickly went far beyond the eastern Mediterranean. Judith Butler, in an online essay entitled 'Jews and the Bi-National Vision', has highlighted Primo Levi's passionate response, who said that after Sabra and Chatila the Israeli state had become morally unaccep-table to anyone who survived the Nazi genocide. Levi signed a petition, with other survivors, to demand the recognition of all peoples of the region.[48] Levi's response was in sharp contrast to that of the philoso-pher Emmanuel Levinas, who in a radio discussion soon after in Paris reacted to Sabra and Chatila by suggesting that the Palestinian was not an Other to whom he is ethically responsible, for the other is composed of neighbours or kin. The Palestinians, he suggested, were a wrong people.[49] In various essays and occasional pieces, Butler has become increasingly critical of the violence embedded in Levinas's philosophy of the encounter between self and Other, and has also spoken of what she regards as Levinas's Eurocentrism and disturbing attitudes to Asians and Muslims.[50]

The Sabra and Chatila massacre revealed and exacerbated a major and continuing cleavage in Jewish intellectual life worldwide, between, let us say, those who in a Periclean spirit believe Israel is composed of honourable culture-bearers bringing Western-style democracy to the Middle East, and those who, in a Thucydidean spirit of fundamental questioning, like Judith Butler, demand a searching examination of the ethical bases of Zionism and its history and consequences. In my own case, my critiques of the violence associated with colonization have increasingly led me to Gandhian perspectives on non-violence, including discourses of non-violence within Jewish tradition, as in the writings of Josephus: Josephus in antiquity as a Gandhian *avant la lettre*.[51] Massa-cres can, we conclude, question humanity at its limits.

Notes

1. Jacques Semelin, 'Towards a Vocabulary of Massacre and Genocide', *Journal of Genocide Studies*, 5 (2003), 204, 208–9.
2. See Mark Levene and Penny Roberts (eds), *The Massacre in History* (New York, 1999), xiv–xv, and 2–3, 6–7, 9, 11, 12, 14, 17, 23–24; Semelin, 'Toward a Vocabulary of Massacre and Genocide', 193–94, 200–2, 204, 207–8.
3. Semelin, 'Towards a Vocabulary of Massacre and Genocide', 208.
4. See Dan Stone, *Constructing the Holocaust: A Study in Historiography* (London, 2003), 16, 21–22, 27, 233, 262–64. See also Ann Curthoys and John Docker, *Is History Fiction?* (Ann Arbor, 2005), 217–19.
5. Dan Stone, *History, Memory and Mass Atrocity: Essays on the Holocaust and Genocide* (London, 2006), 198–99, 206–9.
6. Dan Stone, 'Genocide as Transgression', *European Journal of Social Theory*, 7 (2004), 45–65. See also Semelin, 'Toward a Vocabulary of Massacre and Genocide', 208.
7. Stone, *History, Memory and Mass Atrocity*, 211; George Bataille, *Eroticism*, trans. Mary Dalwood (London, 1987), 186.
8. Levene, 'Introduction', in *The Massacre in History*, 1, 5.
9. Jacques Derrida, 'White Mythology: Metaphor in the Text of Philosophy', in *Margins of Philosophy*, trans. Alan Bass (Chicago, 1986), 258–64; Curthoys and Docker, *Is History Fiction?*, 150–51.
10. Mark Greengrass, 'Hidden Transcripts: Secret Histories and Personal Testimonies of Religious Violence in the French War of Religion', in Levene and Roberts (eds), *The Massacre in History*, 69. Ben Kiernan, *Blood and Soil: A World History of Genocide and Extermination from Sparta to Darfur* (Melbourne, 2008), 16, points to the similarly ambiguous history of the notion of extermination, originally meaning to drive out, expel or banish, only later acquiring another meaning, of abolishing, extirpating, destroying.
11. See Ann Curthoys and John Docker, 'Defining Genocide', in Dan Stone (ed.), *The Historiography of Genocide* (London, 2008), 9–41.
12. Raphael Lemkin, *Axis Rule in Occupied Europe*: *Laws of Occupation, Analysis of Government, Proposals for Redress* (New York, 1944), Ch.IX, 'Genocide', 79–95; for an extended evocation of chapter nine, see Ann Curthoys and John Docker, 'Introduction – Genocide: Definitions, Questions, Settler-colonies', *Aboriginal History*, 25 (2001), 5–11.
13. Lemkin, *Axis Rule in Occupied Europe*, xi, 79–80.
14. Scholars like Tony Barta, Dirk Moses, Dan Stone, Jürgen Zimmerer, Ann Curthoys, and Wendy Lower, in comparative spirit, are interested in exploring relationships between genocide and situations of settler colonialism in world history, including in the history of Nazism and the Second World War. See Dan Stone (ed.), *The Historiography of Genocide*; and A. Dirk Moses (ed.), *Empire, Colony, Genocide: Conquest, Occupation, and Subaltern Resistance in World History* (New York, 2008).
15. Docker, 'Are Settler-Colonies Inherently Genocidal? Re-reading Lemkin', in Moses (ed.), *Empire, Colony, Genocide*.
16. Jane Goodall, *The Chimpanzees of Gombe: Patterns of Behavior* (Cambridge, Mass., 1986), 2–3.
17. Goodall, *The Chimpanzees of Gombe*, 500, 504–14.
18. Goodall, *The Chimpanzees of Gombe*, 532.
19. Goodall, *The Chimpanzees of Gombe*, 532.
20. Goodall, *The Chimpanzees of Gombe*, 530.
21. Jared Diamond, *The Rise and Fall of the Third Chimpanzee* (London, 1992), 251, 261–64.
22. Diamond, *Rise and Fall*, 251, 261–64.
23. Diamond, *Rise and Fall*, 250–59.
24. Diamond, *Rise and Fall*, 164, 166–67. My thanks to Ned Curthoys for alerting me to this chapter on agricultural society.
25. Diamond, *Rise and Fall*, 168–69.

26. Diamond, *Rise and Fall*, 169–72.
27. Diamond, *Rise and Fall*, 171–72. See also Hugh Brody, *The Other Side of Eden: Hunter-Gatherers, Farmers, and the Shaping of the World* (London, 2002).
28. See, for example, David Pritchard, 'War and Democracy in Ancient Athens: A Preliminary Report', *Classicism*, xxxi (April 2005), 16–25; Sophie Mills, *Theseus, Tragedy and the Athenian Empire* (Oxford, 1997).
29. Thucydides, *History of the Peloponnesian War*, trans. Rex Warner (London, 1972), 2.64.
30. Cf. Curthoys and Docker, *Is History Fiction?*, 39–41.
31. Cf. Docker, *The Origins of Violence: Religion, History and Genocide* (London, 2008), 50–53.
32. Cf. Sankar Muthu, *Enlightenment against Empire* (Princeton, 2003); and Ann Curthoys, 'Transnational Scholarship on Race', symposium on Marilyn Lake and Henry Reynolds, *Drawing the Colour Line*, Centre for International and Public Law, Australian National University, 12 June 2008 (unpublished paper).
33. Cf. W.A. Schabas, *Genocide in International Law* (Cambridge, 2000); Martin Shaw, *What is Genocide?* (Cambridge, 2007).
34. See Dirk Moses and Dan Stone (eds), *Colonialism and Genocide* (London, 2007).
35. Lemkin Collection, American Jewish Historical Society, 15 West 16th Street, New York, Box 8, Folder 11, History of Genocide. Projected Book and North American Indian Correspondence, 1947–1949, 1951. See also Ann Curthoys, 'Raphaël Lemkin's "Tasmania": An Introduction', *Patterns of Prejudice*, 39 (2005), 164–66, and also my essay, 'Are Settler-Colonies Inherently Genocidal? Re-reading Lemkin', in Moses (ed.), *Empire, Colony, Genocide*, 81–101.
36. Docker, *The Origins of Violence*, ch.5, 'Victimology and Genocide: The Bible's Exodus, Virgil's *Aeneid*', 113–44.
37. See Anthony D. Smith, *Chosen Peoples: Sacred Sources of National Identity* (Oxford, 2003).
38. Richard Waswo, *The Founding Legend of Western Civilization: From Virgil to Vietnam* (Hanover and London, 1997).
39. See Shino Konishi, 'The Father Governor: The British Administration of Aboriginal People at Port Jackson, 1788-1792', in Matthew McCormack (ed.), *Public Men: Political Masculinities in Modern Britain* (Hampshire, 2007), 54–72, and Julie Evans, 'Colonialism and the Rule of Law: The Case of South Australia', in Barry S. Godfrey and Graeme Dunstall (eds), *Crime and Empire 1840–1940: Criminal Justice in Local and Global Context* (Cullompton, 2005), 57–75.
40. See the essay in this book by Hélène Jaccomard.
41. John Milfull, 'Decolonising Europe? The Colonial Boomerang', *Australian Journal of Politics and History*, 54 (2008), 464–68.
42. Simone de Beauvoir, *Force of Circumstance*, trans. by Richard Howard (London, 1965), 598–601.
43. Milfull, 'Decolonising Europe? The Colonial Boomerang', 467.
44. See Isaac Deutscher, *The Non-Jewish Jew* (London, 1968).
45. Cf. Ann Curthoys, 'Autobiography and Cultivating the Arts of the Female Self', in Jane Bennett and Michael J. Shapiro (eds), *The Politics of Moralizing* (New York and London, 2002), 97–98, 101.
46. A. Dirk Moses, 'The Non-German German and the German German: Dilemmas of Identity after the Holocaust', *New German Critique*, 34 (2007), 45–94.
47. Mark Levene, 'Introduction', *The Massacre in History*, 28.
48. Butler's essay was originally given as a talk at the 2nd International Conference on An End to Occupation, A Just Peace in Israel-Palestine: Towards an Active International Network in East Jerusalem, 4–5 January 2004.
49. Levinas, 'Ethics and Politics', in Seán Hand (ed.), *The Levinas Reader* (Oxford, 2003), 290, 294. Cf. John Docker, 'Sacredness and Uncaring for the Other: Levinas and Pat-

rick White', in Makarand Paranjape (ed.), *Sacred Australia: Post-Secular Considerations* (Melbourne, 2009), 188–209.

50. See Judith Butler, 'Ethical Ambivalences', in Marjorie Garber, Beatrice Hanssen, and Rebecca L. Walkowitz (eds), *The Turn to Ethics* (New York and London, 2000), 15, 24–27; also Butler, *Precarious Life: The Powers of Mourning and Violence* (London and New York, 2004), 134–36, 139–40. See also Butler's talks online, in Nicholas Boston, 'Tackling the West Bank Issue', *Gay City*, 310 (4–10 March 2004), and Samantha Henig, 'Butler Asks for Mideast Dialogue', *The Cornell Daily Sun*, posted 11 November 2005. See also Howard Caygill, 'Levinas's Political Judgement: The *Esprit* Articles 1934–1983', *Radical Philosophy*, 104, (November/December 2000), 6–15.

51. See John Docker, 'Josephus: Traitor or Gandhian avant la lettre?', in Debjani Ganguly and John Docker (eds), *Rethinking Gandhi and Nonviolent Relationality: Global Perspectives* (New Delhi, 2009), 257–79.

Chapter 2

Massacre in the Peloponnesian War

Brian Bosworth

The year 1915 has a significant place in the history of massacre. In our time it conjures up the pointless slaughter of the Gallipoli landings. But the Gallipoli campaigns do not stand alone. The area has vital strategic value, and not surprisingly it has had a long and bloody history. In particular, it became the theatre for the naval war between Athens and the Peloponnesian alliance which brought down the Athenian Empire.

This war ended in late 405 BC with one of the most decisive battles of the ancient world.[1] It was fought off Aegospotami, a stretch of beach on the west side of the Dardanelles, where the Athenians were caught at their moorings. There was little or no hand fighting, because the Athenians had been fooled by one of the oldest ruses in the history of warfare.[2] They and their Peloponnesian adversaries had avoided engagement over a five-day period. The Athenians would put out to sea and challenge the Peloponnesians to leave their base at Lampsacus and fight in the narrows, and each day the Peloponnesians refused battle.[3] Not surprisingly the Athenians lost respect for their enemy, and withdrew in increasing disorder as the days passed. Finally the Peloponnesian fleet, carefully schooled by its admiral Lysander, moved to the attack.[4] It caught the Athenians as they were withdrawing to their base, which was stationed in a highly vulnerable position, completely devoid of fortification. It could not be defended, and there was no space for the Athenians to recover from their blunder. The upshot was total disaster. The Athenians had entered the Dardanelles with 180 warships.[5] Of those only ten managed to escape. The rest fell into Peloponnesian hands. It meant the destruction of Athenian naval power, as the city no longer had the resources to rebuild its navy, which had comprised no less than 300 triremes in battle condition when the war began in 431 BC.[6] As for the rowers, it was relatively easy for them to save their skins. Many of them had taken to flight as soon as they were aware that their own ships were in retreat. They were in no position to put out to sea, as their ships were only partially manned and some were still empty.[7] Other troops were foraging in the hinterland and found it easy to withdraw by land to Sestos, the Athenian occupied fortress at the entrance to the narrows. That left three thousand prisoners of war who had been taken at the landings,[8] and it is their fate that I wish to examine.

At first sight the number seems suspiciously small. The Athenians had 180 warships in commission at Aegospotami, and the complement of each vessel was 200, a total of 36,000 men.[9] If that is correct, the figure seems wholly disproportionate. But as we have seen, a fair number of the Athenian rowers were operating in the countryside. More significantly there is no reason to think that the Athenian fleet was anything like fully manned by the time Lysander made his attack. Xenophon speaks of ships with two banks of oars, others with one and some without rowers at all. It looks as though there were insufficient oarsmen to man the vessels available.[10] The total number can hardly be guessed at, but we cannot assume that the Athenian warships had their full complement. And there is another crucial consideration. After his victory, Lysander had no need of manpower and he was perfectly willing to allow the refugees from the ships to use Sestos as a mustering point.[11] The more extra people that required feeding, the greater the military pressure upon Sestos and the other Athenian possessions in the area. It is interesting to compare Lysander's treatment of Sestos with his actions at Lampsacus, the city captured immediately before the Athenian fleet arrived.[12] Lysander let the Athenian garrison leave in peace, while he 'returned the city to the people of Lampsacus and looted their possessions'. These are typical war measures. The Athenian garrison was simply sent away to be a burden upon the food supply of the main force. The people of Lampsacus appeared to have lost their property: anything that could be used or sold was requisitioned. Lampsacus must have been left an empty shell, stripped of anything of value.[13] Xenophon is rather more specific, adding that the city was full of food, wine and other provisions.[14] Lysander discharged the free population, no doubt leaving the slaves to act as body servants for his troops, or perhaps new helots for the Spartan contingent. Lampsacus paid a bitter price for its strategic position.

There is, then, no valid reason to challenge the figure of three thousand for the Athenian prisoners. It is well attested, except for a variant in Pausanias, who cites four thousand. That is no problem: one must allow for rounding up and down. The question was what to do with the Athenians in Lysander's power. Interestingly, the admiral did not make a decision in his own right. He referred the matter to an ad hoc council of his Peloponnesian allies, which duly condemned the Athenians *en masse*. This was a kangaroo court, the verdict a formality. And the Athenians had not helped their cause by voting that all enemy belligerents should, if captured, have their right thumbs cut off, to incapacitate them for active service. The motion was the work of Philocles, who served as one of the generals of Aegospotami, and there is no reason to doubt that he put his decree into force. That was held against him and justified the wider executions, as did the mass drowning of the crews of two Peloponnesian warships, which had fallen into Athenian hands.

However, the verdict was the responsibility of the Peloponnesians and Lysander was exculpated, in his own eyes at least. His only participation in the trial was to confront Philocles and challenge him to justify his atrocious acts. There is an interesting parallel from the reign of Alexander. In 335 BC he dealt with the Theban revolt, storming the city resulting in a great loss of life. Afterwards he referred the matter to his allies, who were the most inveterate enemies of the Thebans.[15] Another tradition has him approach the council of the Corinthian League,[16] but in both cases the king had nothing to do with the trial. He merely put the verdict into effect.

The result at Aegospotami was a foregone conclusion. The Athenian prisoners were condemned to death and the sentence was enforced immediately. So the sources state,[17] and they read in a very matter of fact way, as though they are recording an everyday affair. We can, however, reconstruct some of the proceedings, and they are extremely grim. The word used for the killing (*aposphattein*) has a sacrificial connotation, the offering of blood at the altar.[18] The victim had its throat cut and the altar received the outpouring of blood. There were human sacrifices, in myth at least, and a favourite theme of Attic vase painters was that of young princesses (notably Priam's daughter Polyxena)[19] sacrificed to procure a favourable outcome from the gods. The human victim would be pinioned and helpless; three men held her horizontally, throat over the altar; she would have her head pulled back by the hair and her throat cut from ear to ear. The sacrificial knife was broad bladed and unlikely to have caused instantaneous death.[20] If we multiply this scene by three thousand, we have some notion of the horror of the execution of the Athenian prisoners. It began in a relatively dignified way. According to Plutarch,[21] Philocles, the general who had been most instrumental in promoting war crimes, was the first victim. He faced out Lysander before his council of allies, then retired for a bath, after which he put on his most splendid cloak and led his men to the slaughter (σφαγή). If the execution began with dignity, it will not have continued so. The killing would have entailed a prodigious amount of physical effort as the Athenian captives struggled against their fate, and one can only guess how much blood was spilled.

It would not be surprising if the Peloponnesian executioners tired of their work, like the *Sonderkommando* that operated in Eastern Europe during the Second World War, and forced their prisoners to do their work for them.[22] For Aegospotami our source is the Greek travel author of the second century AD, Pausanias, who compiled a brief balance sheet contrasting the virtues and vices of Lysander.[23] Not surprisingly the execution of the Athenian captives bulks large in the list. Lysander is said to have killed Philocles and around four thousand prisoners of war. Note here how Pausanias uses a neutral term (*apekteinen*) and says nothing that implies that they had their throats cut. Instead he records a different mode of execution: 'Lysander killed the prisoners of war and heaped earth upon them when they were not even dead'. The passage, however, can be understood in a different way: 'he did not even place earth upon them after they were dead'.[24] In the latter case Lysander was denying the prisoners due burial. That was a serious infraction of Greek morality, which insisted on the token of throwing earth over the corpse. Everyone on both sides would have had vivid recollections of the Battle of Arginusae a year before, when the Athenian commanders won a famous victory but were subsequently condemned to death because they had failed to retrieve their men's bodies.[25] One can well believe that Lysander was eager to make the sharpest contrast with the delinquent Athenian generals; he was certainly not intending to leave thousands of bodies to rot on the beach as a monument of Spartan sacrilege. That takes us back to the first interpretation. What Pausanias seems to be saying is that the Athenians were buried alive. That is not inconsistent with having their throats cut. We should imagine a scenario where the prisoners inaugurated proceedings by digging their own graves, probably long slit trenches close to the shore. Next they would have had their throats cut, quickly and messily, leaving some at least only half dead. Finally the bodies were thrown down into the trenches and the earth fill heaped upon them. Under those circumstances many would certainly have been buried alive.[26] That was the end of Lysander's campaign, a singularly nasty mass killing, which must have had a very strong psychological effect. What advantage would there be in unconditional surrender if the outcome was to be death in any case? The execution of the Athenian prisoners 'was a clue, if one were needed, to the anger of the allies'.[27] So states Kagan, and he is certainly right. The executions at Aegospotami must have sent a shock wave through the whole Greek world. They certainly did in Athens. In a famous passage of Xenophon,[28] we have an emotional description of the arrival of the news of the great defeat:

> the Paralus[29] arrived at Athens at night and announced the disaster, and a wailing came from the Peiraeus, through the Long Walls, to the city, one man passing the word to another, so that on that night no one slept. They wept not only for the men who had been killed but even more for themselves, thinking that they would suffer the kind of fate they had imposed on the

> Melians, colonists of the Spartans, after they had conquered them by siege, and on the people of Histiaea and Scione and Torone and Aegina and many of the other Hellenes.

Xenophon's rhetoric is impressive, but it presses the truth somewhat hard. Take the case of Torone for instance. It was certainly taken by storm.[30] The Spartan commander, the famous Brasidas, had occupied the city by virtue of internal treachery, and a few years later he lost it thanks to a surprise attack by the Athenian general in the area, the infamous Cleon.[31] However, Cleon's treatment of the population of Torone was surprisingly lenient. There were no mass executions. The women and children were enslaved, as was customary (they could be ransomed later),[32] but the men of Torone, along with their Peloponnesian garrison, were sent to Athens where in due course they were repatriated following an exchange of prisoners. Torone then, Xenophon notwithstanding, lost very little from its capture and recapture. The same applied with Histiaea, at the north edge of the large island of Euboea.[33] It had defected from the Athenian alliance in 446 BC and triggered a general revolt against the imperial city, but despite the provocation there was no extermination of the male population. The people of Histiaea were simply dispossessed.[34] This would have caused hardship in plenty, but there were no mass killings.[35] Were the generals in charge, then, reluctant to enforce the supreme penalty?

The explicit case, carefully underlined by Xenophon, is Melos. There is no doubt that the male population was massacred. Thucydides ends his fifth book with a bald statement: 'the Melians surrendered unconditionally to the Athenians, who killed all the men they found who had reached maturity, and enslaved the women and children'.' It is clear then that the males of Melos were largely exterminated, but the story is not quite as simple as it would seem. Thucydides supplies no background information. He does, however, use the generic term for killing and gives no indication that the Melians who surrendered had their throats cut.[36] The same applies to Scione, whose fate is recorded in exactly the same terms as that of Melos.[37] It looks as though the generals who were ordered to carry out the killing found the commotion distasteful and tried to discharge it with as much humanity as they could muster.

There is some corroborative evidence in the famous Melian Dialogue, in which Thucydides portrays the Athenian generals in charge of the expedition arguing with the oligarchic clique that governed Melos.[38] The Athenian commanders, Cleomedes and Teisias, seem to have done everything in their power to save the Melians from their own destruction. They leave the Melian hinterland intact[39] and engage in a long and convoluted debate with the government. They make no bones about the issue; the Melians have to choose between subjection to Athens and destruction. The Athenians for instance insist that it is in their own interests to spare the Melians; they wish to rule them without hardship,

in a way that is expedient for them both.[40] The Melians respond with
total rejection: 'how can it be as useful an outcome for us to be slaves
as it would be for you to rule?' The Athenians have a brutal answer: 'in
your case it would be possible to surrender before suffering the ultimate
penalty, while we would not profit by destroying you'. That puts the
situation in a nutshell. If the Melians persist in their resistance, they
will be destroyed. There is no middle way. The Athenians insist there
is no equality in the relationship. They are far superior and there is no
contest. All through the Dialogue there is an insistence that the Melians
will be destroyed if they refuse to surrender, and the Athenians harp
on the theme continuously. There is real urgency in their final appeal
(5.111.4): 'there is nothing disgraceful in giving way to the greatest of
cities when she is offering reasonable terms – to enter alliance and pay
tribute. Resistance is not merely useless; it is perverse. Think again and
again, keep in mind that you only have a single fatherland, and its very
existence hangs upon the outcome of this one debate.'

The Melians persisted in their resistance, and so came under siege.
It was a protracted affair, from the summer of 416 BC to the spring of
415 BC, and they were able to inflict a number of minor defeats upon the
invading forces. Thucydides (5.115.4) records losses on the Athenian side,
which would hardly have sweetened the temper of the *demos*. It is not
surprising that it voted to execute the male population of Melos. There
were, however, some mitigating factors. Not all of the Melian males were
killed. The city had not been taken by storm. It was surrendered by a
faction inside the walls which negotiated with the Athenian generals
in charge of the siege.[41] They at least should have avoided the death
penalty, and may have been settled elsewhere in the Athenian alliance.
In any case there were survivors who remained to be repatriated by
Lysander.[42] At least one achieved a high status: that was Theopompus,
son of Lapompus of Melos, who fought under Lysander at Aegospotami,
and his statue figured prominently in the great victory memorial erected
at Delphi.[43] Now, compare what we know of Melos before the Athenian
invasion. It was a surprisingly small community, which could only muster
two *pentekonters* (light galleys) for the massive Hellenic fleet that fought
at Salamis (the Athenians alone had enlisted 200 warships). The island
itself measured only 151 sq. km. Its soil is volcanic and fertile, but limited
in area.[44] It cannot have supported a particularly large population (it was
replaced by 500 Athenian settlers after the conquest), and one wonders
how many had remained to be slaughtered by the Athenians. Perhaps
Teisias and Cleomedes were reluctant to carry out the letter of the law
and allowed many of the Melian males to escape. It is a moot point how
far one can call the execution a massacre. It certainly was not exhaustive,
and it looks as though the Athenian generals killed only a fraction of the
potential victims.

The most atrocious act of mass killing on the Athenian side was the
execution of the rebels at Mytilene in the summer of 428 BC. The latter

had led their fellow subjects into revolt,[45] and after its repression they were rounded up and despatched to Athens.[46] There were over a thousand of them, so Thucydides tells us, and they were all killed (Thucydides uses the neutral word διέφθειραν, 'destroyed'). The Athenians were not satisfied with killing the instigators of the revolt. They voted to do away with the entire male population of Mytilene as a collective punishment. The decree, passed in haste, was repented at leisure. According to Thucydides, 'they reckoned that what they had voted was savage and excessive',[47] and after a heated debate an amendment was passed reprieving the mass of the populace which had no part in the revolt. There was a genuine revulsion at the planned execution and the bloodshed it would entail. Nothing shows this better than the dramatic story of the two triremes. The first vessel, transporting the death warrant, was felt to be on an inhuman mission and took its time to arrive, while the crew of the second, carrying the reprieve, strained every nerve to reach Mytilene before the sentence could be implemented.

The execution would have been quite atrocious, exactly parallel to the mass killing after Aegospotami. In both cases there would have been problems with the mode of killing. It looks as though the Athenians had little experience of collective executions, and tended to back away when faced with the reality. That explains to some degree why their victims were relatively small states like Melos[48] and Scione, whose military population could be disposed of quickly. Paradoxically the worst atrocities were inflicted on fellow Athenians. Under the regime of the Thirty (404/3 BC) they are said to have killed more of their own number in eight months than the Peloponnesians did in ten years of warfare.[49] But this was not massed collective killing. Individuals or groups of individuals were confined to state prison and were forced to drink hemlock – a relatively humane way of meeting their end. And it would have been a protracted business. The hemlock could run out, as happened in 317 BC when Phocion and his faction were forced to provide extra supplies at their own expense.[50] The Mytilenean insurgents would have posed a difficult logistical problem, and it is not impossible that some of the one thousand were reprieved. The alternative was to find some other mode of execution, probably a massive throat cutting exercise, and it may well have evoked strong feelings of revulsion. It was one thing to pass a death sentence, but quite another to enforce it. It seems that the Athenians at home and in the field were forced into humane behaviour by the physical constraints of massacre.

Notes

1. For details of the battle see Xenophon, *Hellenica* 2.1.21–32; Diodorus, 13.106.1–7; Plutarch, *Lysander* 10–11, *Alcibiades* 36–37; Frontinus, 2.1.18; Polyaenus, 1.45.2; Pausanias, 9.32.9; Nepos, *Alcibiades* 8. For modern treatments of the episode, see J.-F. Bommelaer, *Lysandre de Sparte* (Paris, 1981), 111–13; D. Kagan, *The Fall of*

the Athenian Empire (Ithaca, 1989), 384–95; A. Andrews, in *The Cambridge Ancient History*, 10 vols. 2nd edn (Cambridge, 1992), 5: 494–96. There is now a chilling analysis of twentieth-century war crimes by Jacques Semelin, *Purify and Destroy* (London, 2005), which provides parallels for every atrocity attested from the ancient world.

2. See the useful compilation by Hans von Wees, *Greek Warfare, Myths and Reality* (London, 2004), 132–33, 286.

3. For an excellent map of the Dardanelles in antiquity, see R.J.A. Talbert (ed.), *Barrington Atlas of the Greek and Roman World* (Princeton and Oxford, 2000), 51, and for a useful outline of the area, see Kagan, *Fall of the Athenian Empire*, 387.

4. This is the crucial manoeuvre. See Xenophon, *Hellenica* 2.1.27–28; Diodorus, 13.106.1–2.

5. Xenophon, *Hellenica* 2.1.20; Diodorus, 13.105.1.

6. See Thucydides, 2.13.8. Pericles is said to have assured the Athenian *demos* that its strength lay in its ships (Thucydides, 2.13.2) and he was also insistent on the invincibility of the Athenian navy (Thucydides, 2.62.2). Athens had a staggering capacity for regeneration. After the disaster of the Sicilian expedition in 413 BC, the navy was able to recover, but ten years of attrition left the city without naval reserves and a single defeat spelled the end, as in 371 BC, according to Aristotle (*Politics*, 2: 1270a 33–35), the single defeat at Leuctra destroyed Spartan hegemony outside the Peloponnese.

7. Xenophon, *Hellenica* 2.1.28.

8. This is the figure given by Plutarch (*Alcibiades* 37.3). Pausanias 9.32.9 claims that there were four thousand deaths. It is likely that the actual figure was somewhere between that and three thousand (cf. Kagan, *Fall of the Athenian Empire*, 394 n. 60).

9. It has even been argued that there were few, if any, executions, and it was only the hard-liner Philocles who suffered the death penalty. See, for instance, C. Ehrhardt, 'Xenophon and Diodorus at Aegospotami', *Phoenix*, 24 (1970), 225–28. It is true that Xenophon (*Hellenica* 2.1.31) and Diodorus (13.106.7) only mention Philocles, but Plutarch (*Alcibiades* 37.3) states explicitly that 'Lysander cut the throats of the 3,000 men whom he had taken alive'. Pausanias represents a different tradition (see below, n.22) but he states explicitly that the Athenian captives were killed, to the number of four thousand.

10. Xenophon, *Hellenica* 2.1.28. The empty warships presumably served as transport vessels. They would have been useful in shipping provisions from the main base at Sestos back to the troops in the field (see below).

11. Diodorus, 13.106.8; Kagan, *Fall of the Athenian Empire*, 398.

12. Diodorus, 13.104.8.

13. Diodorus, 13.104.8. The word 'loot' (ἁρπάσας) is explicitly used. Cf. W. Kendrick Pritchett, *The Greek State at War: Part V* (Berkeley, Los Angeles and Oxford, 1991), 301–2.

14. Xenophon, *Hellenica* 2.1.19. See Pritchett, *The Greek State at War*, 300–3.

15. Arrian, *Anabasis Alexandri*, 1.8.8. The political units at issue included the Phocians, Plataeans, Thespians and Orchomenians, all of which had been annexed and demolished by the Thebans. For details see A.B. Bosworth, *A Historical Commentary on Arrian's History of Alexander*, 2 vols. (Oxford, 1980), 1: 84.

16. Diodorus, 17.14.1: 'convening the delegates of the Hellenes he submitted to the common council the question how they should deal with the city of the Thebans'.' In practice there is little or no difference between the two traditions. The common council comprised delegates who were bitter enemies of Thebes and would press for her destruction.

17. Xenophon, *Hellenica* 2.1.31–2: 'After this Lysander summoned his allies and told them to decide on the fate of the prisoners'; cf. Diodorus, 13.106.7; Plutarch, *Lysander* 13.1.

18. See Pritchett, *The Greek State at War*, 206–16, who lists a dozen or more modes of execution. Throat cutting would have been the most sanguinary, and when

multiplied a thousand times and more, the whole of the killing ground would have been saturated.

19. The *locus classicus* is in Euripides' *Hecabe* 218–20. For more detail, see *LIMC s.v. Polyxene* and the superb sarcophagus discovered in the Troad in 1994, which gives the most terrifying visual depiction of death by throat cutting. It would have been relatively quick, as the carotid artery was severed but the last moments of the victim would have been quite hideous. See the recent article by Brian Rose, 'The Tombs of the Granicus River Valley,' in I. Delemen, ed., *The Achaemenid Impact on Local Populations and Cultures in Anatolia* (Istanbul, 2007), 247–64, with full bibliography.

20. Note the description of the mass killing in Rwanda: 'if they have to slit their victim's throats, the perpetrators know that it is better to make the person kneel down and then to cut his throat from behind, as if they were killing animals' (Semelin, *Purify and Destroy*, 273).

21. Plutarch, *Lysander* 13.3, based on the peripatetic philosopher Theophrastus. As mentioned above, Philocles had previously passed a motion in the Athenian assembly to cut off the right thumbs of all prisoners who were captured, and later he had the crews of two triremes allied against Athens drowned *en masse* (Xenophon, *Hellenica* 2.1.31).

22. There is a large bibliography on the atrocities. See the eye-witness reports compiled by Laurence Rees, *Their Darkest Hour* (London, 2008), 11–15.

23. Pausanias 9.32.9. The passage is ignored by Pritchett, *The Greek State at War*, 218.

24. ὅσον τετρακισχιλίους αἰχμαλώτους ὄντας ἀπέκτεινεν ὁ Λύσανδρος καί σφισιν οὐδὲ ἀποθανοῦσιν ἐπήνεγκε γῆν.

25. On this campaign see CAH² 5.492–4, and on a broader canvas, Kagan, *Fall of the Athenian Empire*, 364–75.

26. Compare the description of a mass execution carried out in Poland by a paramilitary division in November 1914: 'The whole business was the most gruesome I had ever seen in my life, because I was frequently able to see that after a burst had been fired the Jews were only wounded and those still living were more or less buried alive beneath the corpses of those shot later, without the wounded being given so-called mercy shots. I remember that from out of the pile of corpses the SS (*sic*) men were cursed by the wounded' (Christopher R. Browning, *Ordinary Men: The 101ˢᵗ Reserve Battalion of the German Police and the Final Solution in Poland* (New York, 1992), 137–41).

27. Kagan, *Fall of the Athenian Empire*, 399.

28. Xenophon, *Hellenica* 2.2.3.

29. One of the state triremes used for public service in Athens, particularly for carrying dispatches.

30. Thucydides, 4.110–12. This was a particularly bloodless coup. Thucydides gives us a vivid siege description, highlighting the deaths of a handful of soldiers who happened to be sleeping in the agora (4.113.2).

31. Thucydides, 5.1.2–3.5.

32. For a comprehensive list of examples of enslavement for ransom, see Pritchett, *The Greek State at War*, 227, 245.

33. Thucydides, 1.114.3; Diodorus, 12.22.2; Plutarch, *Pericles* 23.3–4. Cf. R. Meiggs, *The Athenian Empire* (Oxford, 1972), 177–81.

34. Thucydides, 1.114.3.

35. Strepsiades, the devious protagonist of Aristophanes' play *The Clouds* (211–14), refers in passing to Pericles' harsh treatment of Euboea, but there is no suggestion that there were mass reprisals.

36. Strabo 10.5.1 (484), writing in the Augustan age in Rome, does use the verb κατέσφαξεν, but he cannot stand against the contemporary Thucydides. It is also worth noting that Strabo states that the Athenians killed the majority of the adult males. It looks as though there were a significant number of survivors.

37. Thucydides, 5.32.1: 'the Athenians forced the men of Scione to surrender: they killed

the men in their prime, enslaved the women and children and gave their land to Plataean settlers to cultivate'.'

38. The so-called Melian Dialogue has given rise to a huge bibliography. For recent discussion, see A.B. Bosworth, 'The Humanitarian Aspect of the Melian Dialogue', *Journal of Hellenic Studies*, 113 (1993), 30–44; Simon Hornblower, *A Commentary on Thucydides: Volume III: Books 5.25–8.109* (Oxford, 2008), 216–56 (esp. 218).

39. Thucydides, 5.84.2. The Athenians here take a leaf out of the Spartans' book, intending to force the Melians into battle to preserve their harvest.

40. Thucydides, 5.91.2, taken up and answered by the Melians at 5.93.

41. Thucydides, 5.116.3–4. It is significant that the Athenians killed all the men of mature age whom they captured. It looks as though Thucydides wished his readers to draw the appropriate conclusion, that there were Melians who escaped the slaughter.

42. Xenophon, *Hellenica* 2.2.9.

43. See the edition by Russell Meiggs and David Lewis, *A Selection of Greek Historical Inscriptions* (Oxford, 1989), 288, no. 95 (f). Theopompus is explicitly termed Melian. It is perhaps unlikely that he was on the island at the time of the invasion, but he could have slipped away with the connivance of the generals.

44. For details of topography and population see Hornblower, *A Commentary on Thucydides*, 256, referring to L. Kallet, *Money and the Corrosion of Power in Thucydides* (Berkeley, 2001), 19, who describes the outcome on Melos as a failure for Athens.

45. For details see Thucydides, 3.2, 3.4.1–6.2.

46. Thucydides, 3.50.1: 'the men whom Paches [the Athenian commander] sent away, regarding them as the most culpable, were killed by the Athenians on the motion of Cleon (there were little more than 1000 of them)'.

47. Thucydides, 3.36.4.

48. The agricultural area of Melos has been estimated at 151 sq. km (C. Renfrew and M. Wagstaff (eds), *An Island Polity: The Archaeology of Exploration in Melos* (Cambridge, 1982)).

49. Xenophon, *Hellenica* 2.4.21.

50. Plutarch, *Phocion* 36.5–6. Phocion was following the heroic examples of Socrates (Plato, *Phaedrus*. 116b–118a).

CHAPTER 3

'THE ABOMINABLE QUIBBLE': ALEXANDER'S MASSACRE OF INDIAN MERCENARIES AT MASSAGA

Elizabeth Baynham

I would like to begin with a quotation from a well known historical novelist, the late Mary Renault, who, despite her innate romanticism, had a considerable gift for recreating the ancient world. The speaker is the young Persian eunuch Bagoas, a servant in the entourage of Alexander the Great. From the safety of Alexander's camp, he has heard his master and lover slaughtering a large company of Indian mercenaries. These men, having made a separate truce with Alexander, had just left the fortress of Massaga in the Swat valley (northern Pakistan), which was under siege at the time. On being informed that the mercenaries were planning to abscond under cover of darkness, the king acted quickly. He surrounded the entire group and had them all killed. Bagoas reflects:

> I lay in my tent, in the cold before the dawn, with the fire dying outside, and I thought, as I had been thinking all night, that the interpreter was Sogdian and no Sogdian will own there is anything he cannot do. Still if the Indians had believed they were free to go, they would have gone by day. Did they know they had broken faith, did they know they had pledged it? Alexander had watched them. They must have looked as if they understood.

I thought of the dead upon the hill, with the wolves and the jackals already tearing them; and I knew that other hands before his had sealed their death; the hand of Philotas; the hands of the dead squires; the hands of all those chiefs and satraps who had taken his right hand, sworn loyalty and had been his welcome guests; then murdered his men whom he'd trusted to them and fallen on his cities.[1]

It seems as though everybody was to blame for this atrocity but Alexander himself. Mary Renault was very likely inspired by Sir William Tarn, the most influential English-speaking scholar on Alexander in the first half of the twentieth century. For Tarn, the incident revolved around whether the Indian mercenaries – a considerable force of between – seven and nine thousand men – had taken an oath to join Alexander's army; if they had, then he was within his rights to kill them for breaking a treaty, but if they had not, then it was 'pure massacre'.[2]

It might be worthwhile to consider whether 'massacre' is an appropriate term for Tarn to have used. According to Jacques Semelin's 'typically sociological' definition, massacre is 'often collective, and aimed at destroying non-combatants'.[3] Although the Indian mercenaries were professional soldiers, at the time of their retreat they were in a non-combatant situation, believing as they did that they were under truce and had leave to go. They had probably sheathed their arms, and almost certainly would have been out of formation and off their guard. In addition, as two ancient authors explicitly state,[4] they had their women and children with them, as they had expected to be at the fortress for some time. When they were attacked by the Macedonian phalanx, they bravely tried a hasty manoeuvre: the classic defensive tactic of forming a circle, with their dependents in the middle. However, the mercenaries were heavily outnumbered; their wicker work shields were useless, their main weapon – the long bow and arrow[5] – was ineffective at close quarters, and they were up against a superior military technology; the phalanx's fearsome five-metre pikes or *sarissae*, with their 55 cm leaf-shaped iron blades. The Indians did not stand a chance.

Tarn went on to suggest that the 'thing may have been a horrible mistake, due perhaps to defective interpreting and Alexander's growing impatience'. I shall address these observations in a later part of this essay. Yet in his summary of Alexander's character, Tarn named the Massaga massacre, together with the destruction of Thebes and the murder of Parmenion, as one of three of Alexander's crimes that he considered particularly heinous: 'the sins of a young and imperious man who meant to rule because he could'.[6] Even allowing for the brutality of ancient warfare,[7] we could add a lot more, such as Alexander's murder of his friend Cleitus in an alcohol soaked rage. The Massaga incident clearly bothered Tarn. Moreover, even though Greek moral views of honouring truces made with native peoples can be ambiguous, the killing of the Indian mercenaries also bothered several of our ancient writers.[8]

As with many atrocities in history – even in our own time, such as the massacre of over seven thousand Muslims by Serbian troops at Srebrenica in 1995 – it is difficult to know exactly how and why the episode occurred.[9] It might also be worthwhile to highlight the main difficulty we encounter in trying to assess any incident from a remove of over two millennia, namely, the type of sources available. There are no inscriptions recording the siege of Massaga, no iconography, archives, diaries, or any of the other data that can often provide information when the opportunities to question either survivors or perpetrators and their descendants have longed passed. To try to understand the massacre at Massaga we need to rely entirely upon ancient historiography, with all its incumbent baggage of bias, selectivity, inaccuracy, conflation, exaggeration and literary aspiration. Some critics might say that literary texts preclude a complete picture, and therefore any interpretation must be invariably skewed. While this might be so, Massaga is also quite richly represented, and interestingly, the details provided by our sources offer answers to many of the issues raised in Semelin's helpful questionnaire, Appendix A, such as the victims, their gender, how and where they were killed, the type of weaponry used, the age, origin and profile of the perpetrators, the motives for the massacre, and its political implications.[10]

Unlike Thucydides who lived through the war that he wrote about, the entire extant tradition on Alexander is derivative, with our earliest source dating from the first century BC. All of our sources mention the siege of Massaga, although they vary considerably on the details of the campaign, the fate of the mercenaries, and their judgements of what happened. Plutarch, in his *Life of Alexander*,[11] describes Alexander's action as a *khlis* (a stain) on the king's conduct as a general; Arrian, in his *Anabasis*,[12] our most detailed source for Alexander's advance into India, does his best to exonerate the king; Diodorus Siculus[13] and the late Latin text, the *Metz Epitome*,[14] emphasize Alexander's savagery and ruthlessness;[15] while two other Roman writers, Justin and Quintus Curtius,[16] omit the massacre altogether. But Curtius offers significant information on the siege itself, and all three Latin texts mention Alexander's attraction to the ruler of Massaga, the sexy Queen Cleophis, by whom (at least according to Justin) Alexander allegedly fathered a son. Plutarch does not mention Cleophis at all, and Arrian only refers to her in passing without stating any activity on her part, or even naming her.[17] Cleophis only makes a significant appearance in the so-called Vulgate, or the tradition represented by Diodorus, Curtius, Justin and the *Metz Epitome*. The latter is a late Latin text that was probably compiled in the fourth or fifth century AD. It consists of two separate ancient works which were bound together in one manuscript, namely, part of a summary of a lost history on Alexander covering his campaigns from about 330 to 325 BC, and the other a fictitious account of Alexander's death and testament. Both treatises are abridged and difficult to read, with many textual uncertainties. They are often overlooked by both students and scholars. However, the historical part of the *Metz Epitome* appears to have used the same sources as the other Vulgate writers, and sometimes offers information not contained in their texts. *The Metz Epitome* will be particularly pertinent to this discussion.

Although Justin himself lived in the late second or third centuries AD, he wrote an epitome, or anthology, what he terms a *florilegium*,[18] 'a little picked bunch of flowers', of a much earlier, universal history, that of Pompeius Trogus, a contemporary of the emperor Augustus.[19] The likely reason for Justin's focus on the seductive Indian queen has been noted by previous scholars:[20] Trogus could have given more emphasis to Alexander's affair with Cleophis, who was subsequently called 'the royal whore' by her own people. Like Trogus himself, the historian's audience would have been all too familiar with the outcome of the battle of Actium in 31 BC. Cleophis' name is very similar to that of another dangerous foreign queen, the infamous 'royal whore of the Canopus',[21] Cleopatra VII. Canopus was in the Nile Delta, and was the heart of Egypt's red light district. An allusion to Cleopatra – and to her children by Julius Caesar and Mark Antony, two of the leading generals in the Roman world – would have been too good to miss. Unfortunately, such colour has also misdirected modern interpretation. However, even if Trogus had included the massacre it is possible that Justin omitted it, out of the need to conserve space or other literary considerations.

However, Curtius wrote a specialist monograph on Alexander, the only Roman whom we know to have done so, and his failure to mention the massacre is decidedly strange. My feeling is that there is probably a lacuna (gap) in Curtius' text at the very point where we would have expected him to include the incident. Sadly, lacunae are all too common in Curtius. The first two books are lost entirely, the end of Book 5 and the beginning of Book 6 are missing, and Book 10 is so riddled with gaps as to render most of it incomprehensible. Lacunae are usually fairly recognizable; the text often becomes broken and choppy and might not make much sense, either linguistically or historically. Lack of continuity is another feature; the text might start up again on a completely different episode. In Curtius' history, there seems to be a rather abrupt change; the historian appears to shift his focus sharply from the Cleophis vignette to the destruction of another Indian city, Nora, and another siege – this time of the great rock fortress of Aornus. Although none of the editors of the various texts of Curtius suggest a lacuna, this is probably because the received text makes perfect linguistic sense, and editors are usually more conscious of linguistic anomalies than they are of historical ones. Moreover, Curtius' text often follows Diodorus' narrative (as well as what survives of the *Metz Epitome*) in that all three sources appear to have drawn on a common tradition. Diodorus' text is peppered with lacunae too. In fact, his entire book is marred by a great gap that takes out the narrative of events from the end of 328 to 327/6 BC and only commences again towards the end of 327, with Cleophis' surrender to Alexander. The city Massaga is not named in the extant part of Diodorus' text, but it is mentioned in the index of Book 17's contents. Cleophis' capitulation is immediately followed by the massacre, and then by the siege of Aornus. The *Metz Epitome* offers a similar order. It seems very likely that Curtius' text did likewise in its original state. Suffice to say that Curtius does not try to whitewash Alexander and the massacre would have also suited his literary considerations. As 'the third son of Jupiter'[22] Alexander would leave his mark – surrender or be destroyed.

We may now turn to the context of the Massaga massacre. The incident took place in the autumn of 327 BC. Massaga was the capital of the Assaceni (the Avaka in Sanskrit), an Indian people who lived in the valley of the Swat River north-east of its confluence with the Panjkora, and about 300 km north of modern Islamabad. The precise location of the site of the fortress is uncertain. There has been some suggestion that Massaga was probably located east of the Katgala Pass, near a natural moat formed by a smaller river, the Wuch Khwar,[23] and in territory intersected by deep ravines.[24] Curtius describes 'towering crags, below which lie caverns and abysses, deeply hollowed by the long lapse of time'.[25]

Alexander's advance into India over the previous summer had been steady and relentless, despite strong resistance offered by the local populations, the Aspasians, Guraei and Assaceni. After reducing the Aspasians, Alexander, having heard that the Assaceni were making extensive preparations for war,[26] moved against Massaga, described by Arrian as the 'greatest city in the region'. Although army figures in ancient sources are notoriously unreliable, both strands of tradition represented by Arrian and Curtius respectively give comparable numbers for the Assaceni infantry – around 30,000. In addition, Arrian states there were about 2000 cavalry and 30 elephants. Massaga was also a strongly fortified place, with some 35 stadia (about 3.5 kilometres) of walls.[27] This was a large, densely populated and formidable city. Alexander, anticipating a siege, had ordered his general Craterus to bring the heavier armed troops of the Macedonian army, together with the siege engines.[28] These were massive wheeled towers, about 15 metres wide and long and 16 metres high, crammed with archers and catapults, and assault bridges that were designed to be lowered at the top level of the wall.[29]

Such technology was unfamiliar to the Indians, and they were terrified. According to Curtius and the *Metz Epitome*,[30] the Assaceni believed supernatural forces were at work, both in the projectiles catapulted from the towers, and the seemingly impossible movement of the towers themselves, which were not being pushed or pulled by anything visible. In fact, the towers' wheels were powered by a large, internal capstan, the like of which are described in our corpus of poliorcic texts, or ancient sources on siege warfare, such as Athenaeus Mechanicus.[31] In his recent fine book, *Into the Land of Bones, Alexander the Great in*

Afghanistan, Frank Holt rightly emphasizes the psychological impact that these machines would have had. Although Holt takes his cue from the Vulgate, he also points out that the siege towers would have been transported in parts and then assembled on site, adding to the impression that the invaders had powers beyond belief.[32]

The siege engines are given as the main reason for Cleophis' capitulation in Curtius and the *Metz Epitome*;[33] according to Arrian, the Indians resisted vigorously until their commander was killed, whereupon they sent a herald to negotiate a truce.[34] It is here that Arrian's text diverges sharply from the other sources. According to Arrian, Alexander 'was glad to save the lives of brave men' – which recalls the king's response to the plight of the Greek mercenaries at the siege of Miletus.[35] He granted them a truce, on the condition that they joined his own army. Arrian says that they camped near the Macedonians, but subsequently intended to slip away during the night and escape. When this was reported to Alexander, he surrounded the mercenaries, cut them down to a man, and took Massaga by assault. For Plutarch, there is no question of treachery on the Indians' part. The responsibility for the massacre lay entirely with Alexander; he made a truce with the mercenaries and then had them killed as they were leaving the camp.[36] In the *Metz Epitome*, Alexander gave the mercenaries permission *exeundi, non abeundi* 'to leave the town, but not to go away from it', a kind of black humoured joke, or the 'abominable quibble' as Tarn described it.[37] According to Diodorus, Alexander concluded a truce with the Indians, but then attacked them, along with their women and camp followers, saying that he had given them the 'right to leave the city, but not of being friends of the Macedonians forever'. The killing at close quarters was horrific, despite the Indians' attempts to defend themselves. Diodorus offers a graphic and moving description of the long *sarissae* of the phalanx piercing through the light shields of the victims and penetrating their lungs.[38] Even the women, who had been goaded by desperation to pick up weapons, were killed.[39]

So which tradition do we accept? Who violated the truce – the Indian mercenaries or Alexander? Was the massacre a deliberate act of terror – as Gerhard Wirth argued – or was defective communication a factor, as Tarn said?[40] *Pace* Wirth, Tarn made a valid point: the Macedonians would undoubtedly have needed to use interpreters and probably relays of interpreters, somebody who could speak not only the Indian dialect, but also another language like Sogdian, Bactrian or Persian, who in turn could communicate with someone else who could speak any of those tongues and Greek. Arrian refers to a man called Pharnuces from Lycia who could speak Sogdian dialects as well as Persian and Greek, and who acted as an interpreter and diplomat during Alexander's campaigns in the eastern part of the Persian Empire.[41] Even allowing for the multi-lingual capacity of traders and other individuals, it was all too likely that in such a situation one or both parties would misunderstand,

and it is possible that the mercenaries had not realized that Alexander expected them to undertake service in his own ranks.

It is also possible, as Bosworth has suggested in a recent conference paper,[42] that Alexander deliberately used ambiguous language to deceive the Indians. A parallel episode is offered by the king's treatment of the Uxians of the Zagros mountains, a people who had been accustomed to extort gifts from the Persian kings in return for safe passage. Alexander made arrangements to meet them at a particular place, so that they 'could take payments from himself', and when a group of them turned up thinking that they would get their money, Alexander attacked their villages and killed many in their homes.[43] So Alexander clearly had a taste for dirty tricks, or what Bosworth calls 'imaginative generalship'. There is also evidence of a particular language itself being used as a means of deception in appropriate circumstances. According to Thucydides, during the Peloponnesian War, the Athenian general Demosthenes tricked a group of Ambraciots (from the far western part of central Greece) into believing Demosthenes' soldiers were their own countrymen by telling the advance troops to speak in Doric dialect.[44]

However, there is another interpretation of the Massaga tragedy. I find myself in this instance drawn to the Vulgate, particularly the *Metz Epitome*, and prefer its account to that of Arrian. It is true that Arrian based his history on eye-witness narratives, especially that of Ptolemy, one of Alexander's generals and bodyguards, and the future king of Egypt, founder of the great Hellenistic dynasty that ended with Cleopatra VII. But it is also true that both Arrian and Ptolemy wanted their histories to celebrate the glorious deeds and achievements of Alexander. This was not an episode which – whatever way it is examined – was particularly glorious. It is highly likely that Arrian (or Ptolemy) knew about Queen Cleophis, and yet downplayed her role, in much the same way that the part played by Ptolemy's mistress, the Athenian courtesan Thais, in burning down Xerxes' palace at Persepolis was overlooked.[45]

This is one of the few instances where one of our most truncated and difficult texts gives the most detailed account of not only Cleophis, but also the massacre, and it has not been given the attention it deserves. According to the *Metz Epitome*, there were two separate arrangements concluded, one with Cleophis and the other with the mercenaries. Assacenus, the homonymous king of the Assaceni and the son of Cleophis, had recently died. She was also taking care of either his infant son, or another child of her own. The texts are divided on the exact relationship: the *Metz Epitome* describes the child as Cleophis' small grandson (*nepos parvus*),[46] whereas Curtius says *parvus filius* (little son).[47]

Amminais, the brother of the late king,[48] had brought in the mercenaries from other regions in India ostensibly to help repel the invader, Alexander. We are not given any details about Amminais, whether he too was a son of Cleophis, or another woman, and hence only a half-brother to Assacenus.[49] Like the Macedonian and Achaemenid kings, the Indian rulers were probably polygamous; they certainly kept harems of concubines.[50] But even if Amminais was Cleophis' son, it is still possible that he was at odds with his mother, and intended the mercenary force to establish his own regime, as the Athenian tyrant Peisistratus[51] and at least two Sicilian tyrants are known to have done. Both Dionysus I of Syracuse[52] and Agathocles used mercenaries to establish and maintain tyrannies.[53]

Cleophis was clearly very uneasy about the Indian mercenaries' presence. At an earlier war council meeting they had proved obstructive and mutinous, and in the queen's subsequent negotiations with Alexander, she blamed the resistance on them.[54] Their suspicion of her was made equally apparent when they learned that Cleophis had been negotiating 'in secret'[55] with the king.

Cleophis already had an alternative male ruler to Amminais in the little boy under her care, and the most likely scenario is that she probably intended to be regent until that child came of age. In something of an ironic phrase, the *Metz Epitome* describes Cleophis as of noble pedigree and well suited for royal power (*nobili loco orta atque imperio digna videretur*). She was not the only Indian ruler who tried to use Alexander for her own ends. Taxiles did likewise, in order to enlist Alexander's aid against his rival, King Porus.[56] Furthermore, Alexander himself had a history of favouring mature, high status women like Barsine, the widow of the influential general Memnon, Sisygambis, the mother of the Persian Great King, Darius, and even female monarchs like Ada, the Hecatomnid queen of Caria, whom Alexander reinstated as ruler of Halicarnassus in 334 BC at the expense of her brother. He showed extraordinary favour to foreign royal women, and it brought rewards. Ada adopted Alexander as her son, which established his legitimacy for the Carians, and also guaranteed Caria's support against Persia's navy.[57] Whereas at Susa in 324 BC, Alexander married Stateira, the granddaughter of Sisygambis in the famous mass weddings conducted between the Macedonian and Persians elites.[58]

It is not known whether ethnic tensions played a part in the Massaga massacre as they have done in many atrocities throughout history. Arrian is the only source who tells us that the mercenaries came from Indian tribes who 'lived beyond',[59] but we are not given any further information. Bosworth suggests that they had most likely come from the neighbouring region ruled by Taxiles, or the areas of the Cophen valley that had already been conquered by Alexander's generals, Hephaestion and Perdiccas.[60] We do not know whether there were any long-standing feuds or hostilities between their tribe and the Assaceni. Nevertheless, a large force of hired military muscle in rival hands was a liability, and one woman saw an opportunity to rid herself of it, as soon as a superior power presented itself at Massaga's door. In turn, Alexander could count on her loyalty and a stable area in his rear when he moved on – a deal that was well worth losing a unit of native fighters over. On this reading, the Indian mercenaries and their families became the expedient victims of a local dynastic struggle in a region which, as recent events have shown, is still deeply and sadly troubled.

Notes

1. M. Renault, *The Persian Boy* (Harmondsworth, 1974), 279. I should like to thank Professor Lyndall Ryan, Assoc. Professor Philip Dwyer, Professors Ben Madley, A.B. Bosworth and Ms Amanda Drummond for their comments and help.
2. W.W. Tarn, *Alexander the Great*, 2 vols (Cambridge, 1948), 1:89.
3. J. Semelin, *Purify and Destroy* (London, 2005), 4.
4. Diodorus, 17.84.3; *Metz Epitome*, 43.
5. Cf. Curtius, 8.9.28; 9.5.9.
6. Tarn, *Alexander the Great*, 125.
7. It is a truism that the ancient world was a violent place, and a general study of massacre would go beyond the parameters of this discussion. Aside from anything else, attitudes to massacre varied among ancient peoples and each culture had different standards. Massacres of civilian populations, including the elderly, women and children (sometimes notwithstanding their value as slaves), often occurred in the Greek world when a city was taken by storm, or when its defences were lax. In the case of the latter, Thucydides highlights the massacre of the inhabitants of the Boeotian town Mycalessus in 413 BC as one of the worst atrocities in relation to the size of population suffered by any Greek community during the Peloponnesian War (see Thucydides, 7.29–30). For discussions of occurrence of massacre and the killing of captives, see W.K. Pritchett, *The Greek State at War*, Part V (Berkeley, 1991) 205–23; Hans Van Wees, *Greek Warfare, Myths and Realities* (London, 2004); also Hans Van Wees (ed.), *War and Violence in Ancient Greece* (London, 2000).
8. See below, n.19.
9. See Semelin's interesting observations; Semelin, *Purify and Destroy*, 195–98.
10. Semelin, *Purify and Destroy*, 376–78.
11. Plutarch, *Alexander* 59.6.
12. Arrian, 4.26–27.4.
13. Diodorus, 17.84.
14. *ME* 44–45.
15. For an alternative view, see the analysis by A. Abramenko, 'Alexander vor Mazagae und Aornus. Korrekturen zu den Berichten über das Massaker an den indischen Söldern', *Klio*, 76 (1994), 192–207, which focuses in particular on Arrian and Diodorus; he argues that these authors confused the siege of Aornus with Massaga.
16. Justin, 12.7.9–11; Curtius, 8.10.22–36.
17. Arrian, 4.27.4.
18. Justin, *Praef* 4.
19. On the dates of Trogus and Justin, see R. Develin's introduction in Yardley and Develin, *Justin: Epitome of the Philippic History of Pompeius Trogus* (Atlanta, 1994), 2–6.
20. W. Heckel in Yardley and Heckel, *Justin Epitome of the Philippic History of Pompeius Trogus*, vol. 1, Books 11–12 (Oxford, 1997), 242; E. Baynham, 'An Introduction to the *Metz Epitome*: Its Traditions and Value', *Antichthon*, 29 (1995), 68–69.
21. Propertius, 3.11.39, 'meretrix regina Canopi'; cf. Pliny, NH 9.119, 'regina meretrix' with Heckel, *Epitome of the Philippic History*.
22. Curtius 8.10.1; cf. *ME* 34.
23. Cf. Curtius, 8.10.23.
24. A.B. Bosworth, *A Historical Commentary on Arrian's History of Alexander*, 2 vols. (Oxford, 1995), 2:169; he is sceptical about accepting the identification but concedes that it has won cautious acceptance.
25. Curtius, 8.10.24.

26. Arrian, 4.25.5.
27. Curtius, 8.10.25.
28. Arrian, 4.25.5.
29. Bosworth, *Historical Commentary*, 2:172–73.
30. Curtius, 8.10.37; *ME* 41.
31. D. Whitehead and P.H. Blyth, *Athenaeus Mechanicus*, On Machines (Stuttgart, 2004).
32. F.L. Holt, *Into the Land of Bones: Alexander the Great in Afghanistan* (Berkeley, 2005), 103. On the dismantling and transportation of the towers, see Whitehead and Blyth, *Athenaeus Mechanicus*, 180–83.
33. Curtius, 8.10.34; *ME* 42.
34. Arrian, 4.27.2.
35. Arrian, 1.19; cf. Bosworth, *Historical Commentary*, 175.
36. Plutarch, *Alexander* 59.6. On the ambiguity in Greek moral views about honouring truces made with 'barbarians', see Paul Goukowsky's comments, *Diodore de Sicile Bibliothèque Historique: Livre XVII* (Paris, 1976), 118–19.
37. Tarn, *Alexander the Great,* 363; see also Baynham, 'Introduction to the *Metz Epitome*', 70.
38. Diodorus, 17.84.4.
39. Diodorus also notes that a few women and 'unarmed' people – presumably children and elderly carers – survived the massacre.
40. Wirth rejects Tarn's explanation, claiming instead that the Massaga massacre was a deliberate slaughter as a warning to other natives, because Alexander's progress had been slowed down by the resistance; see Wirth and von Hinüber, *Der Alexanderzug Indische Geschichte* (Munich, 1985), 915.
41. Arrian, 4.3.7.
42. Bosworth, 'Deceit and Propaganda in the Age of the Successors', in J.H. Kim On Chong-Gossard, A. Turner and F. Vervaet, *Private and Public Lies: The Discourse of Despotism and Deceit in the Ancient World* (Leiden, forthcoming).
43. Arrian, 3.17.2–3.
44. Thucydides, 3.112.
45. For Arrian's notoriously brief account of the destruction of Persepolis, see 3.18.11–12; on Thais' role, see Curtius Rufus 5.7.1–8; Plutarch, *Alexander,* 39; Diodorus, 17.72. Her participation in the arson is a highly controversial issue in modern scholarship. See Bosworth in A.B. Bosworth and E.J. Baynham (eds), *Alexander the Great in Fact and Fiction* (Oxford, 2000), 13–14.
46. *ME* 45.
47. Curtius, 8.10.34.
48. *ME* 39.
49. On Amminais see W. Heckel, *Who's Who in the Age of Alexander the Great* (London, 2006), 22. His territory was to the east of the Swat river basin. See also P.H.L. Eggermont, 'Alexander's Campaign in Gandhara and Ptolemy's List of Indo-Scythian Towns', *Orientalis Lavaniensia Periodica*, 1 (1970), 63–124.
50. Cf. Curtius, 8.9.30.
51. *Athenaion Politeia*.15.2; cf. Herodotus, 1.61.
52. Cf. Diodorus, 13.96.3.
53. Diodorus, 19.6; cf. Thucydides, 4.124–25. In 424 BC, the Macedonian king Perdiccas and Spartan general Brasidas attempted to establish Perdiccas' control of the upper Macedonian region of Lyncus with the help of Illyrian mercenaries. However, the mercenaries changed sides and the attempt failed.
54. *ME* 42.
55. *clam: ME* 42.
56. Taxiles had actually encouraged Alexander to invade India. See Bosworth, *Alexander and the East: The Tragedy of Triumph* (Oxford, 1996), 11, 79–83.
57. On Ada's adoption of Alexander, see Arrian, 1.23.8; cf. Plutarch, *Alexander* 22.7; Bosworth, *Historical Commentary*, 1:154.

58. On Alexander's relationship with Persian women, see E. Carney, 'Alexander and Persian Women', *American Journal of Philology*, 117 (1996), 563–83.

59. Arrian, 4.26.1.

60. Bosworth, *Historical Commentary*, 2:170.

CHAPTER 4

THE ROMAN CONCEPT OF MASSACRE: JULIUS CAESAR IN GAUL

Jane Bellemore

Julius Caesar is regarded as one of Rome's great generals, a reputation he established in the main through his subjugation of Gaul (58–50 BC), but Caesar ensured his place in history by providing a commentary on these campaigns, *Gallic Wars* (*Commentarii de Bello Gallico*), which he published during or just after the period of the campaigns.[1] Although Caesar should be suspected of presenting his actions in Gaul in the best possible light, nevertheless, because of his privileged position as commander of the Roman forces, his view of the motives and strategies used in the deployment of Roman troops is authoritative,[2] and his work provides a unique insight into Roman attitudes to warfare. Since Caesar's military achievements in Gaul became the subject of official praise by the Roman state on three separate occasions in this period (at the end of 57, of 55 and 52 BC),[3] his methods of fighting must have been considered outstanding exemplars of current Roman practice.

Given that Caesar, as the author of the *Gallic Wars*, was in a position to ameliorate the presentation of the events, it comes as a surprise that he describes several occasions when Roman legionaries under his command slaughtered non-combatants, instances that in modern terms would be construed as 'massacres'.[4] An exploration of one episode in particular, supplemented by material from other instances, will reveal Caesar's and hence the Roman attitude to the deaths of non-combatants in the theatre of war. From this we may determine what codes, if any, were observed by the Roman military.[5]

Caesar's Forces Commit a Massacre

In 58 BC, a coalition of Helvetian and other tribes, comprising men, women and children, emigrated from their homelands (in modern Switzerland) with the intention of settling in the far west of Gaul.[6] The most direct route for their migration would have taken them through the Roman province of Gallia Narbonensis, then under Caesar's command, and so they requested Caesar's permission to cross through this territory, but he refused. A number of the Helvetii made a feeble attempt to force their way into the Roman province, but they were kept out by the defences Caesar had put in place. The migrants then decided to change the direction of their trek, and instead of heading due west, they went northwards around the Jura mountains and entered Gaul-proper many hundreds of kilometres to the north of Gallia Narbonensis. Although the Helvetii and their allies had steered well clear of Roman territory, Caesar raised troops and marched out of his province in their direction. When he was informed that the Helvetii were inflicting damage on Rome's allies in Gaul, he decided to put a stop to their depredations by means of an ambush, as he describes:[7]

> The Helvetii were crossing it [the River Saone] on rafts and boats joined together. When Caesar was told by his scouts that three-quarters of the forces of the Helvetii had already crossed the river and that about one-quarter had been left on the near side of the River, at about the third watch [4am], he set off from camp with three legions and reached that contingent which had not yet crossed. He attacked them while they were encumbered with baggage, off their guard, and he killed a large part of them; the rest took to their heels and hid in woods nearby.

Caesar openly acknowledges that three-quarters of the whole tribal force comprised boys, old men and women,[8] and he indicates that the Helvetii were technically non-combatants, as they had no idea that they were enemies of Rome.[9] Although the reason for this military action appears legitimate (to protect Rome's allies), Caesar's failure to declare war, and to distinguish combatants from non-combatants, shows that his attack on the Helvetii, in which up to sixty thousand people were killed, was a massacre.[10] Caesar himself reveals that he considered that some aspects of his attack required explanation, since he goes to great lengths to portray the ambush as 'just'.[11] Let us review these two elements that comprised the massacre, first, the deaths of civilians, and second Caesar's justification for unilateral military action.

Civilian Casualties

In addition to the ambush on the Helvetii, Caesar describes another three occasions when civilians were slaughtered by his troops.

A few weeks after the attack on the Helvetii at the River Saône, the Romans engaged the full army of the Helvetians and their allies in a set battle. After a hard-fought struggle on the field, the Romans drove one section of the enemy combatants back towards their camp, which became the focus of further fighting between the Roman and Gallic forces, but eventually the Romans won the day and took possession of the camp.[12] Caesar reports that the children of one of the Helvetian notables were not killed but were taken captive in the camp,[13] but his comments suggest that the survival of these children was remarkable and that many other non-combatants died in the scrimmage.[14] The figures that Caesar gives for the enemy dead as a whole bear this out, as the migrants had initially totalled 368,000 people, of whom 92,000 were fighting men (about one-quarter of the force),[15] but only 110,000 survived to be repatriated.[16] On this basis, about 250,000 people perished during the course of the campaign,[17] the great majority of whom were civilians.

When Caesar and his Roman legionaries encountered migrating Germans, mainly Suebi, in battle later in 58 BC, non-combatants were also killed. As the Germans took up position, the German fighting men placed their women in wagons and carts around the field of battle,[18] but when their lines broke under pressure from the Romans and the fighting men tried to escape, those in the wagons became caught up in the melee. Caesar claims that the Roman cavalry pursued and killed combatants and non-combatants alike, as he boasts that only a handful of very strong individuals from perhaps as many as eighty thousand men, women and children, escaped the onslaught.[19] As a point of interest, Caesar notes that three royal German women were killed during the pursuit by his cavalry, while one was taken alive,[20] and again the casual nature of his remarks suggests the large numbers of civilians died.

In 55 BC, Caesar reports his interaction with yet another group of migrating Germans, the Usipetes and Tencteri, who had been forced from their homeland and were seeking to settle in northern Gaul near the River Rhine. After these Germans had violated a truce with the Romans, Caesar determined to punish them. When their leaders arrived in his camp to excuse the violation, Caesar arrested them, and used this opportunity to attack their now leaderless tribes:[21]

> My men formed a triple line and quickly marched eight miles. They reached the enemy camp before the Germans could realize that anything was happening. Terrified by this sudden turn of events, by the speed of our arrival and the departure of their leaders, they were thrown into turmoil ... [O]ur men broke into the camp, enraged by the treachery shown the day before. At this point, those who could took up arms ... but the rest of the large horde, boys

and women, began to flee (for the Germans had left their home and crossed the Rhine with all their dependants). Caesar sent his cavalry in pursuit.

Caesar goes on to record that the 'dependants' were killed by his men, and he hints that German losses were close to 430,000.[22] Once again, the majority of these were civilians. The Germans were slaughtered or drowned in the river nearby. Caesar was said to have been attacked by his political enemies in Rome for this instance of violating a truce, but no action was ever taken against him.[23] In any case, Caesar presented a strong case against the Germans for breaking the truce first.

These strikingly similar examples, where the civilians in a camp or in wagons were vulnerable to attack, reveal clearly that Caesar felt no empathy for the plight of civilians caught up in the fighting, and in the last example he presents the women and children as legitimate military targets. While he at times does acknowledge the possibility that non-combatants might be exempted from attack by armed soldiers[24] – and he is offended when Roman and Italian civilians become the object of Gallic attack [25] – his failure to restrain his troops from indiscriminate slaughter indicates that he did not consider himself bound by any convention concerning the protection of civilians. In fact Caesar seems to have inspired his men to slaughter, since he sometimes personally led the charge to cut down fleeing non-combatants,[26] and he boosts the impact of the numbers of the enemy killed by including the deaths of civilians in the overall tally.[27]

Caesar's 'Just War'

Caesar's attitude to the 'rules of war' are best illustrated by two examples, in both of which he used his troops to ambush and wipe out unsuspecting non-combatants.

Although Caesar consistently portrays the Helvetian migration of 58 BC as a major threat to Roman dominion,[28] he shows that his ambush on the Helvetian contingent at the River Saône was not only effective in obviating this threat but was also vengeance for a past wrong.[29] Fifty years before, Caesar reports, this same canton of the Helvetii (called the 'Tigurini'), inflicted a defeat on a Roman army that had inadvertently committed some offence against them. The Tigurini, Caesar complains, did not inform the Romans of their offence but marched out from their territory to set an ambush,[30] and the Romans, being off their guard, had not been in a position to ward off the attack and were easily defeated. Although Caesar admits that he did not know, prior to his own ambush of the Helvetii, that it was the Tigurini he would encounter, he glosses this by suggesting that it was fated that he should attack and punish this canton.[31]

Although Caesar claims that his ambush in 58 BC was modelled on that undertaken by the Tigurini in 107 BC, there are major discrepancies between the two episodes. First, Caesar acknowledges that the 'victim' of the earlier ambush was a Roman army, and that it had committed a serious offence against the Tigurini. What Caesar fails to say, however, is that this Roman army had been actively campaigning outside Roman territory and had pursued the Tigurini across the length of Gaul to the Atlantic ocean,[32] that the 'ambush' had been a military response by the Tigurini, and that this action took place about 500 km from Helvetian territory.[33] Caesar has, therefore, compared the Tigurini in 58 BC, migrants travelling en masse through friendly territory, to a Roman army on campaign in hostile territory. He also claims parity between the offence committed by the Tigurini in 58 BC, when elements of the Helvetii (not necessarily the Tigurini) had briefly tried to get into the Roman province and had later attacked Rome's allies in Gaul, and that committed by the Roman army in 107 BC when it had engaged in a relentless military pursuit of the Tigurini. Caesar also intimates that the Romans in 107 BC had just happened to be in the vicinity of the Tigurini, and that these had then left their home to launch their attack,[34] but it had been the action of the Roman army, in pushing the Tigurini from their homes, that had precipitated their unexpected military response. In 58 BC, however, most of the Helvetii were trying to avoid conflict with the Romans, as in fact the Tigurini had been doing in 107 BC.

On almost every criterion of comparison, the two ambushes were dissimilar, and it seems barely credible to assert that the Romans of 107 BC had been the injured party and that the Tigurini had committed a crime in ambushing them; yet Caesar pursues this line of justification, and he exonerates his ambush of 58 BC by suggesting that his strike prevented a second massacre of a Roman army. To strengthen his case, Caesar claims that the leader of the Helvetian embassy that came to negotiate with him after the ambush of 58 BC was the very same man, Divico, who had led the Tigurini in their ambush fifty years before, and in Caesar's report of his speech, Divico does not complain about the illegality of Caesar's attack but instead recalls the disaster suffered by the Roman army in 107 BC. Divico further boasts that the Helvetii always fought on fair terms, which in this context is clearly a lie, and he threatens Caesar and his army with a massacre (*internecio*), as the army of 107 BC had suffered.[35] Caesar, therefore, makes Divico accept that the Roman ambush of 58 BC was fully justified, that the Helvetii were at fault in 107 BC, and that they were still a threat to the Romans.[36] Although Caesar openly admits that his ambush was a massacre, by his inverted presentation of the ambush of 107 BC, he shows that his attack on the Tigurini was vengeance for a crime committed fifty years before and also a preventive measure to ensure that the Romans not suffer again.[37]

Caesar undertook a second ambush some years later, in 55 BC, which he justifies in terms similar to those used for the earlier occasion. First, he reports that two German tribes crossed the Rhine and, by deception, occupied the lands and possessions of the Gallic Menapii.[38] It is made clear that the Germans were the aggressors in this instance. Second, Caesar claims that these Germans were conspiring against the Romans, since they formed alliances with some of the Gauls whom the Romans had conquered, and he calls this situation war (*bellum*).[39] Caesar raised a levy of Gallic cavalry to wage war against the 'aggressors', but as soon as the Romans approached them, the Germans sent envoys to parley with him.[40] Despite this apparent attempt by the Germans to reach a peaceful agreement with the Romans, in his account of their speech, Caesar has the German envoys indicate that they will resist if attacked, and they suggest that the Romans should ask them to become their allies. To confirm this arrangement, they want to be given land in Gaul, and they conclude by boasting that Germans can easily defeat the Romans.[41]

Caesar refused their terms, and told the Germans to leave Gaul. All the while, Caesar kept moving his forces in the direction of the German forces because he believed that they were being duplicitous and were looking for an opportunity to attack him.[42] When the Germans came to negotiate a second time, Caesar maintained his advance, but at the request of the Germans for a cessation of hostilities, he ordered his cavalry not to engage, and the envoys conditionally accepted the terms he was offering. His fears of treachery proved well-founded, however, since the German army deliberately attacked his cavalry during this period of truce.[43] Because of this treachery, Caesar unilaterally decided to break off negotiations and to retaliate against them.[44] When a delegation of leading Germans came to his camp the following day to apologize for breaking the truce, instead of negotiating, Caesar had these men arrested; he then led out his troops against the German camp, where the ordinary people were awaiting the outcome of the mediation, but he killed these people for the treachery displayed by their leaders (*perfidia*).

In this episode, Caesar shows how he cleverly turns the tables on the Germans, and he includes the key elements of the justification of the earlier ambush. He has argued that the Germans committed an offence against the Romans when they attacked them during a period of truce, and that they deserved to be punished. He also reveals that the Germans were planning an ambush on his forces.

Acceptance of Caesar's Methods

The impact of Caesar's propaganda – that the nations he had overcome in Gaul had been and were still a direct threat to Rome – can be measured in contemporary and later works. The orator Cicero remarked to the Roman Senate in 56 BC and again in 55 BC that Caesar had fought and crushed the fiercest and most important tribes of the Helvetii and Germans, and that his actions were responsible for preventing hostile tribes crossing the Alps and entering Italy;[45] Cicero recalls his full support for the public votes of thanksgiving offered for Caesar's victories of 58 BC and 57 BC.[46] Cicero also reflects Caesar's allusions to the barbarian tribes that attempted to enter Italy at the end of the second century BC, the Cimbri and Teutones, but he claims that Caesar was going one better than the earlier successful commander Marius by seeking out and defeating the Gallic enemy in their strongholds.[47] Cicero promotes the magnitude of Caesar's victories, suggestive of the large numbers of the enemy killed, and he accepts and even advocates the use of pre-emptive strikes as a means of conquering these unrelenting enemies of Rome.[48]

Caesar's later (ca AD 100) Greek biographer Plutarch repeats many of Caesar's claims too. He relishes the fact that Caesar captured more than eight hundred cities in Gaul, killed one million men in battle, and took two million captive,[49] and when he records that Helvetian civilians were slaughtered in large numbers by Caesar's Roman legionaries, he summarizes the action as a 'fine deed', but he adds, by way of clarification, that these women and children had joined in the fray and so were justifiably slaughtered.[50] Plutarch considered, however, that Caesar acted in a better fashion by not killing, but instead repatriating the surviving Helvetians.[51] In terms of civilians, therefore, Plutarch accepts Caesar's right to kill them, but he prefers it if those killed were undeniably combatants and so deserving of their fate.

Plutarch is persuaded by Caesar's justification for his pre-emptive strikes, but he uses his literary skills to sharpen Caesar's military rationale. When describing the events of 58 BC, Plutarch accentuates the threat posed by the Helvetii and Tigurini to Roman dominion by claiming that these tribes had actually entered the Roman province (Gallia Narbonensis), just as the infamous Cimbri and Teutones had done fifty years before.[52] When Plutarch describes the Roman ambush on the Tigurini, he omits most of the detail, and he attributes this attack not to Caesar, but to Caesar's subordinate Labienus, who became renowned for his treachery.[53] Plutarch also suggests that the main force of the Helvetii attacked Caesar without provocation.[54] These modifications present Caesar's military actions against the Helvetii as purely defensive, and so Plutarch has captured the essence of Caesar's justification, while editing the material to present it in a more clear-cut fashion.

Conclusion

The unqualified praise that Caesar received from his fellow Romans for his military actions in Gaul show that Caesar must have been complying with standard Roman practice. As we have seen, Caesar refused to accept that civilians were exempt from attack, and he considered that they comprised a part of an enemy force to be harried, captured and, if required, killed.[55] He did distinguish combatants from non-combatants, but only in the sense that the former were ready for war or were deserving of attack, whereas the latter were not. On this basis, although the Romans killed hundreds of thousands of unarmed and defenceless civilians in Gaul and elsewhere,[56] this was an accepted practice and did not constitute a massacre.

On the other hand, Caesar acknowledges that ambushes entailed not playing by the rules, and so could be interpreted as massacre, but in every instance he constructs strong cases against his enemies to ensure that they were culpable and that the Romans were, or feared to be, the injured party, and Caesar proves to his reader that he and his men never committed a massacre in Gaul.

Cicero reveals the rationale behind this attitude, that Caesar's campaigning methods were never criticized, not just because they were Roman policy, but also because such actions were at the basis of their Empire:[57] 'And so he has, with brilliant success, crushed in battle the fiercest and greatest tribes of Germania and Helvetia; the rest he has terrified, checked and subdued, and taught them to submit to the rule of the Roman people. ... Yet one or two summers, and fear or hope, punishment or rewards, arms or laws can bind the whole of Gaul to us with eternal fetters.'

Notes

1. For a comprehensive discussion of the date of publication of the *Gallic Wars*, see A.M. Riggsby, *Caesar in Gaul and Rome* (Austin, 2006), 9–11. Cicero, Caesar's contemporary, speaks in mid-56 BC of a flood of information about Caesar's achievements, in his speech on the choice of consular provinces (Marcus Tullius Cicero, *de Provinciis Consularibus*, in *Orations*, trans. R. Gardner, 20 vols (Cambridge, Mass., 1958), vol. 13, par. 22).

2. Caesar's accuracy is vouched for by one of his officers Aulus Hirtius (Gaius Julius Caesar, *Gallic War*, trans. H.E. Edwards (London, 1917), book 8 (by Aulus Hirtius), preface 7), but the veracity of the *Gallic Wars* has been hotly debated in modern times. K. Kagan, *Eye of Command* (Ann Arbor, 2006), 108–15, argues for the truthfulness of Caesar's battle descriptions, but Caesar's reliability has been questioned in instances where his leadership or bravery is concerned (J. Collins, 'Caesar as a Political Propagandist', *Aufstieg und Niedergan der römishen Welt* 1.1 (1972), 941–42; A. Powell, 'Julius Caesar and his Presentation of Massacre', in A. Powell and K. Welch (eds), *Julius Caesar as Artful Reporter: the War Commentaries as Political Instruments* (London, 1988), 115–24). Scathing criticisms of Caesar's account have been made by M. Rambaud, *L'Art de la Déformation Historique dans les Commentaires de César* (Paris, 1953), but many of these arguments have been challenged by Collins, 'Caesar', 922–42; see also Riggsby, *Caesar*, 24–45.

3. Caesar, *Gallic War*, book 2, chap. 35, book 4, chap. 37, book 7, chap 90; Cicero, *de Provinciis Consularibus*, 25–26; Plutarch, 'Caesar', in *Plutarch's Lives*, trans. B. Perrin, 11 vols. (London, 1949), vol. 7, chap. 21.

4. For a definition of massacre, see M. Levene, 'Introduction', in M. Levene and P. Roberts (eds), *Massacre in History* (New York, 1999), 5–6; W. Coster, 'The English Civil War', in ibid., 90; J. Semelin, *Purify and Destroy* (New York, 2007), 323–24.

5. For Collins, 'Caesar', 937–38. Moreover, one can argue that Caesar's amoral behaviour and lack of a sense of justice were simply symptomatic of the diminished values of the period. On the other hand, Caesar's enemies were eager to bring him down, and if

Caesar had committed an offence in Gaul that had brought prosecution and condemnation in the past, his enemies would have seized this opportunity to attack him.

6. Caesar, *Gallic War*, 1.2. See Riggsby, *Caesar*, 175–77.
7. This is my translation of Caesar, *Gallic War*, 1.12.1–3.
8. Caesar, *Gallic War*, 1.29, reports that the total of Helvetian fighting men, boys, old men and women numbered 263,000, and later he notes that the fighting men comprised about one quarter of the force (1.29).
9. Caesar, *Gallic War*, 1.7, indicates that his hostility towards the Helvetii was one factor behind his refusal to allow them to cross the Province; yet while he engaged in diplomatic exchanges with them, he made no mention to them of his enmity (ibid., 1.7–8).
10. Caesar, *Gallic War*, 1.29, claims that the Helvetii alone numbered 263,000, and so one-quarter would be approximately 60,000. On the legality of the pre-emptive strike, see Rambaud, *Déformation*, 114–15.
11. 'Justification' must be understood in the broadest possible way, since there was perhaps no one in Rome who needed convincing. See Riggsby, *Caesar*, 157, 171.
12. On the engagement, see Caesar, *Gallic War*, 1.23–26.
13. On the struggle around the camp and its capture along with its contents, see Caesar, *Gallic War*, 1.26.3–4.
14. Caesar reports that about 130,000 Helvetians escaped from the battle, but most later surrendered (*Gallic War*, 1.26–27). Even allowing for those killed in the earlier ambush, this indicates that about 70,000 Helvetii were killed during the battle. Plutarch assumes that most of them were killed in and around the camp at the time of the main battle (Plutarch, 'Caesar,' 18).
15. Caesar, *Gallic War*, 1.29. While the numbers quoted seem large, Caesar is consistent in his claims, and he has won modern support; see C.B.R. Pelling, 'Introduction, Text, and Commentary on Chapters 1–27 of Plutarch's Life of Caesar', (PhD diss., University of Oxford, 1974), 334–35 but also G. Walser, *Bellum Helveticum* (Stuttgart, 1998), 72–74). Caesar was au fait with the approximate number of a Roman legion (5,000), and he had six legions under his command at this time, and so he perhaps estimated numbers of the enemy based on multiples of Roman legions. Even if these figures are too high – and it is also unlikely that these wandering tribes had kept meticulous records of their numbers and classes – Caesar is claiming full responsibility for any and all deaths.
16. One tribe from the migration, the Boii, originally numbering 32,000, settled in Gaul. Therefore, more than 110,000 people survived but not many more (Caesar, *Gallic War*, 7.9).
17. Caesar does not distinguish the status of those who escaped the battle, but he simply records that 130,000 Helvetii got away (*Gallic War*, 1.26). This tally must have included civilians because it is a number larger than the number of fighting men (92,000).
18. There are other mentions of women with the Germans (Caesar, *Gallic War*, 1.50.4; Dio Cassius, in *Dio's Roman History*, trans. E. Cary, 11 vols (Cambridge, Mass., 1914), vol. 3, book 38, chapter 48, verse 1).
19. The cutting down of a fleeing enemy was one of the three recognized stages of a Roman battle (P. Sabin, 'Face of Roman battle', *Journal of Roman Studies*, 90 (2000), 5; Kagan, *Eye*, 120). Plutarch, 'Caesar', 19, states that the bodies and spoils of the Germans littered the ground between the field of battle and the river, and that 80,000 were killed in this engagement. On the numbers of Germans, see Caesar, *Gallic War*, 1.31; on the battle, ibid., 1.51–53.
20. Caesar, *Gallic War*, 1.53.
21. Caesar, *Gallic War*, 4.14–15.
22. Caesar, *Gallic War*, 4.14–15, notes the presence of wagons, baggage, women and children in the camp, which inhibited its defence. Numbers given by Caesar are very large (Collins, 'Caesar', 934).

23. Collins, 'Caesar', 923–26; Powell, 'Julius Caesar', 124–28.
24. In 57 BC, Caesar spared the Bellovaci, a hostile tribe, after approaches had been made to him by its elders and by its boys and women (Caesar, *Gallic War*, 2.13–15). He did not kill Nervian civilians who surrendered to him immediately after the destruction of their army (ibid., 2.16–28). Caesar refrained from attacking the German tribe, the Ubii (ibid., 6.9) and others (ibid., 6.32). During the siege of Gergovia in 52 BC, the women inside the town bared their breasts and leant over the walls, begging the Romans not to kill them (ibid., 7.47), suggesting that these women hoped for mercy.
25. Roman and Italian merchants were slaughtered at Cenabum in 52 BC (Caesar, *Gallic War*, 7.28; also 7.3), which he dubs a particular instance of 'Gallic treachery', *perfidia Gullorum* (ibid., 7.17). Other Romans were taken unawares and killed by the Aeduans (ibid., 7.42). To elevate these deaths to the level of massacre, Caesar uses a word commonly found in the civic sphere to denote 'murder' (*caedes*); e.g. ibid., 6.13, 7.1, which in other contexts suggests unwarranted or undeserved slaughter: ibid., 5.47, 7.28, 7.38 (3 times), 7.42, 7.67, 7.70, 7.88 (2 times).
26. E.g. Caesar, *Gallic War*, 1.12, 1.53, 2.10.
27. Collins, 'Caesar', 933–38. It is likely that all Roman generals inflated the numbers of casualties suffered by the enemy (P.A. Brunt, *Italian Manpower* (Oxford, 1971), 694–97; Pelling, 'Plutarch's Life', 314; see also Powell, 'Julius Caesar', 129, 130, 131).
28. Caesar, *Gallic War*, 1.2, 3, 6–7, 10, 11, 17, 30. Caesar is not alone in his claim that the Helvetii were inveterate enemies of Rome (Marcus Tullius Cicero, *ad Atticum* 1.19.2, 1.20.5, 2.1.11 in *Cicero's Letters to Atticus*, trans. D.R.S. Bailey, 7 vols (Cambridge, 1965), vol. 1, book 1, chap. 19, verse 2, book 1, chap. 20, verse 5, book 2, chap. 1, verse 11). Caesar further claims that the Helvetian leaders were in league with dissident factions within the ranks of his allies (Caesar, *Gallic War*, 1.3, 1.9), which made the Helvetii an even greater threat and his allies potentially disloyal (as we see shown in ibid., 1.15–19). Although Caesar depicts the Helvetii as intent on forcing a passage through the Province, most accepted his refusal and made alternative arrangements to cross Gaul.
29. Cicero, *de Provinciis Consularibus*, 33; Riggsby, *Caesar*, 172.
30. Caesar, *Gallic War*, 1.7–8, 1.12, 13, 14.
31. Caesar, *Gallic War*, 1.12.6, 1.13.4–5. Semelin, 'Purify', 255–56, notes that the perpetrators of massacres often invoke divine sanction for their actions.
32. Other details of the events of 107 BC are scanty. See Titus Livius, *Periochae*, in *Livy, History of Rome*, trans. A.C. Schlesinger, 14 vols (Cambridge, 1959), vol. 14, par. 46; Cornelius Tacitus, *Germania*, in *Agricola. Germania. Dialogue on Oratory*, trans. W. Peterson, 5 vols (Cambridge, Mass., 1914), vol. 1, par. 37; Appian, *Celtica*, in *Roman History*, trans H. White, 4 vols (Cambridge, Mass., 1914), vol. 1, book 1, chap. 3; Paulus Orosius, *Contra Paganos* (Against the Pagans), book 5, chap. 15, verses 23–24, found at http://www.thelatinlibrary.com/orosius/orosius7.shtml.
33. Orosius, *Contra Paganos*, 5.15.23. Although Orosius was writing ca AD 400, he used Livy as a main source (ca 20 BC). Orosius notes that the Tigurini were a military target of the Romans in 107 BC. The ambush occurred in the Guyene district of southern France (Livy, *Periochae*, 65), just north of Gallia Narbonensis.
34. Caesar, *Gallic War*, 1.14.
35. Caesar, *Gallic War*, 1.13.7. Caesar very often associates 'massacre' with the unforeseen deaths of soldiers. When almost ten thousand Roman soldiers died in 55/54 BC, some of them cut down on the march by the enemy, while the rest later took their own lives, their deaths were viewed as massacre, *caedes* (ibid., 5.47). Caesar himself was accused of massacring large numbers of auxiliary Gauls under his command in 52 BC, but he denies this (ibid., 7.38). Cicero too associates massacre in the field with the deaths of Roman soldiers (Marcus Tullius Cicero, *in Pisonein*, in *Orations*, trans. N.H. Watts, 29 vols (Cambridge, Mass., 1931), vol. 14, par. 92). On this definition, see J. Gittings, 'The Indonesian Massacres, 1965–1966', in M. Leven and P. Roberts (eds), *Massacre in History* (New York, 1999), 247.

36. He re-enforces this in a speech in reply, where he claims that the Helvetii were surprised that they had not suffered reprisals for their ambush in 107 BC (Caesar, *Gallic War*, 1.144).
37. After the threat made by the Helvetian legate, Caesar refers once again to the Roman catastrophe of 107 BC, which he claims was undeserved, and he links this to Helvetian aggression against Gallia Narbonensis and Rome's Gallic allies (Caesar, *Gallic War*, 1.14).
38. Caesar, *Gallic War*, 4.4. The Menapii were ambushed when they were unaware of the threat (4.4.5: *inscios inopinantisque*), as had been the Tigurini (1.123: *impeditos et inopinantes*), when attacked by the Romans. On the seizure of land, see Caesar, *Gallic War*, 4.4. Note that Caesar had campaigned successfully in 56 BC against the Menapii and driven them from their territory (ibid., 3.28–29), and it was perhaps for this reason that the Germans were able to take over the region so easily.
39. On the conspiracy and the state of war, see Caesar, *Gallic War*, 4.5–6.
40. Caesar, *Gallic War*, 4.6–7.
41. Caesar, *Gallic War*, 4.7.3, 5 (... esse neminem quem non superare possint: ... 'there was no one whom they could not overcome.')
42. Caesar, *Gallic War*, 4.9.
43. Duplicity (Caesar, *Gallic War*, 4.11); breaking the truce (ibid., 4.9–13). Caesar claims that there were 430,000 Germans (ibid., 4.15). Caesar's breaking of the truce became the subject of criticism in Rome, but no one questioned the military success. In any case, the matter was not pursued. See Collins, 'Caesar', 924–25.
44. Caesar, *Gallic War*, 4.13.1: [Germani] per dolum atque insidias petita pace ultro bellum intulisset: 'since the Germans had deliberately engaged in warfare, although they had sought peace by deception and treachery'. Despite his anger at the deception, Caesar stresses the military advantages to be gained from such a course of action (ibid., 4.13.2).
45. Cicero, *de Provinciis Consularibus*, 33–34; *in Pisonem* 81. See also Cicero, *ad Familiares* in *Letters to Friends*, trans. D.R.S Bailey, 29 vols (Cambridge, Mass., 1958), vol. 25, book 1, chap. 9, verse 12 (December 54).
46. Cicero, *de Provinciis Consularibus*, 25–26; see also Cicero, *in Pisonem*, 59, 61. On the thanksgiving, see also Caesar, *Gallic War*, 2.35.4; Plutarch, 'Caesar', 21.1.
47. Caesar's references to the Cimbri and Teutones are made in the context of his campaigns against the Germans in 58 BC (Caesar, *Gallic War*, 1.33.4, 1.40.5, 2.4.1–3), but Cicero uses these tribes to illustrate the threat that was also posed to Italy by both the Gauls and Germans (Cicero, *de Consularibus Provinciis*, 32–34.; also 19, 26, 27; Cicero, *in Pisonem*, 81).
48. Other Roman writers dwell on the large numbers of the enemy killed by Caesar without thought for their composition (Velleius Paterculus, *Compendium of Roman History*, trans. F.W. Shipley (London, 1924), book 2, chapter 46, verse 1).
49. Plutarch, 'Caesar', 15. The figures had their source in Caesar's account, but they were clearly exaggerated. They are not given any credibility (Pelling, 'Plutarch's Life', 313–15).
50. Plutarch, 'Caesar', 18. Caesar's original report of the episode made no mention of the deaths of women and children (Caesar, *Gallic War*, 1.26), but the overall drop in numbers of the enemy no doubt gave rise to the inference of the destructive outcome of the attack on the Helvetian wagons. He is more discreet later when describing the German campaigns. He reports that eighty thousand Germans died in the engagement, but he refrains from mentioning non-combatants (Plutarch, 'Caesar', 19. Dio Cassius 38.48.1). On this justification, see Semelin, 'Purify', 134–35. Dio Cassius 38.32.5–6, like Caesar, omits the deaths of civilians.
51. Plutarch, 'Caesar', 18.
52. Plutarch assimilates the Helvetii in numbers and courage to the Cimbri and Teutones, and he exaggerates their numbers to 300,000, claiming that over a half – 190,000 – were fighting men.

53. Appian, *Celtica*, 1.3, has followed Plutarch in this instance, whereas the later Dio Cassius 38.32.4 rejects this tradition and has followed Caesar. On the traditions against Labienus, see F.F. Abbott, 'Titus Labienus', *The Classical Journal* 13 (1917), 12–13.

54. Plutarch, 'Caesar', 19, similarly portrays Caesar's attacks on the Germans in 58 BC as legitimate because of the likelihood that they would seize Gaul, and he repeats the comparison of Caesar to Marius, and the Germans to the Cimbri.

55. Consider the unchanging nature of the Roman attitude to non-combatants: in 212 BC, many Syracusans, including Archimedes, were slaughtered when the town was taken (Titus Livius, in *Livy, History of Rome*, trans. F.G. Moore, 14 vols (Cambridge, 1940), vol. 6, book 25, chap. 31); in 102 BC the Romans defeated a tribal army, trapped the remainder against their wagons and slaughtered all the men and the women (Plutarch, 'Marius', in *Plutarch's Lives*, trans. B. Perrin, 11 vols. (London, 1920), vol. 9, chap. 19; see also Velleius Paterculus, 2.12); and in AD 61 the Romans defeated the Britons in battle, forced the men back against their wagons, and there they slaughtered eighty thousand men and women, and even the pack animals (Cornelius Tacitus, *Annals*, trans. J. Jackson (Cambridge, Mass., 1937), book 14, chap. 37). On the massacre of animals, see P. Coates, 'Extermination of the Wolf', in M. Levene and P. Roberts (eds), *Massacre in History* (New York, 1999), 164–65.

56. Roman military brutality was well known to the Greeks by the late third century BC (A.M. Eckstein, 'T. Quinctius Flamininus and the Campaign against Philip in 198 B.C.', *Phoenix*, 30, no. 2 (1976), 126, 134–35, 138, 141; C. Champion, 'Romans as Barbaroi: Three Polybian Speeches and the Politics of Cultural Indeterminacy', *Classical Philology*, 95, no. 4 (2000), 428–29.

57. Marcus Tullius Cicero, 'De Provinciis Consularibus', in *Orations*, trans. R. Gardner (Cambridge, Mass., 1958), par. 33: 'itaque cum acerrimis nationibus et maximis Germanorum et Helvetiorum proeliis felicissime decertavit, ceteras conterruit, compulit, domuit, imperio populi Romani parere adsuefecit.'; par. 34: 'una atque altera aestas vel metu vel spe vel poena vel praemiis vel armis vel legibus potest totam Galliam sempiternis vinculis adstringere.' On Cicero's attitude to Caesar's campaigns, see Riggsby, *Caesar*, 21–24.

CHAPTER 5

ATROCITY AND MASSACRE IN THE HIGH AND LATE MIDDLE AGES

Laurence W. Marvin

If one views 'Western Civilization' as a long but ambiguous continuum, the Middle Ages is often portrayed as its most violent era. When Marcellus the gangster remarks in the film *Pulp Fiction* that he plans to '...git medieval...' on someone, the audience understands he means brutality at the very least, with wholesale slaughter a likely possibility.[1] The terms 'Feudal', 'Medieval' and 'Middle Ages,' are synonymous with arbitrary, extreme forms of violence. This view of course does not square with the facts. Undoubtedly massacre and atrocity formed part of the medieval experience, but the medieval world held no exclusive rights to barbarity on the part of human beings. What I propose to do in this paper is to briefly sketch out how medieval people developed their ideas about massacre and atrocity and explore some attempts to limit it in warfare.

In the still understudied history of atrocity, mass killings and genocide, paradoxically authors usually gloss over the medieval period. Most start with the Bible, swiftly accelerate to the Greeks and Romans and race by with a nod to the Middle Ages before slowing down in the early modern era.[2] Because historical examples provide most of the primary material, this slighting of the Middle Ages seems rather inexplicable. Since genocide usually involves a certain level of technology, perhaps authors justifiably ignore the Middle Ages, yet an examination of recent works reveals that they do not disregard the ancient period on the same grounds.[3]

Medieval people's notions of limitations in war were built on the past but filtered and adjusted for the times. The inheritance from the ancient world emerged from the two distinct trunks of the secular classical and Judeo-Christian traditions. From the classical trunk stemmed three branches of ancient authors who theoretically depicted how warfare should be limited: philosophical writers, like Aristotle[4] and Cicero;[5] military manuals for would-be commanders, by Frontinus,[6] and especially Vegetius;[7] and historical works that discussed contemporary warfare, like Sallust[8] and Julius Caesar.[9]

Ancient philosophers were generally only interested in the causes and who had a right to prosecute war. These authors usually said little to nothing about how combatants, even when fighting a war for just reasons, could or should avoid killing civilians or massacring combatants or non-combatants.[10] Philosophical works therefore tended to focus almost exclusively on the 'just war', or *ius ad bellum* as opposed to the *ius in bello*, or conduct in war.[11] These phrases existed in the ancient and medieval periods but strict definitions for them only emerged in the twentieth century, so we must be careful not to ascribe modern meanings to concepts that really did not exist centuries ago.[12] The second branch, represented by military manuals written by Frontinus and Vegetius, also say surprisingly little about the taking of or arbitrary killing of prisoners, or what it was acceptable to do either to enemy combatants or civilians. The silence on the subject is deafening.[13]

The third branch, composed of ancient authors who wrote histories in which war occupied a central place, represent an entirely different approach. Sallust wrote about real war and Caesar reported his actual experiences. Their accounts of warfare frequently dealt with massacre and atrocity. During the Jugurthine War the famous consul and reforming soldier Marius killed the men and enslaved the women and children of the North African stronghold of Capsa because the town surrendered after a Roman assault breached the gates.[14] Caesar mentions how his legionaries and auxiliaries ravaged Ambiorix's land and people after the chieftain repeatedly eluded a Roman dragnet. Caesar intended to kill as many people and destroy as much property as possible to make the German leader unpopular with a population he could no longer defend.[15] More than a thousand years later medieval readers knew that the slaughter of innocents and prisoners was a regular part of Roman warfare, even though Roman authors themselves tended to view such drastic expedients with regret if not disgust.

The second trunk bequeathed to the Middle Ages was the Judeo-Christian tradition, typified most influentially by St Augustine. Augustine represented a peculiar combination of the pagan classical world and the increasingly Christian one who reconciled that past with the Christian present and future.[16] Unlike the earliest Christian communities, by Augustine's day no one knew when Christ would come back, so one had to worry about the present to some degree, including contemporary problems like excess in warfare. But Augustine avoided this discussion, dealing instead with the same aspect of warfare as classical authors: the just war rather than conduct in war.[17] In fact, Augustine stated that a soldier could serve an unjust ruler and by implication do unjust things if the soldier himself were just.[18]

This dual pagan and Christian tradition that ignored *ius in bello* remained pervasively influential throughout the Middle Ages.[19] By the mid-twelfth century, dozens of clerical writers weighed in on the issue of the just war yet avoided that of the conduct of war, especially against surrendered prisoners or non-combatants.[20] The idea of a 'war crime' would be anachronistic of course, but one might think that more authors would have considered whether arbitrary murder really exhibited Christian charity. In fact, many writers simply reflected St Augustine's idea that a just man serving an unjust ruler in an unjust war should still obey orders even if that led to the death of innocents.[21]

This tradition continued through the Middle Ages. By the fourteenth and fifteenth centuries more secular writers than ever theorized about war, in the vernacular for a lay audience. A lay audience might have been more interested in how war ought to be limited yet authors continued to ignore *ius in bello*, though less so than their forbears. The writings of three of the most noteworthy, Geoffroi de Charny,[22] Honoré Bouvet,[23] and Christine de Pizan,[24] spent considerable effort analysing, paraphrasing, and plagiarizing Vegetius, who had said little about conduct within war, preventing massacre or excesses in warfare. Therefore their writings also tended to lack discussion of *ius in bello*.

Geoffroi de Charny was a knight of the early Hundred Years War who died at the battle of Poitiers in 1356.[25] His most extensive work was *The Book of Chivalry*, written between 1344 and 1352 for the French king and members of the Company of the Star.[26] Because of his experience as a combat-tested knight, one might presume that Charny would have had much to say about limiting combat and protecting the innocent. This was not the case. He only goes as far as to say that men-at-arms (knights) 'should be humble among their friends, proud and bold against their foes, tender and merciful toward those who need assistance, cruel avengers against their enemies, pleasant and amiable with all others'.[27] The closest he got to condemning improper conduct in war was his discussion of those unworthy to be men-at-arms, including those who 'wage war without good reason, who seize other people without prior warning and without any good cause and rob and steal from them, wound and kill them'.[28]

The *Tree of Battles*, written sometime before 1387 by the Benedictine prior Honoré Bouvet, differs from *The Book of Chivalry* only slightly.[29] For example, Bouvet wrote that a man-at-arm's sexual assault of a female was not intrinsically wrong but rather resulted from the war itself either being unjust or the intentionality of the perpetrator being wrong. He stated that 'the good must sometimes suffer by reason of their evil neighbours'.[30] In his chapter on 'How and For what Offences Knights should be punished', he says nothing about military excess, and that if the knight or soldier slaughtered innocent people for a just cause he did nothing wrong.[31] Bouvet maintained that a man captured in a just war was 'the serf of the captor, who could sell him in market as one might sell a horse, or a sheep, or anything else, and who, further, could kill him, or work his will on him in other manner'.[32] The only limitation Bouvet placed on war is when he said that 'to kill an enemy in battle is allowed by law and by the lord, but out of battle no man may kill another save in self-defence, except the lord, after trial', an ambiguous condemnation of the arbitrary killing of prisoners.[33]

Christine de Pizan proffered military advice for the fifteenth-century general when she herself was certainly not a soldier. She was a most unusual author because of her gender, her choice of subject, and because she wrote her works explicitly for payment. In her *Book of Deeds of Arms and Chivalry*, written around 1410, she drew heavily from Vegetius and Bouvet. Like Vegetius, Christine de Pizan said little about *ius in bello*, although she mentioned that prisoners should not be killed, if for no other reason than out of Christian charity.[34]

Formal Movements to Limit Warfare in the Middle Ages

In contrast to writings which were fixated on the just war, attempts were made during the medieval period to limit conditions which might result in atrocities or massacre, the most important being the Peace and Truce of God movements, the first of which began in the late tenth century in southern France.[35] In 989 a bishops' council established exemptions for some members of society from violence associated with warfare or criminality.[36] It was the first major initiative in the Middle Ages concerned with *ius in bello*. Interestingly, its authors were primarily concerned with criminality, asserting that localized warfare involving non-combatants was essentially criminal, not martial, activity. They placed among the protected categories the goods and chattels of peasants and poor people, as well as churchmen and their property. Peasants could still be harmed physically, just not their property. The Peace of God in no way prevented soldiers from fighting but simply represented an attempt to limit violence against a large segment of the population least able to defend itself.[37] The Peace of God movement became popular among all levels of society in southern France but it never became universal across the Frankish realm, let alone Western Europe, and thus only had modest effectiveness.[38]

The eleventh-century Truce of God can perhaps be seen as an extension of the Peace but was in many ways more comprehensive because it prohibited warfare during certain periods of the year, indeed, even certain days of the week. Warfare was suspended from Thursday to Monday morning, on prominent feast days, and during Advent and Lent.[39] The only real personal penalty for breaking the Peace and Truce was excommunication, being cast out of the Christian community by denial of the sacraments and burial in a churchyard, which by our standards was not a powerful disincentive.[40] Added to this, however, was the threat of the suspension of vassals and subjects from their oaths and responsibilities, in effect deposing a ruler or lord, as happened during the famous Investiture Controversy when Gregory VII did so to the German king Henry IV.[41] Clergymen could also impose an interdict, which could penalize everyone in a geographical area by suspending church burials and other services.[42] By holding everyone in a community responsible for the misdeeds of its leaders, the interdict was supposed to add collective coercion against those who broke the Peace and Truce. For a deeply religious society excommunication and interdict were seen as strong inducements to comply, so they should not be discounted. However, the Peace and Truce of God, with their celestial punishments, did not stop warfare at all, let alone the killing or massacring of non-combatants to any great degree, even if they represented an attempt in good faith to restrict warfare and the possibility of killing innocents.

The second attempt to mitigate warfare in the Middle Ages grew out of a code of conduct designed for the knightly class of Europe. This took the form of chivalry, a way of thinking and a genre of literature which developed after 1100.[43] Medieval authors had long artificially divided contemporary society into three groups: those who fought, those who prayed, and those who worked.[44] Among a knight's most important responsibilities was protecting those who could not protect themselves, namely the other two orders.[45] Hence massacre should never occur. Unfortunately the chivalric code only occasionally prevented massacre, atrocity or arbitrary killing between knights.[46] International measures to regulate war and prevent massacre in the Middle Ages therefore did not really exist. Practical measures like the Peace and Truce of God and 'codes' like chivalry were notoriously ineffective. Notwithstanding, medieval warfare had accepted boundaries and chroniclers noted when excesses occurred, increasingly so over the centuries.[47] A brief examination of warfare during the era illustrates these boundaries and excesses.

Sieges

Under certain conditions siege warfare encouraged massacre and atrocity.[48] Unwritten conventions dictated that sieges could end without ill-treatment to the besieged depending on the point at which they surrendered. In the age of the stone castle and before gunpowder, those behind high, thick walls had a remarkable advantage over those trying to get in. By the early thirteenth century Western Europeans were making the most sophisticated stone fortifications in the world. Garrisons quite commonly held out against many times their number.[49] Most blockades and sieges failed because it took too long to bring a town and or its garrison to terms. Because of this, besiegers and besieged understood the consequences were severe when the former successfully stormed a fortification. The earlier the besieged negotiated, the better conditions they got. Before the blockade began, the city or fortification was warned to surrender and could be given the option of marching out with all arms and goods. If, however, that option was not presented or taken and the siege lasted a long time, civilians caught in the middle could expect little mercy. By the time the besiegers stormed the walls, everything fell forfeit to the attackers, including the lives of the losers. This practice was not uniquely medieval: it was an accepted convention going back to the Bible and the Greco-Roman world.[50]

One of the most notorious massacres occurred during the First Crusade. By 1099 the crusaders had endured a three-year death march and perhaps close to ninety per cent of those who had set out from Europe had died.[51] When the crusaders approached their ultimate goal, Jerusalem, they despaired as they realized its substantial defences represented yet one more obstacle which would thin their ranks. Still, this was a tough bunch, hardened survivors of the crucible of war, starvation and disease. After a couple of failed attacks and more than a month-long blockade, they constructed siege towers and assaulted the city. Upon gaining entrance the crusaders massacred the citizens and the garrison, making no distinctions between age, gender or religious affiliation. Several chronicles reported that the crusaders waded in blood up to their ankles or that it reached their horses' bridles; an exaggeration of course, but no chronicler denied that the city's population suffered horribly in the assault's aftermath.[52] Yet the people of Jerusalem could have avoided this had they surrendered earlier. The likelihood of massacre after a siege was a risk accepted by both parties rather than an absolute imperative imposed by one side over another.

Less understandable is what could happen to a captured garrison that had surrendered prior to an assault, but was massacred anyway. A classic case of this occurred in 1219 during the Albigensian Crusade in southern France. At Marmande a huge army led by Louis 'The Lion', heir-apparent to the French crown, frightened the garrison into entering talks to end the siege. The leaders of the garrison, including its commander Centule, Count of Astarac, surrendered themselves to Prince Louis. After the surrender a bishop insisted that the leaders and people be executed because they should have surrendered sooner and because they were heretics.[53] Some secular leaders in the French army supported the bishop, while others reminded Louis that the Count of Astarac had surrendered and therefore deserved to be treated with restraint. When it was pointed out by yet another bishop that executing Centule of Astarac might result in the execution of crusaders in enemy hands, the crusader leadership spared the lives of the count and four other nobles. The men of Louis' army then carried out a thorough massacre of the men, women and children inside Marmande. One chronicler embroidered his account by stating that there were so many corpses that they 'lay on the open ground as if they had rained down from the sky'; another, sympathetic to the French monarchy, stated that Louis' army massacred five thousand people, mostly women and children.[54] We can never know the actual number but the sources agree that an inexcusable massacre of surrendered innocents took place.

Battles

Pitched battles were rare in the Middle Ages for several reasons.[55] The wise commander protected himself behind high, strong walls and allowed his foe to starve or batter himself senseless before giving up. While we cannot know for sure what medieval commanders were thinking, some believed that opting for battle was in fact seeking God's judgement.[56] No one presumed to know what God's judgement might be, so fighting in the field was in fact a great gamble, even if the advantage clearly lay with one side.

The price of God's judgement was high for the loser, especially if they did not share the same social class. By the twelfth century, knights and nobles treated captured opponents of their own social order with some compassion and decency, evidence of the cosmopolitanism existing between warriors who might be friends during a tournament, yet enemies at war, sometimes in the same year.[57] There were exceptions of course, such as the killing of noble prisoners by Henry V at Agincourt.[58] Those not worth ransoming – the vast majority of soldiers in an army – received little sympathy or courtesy if their side lost. For example, during the battle of Muret, fought in southern France in 1213, Simon de Montfort's horsemen encountered the city militia of Toulouse who were bombarding the town. Simon's cavalrymen surprised the hapless militiamen and massacred them as they ran for the Garonne river, many drowning before they reached their boats. Simon's men killed as many as they could; a chronicler stated that every household in Toulouse lost someone at Muret.[59] A year later, in one of the largest battles of the High Middle Ages, Bouvines, whole units of infantry were slaughtered on the field when the battle turned against the Emperor Otto's forces.[60] These events reveal that losing a battle was especially hard for those who were not part of the chivalric class.[61]

Raids/Chevauchées

Scholars now believe that most martial activity during the Middle Ages did not involve knights slugging it out in stylized duels, or even sieges necessarily, but in ubiquitous raiding. Raids occurred constantly during war because they were cheap, allowing a general to support his troops from his enemies' territory instead of his own. More importantly, successful raids indicated to people of the victimized territory how ineffective their own leaders were, thereby undermining confidence in local government.[62]

Terms for raiding differ, though nowadays when scholars use the term '*chevauchée*,' they usually mean a large mounted raid with strategic goals.[63] Raids against agricultural territory, villages and small towns lent themselves perfectly to acts of atrocity and massacre. In fact, it was because of this that the Peace and Truce God had begun in the south of France in the tenth century. Needless to say, independent units and local lords had little incentive to treat those they raided with any sense of decorum, and a recounting of the resulting atrocities and massacres could fill an entire library.

This localized martial activity, and its subsequent atrocities, happened all the time. Orderic Vitalis's *Ecclesiastical History* is a veritable who's who of raids, destruction, despoliation, mutilation and murder as both English and French kings contested control over northern France in the early twelfth century. One of the most infamous raiders, Robert of Bellême, among a long laundry list of transgressions, burned a church with forty-five people inside.[64] Another rebel against the English king, Count Waleran of Meulan, captured a number of peasants cutting wood in 1124 and had their feet chopped off.[65] Later in the century, that supposed paragon of chivalric knighthood, Richard I the Lionheart, retaliated against his enemy Philip Augustus of France by blinding prisoners after the French king had done this to some of Richard's mercenaries.[66]

Endemic raiding and the harsh treatment of non-combatants frequently occurred on frontiers and borderlands. This is true of the margins of the British Isles, both on the western Welsh march and the northern frontier with Scotland. Typically, Celtic peoples were not as well equipped as their English counterparts, so meeting on the battlefield or trying to besiege stone castles had little to recommend it. But the Welsh and Scots became adept at raiding English territory. Terrorizing and massacring villagers formed a standard *modus operandi*. The English of course, did the same thing, with the same results.[67]

Perhaps the most famous medieval raids and massacres occurred during the Hundred Years War. For a variety of reasons the English often conducted *chevauchées*, sometimes to avoid combat against the numerically superior French, and sometimes, ironically, to goad the French into fighting where the English could pick the field.[68] The aim, in part, of this raiding was to demonstrate the French crown's inability to protect its people, since one of King Edward III's ostensible goals was to obtain the French throne. Some of these *chevauchées* lasted for months and were incredibly devastating. One of the most noteworthy was the *chevauchée* conducted by Prince Edward through southern France in 1355. In one sixty-eight day raid, the Black Prince devastated perhaps as much as 18,000 square miles together with its population. [69] Indiscriminate killing, rape and rapine were fixtures of this type of warfare.

As well as all the official activity during the Hundred Years War, the lulls in the fighting saw the destructive work of free companies.[70] Free companies consisted of soldiers of all nationalities who had served in one of the armies employed by the French or English kings. At various points governments either ran out of funds or signed truces with each other, leaving thousands of soldiers unemployed. Unfortunately many had no home or livelihood to return to, so they stayed in their units and continued to do what they did best: raiding, extortion, atrocity and massacre. For several years free companies moved to southern France, Italy, and even Spain. During their operations in Aragon, in 1366, a group of freebooters set a church ablaze in Barbastro, killing two hundred residents in the fire.[71] The trail which the Great Companies left across a large swathe of Western Europe during the 1360s was filled with misery and massacre.

Conclusion

Ancient and medieval philosophers were not normally interested in limiting warfare or discussing proper conduct within it. More practical movements, like the Peace and Truce of God, had little influence. Yet in spite of the lack of formal attention and writing about limiting excesses in warfare, what should be remembered is that in general, warfare in the Middle Ages was no more common or cruel than in any other era. Massacres occurred no more frequently or with any more brutality than those perpetrated at Melos during the Peloponnesian War, Magdeburg in 1631 during the Thirty Years War, or Fort Pillow during the American Civil War.[72] The lack of technology and the limitations of pre-modern government helped to restrict the potential for excesses in war. No western kingdom, not even the pope preaching a crusade, had sufficient authority or the infrastructure to systematically have people massacred, even in such a religiously charged atmosphere as the one which produced the Albigensian Crusade.

That being said, the potential for massacre and atrocity increased under certain conditions, especially on the 'frontiers' of the medieval world. I place 'frontier' in quotation marks because the potential for massacre was greater on political frontiers, such as the English border with Wales or Scotland, or the Middle East.[73] Yet frontiers also existed in the cultural and religious sense. The latter obviously brings to mind the crusades, and some spectacular massacres did take place during the time of the crusades. But massacres could have cultural origins, as in Jewish communities in the Rhineland during the era of the First Crusade. In any place where an actual or metaphorical frontier existed, massacre was more likely to happen in the Middle Ages.

Notes

1. Carolyn Dinshaw, 'Getting Medieval: *Pulp Fiction*, Gawain, Foucault', in Dolores Warwick Frese and Katherine O'Brien O'Keefe (eds), *The Book and the Body* (Notre Dame, 1997), 116–63, especially 116–18; Marcus Bull, *Thinking Medieval: An Introduction to the Study of the Middle Ages* (New York, 2005), 10–13.
2. Martin Shaw, *War and Genocide. Organized Killing in Modern Society* (Malden, MA, 2003); William D. Rubinstein, *Genocide: A History* (London, 2004), 29–34; Daniel Chirot and Clark McCauley, *Why Not Kill them All? The Logic and Prevention of Mass Political Murder* (Princeton, 2006), 14, 39–40, 68, 107, 112–13; Ben Kiernan, *Blood and Soil. A World History of Genocide and Extermination from Sparta to Darfur* (New Haven, 2007), 64–70; Hugo Slim, *Killing Civilians. Method, Madness, and Morality in War* (New York, 2008), 12–13, 47–48, 80–82, 131–33. I note, however, that Steven J. Katz, *The Holocaust in Historical Context I: The Holocaust and Mass Death before the Modern Age* (New York and Oxford, 1994), relies on solid primary sources as well as secondary material written by specialists in the medieval period.
3. Kiernan, *Blood and Soil*, 58–59, 64. For example, Kiernan says 'Imperial expansion was brutal, but medieval warfare rarely reached the level of genocide'.
4. Aristotle, *Politics*, trans. Ernest Barker, rev. R.F. Stalley (New York, 1995); Bernard G. Dod, 'Aristoteles Latinus', in Norman Kretzmann, Anthony Kenny and Jan Pinborg (eds), *The Cambridge History of Later Medieval Philosophy. From the Rediscovery of Aristotle to the Disintegration of Scholasticism 1100–1600* (Cambridge, 1982), 45–53. Direct knowledge of Aristotle only occurred after 1100. References to primary sources are to accessible English translations when available.
5. Cicero, *De Officiis*, trans. Walter Miller (Cambridge, 1913, 2005).
6. Frontinus, *Strategems*, trans. Charles E. Bennett, ed. Mary B McElwain (Cambridge, 1925, 2003).
7. Vegetius, *Epitome of Military Science*, trans. N.P. Milner, 2nd edn (Liverpool, 1996). Vegetius was especially popular throughout the Middle Ages; see Walter Goffart, 'The Date and Purpose of Vegetius' "De Re Militari"', *Traditio*, 33 (1977), 65–100; Charles R. Shrader, 'A Handlist of Extant Manuscripts Containing the *De Re Militari* of Flavius Vegetius Renatus', *Scriptorium*, 33.2 (1979), 280–305 and 'The Influence of Vegetius' *De re militari*', *Military Affairs*, 45.4 (1981), 167–72; Bernard S. Bachrach, 'The Practical Use of Vegetius' *De Re Militari* During the Early Middle Ages', *The Historian*, 47.2 (1985), 239–55; Clifford J. Rogers, 'The Vegetian "Science of Warfare" in the Middle Ages', *The Journal of Medieval Military History*, I (2002), 1–19; Helen Nicholson, *Medieval Warfare. Theory and Practice of War in Europe 300–1500* (New York, 2004), 13–19; David Whetham, *Just Wars and Moral Victories: Surprise, Deception and the Normative Framework of European War in the Later Middle Ages* (Leiden, 2009), 121–22.
8. Sallust, *The Jugurthine War*, trans. S.A. Handford (London, 1963).
9. Julius Caesar, *The Gallic War*, trans. Carolyn Hammond (Oxford, 1996), xxxviii–xxxix.
10. Robert C. Stacey, 'The Age of Chivalry', in Michael Howard et al. (eds), *The Laws of War. Constraints on Warfare in the Western World* (New Haven, 1994), 30; Aristotle, *The Nicomachean Ethics*, trans. H. Rackham (Cambridge, 1926, 2003), 615. I note, however, that in Cicero, *De Offiiciis*, 83, he says, 'As to destroying and plundering cities, let me say that great care should be taken that nothing be done in reckless cruelty or wantonness. And it is a great man's duty in troublous times to single out the guilty for punishment, to spare the many, and in every turn of fortune to hold to a true and honourable course.'
11. Robert Kolb, 'Origin of the Twin Terms *jus ad bellum/jus in bello*', *The International Review of the Red Cross*, 320 (1997), 553–62. See footnote 1, 553. Kolb defines the former as, 'the conditions under which one may resort to war or to force in general' while he defines the latter as that which 'governs the conduct of belligerents during a war'.

12. Kolb, 'Origins of the Twin Terms', 553.
13. Frontinus, *Strategems,* 165–70; Vegetius, *Epitome,* 116.
14. Sallust, *Jugurthine War,* 124, 126–27.
15. Caesar, *Gallic War,* 208–209.
16. Frederick Russell, *The Just War in the Middle Ages* (Cambridge, 1975), 16.
17. Augustine, *Answer to Faustus, a Manichean*, trans. Roland Teske (Hyde Park, 2007), 351–53 and *Concerning the City of God against the Pagans*, trans. Henry Bettenson (London, 1972), 11, 861–62, 866–72; Russell, *Just War*, 16–26; Maurice Keen, *The Laws of War in the Late Middle Ages* (London, 1965); R.A. Markus, 'Saint Augustine's Views on the "Just War"', *The Church and War. Studies in Church History,* 20 (1983), 1–13.
18. Augustine, *Answer to Faustus*, 352.
19. John R. E. Bliese, 'The Just War as Concept and Motive in the Central Middle Ages', *Medievalia et Humanistica,* n.s. 17 (1991), 4–5.
20. Russell, *Just War*, 26, 60, 84–85, 128–29; Whetham, *Just Wars*, 46.
21. John of Salisbury, *Policraticus*, ed. and trans. Cary J. Nederman (Cambridge, 1990), 117–18.
22. Geoffroi de Charny, *The Book of Chivalry of Geoffroi de Charny. Text, Context, and Translation*, trans. Elspeth Kennedy, ed. Richard W. Kaeuper (Philadelphia, 1996).
23. Honoré Bouvet, *The Tree of Battles*, trans. G.W. Coopland (Liverpool, 1949).
24. Christine de Pizan, *The Book of Deeds of Arms and of Chivalry*, trans. Sumner Willard (University Park, 1999).
25. Charny, *Book of Chivalry*, 3–17; Whetham, *Just Wars*, 166–67, 172.
26. Charny, *Book of Chivalry*, 21–22.
27. Charny, *Book of Chivalry*, 129.
28. Charny, *Book of Chivalry*, 177, 179.
29. Whetham, *Just Wars*, 48–49.
30. Bouvet, *Tree*, 125.
31. Bouvet, *Tree*, 132–33.
32. Bouvet, *Tree*, 151.
33. Bouvet, *Tree*, 152.
34. Pizan, *Book of Deeds*, 169–70, 172.
35. Thomas Head and Richard Landes (eds), *The Peace of God. Social Violence and Religious Response in France around the Year 1000* (Ithaca, 1992); Thomas N. Bisson, 'The Organized Peace in Southern France and Catalonia (c.1140–c. 1233)', in *Medieval France and Her Pyrenean Neighbours* (London, 1989): 215–36; Georges Duby, *The Chivalrous Society*, trans. Cynthia Postan (Berkeley, 1977), 123–33; H.E.J. Cowdrey, 'The Peace and Truce of God in the Eleventh Century', *Past and Present*, 46 (1970), 42–67.
36. Head and Landes, *Peace of God*, 327–28; Cowdrey, 'Peace and Truce', 42–43; Duby, *Chivalrous Society*, 125.
37. Duby, *Chivalrous Society*, 129.
38. Head and Landes, *Peace of God*, 4–6.
39. Head and Landes, *Peace of God*, 7, 342.
40. Elisabeth Vodola, *Excommunication in the Middle Ages* (Berkeley, 1986), 19–20.
41. Vodola, *Excommunication*, 21–23.
42. Peter D. Clarke, *The Interdict in the Thirteenth Century: A Question of Collective Guilt* (Oxford, 2007), 59–75.
43. Maurice Keen, *Chivalry* (New Haven, 1984); Richard Barber, *The Knight and Chivalry*, rev. edn (Woodbridge, 1995).
44. Georges Duby, *The Three Orders: Feudal Society Imagined*, trans. Arthur Goldhammer. (Chicago, 1980).
45. Bernard of Clairvaux, 'In Praise of the New Knighthood', in *Treatises III*, trans. Daniel O'Donovan (Kalamazoo, 1977), 134.
46. Richard Kaueper, *Chivalry and Violence in Medieval Europe* (Oxford, 1999), 169.

47. Daniel Baraz, *Medieval Cruelty. Changing Perceptions, Late Antiquity to the Early Modern Period* (Ithaca, 2003), 85–89, 177. Baraz suggests that the idea of atrocity developed during the High Middle Ages as more chroniclers wrote about extreme conduct.

48. John France, 'Siege Conventions in Western Europe and the Latin East', in Philip de Souza and John France (eds), *War and Peace in Ancient and Medieval History* (Cambridge, 2008), 158–72; Keene, *Laws of War*, 119–33; Sean McGlynn, *By Sword and Fire. Cruelty and Atrocity in Medieval Warfare* (London, 2008), 145, 148–49, 151–52.

49. John France, *Western Warfare in the Age of the Crusades 1100–1300* (Ithaca, 1999), 87–95, 126–27; Nicholson, *Medieval Warfare*, 81–86, 128–33.

50. Paul Bentley Kern, *Ancient Siege Warfare* (Bloomington, 1999), 22–25, 135–62, 323–44.

51. John France, *Victory in the East. A Military History of the First Crusade* (Cambridge, 1994), 3–4, 131, 134–42, 330–31; Thomas Asbridge, *The First Crusade. A New History* (Oxford, 2004), 40, 65, 300; Conor Kostick, *The Social Structure of the First Crusade* (Leiden, 2008), 288–90.

52. Albert of Aachen, *Historia Ierosolimitana*, ed. and trans. Susan B. Edgington (Oxford, 2007), 430–33, 436–45; Anonymous, *Gesta Francorum et aliorum Hierosolimitanorum* trans. Rosalind Hill (London, 1962), 90–92; Raymond D'Aguilers, *Historia Francorum Qui Ceperunt Iherusalem*, trans. John Hugh Hill and Laurita L. Hill (Philadelphia, 1968), 125–28; Peter Tudebode, *Historia de Hierosolymitano Itinere*, trans. John Hugh Hill and Laurita L. Hill (Philadelphia, 1974), 118–20; Benjamin Z. Kedar, 'The Jerusalem Massacre of July 1099 in the Western Historiography of the Crusades', *Crusades*, 3 (2004), 15–75; France, *Victory in the East*, 355; Asbridge, *First Crusade*, 316–21; McGlynn, *Sword and Fire*, 152–61; David Hay, 'Gender Bias and Religious Intolerance in Accounts of the "Massacres" of the First Crusade', in Michael Gervers and James M. Powell (eds), *Tolerance and Intolerance. Social Conflict in the Age of the Crusades* (Syracruse, 2001), 3–10.

53. Claire Taylor, *Heresy in Medieval France. Dualism in Aquitaine and the Agenais, 1000–1249* (Woodbridge, 2005), 219.

54. William of Tudela, *Song of the Cathar Wars. A History of the Albigensian Crusade*, trans. Janet Shirley (Aldershot, 1996), 187–89; William of Puylaurens, *The Chronicle of William of Puylaurens*, trans. W.A. and M.D. Sibly (Woodbridge, 2003), 64–65; William the Breton, *Gesta Philippi Augusti. Œuvres de Rigord et de Guillaume le Breton*, ed. François Delaborde (Paris, 1882), 319; Laurence W. Marvin, *The Occitan War: A Military and Political History of the Albigensian Crusade, 1209–1218* (Cambridge, 2008), 298–300.

55. John Gillingham, 'Richard I and the Science of War in the Middle Ages', in John Gillingham and J.C. Holt (eds), *War and Government in the Middle Ages* (Exeter, 1984), 78–91, esp. 81; Bernard S. Bachrach, 'Siege Warfare, A Reconnaissance', *The Journal of Military History*, 58 (1994), 119–33. Rogers, 'Vegetian "Science"', 2–5 and footnote 6 challenges this thesis.

56. Whetham, *Just Wars*, 248.

57. John Gillingham, 'Conquering the Barbarians: War and Chivalry in Twelfth-Century Britain', *Haskins Society Journal*, 4 (1992), 67–84, esp. 79; Matthew Strickland, 'Slaughter, Slavery or Ransom: the Impact of the Conquest on Conduct in Warfare', *England in the Eleventh Century. Harlaxton Medieval Studies*, 2 (Stanford, 1992), 41–59; David Crouch, *The Birth of Nobility. Constructing Aristocracy in England and France 900–1300* (Harlow, 2005), 63–66.

58. Anne Curry, *Agincourt A New History* (Gloucestershire, 2005), 212–21.

59. William of Puylaurens, *Chronicle*, 48–49.

60. William the Breton, *Gesta Philippi*, 289–90; Georges Duby, *The Legend of Bouvines*, trans. Catherine Tihanyi (Berkeley, 1990), 123, 202.

61. Matthew Strickland, *War and Chivalry. The Conduct and Perception of War in England and Normandy, 1066–1217* (Cambridge, 1996), 176–81.

62. France, *Western Warfare*, 9–10, 14; Clifford J. Rogers, 'Edward III and the Dialectics of Strategy, 1327–1360', in Clifford J. Rogers (ed.), *The Wars of Edward III. Sources and Interpretations* (Woodbridge, 1999), 265–83, esp. 273; Whetham, *Just Wars*, 11–12.

63. Rogers, 'Edward III and Dialectics', 266–67.

64. Orderic Vitalis *The Ecclesiastical History of Orderic Vitalis* VI, ed. and trans. Marjorie Chibnall (Oxford, 1978), 63; Christopher J. Holdsworth, 'Ideas and Reality: Some Attempts to Control and Defuse War in the Twelfth Century', *The Church in War. Studies in Church History*, 20 (1983), 59–78, esp. 71–72.

65. Orderic Vitalis, *Ecclesiastical History*, VI, 349.

66. William the Breton, *Philippide, Œuvres de Rigord et de Guillaume le Breton*, ed. François Delaborde (Paris, 1885), 136–37; John Gillingham, *Richard I* (New Haven, 1999), 316; McGlynn, *Sword and Fire*, 61.

67. Henry of Huntingdon, *The History of the English People 1000–1154*, trans. Diana Greenway (Oxford, 1996), 69–70; John of Salisbury, *Policraticus*, 113; Frederick C. Suppe, *Military Institutions on the Welsh Marches, 1066–1300* (Woodbridge, 1994), 9–12, 21–24; R.R. Davies, *Domination and Conquest: The Experience of Ireland, Scotland and Wales 1100–1300* (Cambridge, 1990), 26–27.

68. Rogers, 'Edward III and Dialectics', 267, 272.

69. Clifford J. Rogers, 'By Fire and Sword. Bellum Hostile and "Civilians" in the Hundred Years War', in *Civilians in the Path of War* (Lincoln, 2002), 37–38, 46–48; Christopher Allmand, 'War and the Non-Combatant in the Middle Ages', in Maurice Keen (ed.), *Medieval Warfare. A History* (Oxford, 1999), 259–62.

70. Rogers, *Civilians*, 48; Kenneth Fowler, *Medieval Mercenaries I: The Great Companies* (Oxford, 2001), 1–3, 133, 169; Jonathan Sumption, *The Hundred Years War II: Trial by Fire* (Philadelphia, 1999), 462–67, 533.

71. Fowler, *Medieval Mercenaries*, 169; Sumption, *Hundred Years War II*, 533.

72. Hans Medick, trans. Pamela Selwyn, 'Historical Event and Contemporary Experience: The Capture and Destruction of Magdeburg in 1631', *History Workshop Journal*, 52 (2001), 23–48; John Cimprich, *Fort Pillow, a Civil War Massacre, and Public Memory* (Baton Rouge, 2005).

73. Gillingham, 'Conquering the Barbarians'; Strickland, *War and Chivalry*, 291–312.

Chapter 6

A Sea of Blood? Massacres during the Wars of the Three Kingdoms, 1641–1653

Inga Jones

⚜

Massacres – An Overview

> Atrocity – this close-range murder of the innocent and helpless – is the most repulsive aspect of war, and that which resides within man and permits him to perform these acts is the most repulsive aspect of mankind.[1]

Thus Dave Grossman described atrocity and massacre – issues which are at the centre of this volume. 'To look at the ugliest aspect of war'[2] is its purpose, not only to answer the question of how such human catastrophes are perceived by contemporaries and successive generations, but, perhaps more importantly, to approach an understanding of why they occur.

The seventeenth century is generally regarded as one of academic and technological innovation, not least in the military sphere. This was the century of Hugo Grotius, Maurice of Nassau, Gustavus Adolphus and the development of standing armies. However, it was also an age of religious wars and colonization, and no wars exemplify the conflict between the progressive thinking of the time and the backwardness of religious and ethnic bigotry as well as those that were fought in the three kingdoms of the British Isles. The study of specific acts of extreme violence illustrates this binary conflict particularly well: while the evolving laws of war generally tended to restrain excesses, especially in England, as soon as religious hatred or feelings of ethnic superiority were involved, all moral and legal considerations were abandoned, and prejudice and intolerance reared their ugly head.

From 1637 to 1653 the three Stuart kingdoms were involved in a series of conflicts that were to rupture the fabric of English, Scottish and Irish societies for decades, and, in the case of Ireland, centuries to come. The wars began with the revolt of the Scottish covenanters against their king and his episcopal church government in 1637, followed by the rebellion of Irish Catholics in 1641, who, mimicking their Scottish brethren, sought to obtain freedom of religious practice and a degree of political independence. The outbreak of the Civil War in England in 1642 finally engulfed the entire British Isles. In the ensuing decade all three kingdoms saw both phases of continuous warfare and periods of relative calm. Due to the nature of these conflicts the sides were far from cleanly delineated, with political, cultural and religious loyalties working against each other. The complexities of allegiance and causes ensured that all three kingdoms – all subjects of King Charles I[3] – fought a series of different conflicts at the same time: civil or civic wars within each kingdom were often conducted alongside conflicts between the kingdoms. Ireland, for example, saw four different armies fighting against each other at one point, while the Scots intervened in English and Irish wars.

This chapter is a distillation of atrocities committed in the three Stuart kingdoms between 1641 and 1653. As such, it is necessarily brief, and avoids detailed discussion of individual cases.[4] Fifteen incidents of massacre committed in England, Scotland and Ireland in the historical episode that is commonly termed the Wars of the Three Kingdoms were analysed and contrasted, with the aim of determining parallels, differences and underlying causes – an approach which allows us to glean the true character of this complicated set of wars. The incidents (displayed in Table 6.1) were selected on the basis of specific criteria such as historical notoriety, evidence of extraordinary cruelty or quantitative considerations, resulting in the selection of four incidents for each of England and Scotland, and seven for Ireland. The inclusion of a larger number of incidents from Ireland reflects the fact that in Ireland, unlike in the other two Stuart kingdoms, the wars were marked by two different phases of particularly violent warfare: the period of the Irish uprising in the winter of 1641–1642 and Cromwell's subsequent subjugation of the country in 1649–1650.

As is the case with modern-day conflict, in seventeenth-century warfare military expediency, strategic considerations and the mode of warfare were all important factors determining where, when and how massacres and atrocities occurred. Assaults on fortified places were especially conducive to the occurrence of massacres, with ten of the fifteen incidents analysed resulting directly or indirectly from such episodes. The spatial constraints of the combat and the absence of the option of flight, combined with the fact that the attackers were facing an enemy which had to that point been safely entrenched behind fortifications while they themselves had to undergo the hardships of a prolonged siege or a physically and mentally demanding assault, contributed to the escalation of violence into uncontrolled slaughter. High numbers of casualties on the part of the attackers, as well as pre-existing animosities and prejudices against their opponents, further increased their determination to fight, thus making the combat especially vicious.[5] As Charles Carlton put it, 'when cornered the weak frequently hide, using the natural features to overcome an enemy's strength'.[6] Accordingly, and particularly towards the latter stages of the Wars of the Three Kingdoms when the parliamentarians began to gain the upper hand, the royalists and their associates throughout the three kingdoms tended to be the besieged (as Table 6.1 demonstrates).

Despite their severity, most of these incidents remained within the permissible boundaries of the internationally accepted codes of conduct, which deemed the annihilation of an entire garrison in the case of a successful assault to be legitimate. It was only at Wexford, where Cromwell's men attacked the stronghold while the negotiations were still in progress, that the rules of war were breached. At Cashel and Drogheda the transgressions were of a different kind. While the killings that took place during the assault in hot blood were perfectly legitimate, the killing of prisoners that occurred in both cases afterwards was widely acknowledged to be a gross violation of the war convention. However, these were not the only transgressions in this particular group of military actions: massacres which were the consequence of breached surrender terms or unmerciful killing of a surrendered garrison were equally common.[7] Such lapses, when they occurred, further contributed to the notoriety of the atrocities in question. Notably, the English incidents stand out for the extent to which the laws of war were observed, a singularity which is confirmed by Barbara Donagan's recent book.[8] Given the predominance of sieges and assaults in the wars of the Stuart dominions, particularly in England and Ireland, combined with the potential dangers and intensity of such military encounters, it is not surprising that a large number of the massacres committed in these wars occurred as a consequence of such engagements. As such, the wars in Britain displayed remarkable continuity with European warfare of the early modern period, with incidents such as the Sacco di Roma (1527), Sacco di Mantova (1630), and the destruction of Magdeburg (1631) constituting Europe's dark exemplars of the brutality that followed the taking of strongholds.[9]

Battles form a further group of military engagements which proved particularly conducive to the occurrence of excessive violence. Amongst the battles fought in Britain at the time, the battles of Aberdeen, Naseby and Philiphaugh stand out for the brutality meted out to the losing side

Table 6.1 Incidents of Massacre during the Wars of the Three Kingdoms

Incident	Perpetrators	Victims	Victims' religion	Hot/Cold Blood	Authorised or not	Military method
Lisgoole (1641) (I)	Irish Rebels	c. 70	protestant	hot blood	yes	siege
Tully (1641) (I)	Irish Rebels	c. 75	protestant	cold blood	no	siege
Islandmagee (1642) (I)	Civilian Ulster Scots + British soldiers	45-70	catholic	cold blood	no	premeditated
Shrule (1642) (I)	Irish Rebels	c. 60	protestant	cold blood	no	premeditated
Barthomley (1643) (E)	Royalist forces	12 villagers	protestant	hot blood	yes	assault
Bolton (1644) (E)	Royalist forces	800–1,000 (72+ civ.)	protestant	hot blood	yes	sack
Aberdeen (1644) (S)	Royalist forces	140–160	protestant	hot blood	no	battle & sack
Naseby (1645) (E)	Parliamentarian forces	c. 100	(likely protestant)	hot blood	no	battle
Philiphaugh (1645) (S)	Scottish Covenanters	c. 350	catholic	hot & cold blood	yes	battle
Basing House (1645) (E)	Parliamentarian forces	c. 100	catholic	hot blood	yes	siege
Lamont (1646) (S)	Scottish Covenanters (Clan Campbell)	c. 100	(protestant)	hot & cold blood	yes	premeditated (siege)
Dunaverty (1647) (S)	Scottish Covenanters	c. 300	catholic	cold blood	yes	siege
Cashel (1647) (I)	Parliamentarian forces	500–700	catholic	hot & cold blood	no	sack
Drogheda (1649) (I)	Parliamentarian forces	3,000–3,500	catholic & protestant	hot & cold blood	yes	siege
Wexford (1649) (I)	Parliamentarian forces	c. 2,000	catholic	hot blood	no	siege

Legend: I = Ireland, E = England, S = Scotland.

(Table 6.1).[10] In all three cases the massacres that took place were to a great degree the consequence of the disintegration and flight of the losing side, the relief and elation felt by the victorious party at survival, and the helplessness of the fleeing soldiers and their camp-followers. Such excesses as occurred, for example, at Aberdeen, where the winning army was not restrained from storming the town following their victory, were permitted by the war convention. By contrast, the killings of the women at Naseby and the camp-followers at Philiphaugh, despite having occurred in hot blood, were clear breaches of the laws of war, directed as they were against women and children who should have been protected by their non-combatant status. Even more indefensible, however, was the cold-blooded killing of the Irish prisoners and the drowning of female and children camp-followers that followed the covenanters' victory at Philiphaugh – both chilling examples of humanity's capacity for unbridled cruelty.

The cases of premeditated massacre, however, are even more disturbing, particularly when it is considered that they were usually committed by people who knew their victims, and often had lived as neighbours for decades,[11] thus vindicating Will Coster's statement that 'the prevalence of certain types of military conflict does not in itself explain why massacres occurred'.[12] Careful analysis of such incidents shows that the predominant factors that contributed to the escalation of violence were the sectarian antagonism between Protestants and Catholics, as well as the cultural and ethnic conflict between the English and Scottish societies and the Gaelic population of the British Isles. The massacres at Shrule and Islandmagee in early 1642 are amongst the best examples of such hatreds, which had been nurtured for decades until they finally found an outlet amidst the breakdown of the social order in Ireland following the Rebellion of 1641.[13] In Scotland, the feelings between the warring parties were heated by age-old clan hatreds, such as persisted between Clan Donald and their associates (including Clan Lamont) and Clan Campbell. The case of Clan Lamont demonstrates how massacres could be carefully planned and executed to achieve specific aims, in this case the annihilation of a rival clan and the seizure of its lands, without any danger of intervention by the government. Quite the opposite in fact: appeals by the surviving members of the clan to the covenanting government remained fruitless, and only with the return of the king in 1660 was a successful suit brought forward against the Marquess of Argyle,[14] resulting in the partial restoration of property to the extremely diminished clan.[15]

The absence of such premeditated atrocities in England, and the fact that all four of the incidents that took place there were committed in hot blood, is significant. Despite the fact that the hostilities were dominated by religious animosities, the survival of what Quentin Outram defined as 'an *imagined community* shared by many soldiers and civilians' contributed to the comparative restraint that can be observed in the English wars.[16] Only where the English were directly confronted with the Irish – in their eyes not only papists and barbarians, but also rebels responsible for the 'Bloody Massacre' of thousands of innocent British Protestants in the winter of 1641–1642 – did the conflict escalate into extreme and unrestrained violence of the kind seen at the battle of Naseby, for example.

There were, therefore, considerable differences in the levels of violence seen in the wars across the individual kingdoms, with the warfare on the Celtic fringes of the Stuart dominions being considerably more severe. Table 6.1 shows that only in Scotland and Ireland were massacres committed in *sang froid*: eight out of eleven incidents examined in these two countries were cold-blooded, calculated killings of prisoners and non-combatants. The correlation between the cold-bloodedness and the extent of authorization for the massacres is also interesting. We find that out of four incidents of unauthorized killing in cold blood, three occurred in Ireland during the first months of the rebellion, a period marked by the total breakdown of order in every sphere of society, and the inability of either side to control their soldiers. Tellingly, the majority of the four authorized massacres in cold blood occurred in Scotland, with the incidents at Dunaverty and Dunoon being the result of the ancient clan feuds between Clan Campbell and the MacDonalds and Lamonts respectively.

The killings that took place after the battle of Philiphaugh were fuelled by the religious and ethnic prejudices of the covenanters towards their Irish enemies and their followers. Of the seven unauthorized massacres, it is only at Shrule that some of the leading personalities intervened in an attempt to stop the carnage. The military commanders of the armies who displayed such brutality at Aberdeen, Naseby, Cashel, and Wexford abstained from restoring order. In fact, they were not even disciplined for failing to do so. It is one of the paradoxes of seventeenth-century warfare that officers who attempted to save their men by surrendering garrisons were usually summarily executed, while commanders who allowed excesses to happen enjoyed impunity or were in fact applauded for the results of their acquiescence.[17]

The numbers of victims allow further conclusions to be drawn as to the degree of violence seen in each of the three theatres of warfare. Surprisingly, it appears that the lowest average of casualties is to be found amongst the Irish incidents of 1641–1642, ranging between 60 and 75 (100, if we consider Portadown, possibly the most infamous incident of this period). This confirms Hilary Simms' argument that the numbers of Protestants killed in the first months of the rebellion were far lower than alleged by outraged contemporaries, who insisted that hundreds of thousands of Protestants were murdered.[18] In England the average lies in a similar range, with Bolton sharply standing out with eight hundred to a thousand deaths. This can be explained by the particularly bitter conflict between the puritan garrison and the strongly anti-puritan royalist forces, which was intensified by local quarrels and the strong desire for revenge on the part of the royalists.

In Scotland, the casualty rate is considerably higher on average, with 160 to 180 people killed at Aberdeen, 300 executed at Dunaverty, and about 350 men, women and children massacred at Philiphaugh. In the case of Clan Lamont about 100 were killed. But however severe the warfare was in Scotland, the most dramatic figures can be found in the later stages of the Irish campaigns when death tolls leapt from hundreds to thousands, Drogheda marking the zenith with 3,500 fatalities. A variety of factors, such as military expediency and strategic considerations, contributed to the severity of the treatment dished out by men such as Oliver Cromwell and Lord Inchiquin at Cashel, Drogheda and Wexford. It is, however, undeniable that religious hatred between Protestants and Catholics, sharpened by ethnic hatred towards the Irish, was the most powerful motivation behind these incidents, arousing as it did passions which were difficult to restrain, particularly when the participants' adrenaline was stirred up by an all-consuming sense of danger and excitement in the heat of combat.

But whatever the specific combination of internal and external factors which led to the massacres discussed in this study, all of them share one particular attribute: in all the desire for revenge was present in one guise or another, ranging from the natural yearning to seek redress for specific grievances or incidents of atrocity, to the urge, fuelled by feelings of sectarian solidarity, to avenge what most Protestants firmly believed to be the massacres of hundreds of thousands of Protestants in 1641. Thus the saying that atrocity begets atrocity was fully vindicated, with the wars of the seventeenth century being guided by the vindictive spirit of the Old Testament.[19]

Massacre and Religion

While several factors contributed to the occurrence of massacres during the Wars of the Three Kingdoms, detailed analysis of specific incidents shows that the element of religious hatred between the opponents, coupled with ethnic prejudice towards the Irish, were undeniably the most powerful incentives behind the atrocities committed during these wars.

Spearheaded by John Morrill, in the past three decades British and Irish historiography has undergone a move away from Marxist attempts to minimize the role played by religion in the wars of the 1640s. There is now a greater recognition that these wars have to be viewed in the context of the series of conflicts raging on the continent. These were fought for many reasons, but the perceived international struggle between the true religion and the forces of Antichrist appeared to be the salient causal factor.[20]

The outbreak of the British troubles in 1637 was precipitated by this binary opposition, as perceived by the majority of the population of the three Stuart kingdoms. Anti-popery thus defined one of the major aspects of the English brand of Protestantism, and of puritanism in particular. The combined effect of the continental wars against the forces of the papal enemy and the ecclesiastical innovations of Archbishop William Laud intensified the existent siege mentality of English puritans in the 1630s.[21] The mere existence of English Catholics (albeit enormously exaggerated in their numbers and their potential threat)[22] led to the labelling of anyone whose religious views were even vaguely suspect as crypto-papists. The imposition of Laudian reforms in all three Stuart kingdoms provoked the repoliticization of the religious scene.[23] Anti-popish hysteria swept through the country as one popish plot after another, centred on the figure of the king and his court, was 'uncovered', culminating in the outbreak of the Irish Rebellion in October 1641. The fear that the Irish rebels, assisted by English and Welsh Catholics, were plotting the looming invasion of England and the extermination of Protestantism, was rampant.[24] The widespread anti-Catholicism thus not only widened the rift between Charles I and his parliament, but also generated the belief that an army was needed for the defence of the country and true religion.[25]

In Scotland the wars were more explicitly religious in character from the start. The National Covenant, which was signed by the majority of Scots in February 1638, was a document deeply embedded in religious rhetoric, vehemently anti-Catholic, and committed to the preservation of presbyterianism.[26] By the time the Scots entered the wars in England and Ireland in 1642–1643 they had already made the leap from their initially narrow demands to the insistence on the establishment of presbyterianism as state church in all three Stuart kingdoms.[27] From the start the covenanters fought a religious war, which in their eyes justified the use of excessive violence against perceived enemies of God and the true religion. This, in turn, meant that when the Irish soldiers surrendered at Philiphaugh, it was not very difficult for the presbyterian clergy to convince General Leslie[28] to deny the prisoners their rights accorded them by the international war convention of seventeenth-century Europe and order their execution. Two years later at Dunaverty it was again Leslie's inability to withstand the demands of clergy which led to the extermination of the major part of the surrendered garrison. As Andrew McKerral put it, such massacres as occurred at Philiphaugh and Dunaverty were fuelled by 'fanaticism pure and simple'.[29]

In Ireland, the situation was different: it appears that in the British Isles it was only here that Protestants and Catholics collided 'head-on' in an attempt to annihilate what each side considered to be God's enemies. Stuart policies of tacit toleration of Catholics, combined with the limited success of the Reformation in large parts of Ireland, created a unique environment in which two rival churches were allowed to flourish.[30] In the long run the divisions between the two evolving societies proved irreconcilable, the pent-up tensions having found their outlet in the outbreak of the Rebellion in October 1641 and the wars that followed. The religious character of these events was apparent from the start: the rebels insisted that they had 'been forced to betake our selves to our Armes, to defend our Religion and liberty'.[31] The attempt to imitate the covenanters' revolt of 1637 is unmistakable.[32] Their deeds confirmed the rebels' words: as early as 25 October it was clear to the Lords Justices of Ireland that Protestants were the primary target of the rebels, who 'robbed and spoiled many English, and none but Prot-estants, leaving the English Papists untouched as well as the Irish'.[33] David Edwards has recently argued that the tendency in late 1641 was indeed 'towards a purely religious war', with English Catholics forming a significant minority of rebels named in the 1641 Depositions, and of every level of the wartime administration of the Confederacy of Kilk-enny, the temporary Irish Catholic government.[34]

The Depositions, a controversial collection of over 3,000 statements taken in the course of over eleven years for the purpose of levelling charges of rebellion and massacre against the Irish rebels and obtaining compensation for their victims,[35] provide ample evidence of the sectarian character of the initial onslaughts on the English and Scottish popula-tion of Ireland. Interpersonal violence against Protestants was accom-panied by the destruction and desecration of churches and Protestant insignia, while the rebels appear to have singled out Protestant clergy for particularly brutal treatment, especially at Shrule, where more than six Protestant clergymen were killed during the onslaught, while others were stripped, and in many cases wounded.[36] In many places the rebel-lion was marked by the attempts of the Catholic clergy to direct the violence towards religious purposes: before Protestants were forced out of their habitations they were often offered the option of converting to Catholicism. Some of the deponents were told by their neighbours that only 'by going to mass' was it possible to save their lives – a warning which proved effective in many cases.[37]

It appears, therefore, that it was only in Ireland that the religiously motivated violence took the form of what Natalie Zemon Davies has defined as a religious riot – the similarities to the riots in sixteenth-century France are indisputable.[38] The expulsion of Protestants, just like the attempts to recover formerly Catholic churches, took the form of a ritualized 'cleansing of heretical pollution' – a 'rite of purification' – which dominated the early stages of the rebellion.[39] The stripping of the British in particular was not only emblematic of the desire of the Irish to send the British colonists home as naked and impoverished as they had arrived, but above all was intended to humiliate the people whom they considered heretics, and therefore a 'polluting' element.[40] Zemon Davies pointed out the religious significance of destruction by water and fire as rites of purification: the rivers not only served as 'convenient mass graves', but they temporarily represented 'a kind of holy water, an essential feature of Catholic rites of exorcism', while fire is considered a 'sacred means of purification' by both Catholics and Protestants.[41] Thus the burning of British Protestants following the siege at Lisgoole and the drownings at Shrule and Portadown can be viewed as attempts on the part of the rebels to cleanse Ireland of the polluting elements.

Nicholas Canny has argued that, despite the involvement of the Catholic clergy in the rebellion, their efforts (at least amongst the higher ranks) were directed less at inciting violence than at directing it towards purely religious purposes, and, where possible, preventing the rebellion from turning into bloodshed. However, he has also shown that more often than not these attempts failed.[42] The lower ranks of the clergy, in particular, whose poverty and frustration were more crippling than that of their superiors, tended to derive 'their own crude interpretations from the justifications for action being outlined by the continentally-trained priests', thus steering the rebels away from the more peaceful objectives of their superiors.[43] Additionally, the rebels very often proved to be beyond the control of the clergy and their military leaders alike. There were men such as the Catholic friar at Shrule, who attempted to save the afflicted Protestants, but more often than not the rebels, frequently motivated by more secular grievances against their captives, took matters into their own hands.[44]

Where the collapse of order was not as complete as in Ulster, the parties opposing each other were in no doubt about the strictly sectarian lines of division.[45] Convinced of the culpability of the Irish Catholics, the Protestants repaid in kind once they recovered from the initial shock. As a result, the parties increasingly became absorbed in a cycle of unparalleled brutality, which was often directed against the innocent population.

The wars that troubled Ireland in the course of the next decade retained this sectarian character. Lord Inchiquin's campaign against the confederate forces in Tipperary in 1647 targeted Catholic clergy in particular, and the desecration of the cathedral and the acts of sacrilege committed by his men following the successful storm of the Rock of Cashel add further weight to the notion of the Irish wars as wars of religion. Compared to what Canny called 'a plethora of experiences on the Continent', the wars that engulfed Ireland in the 1640s were a rather belated release of the tensions and conflicts which had been accumulating in the course of a century. When this release came, however, it did so with a vengeance. In Britain it was only here that Protestantism and Catholicism confronted each other directly, and the passions which were thus released proved incapable of being controlled, plunging the country into what Walter Love described as a time of 'indiscriminate blackness'.[46]

In such an atmosphere it was inevitable that the passions that were thus aroused would ultimately spill over into religiously motivated atrocities. While all of the incidents analysed were the result of the interaction between various factors, the religious character of many of them is unmistakable. While Cashel was an important centre of Munster Catholicism, Bolton and Barthomley were known for their puritanism, with the former regarded by contemporaries as the 'Geneva of Lancashire'.[47] Basing House was not only a known place of refuge for numerous Catholics, but since May 1645 was officially a purely Catholic garrison. The reports that were circulated in the aftermath of these incidents in particular stress the centrality of religious prejudice to the commission of the atrocities: Cromwell's description of Basing House as 'a nest of Romanists'[48] made it sufficiently clear that in the eyes of the parliamentarians, their religious affiliation relegated the inmates of the garrison to sub-human status; in a similar vein the parliamentarians rejoiced at the reports of the execution of the Catholic clergy at Cashel. In Bolton the presence of the Catholic Lancashire troops in Rupert's army ensured that the attack on the stronghold would take the form of what G.M. Trevelyan termed a 'local feud between Catholics and Protestants'.[49] Additionally, Rupert was accused of having singled out several 'godly and zealous Preachers'[50] for particularly gruesome deaths. Even though such reports were often exaggerated, and the said clerics were found alive in 1647, for the parliamentarians there was no question that it was their religion that had made so many puritans victims of the royalist army.[51] At Naseby the killing of the women in the royalist baggage train was motivated primarily by the fact that they were considered to be Irish prostitutes.

In the mind of seventeenth-century Englishmen, however, being Irish was inextricably connected to being Catholic, and seen from this perspective the massacre that took place can be considered as having been motivated by, amongst other reasons, the anti-Catholicism of the parliamentary soldiers. Likewise, it was the covenanting clergy who persuaded Lesley to authorize the massacre of the Irish prisoners after the battle of Philiphaugh, without as much as a hint of remorse on the part of the perpetrators. In their persuasion all these parties were acting in the name of God, exacting just and deserved punishment on what they considered the spawn of Antichrist. As John Morrill has observed, religion has the capacity to arouse passions which go beyond what political or localist concerns can stimulate; a passion which, as the incidents in question amply show, could and did spill over into unrestrained slaughter.[52]

Massacre and Ethnic Prejudice against the Irish

The incidents under review have further emphasized the tremendous effect that the Irish Rebellion of 1641 had on the collective mind of the non-Gaelic population of the British Isles. Not only was the fear of a Catholic invasion paramount, but the extreme hibernophobia was so deeply embedded in the minds of the English and the Scots that the Irish became the scapegoat for much of what occurred. Accounts of atrocities perpetrated by the Irish rebels spread like wildfire and, despite exaggeration and fabrication, they were generally believed, not least because of oral confirmation given by refugees. Bearing in mind that the English public was well informed about the atrocities that took place on the continent, and allowing for the widespread prejudices against Catholics and the Irish in particular, the fear of similar atrocities being perpetrated in England, Wales and Scotland was very real, causing widespread alarm and panic. The severity of the parliamentarian action against the alleged Irish rebels who landed on English soil from 1643 onwards testifies to the continued intensity of the feelings of revulsion and horror that had been aroused by the Irish risings of 1641.[53] In Scotland, the first-hand experience of cruelties committed by the Irish troops only confirmed the existing prejudices against the Irish amongst the Scottish population. It was this intervention more than anything that ultimately made it possible for their inherent contempt towards their fellow Scots from the Highlands to be superseded by this blatant hibernophobia.

These sentiments found their most draconian expression in the parliamentary ordinance of 24 October 1644.[54] The result of the countrywide panic and fear that followed the arrival of royalist soldiers from Ireland in late 1643,[55] such legislation not only excluded the Irish from the right of quarter granted by the contemporary laws of war, but effectively made the killing of the Irish, which would otherwise have been considered a clear breach of the accepted codes of conduct, legitimate, thus formally relegating them to subhuman status. A year later the Scottish Parliament followed suit, by which point the killing of Irish prisoners had already become routine.[56] It was this 'licence to kill' that provided the parliamentary propagandists with a justification for what had happened at Naseby, by maintaining that the women who were killed in the aftermath of the battle were armed and Irish. Such dehumanization and demonization of the Irish thus not only effectively reduced the natural barriers which under other circumstances may have prevented excessive violence, but coupled with their supposed culpability for the alleged massacres of 1641 provoked the worst atrocities of the long war period, and further deepened the rift between the Irish and their English and Scottish counterparts.

Conclusion

The wars fought in the three kingdoms during the 1640s were fought for many reasons, but, in an age when religion was inextricably bound to every aspect of life, it was the beliefs of the people and their fears of change and disruption of their religious liberties which aroused passions strong enough to motivate them to take up arms. This article has shown that this kind of religious motivation lay behind the wars in each of the three Stuart dominions, thus considerably increasing the potential for violence. In situations dominated by strong sectarian hatred, members of the clergy were routinely subjected to mockery and humiliation, and were singled out for especially harsh treatment. With this, a strong case can therefore be made for the Wars of the Three Kingdoms to be regarded as Wars of Religion, this term encompassing not only the justifications used by the warring parties, but also the motivation behind the actions of the belligerents and their behaviour towards their opponents. Bearing in mind the international dimension of religious communities in seventeenth-century Europe, these wars have to be viewed in the context of the international war of the godly against the forces of Antichrist which devastated the continent in the form of the Thirty Years' War – a war whose sectarian character is denoted by Heinz Schilling's term 'konfessionelle Glaubenskriege'.[57]

Coupled with the extreme hibernophobia of the non Gaelic population of the British Isles, the religious hatred contributed considerably to the escalation of the conflicts into unbridled violence, a fact which endangers the very concept of the English Civil Wars as being comparatively benign. Despite the desperate attempts of the English to prevent England from 'turning Germany'.[58] the wars that were fought on English territory turned out to be very violent. Quentin Outram argued that, unlike in Germany, the absence of mercenaries reduced the potential for conflict and thus contained the viciousness of the warfare.[59] As has been shown, however, the English and Scots proved as capable of committing massacres and atrocities as their counterparts on the Celtic fringe and on the continent, and they demonstrated this in abundance during their exploits in Ireland as well as in their own countries. In the mid-seventeenth century the three Stuart kingdoms therefore found themselves immersed in what a contemporary described as a 'sea of blood'.[60] the repercussions of which were to determine the relationships between the three entities for centuries to come.

Notes

1. Dave Grossman, *On Killing. The Psychological Cost of Learning to Kill in War and Society* (New York, 1996), 227. I am grateful to Joel Halcomb and Neil Jones for reading and commenting on the various drafts of this article.
2. Grossman, *On Killing*, 227.
3. Mark A. Kishlansky John Morrill, 'Charles I (1600–1649)', *Oxford Dictionary of National Biography* (Oxford, 2004).
4. Detailed analyses of each incident is provided in my doctoral dissertation, Inga Volmer, 'A Comparative Study of Massacres during the Wars of the Three Kingdoms, 1641–53', PhD, University of Cambridge, 2006.
5. This could be observed most clearly in the sieges at Lisgoole, Bolton, Basing House, Cashel, Drogheda, and Wexford (Volmer, 'Comparative Study', chaps. 3–4).
6. Charles Carlton, *Going to the Wars. The Experience of the British Civil Wars 1638–1651*, 2nd edn (London, 1995), 154. Carlton calculated 198 sieges out of 645 incidents, resulting in 20,981 deaths.

7. Such transgressions occurred at the sieges of Tully, Toward, Ascog, Dunaverty, and the sack of Barthomley (Volmer, 'Comparative Study', chaps. 3–4).

8. Barbara Donagan, *War in England 1642–1649* (Oxford, 2008).

9. P. Burschel, 'Das Heilige und die Gewalt. Zur frühneuzeitlichen Deutung von Massakern', *Archiv für Kulturgeschichte*, 86.2 (2004), 344–47, 354–57; Julius R. Ruff, *Violence in Early Modern Europe* (Cambridge, 2001), 56.

10. Volmer, 'Comparative Study', ch. 2.

11. This is true for both the Islandmagee and the Clan Lamont massacres (Volmer, 'Comparative Study', ch. 5).

12. Will Coster, 'Massacre and Codes of Conduct in the English Civil War', in Mark Levene and Penny Roberts (eds), *The Massacre in History* (New York, 1999), 91. For detailed discussion of premeditated massacres, see Volmer, 'Comparative Study', ch. 5.

13. Volmer, 'Comparative Study', chs. 5.2, 5.3.

14. David Stevenson, 'Campbell, Archibald, Marquess of Argyll (1605/7–1661)', *Oxford Dictionary of National Biography* (Oxford, 2004).

15. Volmer, 'Comparative Study', ch. 5.4.

16. Quentin Outram, 'The Demographic Impact of Early Modern Warfare', *Social Science History*, 26.2 (2002), 247.

17. As happened after Naseby, Cashel and Wexford (Volmer, 'Comparative Study', chs. 2.4, 3.5, 4.4).

18. H. Simms, 'Violence in County Armagh, 1641', in Brian Mac Cuarta (ed.), *Ulster 1641. Aspects of the Rising* (Belfast, 1993), 123–38.

19. The Books of Joshua and Esther, Old Testament, are amongst the best examples for this; for current criticism of this aspect of the Old Testament see amongst others Richard Dawkins, *The God Delusion* (London, 2006), and Christopher Hitchens, *God is Not Great* (London, 2007). For one of the best depictions of the influence of the Old Testament on seventeenth-century minds see especially John Morrill, 'How Oliver Cromwell Thought', in John Morrow and Jonathan Scott (eds), *Liberty, Authority, Formality. Political Ideas and Culture, 1600–1900* (Exeter, 2008), 89–111.

20. See especially John Morrill, *The Nature of the English Revolution. Essays by John Morrill* (London, New York, 1993), 31–176; Christopher Hibbard, *Charles I and the Popish Plot* (Chapel Hill, 1983). For Ireland see especially the work of Nicholas Canny (cited below).

21. Anthony Milton, 'Laud, William (1573–1645)', *Oxford Dictionary of National Biography* (Oxford, 2004).

22. John Bossy calculated that by 1641 the number of known recusants had reached sixty thousand (*The English Catholic Community, 1570–1850* (London, 1975), 182–94).

23. Patrick Collinson, 'Wars of Religion', in idem., *The Birthpangs of Protestant England. Religious and Cultural Change in the Sixteenth and Seventeenth Centuries* (London, 1988), 140, 133, 147–48; John Morrill, 'The Attack on the Church of England in the Long Parliament', in idem., *The Nature of the English Revolution*, 69; and John Morrill, 'The Religious Context', in idem., *The Nature of the English Revolution*, 53–56.

24. For the impact of the Irish rebellion on English society see Keith J. Lindley, 'The Impact of the 1641 Rebellion upon England and Wales', *Irish Historical Studies*, 18.70 (1972), 143–76, and Ethan H. Shagan, 'Constructing Discord: Ideology, Propaganda, and English Responses to the Irish Rebellion of 1641', *Journal of British Studies*, 36.1 (1997), 4–34.

25. Robert Clifton, 'The Fear of Catholics in England, 1637–1645', DPhil diss., Oxford University, 1967, 351.

26. Neil Grant, *The Campbells of Argyll* (London, 1975), 46; Caroline Bingham, *Beyond the Highland Line: Highland History and Culture* (London, 1991), 121.

27. John Morrill, 'The Scottish National Covenant', in idem., *The Nature of the English Revolution*, 114.

28. T. F. Henderson, 'Leslie, David, first Lord Newark (1601–1682)', rev. Edward M. Furgol, *Oxford Dictionary of National Biography* (Oxford, 2004).

29. Andrew McKerral, *Kintyre in the Seventeenth Century* (Edinburgh, 1948), 64.
30. Nicholas Canny has widely written on this topic. See also Hugh F. Kearney, *Strafford in Ireland 1633–41: A Study in Absolutism*, 2nd edn (Cambridge, 1989), 19–20, 109; and Michael Perceval–Maxwell, *The Outbreak of the Irish Rebellion* (Dublin, 1994), 20–27.
31. *The true Demands of the Rebells in Ireland. Declaring The Causes of their taking up Armes...* (London, 1642).
32. Perceval-Maxwell, *Outbreak*, 179–80; Nicholas Canny, *Kingdom and Colony. Ireland in the Atlantic World 1560–1800* (Baltimore, 1988), 60.
33. Lords Justices and council to the Earl of Leicester, Dublin, Dublin, 25 October 1641, in *Calendar of the Manuscripts of the Marquis of Ormonde, N.S.*, ed. H.M.C., 8 vols. (London, 1902–1920), 2:3, 34–39.
34. David Edwards, 'A Haven of Popery: English Catholics' Migration to Ireland in the Age of Plantations', in Alan Ford and John McCafferty (eds), *The Origins of Sectarianism in Early Modern Ireland* (Cambridge, 2005), 124–26.
35. This collection is located in Trinity College, Dublin, and is currently being prepared for digital publication.
36. For the correlation of religion and violence see the work of Nicholas Canny, and especially *Making Ireland British, 1580–1650* (Oxford, 2001), ch. 8, passim, and 'Religion and Violence in Early Modern Ireland', in Kasper von Greyerz and Kim Siebenhüner (eds), *Religion und Gewalt. Konflikte, Rituale, Deutungen (1500–1800)* (Göttingen, 2006), passim.
37. TCD MS 831, fols. 193v–4, deposition of John Gouldsmith.
38. Nathalie Zemon Davis, 'The Rites of Violence: Religious Riot in Sixteenth-century France', *Past and Present*, 59 (1973), 55–59.
39. Canny, 'Religion and Violence', 192; idem., *Kingdom and Colony*, 62.
40. Canny, *Kingdom and Colony*, 61–62; Davis, 'Rites of Violence', 59, 84.
41. Davis, 'Rites of Violence', 82.
42. N. Canny, 'Religion, Politics and the Irish Rising of 1641', in J. Devlin and R. Fanning (eds), *Religion and Rebellion* (Dublin 1997), 58, 62–63.
43. Canny, 'Religion, Politics and the Irish Rising', 63.
44. Volmer, 'Comparative Study', chap. 3.
45. Canny, 'Religion, Politics and the Irish Rising of 1641', 54–55.
46. W.D. Love, 'Civil War in Ireland: Appearances in Three Centuries of Historical Writing', *The Emory University Quarterly*, 22 (1966), 57.
47. W. Beamont, ed., *A Discourse of the War in Lancashire* (Chetham Society, 1864), 48–49.
48. *Moderate Intelligencer*, No. 33, 09–16.10.1645 (TT E.305[3]), n.p.
49. George Macaulay Trevelyan, *England under the Stuarts* (London, New York, 2002), 220.
50. *The Scottish Dove*, No. 34, 31.05.–07.06.1644 (TT E.50[21]), 269.
51. Volmer, 'Comparative Study', 162.
52. Morrill, 'The Religious Context', 68.
53. Lindley, 'The Impact of the 1641 Rebellion', 176. For the very real fear of Catholics and the Irish please refer to the work of Robin Clifton. For the reaction of the English towards the arrival of soldiers from Ireland see Mark Stoyle, *Soldiers and Strangers. An Ethnic History of the English Civil War* (New Haven, London, 2005), 53–72.
54. 'The Lords and Commons assembled in the Parliament of *England*, do *Declare*, That no Quarter shall be given hereafter to any *Irishman*, nor to any Papists whatsoever, born in *Ireland*, which shall be taken in Hostility against the Parliament, either upon the Sea, or within this Kingdom, or Dominion of *Wales*' (24 October 1644, C.J., 3:676). The Scottish followed this example a year later, after the killing of Irish prisoners had become a routine.
55. See Volmer, 'Comparative Study', chs. 2.4, 4.2.

56. This is particularly evident in the massacre after the battle of Philiphaugh, which preceded the legislation ('Two orders of 23 December 1645 concerning the prisoners being held at Selkirk and Jedburgh', in *APS*, 6.1:492–3).

57. Heinz Schilling, 'Die konfessionellen Glaubenskriege und die Formierung des frühmodernen Europa', in Peter Herrmann (ed.), *Glaubenskriege in Vergangenheit und Gegenwart* (Göttingen, 1996), 123–37, esp. 134–35.

58. Ian Roy, 'England Turned Germany? The Aftermath of the Civil War in its European Context,' *Transactions of the Royal Historical Society*, 5th series, 28 (1978), 127–44.

59. Outram, 'The Demographic Impact', 247.

60. Edmund Borlase, *The History of the Execrable Irish Rebellion* (London, 1680).

PART II

THE COLONIAL FRONTIER

CHAPTER 7

LOOKING THE OTHER WAY:
THE GNADENHÜTTEN MASSACRE AND
THE CONTEXTUAL INTERPRETATION
OF VIOLENCE[1]

Rob Harper

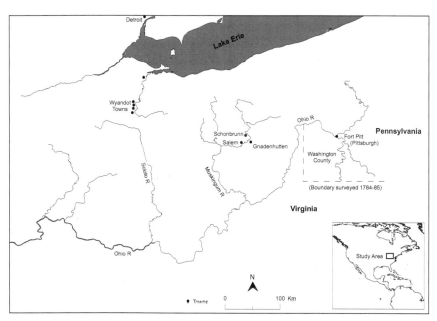

Map 7.1   The Ohio Country, 1782. © 2011 Robert J. Anders.

Data sources: Helen Hornbeck Tanner (ed.), Atlas of Great Lakes Indian History (Norman: University of Oklahoma Press, 1987), maps 15 and 16. Base data: US National Atlas (USGS).

In early March 1782, roughly 160 western Pennsylvania militia marched to eastern Ohio in search of American Indian warriors responsible for attacks on white settlements. According to rumours, the warriors had occupied the town of Gnadenhütten, a recently abandoned mission of the Church of the United Brethren (more commonly known as Moravians). When they arrived, the Pennsylvanians found not warriors, but almost one hundred Moravian Indian converts, who had returned to their former homes to find food. The militia initially offered the Indians safe passage to Fort Pitt, but then accused them of aiding enemy war parties and condemned them to death. Using a Moravian Indian's cooper's mallet, the militia killed and scalped nearly one hundred unarmed captives, including over thirty children. They then plundered and burned the town. They never faced any punishment for their actions.

The Gnadenhütten massacre illustrates a common pattern of frontier violence. During the latter half of the eighteenth century, white settlers repeatedly retaliated for enemy Indian attacks by killing neutral or allied Indians. This series of murders reshaped the trans-Appalachian west, dooming attempts at intercultural accommodation and setting the stage for ongoing war, dispossession, and colonization.

Most explanations of these events place a heavy emphasis on motive, usually attributing them to a deep and abiding hatred of Indians that permeated the colonial backcountry. This focus, however, offers at best a partial and often distorted understanding of how such atrocities came about. In particular, the prevailing concern with why murderers chose to kill has precluded close study of the circumstances that made this choice possible. Most studies seem implicitly to assume that motive constituted a sufficient condition for murder, obviating any further study of causation. In consequence, the scholarly literature on anti-Indian violence tends to obscure rather than explain the social and political context in which these atrocities took place. This reassessment of the Gnadenhütten massacre illustrates the inadequacy of motive-centred interpretations and offers a model for more contextually grounded studies of violence.

Existing interpretations of the massacre are limited in several respects. Most accounts treat the militia as an undifferentiated mob – save for a handful of impotent dissenters – rather than as a collection of individuals with diverse interests and priorities. Also, the persistent emphasis on the murderers' motives has led historians to overlook many contextual concerns. In particular, they neglect to explore either the immediate circumstances that brought the militia to Gnadenhütten or how others enabled or overlooked their actions. This account addresses these problems by exploring why the massacre occurred when it did, how and why the militia resolved upon mass murder, and, after the fact, why civil and military authorities chose to look the other way.

White settlers had suspected the Moravian Indians of treachery for much of the Revolutionary War, but until 1782 the missions were protected by allies in the backcountry military. That changed in early March, when James Marshel, the militia commander of Washington County, Pennsylvania, 'ordered out the militia to go to Muskingum' and investigate the Moravian towns.[2] In doing so, Marshel eliminated obstacles that had faced earlier advocates of an attack, such as how to convince a critical mass of comrades to join them and how to organize a large-scale venture without alerting the Moravians' army allies. An assault on the missions, formerly the project of only the most militant settlers, now acquired the stamp of official policy, attracting individuals who were not interested in persecuting the Moravians but were eager to participate in the collective defence of their homes. Where other military leaders had ignored or suppressed calls for an attack on the mission towns, Marshel used his authority to make them a reality.

Part of the explanation for Marshel's actions lies in the politics of the upper Ohio Valley, where he occupied a particularly precarious position. In early 1781, Pennsylvania had granted Marshel some of the most important offices in a new county government, most notably that of militia commander, but he had since faced many challenges to his authority. Popular resistance sabotaged his attempts to organize militia companies, while voters elected his chief rivals to high office.[3] These difficulties made Marshel's political prospects increasingly doubtful. A report of suspicious activity at the mission towns and subsequent calls for a campaign against them enabled Marshel to show that he could do more than hold unruly musters and guard ineffectual stockades: he would send an expedition into Indian country. By encouraging aggression against Indians, Marshel reasserted his authority as commander while diverting settler hostility away from himself and the government he served. In the process, he helped turn the familiar anti-Moravian rhetoric into gruesome reality.

By ordering an expedition, James Marshel made the massacre possible but not inevitable. When the militia reached the mission towns, they chose how to proceed. Their decision stemmed not from a collective desire to kill, but from widespread deference to the demands of an especially vocal and bloodthirsty faction. In the chain of events that culminated in the massacre, this passive acquiescence mattered as much as the murderers' consuming hatred.

The published histories of Moravians George Henry Loskiel and John Heckewelder attributed the Gnadenhütten massacre to the general contempt felt by frontier settlers for Indians. While both authors noted that some expedition members opposed the slaughter, they stressed that 'the majority remained unmoved, and only differed concerning the mode of execution.' The Indians' few defenders could do nothing but wring their hands, 'calling God to witness' that they took no part in the atrocity.[4] This explanation of the militia's actions established the model that nearly all subsequent accounts have followed.

Heckewelder had described these events rather differently, however, in an earlier and more detailed manuscript entitled 'Captivity and Murder'. According to this account, 'the Major part' of the militia 'were very much against hurting' the captives, who 'were not only declared Innocent by many, but recommended to the Protection and Charity of all as good and true Christians'. These protests, however, failed to move those intent on bloodshed, who 'positively declared that they must Dye'. In this narrative, Heckewelder stated that the passion of a relatively small pro-massacre faction overcame the misgivings of their more numerous companions. This version of events is corroborated by several early sources based on reports from both expedition members and massacre survivors.[5]

Several other details about the event fit well with these reports of significant internal division. However many expedition members supported the massacre, their decision came slowly. Two early sources indicate that the expedition members lingered with their captives for two or three days. Williamson's men had ample reason to hurry: the preceding August, British-allied Indians had ambushed and destroyed a similar force of Pennsylvania militia on the Ohio River.[6] The delay suggests that the militia's decision was neither hasty nor preordained. In addition, expedition members reportedly identified about ten non-Moravian men among their captives. One later source states that these ten, whom the militia presumed to be enemy warriors, were murdered apart from the mission inhabitants. This distinction between 'warriors' and Moravians indicates that some of the militia contemplated killing the former but not the latter. The militia also separated their adult male captives from the women and children, suggesting that at least part of the militia considered indiscriminately slaughtering the men only, as had been done on a campaign the previous year.[7]

The Moravian Indians' remarkable trust in the militia raises further doubts about the breadth of support for the massacre. When the militia arrived at Gnadenhütten, most of the eventual victims were at the neighbouring mission of Salem, several miles downriver. They first learned of Williamson's arrival from John Martin, one of the missionaries' Indian helpers, who had seen the people of Gnadenhütten 'up & down the Streets together with the white People, & as he thought quite merry together'. This sight convinced him that 'their Friends [meaning the Americans] were come out of Love & Friendship, to take them under their Protection & Care'. On receiving this news, the people of Salem sent three men to Gnadenhütten to test the waters. They returned with a number of expedition members, who had 'desired them to Show them the place & People the[y] belonged to'. The Salemites welcomed and fed their guests, who convinced them to join the people of Gnadenhütten for the promised journey to Fort Pitt. On the way to Gnadenhütten, three of the missionaries' Indian assistants conversed extensively with 'such of the white People, who appeared to be religious'. Their interlocutors acknowledged 'that the Indians not only perfectly understood the

Scripture, but indeed were without doubt good Christians'. Two other Moravians spoke with expedition members 'who were inquisitive as to politicks', so that the militia 'became fully acquainted with these Christian Indians in every Respect'. Meanwhile, some of the Moravians' 'big Boys ... were playing all the way with some of the White Lads'.[8] According to Heckewelder, at no point during these events did any militia members threaten or coerce the Salemites. The Moravians had ample opportunities to size up their visitors, and they undoubtedly did so carefully. Tragically, they concluded that Williamson's men could be trusted.

After assembling the Moravians at Gnadenhütten, David Williamson, the expedition commander, instructed the militia to choose 'either to carry the Indians as prisoners to Fort Pitt, or to kill them'. Williamson's decision to entrust the captives' fate to his men reflected the politics of the upper Ohio militia, the commander's recent experiences, and concern for his own popularity and reputation. The previous fall, Williamson had led the expedition that captured a handful of Moravians at the mission towns. On that occasion, he delivered his prisoners to the Continental commander at Fort Pitt, who promptly freed them. Williamson subsequently found himself subject to 'severe animadversions on account of his lenity' to the captives from those who believed that they 'ought to have been killed'. When he returned to Gnadenhütten in March, such criticisms likely gave him pause. Equally important, Williamson's influence over his men was tenuous at best. His wealth and social prestige had secured him a leading position in the local militia, but his actual power extended only as far as his followers' willingness to obey him. Wary of alienating his men and of injuring his reputation at home, he left the fateful decision to a vote.[9]

The political culture of the Pennsylvania backcountry helps to explain how those advocating massacre prevailed in this vote. In their actions, the settlers of this region exhibited a brash majoritarian localism that Saul Cornell has called 'plebeian populism'. In the 1780s and 1790s, plebeian populists fiercely opposed the growing power of both state and federal governments. For them, 'local institutions such as the jury, the militia, or the crowd embodied the true voice of the people'. Rejecting the need for 'any mediating class of political leaders', they held that only the will of the local majority could adequately protect their communities from corrupting private interests. Because of their high regard for popular opinion, these radical localists had little respect for the rights of those who deviated from it. The traumas of war, together with the chronic insecurity of frontier existence, magnified such suspicion and intolerance, leading to hostility and even violence against dissenters.[10]

Widespread fears that conniving enemies of the people could manipulate the democratic process led to widespread suspicion and controversy surrounding militia elections. In early February 1782, 'a Large Mob' at a Washington County militia election prevented the use of the secret ballot, forcing voters to declare their preferences publicly. And in May, another militia expedition nearly collapsed before it began because of infighting over the election of officers.[11] Forbidding the secret ballot enabled the mob to intimidate voters into supporting its candidates. This bullying approach to democracy worked especially well in a society suspicious of difference and hostile toward dissent. In the upper Ohio settlements, separating oneself from the crowd was not merely intimidating but dangerous. Ironically, an ideology that celebrated majority rule could enable a particularly determined or outspoken cohort to cow its opponents into silence, thereby hijacking the much heralded 'will of the people'. A minority faction could thus turn itself into a majority, while a slim majority could become a virtual consensus.

The only detailed account of the fatal vote comes from the account of Joseph Doddridge, a dubious source written decades after the event. According to Doddridge, when the militia met to decide the issue, Williamson simply asked that all those 'in favor of saving [the Moravians'] lives' step forward to be counted. 'On this sixteen, some say eighteen, stepped out of the rank, and formed themselves into a second line; but alas! This line of mercy was far too short for that of vengeance.' Most of those opposed to the slaughter succumbed to 'the fear of public indignation' and 'had not heroism enough to express their opinion'. Doddridge concluded that 'the justice and humanity of a majority [was] silenced by the clamor and violence of a lawless minority'.[12]

These vivid details may well be apocryphal and are probably coloured by the author's desire to uphold 'the honor of my country'.[13] But this account generally fits with other more reliable evidence and helps to illustrate how the fatal decision might have come about. Whether or not most expedition members cherished what Doddridge called justice and humanity, Heckewelder's manuscript and other sources indicate that only a minority endorsed indiscriminate slaughter. Whether or not Williamson asked massacre opponents literally to step forward, the region's intolerant, bullying political culture surely discouraged them from speaking out. It is not hard to imagine how any number of men caved under the pressure, each persuading himself that his lone voice could do little to turn the tide. Other considerations may have contributed as well: an unwillingness to challenge men seeking vengeance for the loss of their families; doubts about the Moravians' innocence; the unpleasant prospect of escorting nearly one hundred captives to Pittsburgh; the desire to share in the loot from the missions; or the belief that Indian lives were less worth defending than white ones. All of these factors encouraged expedition members to follow their commander's lead and decline to take a stand.

In sum, the sources available cast doubt upon the Moravian historians' depiction of an imbalanced, two-sided debate between the mass of Indian haters and a few more humane souls. Heckewelder's manuscript states that the misgivings of the majority gave way to the murderers' resolve. Other evidence suggests that different expedition members had widely varying ideas and expectations about their captives' fate. Williamson's abdication of leadership and a local political culture intolerant of dissent help to explain how the massacre proponents suppressed opposition. These considerations all point to an alternative explanation of how the militia chose mass murder: a relatively small pro-massacre faction prevailed not because of the popularity of their proposal but because those who could have stopped them chose to look the other way.

On learning of the massacre, both Congress and the state of Pennsylvania called for an investigation.[14] The men who led the inquiry, Dorsey Pentecost and William Irvine, chose to suppress the controversy rather than attempt to bring any of the perpetrators to justice. Like James Marshel's decision to order out the Williamson expedition, Irvine and Pentecost's choice reflected particular political predicaments that confronted them at the time.

Since 1774, Virginian Dorsey Pentecost had supported his home province's claim to the upper Ohio Valley. In 1781, after Virginia relinquished that claim to Pennsylvania, Pentecost won election to his new state's highest governing body.[15] This success put him in an awkward position. Notwithstanding his long opposition to Pennsylvania's government, he now found himself among its leading officeholders. He had attained that status, however, only because of popular support in the West – support he owed, at least in part, to his well-known defiance of Philadelphia's authority. Pentecost attempted to finesse this conflict. With his new colleagues in the East, he played the dutiful civil servant. When he returned home, however, he advised his neighbours to resist state taxation, questioned Pennsylvania's claim to the region, and suggested that westerners secede to form a new state.[16] Pentecost presumably hoped that, if such a state came into being, this early support would increase his influence in it. If, on the other hand, the region remained part of Pennsylvania, maintaining good relations with Philadelphia officials would safeguard his political future there. In the spring of 1782, then, he found himself walking a tightrope, seeking to demonstrate his allegiance to both state and settlers. Under such circumstances, the last thing he needed was a controversy that would force him to declare his loyalties openly.

William Irvine found himself in a similarly tenuous position, though for different reasons. An upwardly mobile Scotch-Irish immigrant and physician-turned-soldier, Irvine had grudgingly assumed command of the Continental Army's paltry western forces the previous winter. He resented his assignment to a remote frontier outpost, worried about his ambiguous social standing, faced near mutinous resentment among his troops, and feared that antagonizing the local militia might jeopardize his command. A few weeks after the Gnadenhütten massacre, a group of militia members – probably veterans of Gnadenhütten – attacked the United States' few remaining Indian allies outside the walls of Fort Pitt and threatened to seize the fort itself. They also declared they would scalp

Irvine's second-in-command, John Gibson, Gibson's Native American wife, and their children.[17] Under these circumstances, Irvine had good reason to fear that his western career might end in humiliating failure. Like Pentecost and Marshel, he found that to become an effective leader in the region, he needed to cultivate the support of local inhabitants.

The Philadelphia officials who ordered an inquiry into Gnadenhütten could hardly have chosen two men more reluctant to lead it. Irvine desperately wished to avoid taking any public position on the massacre. He implored his wife, over one hundred miles to the east, to keep her feelings on the matter to herself. Pentecost similarly wished to convince his constituents that he was on their side without alienating his new colleagues in Philadelphia. Whatever credit he earned by quietly encouraging a tax revolt might well vanish if he became embroiled in a public investigation of the militia. Upper Ohio settlers' responses to Gnadenhütten were sharply divided, with 'some condemning, others applauding the measure'. Militia officer Edward Cook claimed that 'the Better Part of the Community' thought that 'the Perpetrators of that wicked Deed ought to be Brought to Condein [appropriate] Punishment'.[18] Irvine and Pentecost's political vulnerabilities, however, made the existence or extent of such feelings irrelevant. Whatever the balance of public opinion, they had good reason to believe that the murderers' defenders were sufficiently passionate and vocal to create a fierce and potentially violent public controversy – an outcome that neither man could afford.

On 7 May the two men met with John Gibson to discuss how to proceed. In their initial inquiries, both Pentecost and Gibson had found that the members of the Williamson expedition differed among themselves about the massacre and that only a minority of the group had supported it. Gibson believed that those who had opposed the murders might be convinced to testify against their companions. Two days later, however, Irvine and Pentecost met again without Gibson and called off the investigation. The political costs of pursuing justice, they concluded, were too great, as the inquiry might 'produce a Confusion, and Ilwill amongst the people'. Rather than stir up further conflict within the region – and risk their own careers in the process – they suggested that the state overlook the massacre while attempting to prevent similar atrocities in the future.[19]

Irvine's experience illustrates how political conflict among colonists could induce those who might otherwise condemn the murderers to tolerate their actions. Early in his tenure at Fort Pitt, he voiced sympathy and admiration for the Moravian congregations. Just two months before the massacre, he sharply rebuked two soldiers accused of attempting to murder an Indian and lamented 'that any person who bears the name of a soldier should be so destitute of humanity or the manly virtues necessary to stamp the profession as to do or say anything even to create a suspicion of so base an act'. During the following months, Irvine grew increasingly wary of making such sentiments public. He worried that the 'general and common opinion of the people of this country [the upper Ohio settlements] is that all Continental officers are too fond of Indians' To gain 'the confidence and esteem of the people', he felt he had to show 'no partiality, favor, or affection to any color'. In practice, this high-minded euphemism meant scrupulously avoiding any hint of criticism of the Gnadenhütten murderers.[20]

Such fears drove Irvine to align himself with, rather than against, the men who helped bring about the massacre. In the weeks and months that followed, he collaborated with James Marshel, David Williamson, and other militia leaders in planning campaigns against British-allied Wyandots. '[I]f they [the militia] behave well on this occasion,' he reasoned, 'it may also, in some measure, atone for the barbarity they are charged with at Muskingum.' These hopes proved illusory. By scrawling on trees and 'exposing Effegies which they left hanging by the heels in every camp' militia members openly mocked Irvine's orders to spare Wyandot prisoners, announcing that 'No quarters [were] to be given to an Indian, whether man, woman, or child' and pledging 'to extermenate the whole Wiandott Tribe.'[21] After the Wyandots and their allies routed one expedition, Irvine agreed to command another one personally. Though 'doubtful of the consequences' he noted that the 'clamorous' settlers 'charge continental officers with want of zeal, activity, and inclination of doing the needful for their protection'. Failing to participate, he feared, could only further jeopardize his own legitimacy – and that of the Congress he served. He even cautiously endorsed settler calls for 'the total destruction of all the Indian settlements within two hundred miles', explaining that their 'dear-bought experience' vindicated this attitude.[22]

Irvine's collaborations with the upper Ohio militia had little military impact but they significantly influenced Irvine himself. In January 1782 he condemned an attack on one Indian; in May, he chose to disregard the slaughter of nearly one hundred. Over the ensuing summer, as he witnessed the toll of Indian attacks on the upper Ohio frontier, his letters increasingly rationalized and defended the attitudes of militant settlers. By the following spring, Irvine embraced their views wholeheartedly, arguing that 'nothing short of a total extirpation of all the western tribes of Indians, or at least driving them over the Mississippi and the Lakes, will insure peace'.[23] Irvine never actually approved of the Gnadenhütten massacre, but he did not have to. Political expediency, together with growing sympathy for the settlers' plight, convinced him not only to let the slaughter go unpunished but to identify ever more closely with those responsible.

Irvine's experience illuminates an important part of the context that made anti-Indian violence possible: the process by which experience, perception, and crisis together created a tolerance for horrific savagery. While we lack the sources necessary to know whether many of his contemporaries underwent a similar transformation, the circumstances of frontier war – widespread terror, doubts about the loyalty of supposed friends, the weakness of civil and military authorities – likely made such experiences commonplace. While stopping short of endorsing mass murder themselves, Irvine and others like him acquired a sinister willingness to overlook the acts of those who did.

Historians' questions about anti-Indian violence have often posited an implicit but sharp distinction between Indian haters and non-Indian haters. Scholars have asked whether the Gnadenhütten murderers were an unfortunate aberration or if they reflected a generally shared racism. This emphasis on the presence or absence of hatred reflects broader questions about the nature of Anglo-American colonialism: whether colonists were mostly good folks or the perpetrators of an eighteenth-century ethnic cleansing; whether the expansion of the United States was heroic or genocidal. These debates over colonists' relative virtue or barbarity are provocative and compelling, but they offer little insight into why certain encounters between Indians and settlers produced mass murder, while countless others did not. For purposes of historical explanation, rather than moral evaluation, an easy distinction between 'haters' and 'non-haters' proves arbitrary and unhelpful.

In this case, many individuals with widely varying motives made choices that enabled the killers to commit their crime and escape unpunished: Marshel, who sent the militia to the mission towns; Williamson, who put the Moravians' fate to a vote; the other expedition members, who chose to let the massacre proceed; and Irvine and Pentecost, who decided to ignore it after the fact. These findings suggest a need to extend the study of anti-Indian violence beyond the motives of perpetrators and a generalized notion of 'Indian hating' to include a closer assessment of the historical context in which it took place.

More specifically, this case points to several aspects of that context that warrant attention. It illustrates the importance of political circumstances: Marshel's and Pentecost's tenuous authority as local leaders, the leadership vacuum fostered by Irvine's recent assumption of command and his absence at the time of the massacre, and the controversy surrounding the release of Moravian prisoners the previous fall. In early 1782 these developments coalesced, seriously weakening the institutions and hierarchies that had previously protected the Moravians from similar attacks. In addition, the willingness of so many individuals to look the other way, exemplified by the shifting attitudes of Irvine, show how people who did not sanction the massacre nonetheless helped to make it possible. Their ideologies shaped and were shaped by the political circumstances of the moment, as Irvine and others sought out, articulated, and ultimately internalized rationales for morally dubious decisions. The complexity and dynamism of these ideas underscores the inadequacy of the catch-all label 'hatred' for explaining the causes of violence.

Finally, historical circumstances, fluctuating ideologies, and the choices they informed all reflected the larger structural context of settler colonialism in the upper Ohio Valley. Many characteristics of the region were typical of settler frontiers: a colonial population rapidly moving beyond the limits of government power; governments attempting, often unsuccessfully, to achieve effective sovereignty; and indigenous peoples intent on protecting their autonomy and the resources on which they depended. These factors combined to undermine the legitimacy and effectiveness of customary legal, political, and military hierarchies among both colonists and Indians, rendering conflict between the two – and between colonists and the governments seeking to rule them – all but inevitable. Officials in London, Philadelphia, and other administrative centres effectively promoted such conflict through ongoing attempts to establish state control over key resources (most notably land), tactics which threatened the economic futures of both natives and settlers while raising the stakes of struggles between them. Such officials typically, and sometimes sincerely, condemned atrocities like the Gnadenhütten massacre, and cited them as further justification for the expansion of state power, but that very expansion had itself created the context that made such crimes possible.[24]

The political predicaments of Marshel, Irvine, and Pentecost reflected this structural context, which placed them in an uncomfortable intermediary position between the governments they represented and the people they were supposed to govern. In many cases, their official duties brought them into direct conflict with settlers' interests and priorities, yet they lacked either the popular legitimacy or the means of coercion necessary to secure popular compliance. Moreover, the resulting struggles infused into the colonial population a strong suspicion of official authority as well as an inclination to support fellow settlers who clashed with it. Many of the factors that made Gnadenhütten possible thus flowed directly from fundamental attributes of colonial society. Colonial structures did not make the massacre inevitable – it resulted from a series of individual decisions, including the murderers' – but the nature of settler colonialism created circumstances that made such choices more likely. Though this structural context did not dictate people's actions, it curtailed their options, skewed their perceptions, and created strong incentives to choose as they did. Further studies of such relationships among ideology, agency, and historical context may shed considerable light on both the causes of violence and the willingness of so many to tolerate it.

Attributing events like the Gnadenhütten massacre to perverse genocidal fantasies can be reassuring. Dwelling on the brutality of perpetrators sets them apart; by contrast, linking mass murder to familiar human frailties such as ambition, insecurity, and cowardice brings the horror ominously close to home. But fully explaining such violence in the past, let alone the present, demands closer attention to how and why individuals look the other way. Widespread willingness to blame atrocities on exotic hatreds only magnifies the need for a more context-sensitive historiography of violence that makes sense of not only the desire to kill, but also the circumstances that turn such dark dreams into reality.

Notes

1. This chapter is a revised and updated version of an article published as 'Looking the Other Way: The Gnadenhutten Massacre and the Contextual Interpretation of Violence', *William and Mary Quarterly*, 64, no. 3 (2007), 621–44.
2. William Irvine to William Moore, 3 May 1782, *Washington-Irvine Correspondence*, ed. C.W. Butterfield (Madison, WI, 1882), 239.
3. Marshel to Joseph Reed, 5 and 27 June 1781, Isaac Mason to Reed, 1 July 1781, Pentecost to Reed, 27 July 1781, and Marshel to William Moore, 4 February 1782, *Pennsylvania Archives*, 12 vols., ed. Samuel Hazard (Philadelphia, 1852–1856), 9:193–94, 233–34, 238–39, 315–19, 484–85; Pentecost to Moore, 25 March 1782, Records of Pennsylvania's Revolutionary Governments, 1775–1790, RG 27, Pennsylvania State Archives, Harrisburg, reel 19, frames 601–604, Microfilm; Lewis Clark Walkinshaw, *Annals of Southwestern Pennsylvania*, 2 vols. (New York, 1939), 2:153–55.
4. George Henry Loskiel, *History of the Mission of the United Brethren Among the Indians in North America*, 3 pts., trans. Christian Ignatius La Trobe (1789; London, 1794), 3:175–81, quotation 179; John Heckewelder, *Narrative of the Mission of the United Brethren Among the Delaware and Mohegan Indians* (1820; New York, 1971), 311–24.
5. 'Captivity and Murder', in Paul A.W. Wallace (ed.), *Thirty Thousand Miles with John Heckewelder* (Pittsburgh, 1958), 194; Dorsey Pentecost to William Moore, 8 May 1782, *Pennsylvania Archives*, 9:540; *Pennsylvania Packet*, 7 November 1782; *Diary of David Zeisberger a Moravian Missionary Among the Indians of Ohio*, 2 vols., ed. and trans. Eugene F. Bliss (1885; St. Clair Shores, MI, 1972), 1:85.
6. William Irvine to George Washington, 20 April 1782, *Washington-Irvine Correspondence*, 99; *Pennsylvania Packet*, 7 November 1782. For the August 1781 ambush, see Thompson and McKee to De Peyster, 29 August 1781, *Washington-Irvine Correspondence*, 230 n. 2.
7. *Diary of David Zeisberger*, 1:79, 85; *Pennsylvania Packet*, 7 November 1782; Joseph Doddridge, *Notes on the Settlement and Indian Wars of the Western Parts of Virginia and Pennsylvania, from 1763 to 1783, Inclusive*, ed. J.S. Ritenour and W.T. Lindsey (1912; Parsons, WV, 1960), 192 (quotation).
8. Heckewelder, 'Captivity and Murder', 191–93.
9. Relation of Frederick Lineback, [April 1782], *Pennsylvania Archives*, 9:524; Doddridge, *Settlement and Indian Wars*, 199.
10. Saul Cornell, *The Other Founders: Anti-Federalism and the Dissenting Tradition in America, 1788–1828* (Chapel Hill, NC, 1999), 109–14, 208–10, quotations 109, 111.
11. Marshel to Moore, 4 February 1782 (quotation); John Rose to William Irvine, 24 May 1782, *Washington-Irvine Correspondence*, 364–65.
12. *Settlement and Indian Wars*, 191, 201.
13. Doddridge, *Settlement and Indian Wars*, 201.
14. Charles Thompson to William Moore, 9 April 1782, and Council to William Irvine, 13 April 1782, *Pennsylvania Archives*, 9:523–24.
15. Thomas Scott to Joseph Reed, 24 January 1781, and Marshel to Reed, 5 June 1781, *Pennsylvania Archives*, 8:715, 9:193; Minutes of the Supreme Executive Council, 19 November 1781, *Colonial Records of Pennsylvania*, 16 vols. (Harrisburg, PA: Theo. Fenn & Co., 1838–1853), 13:119.
16. Pentecost to William Moore, 8 and 9 May 1782, Pentecost to Moore, 18 May 1782, and Depositions of John Robinson and Hugh M. Brackenridge, 20 June and 4 July 1782, in *Pennsylvania Archives*, 9:540–42, 545–46, 572–73.

17. Irvine to Washington, 2 December 1781, and Irvine to Board of War, 25 September 1781, *Washington-Irvine Correspondence*, 78, 157–58; John Finley to Irvine, 2 February 1782 and soldiers of the 7th Virginia Regiment to Irvine, n.d., *Washington-Irvine Correspondence*, 351–53 and 103 n. 1; William Irvine to Ann Irvine, 12 April 1782, 2AA:17–21, Lyman C. Draper Manuscripts, Wisconsin Historical Society, Madison; Irvine to George Washington, 20 April 1782, *Washington-Irvine Correspondence*, 99–103; Joseph Nevill to George Rogers Clark, 14 April 1782, *George Rogers Clark Papers*, ed. James Alton James, Collections of the Illinois State Historical Library, vols. 8, 19 (Springfield, IL: Illinois State Historical Library, 1912–1924), 19:57–58; Irvine orderly book, 25 March 1782, 2NN:217–18, and Irvine to [Isaac Craig], September 1782, 1AA:316–19, Draper Manuscripts; Judith Ridner, 'William Irvine and the Complexities of Manhood and Fatherhood in the Pennsylvania Backcountry', *Pennsylvania Magazine of History and Biography*, 125 (2001), 5–34.

18. Pentecost to Moore, 8 May 1782, 540 ('some condemning'); Cook to Moore, 2 September 1782, *Pennsylvania Archives*, 9:629 ('the Better Part'); William Irvine to Ann Irvine, 12 April 1782; William Croghan to William Davies, 6 July 1782, *George Rogers Clark Papers*, 19:71–73; Nevill to Clark.

19. Pentecost to Moore, 8 and 9 May 1782, Irvine to Moore, 9 May 1782 and Gibson to Nathaniel Seidel, 9 May 1782, *Washington-Irvine Correspondence*, 241–45, 362n.

20. William Irvine to Ann Irvine, 29 December 1781, *Washington-Irvine Correspondence*, 341–42; Irvine orderly book, 12 January 1782, 2NN:206, Draper Manuscripts ('that any person'); William Irvine to Ann Irvine, 12 April 1782 ('general and common opinion').

21. Irvine to Moore, 9 May 1782, and Irvine to commander of volunteers, 14 May 1782, *Washington-Irvine Correspondence*, 243–44, 119 n; Arent De Peyster to Frederick Haldimand, 18 August 1782, *Historical Collections: Collections and Researches Made by the Michigan Pioneer and Historical Society*, 40 vols. (Lansing, MI, 1874–1929), 10:628–29; and Heckewelder, *Narrative of the Mission*, 341–42.

22. Irvine to Benjamin Lincoln, 1 July 1782, *Washington-Irvine Correspondence*, 175.

23. Irvine to Lincoln, 16 April 1783, *Washington-Irvine Correspondence*, 187.

24. John C. Weaver, *The Great Land Rush and the Making of the Modern World: 1650–1800* (Montreal, 2003); Cole Harris, 'How Did Colonialism Dispossess? Comments from an Edge of Empire', *Annals of the Association of American Geographers*, 94 (2004), 165–82; David L. Preston, 'Squatters, Indians, Proprietary Government, and Land in the Susquehanna Valley', in *Friends and Enemies in Penn's Woods: Indians, Colonists, and the Racial Construction of Pennsylvania*, ed. William A. Pencak and Daniel K. Richter (University Park, PA, 2004), 180–200; Patrick Wolfe, 'Settler Colonialism and the Elimination of the Native', *Journal of Genocide Research*, 8.4 (2006), 387–409. Cf. Elizabeth Elbourne, 'The Sin of the Settler: The 1835–36 Select Committee on Aborigines and Debates Over Virtue and Conquest in the Early Nineteenth-Century British White Settler Empire', *Journal of Colonialism and Colonial History*, 4.3 (2003), 1–49.

CHAPTER 8

SETTLER MASSACRES ON THE AUSTRALIAN COLONIAL FRONTIER, 1836–1851

Lyndall Ryan

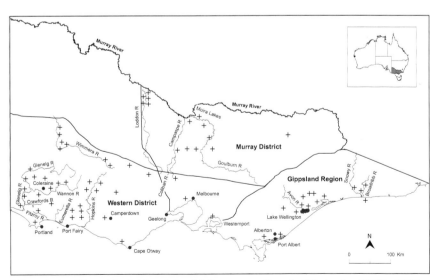

Map 8.1 Identified Aboriginal Massacre sites in Victoria, 1836–1851. © 2011 Robert J. Anders.

Base data: © Commonwealth of Australia (Geoscience Australia) 2003.

Introduction

In 2005, Richard Broome, one of the most respected historians of the Australian colonial frontier, published his long awaited history of the Aboriginal people of the colony of Victoria.[1] As the first sustained narrative of their historical experiences from the British colonization of their country in 1836 to the present, it is, by necessity, an account of how they survived against the odds, because from the outset it appears that the British settlers did everything possible to eradicate them.

The grim statistics leave the reader in no doubt about what happened. Broome estimated that there were at least 10,000 Aboriginal people in the colony in 1836 and that by 1853 their number had fallen to 1,907, a decline of eighty per cent in just under twenty years. How then did they nearly 'vanish' so rapidly? He estimated that 1,500–2,000 died violently at white and black hands and that perhaps a further 1,000 to 1,500 died of natural causes, leaving 4–5,000 who fell to diseases, disruption of food supplies and the impact of cultural dislocation. This was exacerbated by the dramatic decline in the birth rate. Broome concluded: 'An unintended and almost literal decimation of Aboriginal people occurred as two different peoples and their cultures clashed, and the more powerful invader, bearing unfamiliar diseases, dispossessed indigenous peoples of their land. Thus the misadventure of foreign microbes and the impact of colonialism caused an unintended outcome not dissimilar to genocide.'[2]

Was the outcome completely unintended? Broome's account of the dramatic population collapse has many important components, but it tends to overlook the possible impact of the phenomenon of settler massacre, that is the killing of an undefended group of Aborigines in one action. Unlike the sporadic killing of one or two Aborigines, a massacre makes an immediate impact on the long-term survival of the targeted Aboriginal group. Could settler massacres have been a critical factor in the Aboriginal population collapse in the colony of Victoria?

Over the last forty years, many historians have grappled with the question but except in a few cases, they have tended to underplay the possible significance of settler massacre. Of the five colony wide studies, three of them, by Michael Christie, Michael Cannon and A.G.L. Shaw have argued in support of widespread settler massacres but they have insufficient evidence to prove their case.[3] The best known studies of two of the colony's three major pastoral regions where most of the recorded violence took place – the Western District and Gippsland – have been more forthcoming in detailing specific incidents but have been reluctant to claim their widespread use.[4] Yet other studies of the colony's key institutions, the Aboriginal Protectorate and the Native Police Force, whose purpose was to 'protect' Aboriginal people from the slaughter, have either ignored the question, or denied that they were a possibility.[5] This diversity of opinion suggests that, as Broome points out, none of them have addressed the issue within a coherent framework or methodology.[6] Yet in 1995, geographer Ian D. Clark published a register of massacre sites in Western Victoria covering the period 1803–1859 and made the issue of settler massacre a subject in its own right.[7]

Clark was the first scholar to offer a definition of massacre on the Australian colonial frontier as 'the unnecessary, indiscriminate killing of human beings, as in barbarous warfare or persecution, or for revenge or plunder' and to consider that a minimum number of five Aborigines killed in one operation, constituted a settler massacre.[8] He did not make a tally of the death tolls in the settler massacres he recorded in his register, but he did identify three of their characteristics that add considerably to our understanding of the subject: a massacre takes place in secret; its intention is to destroy or eradicate the victims; and 'a code of silence' to preserve the anonymity of the perpetrators makes detection extremely difficult. These factors were compounded by the colonial legal system which prevented Aboriginal witnesses from presenting evidence in court, enabling many massacre perpetrators to escape conviction.[9]

In 2003, Richard Broome analysed Clark's data and estimated that a total of 430 Aborigines had been killed in 107 fatal attacks in Western Victoria; that in fifty-five of these incidents, one to three victims had been killed, totalling eighty-eight people; that in each of twenty more cases, four people had been killed (eighty victims); and that in a further thirty-two incidents, five or more had been killed (262 victims).[10] In other words, more Aborigines had been killed in thirty-two mass killings than in the fifty-five small-scale incidents. This astonishing finding had the potential to reframe our understanding of the impact of settler massacres. But, when Broome reviewed Clark's data two years later, he was not convinced that every one of the thirty-two incidents in which five or more Aborigines had been killed necessarily constituted a massacre:

> Such killings are often termed 'massacres' – the killing of defenceless or beaten people ... the word is overused and portrays Aboriginal people as passive victims. Some incidents were not 'massacres' but battles in which one side suffered severe losses. The details of the action are too vague in many incidents to confidently label them 'massacres' rather than 'defeats'.[11]

Broome appears to regard these two labels as mutually exclusive.

Rather, he considered that only three incidents of massacre in Western Victoria , in each of which thirty or more Aboriginal people were killed, more readily fitted his understanding of the concept. Yet he accepted that the Aboriginal killing of seven white male settlers in what is known as the Faithfull Massacre at present-day Benalla in April 1838, did constitute a massacre (rather than a 'defeat'). In the apparent confusion of different concepts of massacre, he appeared to give the impression that on the Victorian colonial frontier, settler massacre was a rarer event than Clark believed.[12] He pointed out that Aborigines had also died from two other causes: from inter-tribal violence which he believed had dramatically increased after the British colonizers arrived in 1836; and from introduced disease, even though the medical records of the Aboriginal Protectorate and other sources revealed that before 1850, the Aborigines in the three pastoral regions experienced a constant trickle of deaths from exotic diseases rather than a large number of fatalities resulting from epidemics.[13]

Broome's reluctance to accept Clark's criteria for settler massacre, has arisen I believe, from the fact that like many academic historians of the Australian colonial frontier, including Henry Reynolds and myself, he has relied on the Aboriginal resistance model to construct his narrative of Australian frontier conflict.[14] The model is used to argue that Aborigines actively resisted the British settler invasion of Australia and employed a range of guerrilla war techniques to harass and oppose the settlers, even though, in the end, they were defeated. But the model also discourages historians from questioning the nature of settler response to Aboriginal resistance.

So it is not surprising that Broome has been unwilling to take up Clark's challenge to seriously consider the subject of settler massacre. Yet the latter's evidence for its widespread practice in Western Victoria, and his observation that a conspiracy of silence surrounds its incidence, cannot be dismissed. Rather, it indicates that the subject is long overdue for serious consideration by historians of the Aboriginal resistance school. This chapter starts the process by revising the resistance model to gain new insights into how the colonial frontier worked in Victoria during the period 1836–1851. The region has been selected because it was the first colony in Australia to establish an Aboriginal Protectorate and the first to experience massive pastoral expansion across a very wide region before the gold rushes began in 1851. The findings could become the basis for comparable research into the possible use of settler massacres in other regions in Australia and in other British colonial settler societies before 1850.

Approach and Method

As mentioned earlier the resistance model is focused more on Aboriginal than on settler actions. By expanding the model to include settler activism and Aboriginal resistance within a framework that considers the British colonization of Australia as a dynamic, contested and ongoing process, the Victorian colonial frontier could be a useful case study of that period of massive pastoral expansion before the gold rushes began in 1851. As Jessie Mitchell has recently pointed out, during this period the colony was the site of colliding expectations between two groups of colonizers. On one hand there were the settlers who believed that they were entitled to the unfettered occupation of the land by virtue of their perceived racial superiority to the Aborigines; and on the other there were the various agents of the British government, some of whom believed that they had a responsibility to 'protect' Aborigines from violent dispossession.[15] In this dynamic tableau of conflicting interests, the diverse array of sources of frontier violence, many of which have now been published, should be read, not at face value, but as contradictory clues each of which tells a different story.

By adopting this approach, it is possible to develop a coherent method to investigate the possible incidence of settler massacre. In this case the typology of massacre developed by the French historical sociologist Jacques Semelin could be useful. He considers that the act of massacre is usually a response to a certain political event, such as the killing of a prominent person, or the unlawful appropriation of property and that it has two objectives: to impose political domination by submission, and to eliminate or eradicate the group in and of itself. To this end, the massacre event is carefully planned rather than a spontaneous response and it tends to suppose a relationship of proximity between the assassins and their victims. Thus, the act of massacre is not so much an expression of power by a strong regime but an expression of a position of weakness subsumed by the recourse to massacre: 'a quick means of appropriating the riches of the massacred group and/or to take the territory on which it lived'. In Victoria it would appear that this also involved eradicating the Aboriginal people. Finally, as has already been pointed out by Ian Clark in relation to Western Victoria and Peter Gardner in relation to the colony's Gippsland region, settler massacres on the Victorian colonial frontier tended to be carried out in secret. It is here that the key question of a witness arises: 'If no witness is intended or present, who will be believed? This problem is of central concern to historians. The nature of the event often leads to silence in the immediate aftermath. However, witnesses and perpetrators sometimes speak about massacre long after it is over, when they are immune from prosecution or removed from fear or reprisal from other perpetrators.'[16] The task for historians, Semelin points out, is to immerse themselves in the collective representations of the groups in conflict and to understand the 'weight of fear and the imaginary that seem to be ever present before the massacre, thus encouraging the perpetration itself, because the role played by fear and the imagination are obviously correlated'.[17]

Semelin also considers that a massacre is not an aberration in the process of dispossession and destruction of targeted groups, but 'one of the dimensions to hasten the capitulation of the enemy'. Thus, settler massacres can be investigated, not only as a series of isolated incidents but also as elements of an 'organized process' of destruction by targeting particular groups. In the context of the settler colonizing states where 'target populations' are perceived as threatening, settler massacres are more likely to become a series of incidents carried out by young men responding to a specific event in a haphazard way at the behest of a weak rather than a strong state.[18] As a result, the focus on evidence for particular incidents of settler massacre often overlooks the process that led to the slaughter and its intended effects.[19]

This chapter applies Semelin's typology to assess a limited but diverse range of published sources for colonial Victoria during the period 1836–1851 for evidence of settler massacres of Aboriginal Victorians.[20] During this time the colony was characterized by rapid pastoral expansion in the three regions which comprised more than sixty per cent of the land overall. It began in the Western District even before 1836, and by 1844 there were more than one million sheep. It continued in the Murray District in 1838 with at least 500,000 sheep by 1844 and climaxed in 1841 in Gippsland where by 1846, more than 100,000 head of cattle were grazed.[21] During the same period the settler population of Victoria had increased from 224 to 77,345.[22] It was in these regions, remote from Melbourne, the colony's capital, that the settlers, police and military used settler massacre as a strategy to eradicate the Aboriginal Victorians and take control of their land.

To assess the scale, preconditions, type and evidence of settler massacre, the chapter adopts Ian Clark's definition of massacre and increases the number he considers constitutes a settler massacre, from five people killed in one operation, to six people which matches the number agreed upon by other Australian historians.[23] I have also employed Semelin's massacre typology to extract data about settler massacre from the printed sources referred to earlier.[24] I have then applied to the evidence the same criteria that I used to construct a chronology of settler massacre in Tasmania in the *Online Encyclopaedia of Mass Violence*.[25] In that project, the criteria for settler massacre included the date and place of the incident, corroborating evidence from other sources, the identity of the victims and/or the names of the perpetrators. From the data collected for this project, I have constructed a chronology of settler massacres in each of the three pastoral regions in the Port Phillip District and then consolidated them to produce a tally of known settler massacres overall from which an estimate has been made of the number of Aborigines known to have been killed. I have then further analysed the evidence to determine the preconditions for massacre. The results of the analysis overall is reproduced in Table 8.1.

As is shown by Table 8.1 and also Map 8.1, sixty-eight known settler massacres (each involving six or more Aborigines killed) were recorded in the three pastoral regions in the period 1836–1851, with an average of more than four massacres per year, and in which 1,169 Aborigines are estimated to have lost their lives. The tally comprises more than eleven per cent of the estimated Aboriginal population of Victoria in 1836. It does not include the number of other Aborigines killed in incidents in the three pastoral regions in which fewer than six were killed by settlers. Nor does it include an estimate of the number of Aborigines killed in the areas outside of the three pastoral regions or other evidence of settler massacres that may be found in other sources. Even so, the tally does

Table 8.1 Tally of Known Massacres in Victoria 1836–1851

| Year | No. of massacres | No. Est. Killed | REGIONS | | | PRECONDITIONS | | |
			Western District	M D	Gippsland	Killing or Harrassing Colonists	Killing or Harrassing Livestock/ property	Pre-emptive Strikes
1836	2	20	2 (20)			1 (10)	1 (10)	
1837	1	10		1 (10)			1 (10)	
1838	6	115	3 (84)	3 (31)		2 (50)	3 (45)	1 (20)
1839	6	103	4 (53)	2 (50)		1 (40)	1 (30)	4 (33)
1840	12	235	8 (182)	2 (13)	2 (40)	5 (73)	5 (128)	2 (34)
1841	9	102	6 (52)		3 (50)	2 (20)	4 (52)	3 (30)
1842	6	60	5 (50)		1 (10)	3 (35)		3 (25)
1843	6	225	4 (45)	1 (10)	1 (170)	2 (179)	4 (46)	
1844	2	15	1 (10)		1 (6)		1 (6)	1 (10)
1845	4	40	2 (25)	1 (6)	1 (10)	2 (30)	1 (6)	1 (6)
1846	6	92	2 (19)	1 (20)	3 (53)	3 (39)	2 (30)	1 (23)
1847	3	70	2 (60)		1 (10)	2 (40)		1 (30)
1848	1	20		1 (20)				1 (20)
1850	3	40	1 (19)		2 (21)		1 (16)	2 (24)
1851	1	20			1 (20)	1 (20)		
Total	68	1169	40 (619)	12 (160)	16 (390)	24 (536)	24 (379)	20 (254)

Key: Numbers in parentheses indicate the estimated number of Aborigines killed.
MD: Murray District

suggest that settler massacres were responsible for more half of the Aboriginal deaths in Broome's estimate of 1,500 to 2,000 deaths in the entire district from large- and small-scale killings and inter-tribal deaths.[26]

Of the three major pastoral regions in colonial Victoria, forty settler massacres were identified in the Western District, in which an estimated total of 619 Aboriginal people were killed; twelve massacres were identified in the Murray District, in which an estimated total of 149 Aboriginal people were killed; and sixteen massacres were identified in Gippsland, in which an estimated total of 389 Aboriginal people were killed. The data for Western District is the most comprehensive; it is less coherent for Gippsland and least developed for the Murray District. Despite the discrepancies and the conservative estimates, the data are sufficiently consistent overall for Semelin's typology to be used to identify the pre-conditions for settler massacre; the types that were employed; the years in which they were most prevalent; and the kinds of evidence used to explain their incidence.

Pre-conditions

As Semelin pointed out, the act of massacre is usually a response to a certain political event, such as the killing of a prominent person, or the unlawful appropriation of property and it has two objectives: to impose political domination by submission and to eliminate or eradicate the group in and of itself.[27] On the Victorian colonial frontier, it would appear that the eradication of the Aboriginal people was the chief priority. In all three pastoral districts, the killing of any settler or the appropriation by Aborigines of settler property such as sheep and cattle, or food stores, was considered by the settlers as sufficient pre-conditions for massacre and in many cases the mere presence of Aborigines in the area was often a sufficient pre-condition for a pre-emptive strike.

Of the first pre-condition, the killing of a settler or settlers by Aboriginal men generated the most ferocious response and catalyzed the most lethal settler massacres in Victoria. The data shows that there were twenty-three incidents of settler massacre in response to the killing or alleged killing of a settler, with an estimated loss of 526 Aboriginal lives. The data also shows that most settlers were killed in ones and twos by Aboriginal men, except in one known case of the massacre of settlers, known as the Faithfull Massacre, already referred to, in which Aboriginal men killed seven settlers. Of the eighty white men that were known to have been killed overall by Aboriginal men in the period under review, twenty-four of them have been identified. They comprise six settlers, an overseer, two hut-keepers, a cook, four stockmen, and ten shepherds. In every case, it would appear that the murdered men had earlier been in contact with a local Aboriginal group and had either killed or abducted Aboriginal women for sexual purposes, or, in the case of the cook, had poisoned a group of Aboriginal women. These men were thus likely killed in retaliation for breaking Aboriginal customary law.

The settlers however, considered the murder of their friends, comrades, or employees as a call for mass revenge. As Semelin pointed out, in this context, the settlers felt vulnerable and believed they were in a position of weakness that could only be reversed by what historians of the Australian colonial frontier know as 'teaching the Aborigines a lesson'.[28] This was especially the case where two settler massacres were conducted in response to the alleged kidnapping of a white child aged two, in the Western District in September 1843; and a white woman aged in her twenties in Gippsland in October 1846. In the former case, the disappearance of the little girl was the call to continue a Native Police campaign that had begun in the area a month earlier and led to the killing of at least nine Aborigines.[29] In the latter case, it was the call for at least two settler reprisal parties and a detachment of Native Police to carry out revenge massacres in which at least fifty Aboriginal people lost their lives.[30] Neither female was ever found nor is there evidence that either of them was ever abducted let alone killed by Aboriginal people.

Of the second pre-condition, the assault and or stealing of colonial livestock and property, twenty-four incidents were identified in which an estimated 377 Aborigines were killed. Due to insufficient and extant primary and secondary sources recording livestock theft, it has not been possible to estimate the number of sheep and cattle killed, stolen or driven off by Aboriginal men, apart from noting that in Western Victoria and in the Murray District, Aboriginal men were more likely to drive off sheep and in Gippsland they were more likely to attack cattle.

Of the third pre-condition, the act of massacre as a pre-emptive strike, that is, perpetrated without a clear motive, twenty incidents were identified from the data with the estimated loss of 254 Aboriginal lives. Most of these incidents were recorded in the Western District and in Gippsland and could be considered as evidence of the fear and uncertainty with which the settlers regarded Aborigines.

Types of Massacre

As Semelin pointed out, one of the purposes of massacre is to eliminate or eradicate the group in and of itself. To this end, a settler massacre is a carefully planned event rather than a spontaneous response and it tends to suppose a relationship of proximity between the settlers and the Aborigines. Thus, the act of settler massacre is not so much an expression of their power as the settlers perceive it, but the reverse – an expression of their perceived weakness which is overcome by their recourse to massacre.[31]

The data identified four types of settler massacre that were common in all three regions. By far the most common, comprising at least forty of the estimated sixty-eight known massacres, was the 'hunting party' which usually consisted of between seven and seventeen armed male settlers aged between seventeen and forty and mounted on horseback. It would usually be formed by a landowner or lessee, or his overseer, following the Aboriginal killing of a settler or the appropriation of live-stock. He would call together a party of stockmen and shepherds to exact revenge. The party would convene the night before their planned reprisal, prepare their weapons, ammunition and horses and set off before dawn to mount a surprise daybreak attack on the camp where the alleged Aboriginal offender(s) were sleeping and then shoot, kill and wound Aboriginal men, women and children at random. In the imme-diate aftermath, the perpetrators would either remain silent or recon-struct the incident as a 'battle' or 'rencontre' between themselves and a large group of Aboriginal men armed with spears and waddies (clubs). For example, following the discovery of the mutilated bodies of settler Mr Charles Franks and his shepherd on 9 July 1836 near Gellibrand Point, near the western entrance to Port Phillip Bay in the Western District, a party of seventeen men armed with muskets 'proceeded in search of the natives whom they supposed to be the murderers'. John Montagu, the Colonial Secretary in Tasmania, wrote about the incident to his counterpart in New South Wales on 18 August 1836:

> They came up with the tribe, consisting of men, women and children, to the number of about fifty to one hundred, and perceiving upon the persons of some of them articles which were recognized as having belonged to Mr Franks, a 'rencontre' followed. It is not stated however what resistance the natives made, but none of the opposing party were injured, although it is feared that there can be little doubt that ten of the tribe of Port Phillip [Vic-toria] natives were killed.[32]

The second type was the daylight ambush or entrapment. The data indi-cates there were at least five cases of these kinds of settler massacre. For example, in May 1845, a group of James Cowper's shepherds, employed at his outstation at the junction of the Loddon and Murray Rivers in the Murray District, decided to kill a group of Aborigines camped on the far side of Murrabit Creek. They concealed their guns and called out in friendly fashion to come across for food. While the Aborigines were crossing in a canoe, the shepherds uncovered their guns and according to the settler who later reported the incident, 'they let fly'.[33] It is not known how many Aborigines were killed.

The third type of settler massacre was the poisoning of Aboriginal people. The data identified five incidents of poisoning in which fifty-nine people were known to have died. Most poisonings were perpetrated by the station cook on remote pastoral runs who would give Aborigines flour or damper laced with arsenic, although there was one case where 'a mixture of flour and plaster of Paris was used'.[34] In another case, at one of the

Henty Brothers stations on the Wannon River in the Western District in October/November 1840, a cook gave a group of visiting Aborigines some damper. Soon afterwards they were 'seized with violent pains in the stomach accompanied by retching' before seventeen of them died. When news of the poisoning reached the authorities in Melbourne and the Chief Protector of the Aborigines, G.A. Robinson was sent to investigate, the Hentys dispatched the culprit to another colony to avoid arrest.[35]

The fourth type was the military-style massacre perpetrated by officials of law and order by day and at night. The data shows that the Native Police carried out eleven massacres and Mounted Police at least two others. Of these, the Native Police conducted four massacres in reprisal for the alleged killing of settlers and seven others as reprisals for killing or stealing sheep and cattle. The data indicates that they killed more than one hundred Aboriginal people overall. Broome's belief that intentional killing was largely carried out by the settlers overlooks the active role played by the Native Police Force and the Mounted Police in eradicating Aboriginal people through the use of massacre.[36]

Prevalence and Evidence of Massacre

Of the number of known settler massacres overall, Table 8.1 shows that most took place between 1838 and 1843 when an estimated 839 Aborigines were killed in forty-five incidents across the three pastoral regions. Thirty took place in the Western District, eight in the Murray District and seven in Gippsland. They include twelve incidents of settler massacre in reprisal for killing male settlers in which 397 Aborigines were killed, seventeen reprisal killings for the appropriation of livestock and other property in which 301 Aborigines lost of their lives, and thirteen pre-emptive strikes, including four cases of poisoning, in which 142 Aborigines were killed. As Clark points out, this was the period when the greatest number of settlers and their sheep and cattle occupied Aboriginal land and when the drought of 1840 and the financial crash of 1842 had the greatest impact.[37]

As Clark, Gardner and Semelin have argued, an act of massacre often leads to silence in its immediate aftermath. However, Semelin also explained that 'witnesses and perpetrators sometimes speak about massacre long after it is over, when they are immune from prosecution or removed from fear or reprisal from other perpetrators'[38] This appears to have been a general rule in relation to settler massacre in the three pastoral regions in Victoria.

Evidence for settler massacres fall into two categories. In the first, three kinds of contemporary evidence were found: settler accounts; contemporary Native Police reports; and contemporary Aboriginal Protectorate reports. In the second category only one kind of evidence was found and that was elicited from settlers long after the event.

Of the contemporary evidence, settler accounts appear to be the most unreliable. Some of them reported engaging in 'pitched battles' or 'clashes' with groups of Aboriginal men whom they considered had stolen their cattle. But these reports were rarely believed, even at the time. For example, on 6 July 1841, Robert W. Knowles, the manager of Robert Martin's Mount Sturgeon Station in the Western District, informed G.A. Robinson of such a 'clash'. The latter was unimpressed: 'Knowles said that he lost some cattle a short time since and went after them. He came to a blacks' camp and they threw spears at him and his stock keeper. He thought they had his bullock. This attacking the camp of the natives under the pretence of looking after stolen property is a system that ought not to be tolerated, it is provoking hostility and would not be allowed in civilized society.'[39]

The second type of contemporary evidence, comprising seventeen reports from officers of the Mounted Police and the Native Police, appear equally unreliable. They frequently reported 'encounters', 'melees', 'collisions' and 'skirmishes' with large groups of Aboriginal men armed with spears and clubs. For example, in June 1839 at the Campaspe Plains in the Murray District, following the murder by a group of Aboriginal men of two shepherds at Captain Charles Hutton's station, a neighbouring squatter, W.H. Yaldwyn called on the mounted police to search for the offenders. According to the official report, a party of mounted police, led by Sergeant Dennis O'Leary, 'went after' the Aboriginal group whom they encountered one hundred and twelve kilometres away. His report said that a 'pitched battle' ensued and at least six Aboriginal people were killed. Some months later, Hutton privately informed E.S. Parker, Assistant Protector of the Aborigines, that O'Leary and his troopers 'rode down to Campaspe Plains, opening fire on the first six Aboriginal people to cross their path. The chase and the gunfire went on for half an hour.' They killed the entire group of forty Aboriginal people, including women and children, and only one woman and a child survived.[40] A few years later, Hutton changed his story and told Lieutenant Governor Charles La Trobe that the Aborigines had 'suddenly disappeared' and died from influenza.[41]

The third kind of contemporary evidence – nineteen reports by Aboriginal Protectorate officers – appears to be more reliable. The officers were often alerted to the incidence of massacre by Aboriginal witnesses. For example, in July 1841 G.A. Robinson was travelling in the Mount William region in the Western District and heard from an Aboriginal woman and then a settler that in November 1840 a hut keeper employed by settler Horatio Spencer Wills had been killed by three Aboriginal men in revenge for killing an Aboriginal man and an Aboriginal woman. In reprisal Wills and two other settlers, first attacked the Aboriginal camp and shot two women and their 'infants left without milk' and then with three other settlers, shot another three Aboriginal men and two women. A few days later three other settlers shot three Aboriginal men. In all twelve Aborigines were killed.[42] Robinson knew that his report would not be followed up because the testimony of the Aboriginal woman would not be admissible in court and the un-named settler would not make a statement incriminating his neighbours.

The second category of evidence, elicited by settlers long after the event, also appears more reliable. For example, in July 1843, following the murder of wealthy squatter, Donald Macalister in Gippsland, a reprisal massacre was organized by his friend and colleague, Angus McMillan.[43] The latter took the law into his own hands and then went to extraordinary lengths to cover up his actions. local historian Peter Gardner, who has spent decades searching a wide array of sources about the incident, has now pieced together the sequence of events. According to him, McMillan collected a party of seventeen mounted stockmen, later known as the 'Highland Brigade', and after having sworn each man to secrecy, he then led them on a massacre rampage. Over the next few days the brigade attacked at least five Aboriginal camps in the area with the aim of eradicating every Aboriginal person who was present. Gardner estimates that overall 170 Aborigines from an entire clan were killed, making it one of the most violent episodes in Australian history. Evidence of the carnage remained hidden for several decades and finally emerged in two separate accounts published by a later generation of settlers, Charles Lucas and Willy Hoddinott. They had arrived in the region as young boys, a year or so after the massacres and had grown up with two Aboriginal boys who were survivors of the massacres. Over the next thirty years they each separately pieced together their accounts based on interviews with their Aboriginal informants who showed them some of the massacre sites, and with other settlers in the region who showed them the remains of burnt bodies. But it was another decade before they were brave enough to publish them separately and anonymously in colonial newspapers and magazines. One of the Aboriginal boys had been wounded in the attack on the first camp and then dragged away by the perpetrators and made to act as a guide to all the others. The other boy had been wounded in the attack on one of the other camps and had hidden in the reeds until the carnage was over.[44] This horrifying incident, the details of which have been questioned by Broome, on the grounds that the estimate of the number killed was far too high and made the Aboriginal people into passive victims, more readily fits Semelin's category of massacre as an 'organized process'.[45]

From the analysis of the data, it is now possible to identify the key characteristics of settler massacres on the Victorian colonial frontier. First, they were widespread across the three pastoral regions and took the lives of more than eleven per cent of the total Aboriginal population in Victoria, although there could be a different percentage for each of the three regions. Second, three pre-conditions for settler massacre were identified: the alleged Aboriginal killing of a settler; the alleged Aboriginal attack on livestock and other property; and the pre-emptive strike by the settlers. Third, four types of settler massacre were identified across all three regions: night attacks by the settler 'hunting party'; the daylight ambush or entrapment organized by shepherds; poisoning of Aboriginal people by station cooks; and military-style massacre by day and by night carried out by the official forces of law and order. Fourth, the data confirmed that settlers were the major perpetrators, but that the Native Police Force and the Military Police also played a key role. Finally, of the four categories of evidence that were identified only two – reports by officers of the Aboriginal Protectorate and by settlers long after the event – can be considered reliable. A further interrogation of the evidence suggests that contemporary settler accounts, of 'clashes' and 'pitched battles' between large mobs of Aboriginal men armed with spears and small groups of settlers on horseback armed with guns which rarely fired, had little basis in fact. Rather, the evidence suggests these accounts were fabricated to cover up the settlers' well-planned attacks on undefended Aboriginal camps at daybreak in which Aboriginal men, women and children were killed. Finally, if the tally of 1,167 Aborigines killed by settler massacres is included in Broome's estimate of 2,000 Aborigines killed in this period, then it would comprise more than fifty per cent of entire number killed overall. This would suggest that settler massacre was a critical component in the dramatic Aboriginal population decline and that the number of Aborigines killed overall has been considerably under-estimated.

Conclusion

Richard Broome's concern that the word 'massacre' was 'overused' to describe conflict on the colonial frontier in Victoria between 1836 and 1851 appears unfounded. By employing Semelin's typology to consider the available primary sources, this chapter has demonstrated that contrary to Broome's concern, the word 'massacre' has actually been under-used. Moreover, the 'details of the action' are not as vague as he believes. There appear to have been very few known 'battles in which one side suffered severe losses'. Rather, the incidents described as battles were, in reality, settler massacres in which Aboriginal men, women and children were indiscriminately slaughtered. Furthermore, the careful analysis of the available data suggests that massacre was a common tactic used by settlers and the agents of law and order to achieve the overall strategic objective of eliminating Aboriginal Victorians when they contested British settler occupation of their land.

The sudden disappearance of entire groups of Aboriginal Victorians as a result of settler massacres in the three pastoral regions on the Victorian colonial frontier suggests that the survivors, as in any community devastated by mass killings over a short period, were extremely vulnerable to disease, which in turn led to the dramatic population collapse.

If this is the case, then settler massacre, rather than disease alone, emerges as a critical factor in accounting for the eighty per cent drop in the Aboriginal Victorian population in fifteen years.

Notes

1. Richard Broome, *Aboriginal Victorians: A History Since 1800* (Crows Nest, NSW, 2005). Before 1850, the colony of Victoria was known as the Port Phillip District of New South Wales. I would like to thank Tony Barta, Richard Broome, Raymond Evans, Ben Kiernan and Benjamin Madley for their editorial advice and insights on earlier drafts. Any errors of fact and interpretation are, of course, my own.
2. Broome, *Aboriginal Victorians*, 91–93.
3. Michael F. Christie, *Aborigines in Colonial Victoria, 1835–86* (Sydney, 1979); Michael Cannon, *Who Killed the Koories?* (Melbourne, 1990); Alan George Lewers Shaw, *A History of the Port Phillip District: Victoria before Separation* (Melbourne, 1996); Broome, *Aboriginal Victorians*; Geoffrey Blainey, *A History of Victoria* (Melbourne, 2006).
4. Peter Corris, *Aborigines and Europeans in Western Victoria* (Canberra, 1968); Phillip Pepper in collaboration with Tess de Araugo, *What Did Happen to the Aborigines of Victoria Volume I: The Kurnai of Gippsland* (Melbourne, 1985); Jan Critchett, *A Distant Field of Murder: Western District Frontiers 1835–1844* (Melbourne 1990): Peter Dean Gardner, *Gippsland Massacres: The Destruction of the Kurnai Tribes 1800–1860*, 3rd edn, (Ensay, Victoria, 2001).
5. Vivienne Rae-Ellis, *Black Robinson: Protector of the Aborigines* (Melbourne, 1988); Marie Hansen Fels, *Good Men and True: The Aboriginal Police of the Port Phillip District 1837–1853* (Melbourne, 1988).
6. Broome, *Aboriginal Victorians*, 95.
7. Ian D. Clark, *Scars in the Landscape: A Register of Massacre Sites in Western Victoria, 1803–1859* (Canberra, 1995).
8. Clark, *Scars in the Landscape*, 7.
9. Clark, *Scars in the Landscape*, 2–3.
10. Richard Broome, 'The Statistics of Frontier Conflict', in Bain Attwood and S.G. Foster (eds), *Frontier Conflict The Australian Experience* (Canberra, 2003), 94.
11. Broome, *Aboriginal Victorians*, 81.
12. Broome, *Aboriginal Victorians*, 81.
13. Broome, *Aboriginal Victorians*, 90.
14. Lyndall Ryan, *The Aboriginal Tasmanians* (Vancouver, 1981); Henry Reynolds, *The Other Side of the Frontier* (Ringwood, Vic. 1982): Richard Broome, *Aboriginal Australians* (North Sydney, 1982).
15. Jessie Mitchell, '"The Galling Yoke of Slavery": Race and Separation in Colonial Port Phillip', *Journal of Australian Studies*, 33.2 (June 2009), 127–28.
16. Jacques Semelin, 'In Consideration of Massacre', *Journal of Genocide Research*, 3.3 (2001), 383.
17. Semelin, 'In Consideration of Massacre', 384.
18. Jacques Semelin, 'From Massacre to the Genocidal Process', *UNESCO*, (2002), 435–36.
19. Semelin, 'In Consideration of Massacre', 381–82.
20. The published sources consulted include those in Cannon, *Who Killed the Kooris?*, Clark, *Scars in the Landscape*, Critchett, *A Distant Field of Murder*, Gardner, *Gippsland Massacres*, Shaw, *A History of the Port Phillip District*, and Michael Cannon (ed.), *Historical Records of Victoria, Foundation Series, Volume 2A: The Aborigines of Port Phillip 1835–1839* (Melbourne, 1982) and *Volume 2B: Aborigines and Protectors 1838–1839* (Melbourne, 1983).

21. Broome, *Aboriginal Victorians*, 20.
22. Wray Vamplew (ed.), *Australians: Historical Statistics* (Broadway, New South Wales, 1987), 26.
23. Keith Windschuttle, 'The Myth of Frontier Massacres in Australian History, Part II: The Fabrication of the Aboriginal Death Toll', *Quadrant*, November 200018; and Ben Kiernan, 'Australia's Aboriginal Genocide', *Yale Journal of Human Rights*, vol.1, no.1, (2000), 52.
24. See footnote 20 for the list of published sources.
25. Lyndall Ryan, 'Chronological Index: List of Multiple Killings of Aborigines in Tasmania: 1804 1835', *Online Encyclopaedia of Mass Violence*, ed Jacques Semelin (Paris, 2008) http://massviolence.org/+-Tasmania
26. Broome, *Aboriginal Victorians*, 81.
27. Semelin, 'In Consideration of Massacre', 383.
28. See Charles Rowley, *The Destruction of Aboriginal Society: Aboriginal Policy and Practice –Volume I* (Canberra, 1970), 157.
29. Clark, *Scars in the Landscape*, 46–47.
30. Gardner, *Gippsland Massacres*, 69–72.
31. Semelin, 'In Consideration of Massacre', 383.
32. Cannon, *The Aborigines of Port Phillip 1835–1839*, 42.
33. Cannon, *Who Killed the Kooris?*, 221.
34. Clark, *Scars in the Landscape*, 97.
35. Clark, *Scars in the Landscape*, 28–30.
36. Broome, *Aboriginal Victorians*, 84.
37. Clark, *Scars in the Landscape*, 9.
38. Semelin, 'In Consideration of Massacre', 383.
39. Clark, *Scars in the Landscape*, 72.
40. Clark, *Scars in the Landscape*, 94–96.
41. Shaw, *A History of the Port Phillip District*, 134.
42. Clark, *Scars in the Landscape*, 73, 77.
43. A 'squatter' was the name given to a settler of wealth and prestige.
44. Gardner, *Gippsland Massacres*, 62, 64.
45. Broome, *Aboriginal Victorians*, 81; Semelin, 'From Massacre to the Genocidal Process', 435–36.

CHAPTER 9

TACTICS OF NINETEENTH-CENTURY COLONIAL MASSACRE: TASMANIA, CALIFORNIA AND BEYOND[1]

Benjamin Madley

Camped under Sally's Peak near the eastern Tasmanian coast, the Paredarerme slept. They did not know that some thirty white men – soldiers, police and colonists – were marching toward them on that November night in 1823. Years later, one of the attackers explained how expedition members 'proceeded stealthily as they neared the spot; and, agreeing upon a signal, moved quietly in couples, until they had surrounded the sleepers.' Then 'The whistle of the leader was sounded, and volley after volley of ball cartridge was poured in upon the dark groups around the little camp-fires.' The eyewitness concluded: 'The number slain was considerable.'[2] During the 1820s similar attacks would become increasingly common in Tasmania, an island roughly the size of Ireland some 150 miles south of mainland Australia.

Three decades later and eight thousand miles away, comparable attacks came out of the California darkness in the early 1850s. On 6 January 1851, Mariposa County Sheriff James Burney raised a posse of over seventy men from around Agua Fria and marched into the Sierra Nevada Mountains.[3] At 2 a.m. on 8 January, a scout returned to Burney's main force 'and reported the village near, as he had heard the Indians singing'.[4] Burney now prepared to silence these Indians, whom an eyewitness called 'Kee-chees … Chow-chil-la[s and] Chuc-chan-ces'.[5]

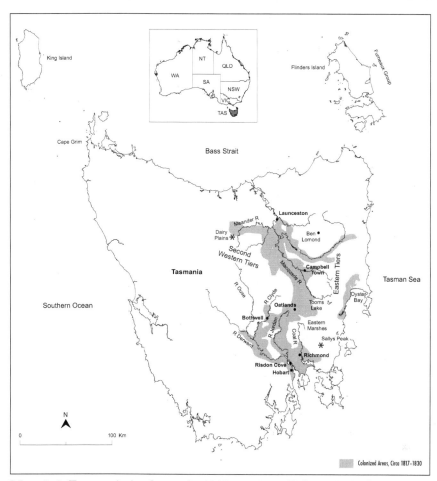

Map 9.1 Tasmania in the early 1800s. © 2011 Robert J. Anders.

Base data: © Commonwealth of Australia (Geoscience Australia) 2008.

The attack commenced at dawn and while surprised Indians wounded seven attackers, they suffered a massacre.[6] Burney reported: 'We killed from 40 to 50.'[7] Another participant explained: 'fifty killed and wounded would be a moderate estimate.'[8] Much as the November 1823 assault on the Paredarerme would become paradigmatic of later Tasmanian massacres, Sheriff Burney's January 1851 operation exemplified a tactical pattern that would become prevalent in California throughout the 1850s and 1860s.

The nineteenth century was an age of empire and a time of massacre.[9] As European powers and their offspring settler states expanded and intensified their control over vast areas of the earth, colonists and their backers sometimes massacred indigenous peoples. Settlers, soldiers, law enforcement officers, businessmen, and others used massacres to quell uprisings, to expedite forced removal and dispossession, to oblige indige-

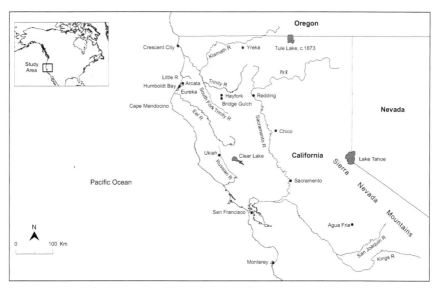

Map 9.2 California in the 1850s and 1860s. © 2011 Robert J. Anders.
Base data: US National Atlas (USGS)

nous people to comply with systems of servitude, or simply to annihilate them. As scholars map the violence at colonialism's dark heart, studies of the economic, ideological, and political motives behind such violence continue. However, scholars have yet to theorize on the military logic, axioms, and tactics underpinning nineteenth-century colonial massacres targeting indigenous peoples. By exploring massacres in Tasmania, California, and beyond, this chapter attempts to shed new light on the tactics of nineteenth-century colonial massacres and how permissive colonial legal regimes encouraged and supported such tactics. So, why extrapolate from Tasmania and California?

Nineteenth-century colonists and their advocates perpetrated massacres – defined here as largely one-sided intentional killings of five or more non-combatants or relatively poorly armed or disarmed combatants, often by surprise and with little or no quarter – in Africa, Asia, Australia and the Americas. Massacres were particularly prevalent in settler colonies where colonists sought not only to extract wealth from the land using indigenous labour but to take the land for themselves, frequently attempting to clear it of indigenous people and sometimes trying to obliterate them all together. As settler societies with relatively little use for indigenous people and a penchant for considering Aborigines and American Indians as impediments to progress, Australia and the United States saw a particularly high number of massacres. Of these two settler projects, Tasmania and California were stained by an extraordinary number of massacres, and both were sites of genocide.

Constables, convict servants, escaped convicts, free colonists, and British soldiers perpetrated dozens of massacres against Tasmanian Aborigines between 1804 and 1831. In 2008 I provided evidence of at least twelve such incidents, but historian Lyndall Ryan has gone further, providing evidence of twenty-eight 'mass killings of Aborigines' between November 1823 and October 1830 alone.[10] With perhaps ten times more indigenous people than Tasmania and hundreds of thousands of nineteenth-century immigrants, California under United States rule was an even bloodier killing field.[11] In my forthcoming *American Genocide: The California Indian Catastrophe, 1846-1873* I present evidence of hundreds of massacres and mass killings perpetrated against California Indians.[12]

An analysis of massacres launched against Tasmanian Aborigines under British rule and California Indians under United States rule reveals surprisingly congruent tactics despite the fact that they occurred decades apart on separate continents and under different regimes, while targeting dozens of different indigenous peoples. In both cases colonizers and their advocates developed aggressive martial tactics intended to maximize the advantages of their longer-range, more lethal firearms, while neutralizing Aborigines' and Indians' faster-firing weapons, ability to live off of the land, intimate geographic knowledge, internal lines of communication, guerrilla warfare, disinclination to fight set-piece European-style battles, and sometimes superior numbers. On both frontiers immigrants and their supporters realized – after some years of trial and error – that by combining stealth, surprise, physical entrapment, and indiscriminate killing they could wage a form of asymmetric warfare that played to their strengths and downplayed indigenous advantages, thus minimizing their losses while maximizing indigenous casualties. Of course, central to these tactics was an acceptance of or an interest in inflicting substantial civilian casualties upon indigenous communities.

The shared massacre tactics – which evolved into a kind of unwritten tactical doctrine – can be divided into four phases: night reconnaissance and envelopment, long-range small arms barrage at night or dawn, close-range attack, and executionary non-combatant killing. This chapter will discuss each phase before briefly exploring exceptions and how this tactical doctrine may apply to nineteenth-century mainland Australia and the nineteenth-century United States as a whole. Finally the chapter will explore how permissive legal systems encouraged and supported this tactical doctrine.

Night Reconnaissance and Envelopment

In Tasmania and California whites often had difficulty finding and engaging highly mobile Aboriginal and Indian communities during daylight hours. For example, Tasmanian surveyor J.H. Wedge wrote: 'The Natives are ... very expert in eluding ... White men.'[13] Colonist James Ross agreed that Aborigines had 'the wonderful facility ... of disappearing on a sudden from the view'.[14] Another colonist recalled, 'I saw one, and, while in the act of leveling my gun at him, he disappeared as if by magic.'[15] Those seeking to engage California Indians were often similarly confounded. As United States Indian Agent Redick McKee reported in 1852, 'As a general thing, the Indians of this country are not disposed to war with the whites; they are afraid of our long rifles.'[16]

Nocturnal reconnaissance and envelopment became a popular tactical response to Tasmanian Aborigines' and California Indians' disinclination to fight set-piece European-style daylight battles. Although night marches toward an enemy were unusual among nineteenth-century Western forces – due to the high potential for disorientation, separation, and friendly fire – they did allow attackers to search for indigenous people when they were least mobile and most willing to stand and fight in order to protect their homes, possessions, food stores, friends and families.[17] In addition, while night reconnaissance was often challenging, it could make Aborigines and Indians easier to locate and target due to their singing or the beacons created by their campfires. Finally, stealthy nocturnal approaches also helped to maximize surprise, confusion, and, perhaps most importantly, casualties.

Having located a village or encampment, attackers typically sought to envelop it in one of three ways. With sufficient men and appropriate terrain they could literally surround their target with attackers. Alternatively, they might form a crescent around Aborigines or Indians and use a geographical feature, such as a cliff or water body, to eliminate the possibility of retreat. Finally, attackers sometimes tried to catch a community in a pincer movement, often using physical terrain to cut off escape.

Britons recorded numerous instances of night reconnaissance and encirclement in Tasmania. The colonist James George recalled that after Aborigines killed two whites in April 1827 other whites pursued them. Soon the pursuers seem to have arrived at the camp of some members of the Oyster Bay nation. 'Having seen their fires in a gully near the River Macquarie, some score of armed men, Constables, Soldiers and Civilians, and Prisoners (convicts) or assigned Servants ... fell in with the Natives when they was going to Breakfast. They fired volley after volley in among the Blackfellows, they reported killing some two score.'[18] Two months later, on 12 June 1827, Pallittorre Aborigines ransacked David Gibson's Dairy Plains hut and tried to spear Thomas Baker. In response, whites tracked them 'and at night, seeing their fires, they went out and shot nine of the natives'.[19] Later, in December 1827, colonist George Hobler wrote, after an Aboriginal attack: 'I have armed four men who I hope will get sight of their night fires and slaughter them as they lie round it.'[20] Journalist Henry Melville arrived on Tasmania in 1828 and later concluded, with some irony, that: 'at this point it was common for parties of the *civilized* portion of society to scour the bush, and falling in with the tracks of the natives, during the night to follow them to their place of encampment, where they were slaughtered in cool blood.'[21]

Night scouting and envelopment were also popular with those seeking to kill California Indians. When horses and mules were stolen from Canadian trappers on the Trinity River in 1850, the Canadians marched to a 'village under suspicion, before daybreak, surrounded it, and set the huts on fire. Then, hiding in the underbrush, they shot down [fifteen Tsnungwe] Indians as they ran from the flaming huts.' Frenchman Ernest De Massey concluded: 'This is typical of the tales we hear around here.'[22] That summer, a Mexican and Anglo-American force tracked stolen horses to a Mattole or Wiyot village near Cape Mendocino and launched a predawn attack, after which one participant ominously reported, 'As "order reigned in Warsaw", so did it in the little "rancheria" when resistance ceased.'[23] These early examples represent the beginning of a tactical trend that would continue in California for decades.

Still, massacre was a choice not always taken. Surrounding a camp containing both civilians and possible combatants provided a moment at which pursuers could authoritatively ask the people in their gun sights to surrender in accordance with long-standing European traditions of martial conduct. Pursuers sometimes did just that. For example, after Tasmanian Aborigines—likely members of an Oyster Bay clan— 'plundered Mr. Ansteys men's hut' near Oatlands in July 1830, whites tracked them through the snow, located their camp, 'squatted down for the night, waiting in the cold with the utmost patience until daylight the next morning, and rushed upon the Aborigines when ... four were captured, and the rest fled; these might have been shot, but Mr. Anstey did not think himself justified in so doing.'[24] Likewise, primary sources record several similar instances in California. For example, in August 1859 state militia General William Kibbe reportedly surrounded a Konkow Maidu village near Chico 'at daybreak' and captured 'about thirty Indians ... without firing a gun.'[25]

Unfortunately, Tasmanian Aborigines and California Indians were not generally accorded the right to surrender, even if surrounded. Attackers' reluctance to grant Tasmanian Aborigines and California Indians rights associated with customary Western laws of war was hardly surprising. For decades, the British administration in Tasmania and its United States counterpart in California made Tasmanian Aborigines and California Indians essentially non-citizens: they were effectively barred from voting, serving as jurors, or acting as witnesses in court cases against whites. Compounding this status, California courts and law enforcement officers rarely punished whites for killing Indians while in Tasmania British administrators never executed a white for killing an Aborigine, despite repeatedly hanging Aborigines for killing whites.[26] Under such permissive regimes, many whites in Tasmania and California employed tactics that minimized their exposure to physical danger and helped to ensure that a minimum number of indigenous people would escape. Others were bent upon extermination and wanted to maximize casualties, both combatant and non-combatant alike.

Long-Range Small-Arms Barrage at Night or Dawn

Firearms were the nineteenth-century colonizers' single greatest military asset in engagements with indigenous peoples. More accurate and deadly over a longer range than most indigenous weapons, muskets – and especially rifles – allowed colonizers to shoot indigenous warriors from beyond the range of most Aboriginal spears and *wadis* (wooden spear-throwing devices) or Indian arrows. Guns were a powerful force multiplier that frequently helped colonizers to defeat numerically superior indigenous forces. However, both the musket and the single-shot rifle were heavy, slow to load, and quick to jam, clog, or overheat. Thus, these weapons could be used to full advantage only under certain conditions. In response, some whites in Tasmania and California developed tactics that optimized the advantages of the musket and single-shot rifle while minimizing their disadvantages.

Attackers generally initiated massacres with a barrage of long-range, small-arms fire at night or at dawn. This timing frequently caught victims unprepared or asleep while the dark of night and grey of dawn concealed attackers' positions, thus helping to neutralize the more rapid rate at which Tasmanian Aborigines could hurl spears and *wadis* and at which California Indians could fire arrows. Low-light conditions also provided cover under which attackers could carefully aim, fire, and reload their relatively cumbersome, slow-firing weapons. Campfires, meanwhile, illuminated Aborigines' and Indians' positions while making it difficult for them to see from the area illuminated by their fires into the darkness, where their attackers were hiding. Finally, encirclement created an interlocking field of fire that maximized casualties and confusion, making it difficult for Aborigines and Indians to know where to aim their spears, *wadis*, and arrows or in what direction to run. Again, such tactics were based upon an acceptance of or interest in inflicting substantial civilian casualties, since low-light conditions made it difficult for attackers to discriminate between armed warriors and unarmed men, women, and children.

Low-light, long-range, small-arms barrages were common in Tasmania. On 6 July 1827, the *Colonial Times* printed a letter reporting that: 'The people over the second Western Tier have killed an immense quantity of the blacks this last week ... They were surrounded whilst sitting around their fires, when the soldiers and others fired at them about 30 yards distant. They report there must have been about sixty [Pallittorre] killed and wounded!'[27] On 9 December 1828, guide John Danvers reported a dawn encirclement massacre he had participated in three days earlier near 'Tooms Lake': 'one of them getting up from a small fire to a larger one discovered us and gave the alarm to the rest, and the whole of them jumpt [sic] up immediately and attempted to take up their spears in defense, and seeing that, we immediately fired and repeated it because we saw they were on the defensive part, they were about twenty in Number and several of whom were killed'.[28] According to another description of this attack: 'Ten of the Natives [probably Oyster Bay clan members] were killed on the spot.'[29] Low-light attacks were, in fact, so common that Lyndall Ryan has concluded: 'most [Tasmanian] Aborigines were killed in groups of five or more at night'.[30]

California massacres often began in a similar fashion. In May 1850 United States Army soldiers struck a Russian River Pomo village and 'dragoons ... fired the brush woods through and through' before 'the infantry entered and picked off every Indian that could be found'.[31] After volunteers had surrounded a Nor-rel-muk Wintu village at night on 22 April 1852, the Bridge Gulch Massacre began at dawn the next day when 'Each rifle marked its victim with unerring precision'.[32] Likewise, after surrounding a Konkow Maidu camp near Chico Creek 'before daylight' in 1859, attackers opened fire from a ring of positions around the camp. Pinned down by crossfire, few Konkow Maidus escaped and one assailant recalled 'about forty' killed.[33]

The conclusion of a devastating initial surprise barrage from positions surrounding a mixed group of civilians and warriors provided a second point at which attackers might logically have asked Tasmanian Aborigines or California Indians to surrender. Yet, it seems that in many cases attackers made no such offers.

Close-Range attack

Following an initial small-arms barrage, assailants usually stormed the camp or village. Attackers typically advanced when they felt it was safe to do so, when their victims began retreating, when they ran out of ammunition, or when their weapons jammed, overheated or became clogged with burnt powder. Once inside the village or encampment, assailants frequently switched from their heavy, slow-firing muskets and rifles to bayonets, knives, pistols, rocks, tomahawks or other hand-held weapons.

The bayonet seems to have been a favoured close-quarters killing tool in Tasmania, at least in the territory of the Oyster Bay nation. Former chief constable Gilbert Robertson reported that in 1827 'The Richmond police ... killed 14 of the Natives, who had got upon a hill ... the police expended all their ammunition, and being afraid to run away, at length charged with the bayonet'.[34] In a November 1827 incident, 'at the Brown Mountains' near the Eastern Marshes, 'Field Police expended seventeen rounds of ball cartridge' before 'fixing their bayonets and charging', upon which 'the natives retreated'.[35] In 1830, after overhearing soldiers and constables describe a July 1828 Eastern Tiers attack on Aborigines in which 'Sixteen of them were massacred', Robert Ayton reported how: 'one man in particular boasted that he had run his bayonet through two of them'.[36]

Soldiers and others in California used a variety of weapons for close-quarters killing. During the 1850 Bloody Island Massacre, for example, following barrages of weapons fire, regular soldiers hunted down Pomo survivors, killing them with bayonets, rifle butts, and oars.[37] Likewise, in the 1852 Bridge Gulch Massacre attackers unleashed a salvo of rifle fire from positions surrounding their victims before moving into the Nor-rel-muk Wintu village where 'the pistol and the knife completed the work of destruction', ultimately leaving over 140 people dead.[38] As we shall see, in other massacres attackers also killed California Indians at close quarters with hatchets.

Executionary Non-Combatant Killing

Having broken all meaningful Tasmanian Aborigine and California Indian resistance to their assault and having taken physical control of a village or camp, attackers were once again in a position to offer terms of surrender in accordance with customary Western martial conduct codes. This they sometimes did. However, in many cases, during this fourth phase, assailants deliberately continued killing non-combatants and prisoners.

Melville provided an account of one Tasmanian attack from an eyewitness: 'some score or so of natives, men, women, and children, had been discovered by their fires, and a whole parcel of the Colonists armed themselves, and proceeded to the spot. These advanced unperceived, and ... the signal for slaughter was given, fire-arms were discharged, and those poor wretches who could not hide themselves from the light thrown on their persons by their own fires, were destroyed.' The attackers 'then ... found ... an infant sprawling on the ground, which one of the party pitched into one of the fires'.[39] According to John Batman, on the night of 1 September 1829 he and others attacked and killed or mortally injured thirteen presumably Ben Lomond clan members near Ben Lomond before murdering two captured during the attack.[40] Meanwhile, Oyster Bay chief Tongerlongter recollected that in 1829 his people had encountered two woodcutters. 'At night they came ... and saw our fires. Then they shot at us, shot my arm, killed two men and three women.' Apparently, 'The women they beat on the head and killed.'[41] In another example of deliberate non-combatant killing, on 3 March 1830, Robertson reported that 'a party of constables and some of the 40th Regiment, sent from Campbell Town ... got the Natives [likely members of the Oyster Bay nation] between two perpendicular rocks [and killed] 70 by firing all their ammunition upon them, and then dragging the women and children from the crevices in the rocks, and dashing out their brains.'[42]

California killers also frequently murdered non-combatants in the final stage of massacre. For example, in September 1859 a death squad assaulted a Pit River Achumawi village at dawn: 'The attacking party rushed upon them – blowing out their brains and splitting open their skulls with tomahawks. Little children in baskets, and even babes, had their heads smashed to pieces or cut open ... Guns, knives, and hatchets were used ... and more than sixty squaws and children, and ten Indian men were found dead.'[43] The following year, an eyewitness described the aftermath of the Indian Island Wiyot Massacre on Humboldt Bay: 'Here was a mother fatally wounded hugging the mutilated carcass of her dying infant to her bosom; there a poor child of two years old, with its ear and scalp torn from the side of its little head. Here a father frantic with grief over the bloody corpses of his four little children and wife ... and in every lodge the skulls and frames of women and children cleft with axes and hatchets, and stabbed with knives, and the brains of an infant oozing from its broken head to the ground.'[44] The deliberate murder of non-combatant Indians, even after all effective resistance to attack had been broken, was common in California.

Exceptions

There were, unsurprisingly, exceptions to the massacre tactics described above. While widespread practice suggested an unwritten tactical doctrine in Tasmania and California, attackers did deviate from its precepts. Reconnaissance and troop movements were not always nocturnal and whites sometimes killed Tasmanian Aborigines and California Indians during full daylight hours. For example, Tasmania's infamous Risdon Cove killings of 3 May 1804 began at approximately 11 a.m. while in 1841 clergyman John Lang was shown 'a spot ... where seventeen [Aborigines, perhaps of the Big River or Oyster Bay nation] had been shot in cold blood [in 1828]. They had been bathing in the heat of a summer's day, in the deep pool of a river ... when ... surprised by a party of armed colonists.'[45] However, daytime massacres were highly unusual in Tasmania.

Whites also occasionally massacred California Indians during the day. For instance, at 3 p.m. on 24 August 1862, soldiers and volunteers located 'about fifty Indians' along Little River, near Arcata. They then surrounded the encampment and unleashed a barrage of rifle fire, killing at least twenty-two Indians—possibly Yuroks— and perhaps 'as many as 35 or 40'.[46] Such daytime attacks – which were relatively infrequent in California – were usually opportunistic, rather than carefully planned. Low-light dawn attacks seem to have been the preferred time for massacres, given that they were less difficult, less dangerous, and more likely to yield substantial casualties.

In a handful of instances artillery supplemented or replaced the initial long-range small-arms barrage. On 3 May 1804, British soldiers killed at least three and possibly as many as fifty Tasmanian Aboriginess—likely of the Big River nation—at Risdon Cove with 'grape shot' and/or small-arms fire while in August 1830 George Robinson recorded hearing that a 'stockkeeper called Paddy Heagon ... had shot nineteen of the western natives [possibly Pallittorre] with a swivel [or whaling gun] charged with nails.'[47] These seem to be the only extant reports of artillery used against Tasmanian Aborigines. Decades later, United States Army soldiers in California used mountain howitzers against Indians in perhaps half a dozen attacks. For example, in December 1864 soldiers fired cannons at Indians' log houses near Arcata and in April 1873 bombarded the Modocs' stronghold south of Tule Lake for days.[48] Still, because cumbersome artillery and its heavy ammunition hindered stealth and speed, especially in rugged, road-less terrain, it rarely figured in Tasmanian or Californian massacres.

Finally, as mentioned earlier, there were cases in which attackers did not deliberately kill non-combatants but instead adhered to conventional rules of engagement. In Tasmania, George Robinson repeatedly captured Aborigines using threat and diplomacy. Later, in California, army officers occasionally captured large numbers of Indians without firing a shot. For example, in 1864, Captain John Simpson surrounded Indians along Eel River and 'told them through Indian interpreters to surrender and they would not be killed.' Although some tried to escape Simpson would not let his men fire and eventually captured eighty-eight people.[49] Regrettably, such bloodless diplomacy was relatively rare due to racism, dehumanization, and permissive legal regimes that failed to protect their indigenous subjects.

Mainland Australia and the United States as a Whole

The pattern of night reconnaissance and envelopment, long-range small-arms barrage at night or dawn, close-range attack, and executionary non-combatant killing was – with variations and exceptions – common in Tasmanian and Californian massacres. Yet, how applicable is this model to other nineteenth-century colonial massacres? Examples from mainland Australia and the United States as a whole suggest that these tactics may have been widely applied.

In mainland Australia whites perpetrated several massacres along roughly Tasmanian lines. For example, on 17 April 1816, Captain James Wallis 'came across an Aboriginal camp on the cliffs above a creek' near Appin, in New South Wales. Presumably using the cliff to help surround the Dharawal camp, Wallis 'ordered his troops into a line and advanced into the camp in the moonlight, killing seven Aborigines' while, according to Wallis, seven more 'met their fate by rushing in despair over the precipice.'[50] In Victoria, following an 1836 raid that left at least two whites dead at Port Philip, 'the avenging party fell upon the guilty tribe about daylight in the morning, having watched them the previous night, and putting into effect a preconcerted plan of attack, succeeded in annihilating them.'[51] In all, perhaps ten 'Port Philip natives were killed.'[52]

Fifty years later, after Aborigines mortally wounded a colonist, Native Police and stockmen located a Gudanji camp at Malakoff Creek, in what later became the Northern Territory, by the light of its campfires. Participant Charles Gaunt recalled that after 'taking up positions at every vantage point' the shooting began about dawn. 'When the melee was over we counted fifty-two dead and mortally wounded. For mercy's sake we dispatched the wounded. Twelve more we found at the foot of the cliff fearfully mangled.'[53] Tasmanian style massacres were also apparently common in neighbouring Queensland. According to historian Jonathan Richards, Queensland Native Police repeatedly tracked Aborigines to their camps. Then, 'once they had been located, the troopers surrounded the camp', presumably at night, before 'firing their rifles into the sleeping people at dawn ... killing men, women and children.'[54]

In the United States as a whole, several nineteenth-century American Indian massacres involved night reconnaissance and marching, envelopment, pre-dawn or dawn attacks, small-arms barrages, and executionary non-combatant killing after all resistance had ceased. For example, on 23 December 1855, Oregon volunteers marched by night to a Tututni and Takelma camp, presumably used the Rogue River to help facilitate encirclement, and at dawn killed nineteen to twenty-six people.[55] Nine years later, after marching through the night, Colonel John Chivington positioned his Colorado and New Mexico Volunteers around a peaceful Arapaho and Cheyenne camp along Sand Creek, Colorado. Chivington then attacked 'about daylight' on 29 November 1864. Over several hours, his force reportedly massacred as many as six hundred men, women, and children.[56] Such massacres continued. At 11 p.m. on 8 August 1877, United States Army troops began marching towards Nez Perce bivouacked at Big Hole, Montana. Colonel John Gibbon later described how he located the camp by its night fires, unleashed a dawn rifle barrage, 'slaughtered' many Nez Perce in a pincer movement, and eventually killed at least eighty-nine men, women and children.[57] South Dakota's infamous 1890 Wounded Knee Massacre also generally fits the pattern. After Miniconjou Sioux surrendered to the Seventh Cavalry on 28 December they were surrounded by reinforcements during the night. Then, on the morning of 29 December cavalrymen began disarming the Miniconjou when a single shot rang out. Who pulled that trigger remains uncertain, but the soldiers began firing on the camp with rifles and light artillery.[58] Cavalrymen then pursued the fleeing Miniconjou for hours, ultimately killing or mortally wounding up to three hundred men, women and children.[59]

These examples of mainland Australian and extra-Californian United States massacres provide intriguing, but inconclusive, evidence that the Tasmanian and Californian massacre pattern was prevalent elsewhere. Massacre studies are far from mature and much more data is necessary in order to gauge the applicability of the colonial massacre model to mainland Australia, the United States as a whole or other nineteenth-century colonial projects. Still, it is clear that in Tasmania and California legal regimes encouraged and supported such massacre tactics.

Colonial Legal Regimes and Massacres Tactics

Built upon the foundations of conventional nineteenth-century European warfare, Tasmanian and Californian massacre tactics emphasized conventional battle tactics, such as surprise, encirclement, an initial barrage, switching to smaller weapons for close-quarters fighting, and attempts to make engagements as asymmetric as possible. However, there were also crucial differences. Tasmanian and Californian massacre tactics routinely emphasized nocturnal reconnaissance and troop movements, and sometimes night attacks, all of which were unusual for the era. More importantly, they emphatically rejected standard nineteenth-century rules of engagement and conduct. In so doing, they intentionally violated conventional Western laws of war, or *jus in bello*.

Massacre perpetrators in Tasmania and California routinely failed to offer quarter and frequently murdered non-combatants and prisoners even after extinguishing all resistance. These violations of customary Western *jus in bello* were, in part, due to the fact that, as historian Paul Kennedy and jurist George Andreopoulos have suggested, 'North American Indians and other aboriginal peoples in the way of European expansion' were 'excluded from *jus in bello* considerations' and that, as a result, 'Time and again there occur cases of people slaughtered indiscriminately on the grounds that they were not considered part of the international community'.[60] Still this exclusion from *jus in bello* considerations was hardly universal. Not every colonizing project or colonial war saw indiscriminate massacres of indigenous peoples. Many settler societies – including Tasmania and California – had legal systems that, at least theoretically, designated indigenous people as subjects and accorded them (extremely limited) rights. Moreover, few colonial administrations or metropolitan colonial governments openly condoned massacring indigenous peoples. Policies written and unwritten were crucial to unlocking the potential for rejecting traditional Western *jus in bello*.

Colonizers and their advocates in Tasmania and California were well aware of what historian Michael Howard has called the 'Western ... "cultural regulations of violence"; what was, in the old-fashioned phrase, "done" and "not done" in war.'[61] The widespread rejection of these norms by colonizerssts and their advocates was possible only because the British administration in Tasmania and its United States counterpart in California – like many colonial regimes – effectively barredstheir indigenous subjects from the protection of their legal systems. By failing to punish mass murderers, both administrations reinforced their white subjects' dehumanization of indigenous people while making their indigenous subjects extremely vulnerable to attack and massacre. There were almost no official repercussions for white crimes against Tasmanian Aborigines or California Indians, even for intentional mass murder.

Nineteenth-century Colonial massacre tactics were conventional battle tactics unconstrained by the customary Western laws of war. Rather than force the enemy to surrender the field or themselves, nineteenth-century colonial massacre tactics – as implemented in Tasmania and California – were designed to annihilate some or all of the enemy, often with little or no distinction between combatants and non-combatants. Thus, the massacre tactics described in this chapter effectively grew out of a second, informal code of nineteenth-century colonial military conduct applied to conflicts with indigenous peoples who had almost no legal rights and were thus effectively reduced to the status of 'alien peoples'. This was the form of warfare described by Kennedy and Andreopoulos which 'excluded *jus in bello* considerations where alien peoples' were concerned.[62] Colonizing powers' policies – at least in Tasmania and California – allowed for a reformulating of conventional battle tactics that, unconstrained by law, traditional Western *jus in bello*, or concern for human life, gave rise to the tactics of colonial massacre and, ultimately, genocide. The nineteenth-century colonial massacre was not, of course, ubiquitous. Yet, where colonizinl regimes were permissive and supportive of violence against indigenous peoples, nineteenth-century colonial massacres could proliferate, even to a genocidal degree. Systematic mass murder rarely takes place without government approval.

Notes

1. The author thanks Alison Alexander, Robert Anders, Philip Dwyer, Paul Kennedy, Ben Kiernan, Piotr Kosicki, Timothy Macholz, Michael Morgan, Nicki Ottavi, Ian and Kim Pearce, Jesse and Matthew Philips, Lyndall Ryan and Owen Williams for their help.
2. James Bonwick, *The Last of the Tasmanians* (London, 1870), 99.
3. California Adjutant General's Office, *Military Department, Adjutant General, Indian War Papers*, California State Archives, F3753:48. hereafter *IWP*; Lafayette Bunnell, *Discovery of the Yosemite and the Indian War of 1851 Which Led to That Event* (Los Angeles, 1911), 30.
4. *IWP* F3753:48.
5. Bunnell, *Discovery of the Yosemite*, 31.
6. *IWP* F3753:48; Bunnell, *Discovery of the Yosemite*, 32.
7. *IWP* F3753:48.
8. Bunnell, *Discovery of the Yosemite*, 32.
9. Eric Hobsbawm minted the phrase 'age of empire' in his *Age of Empire: 1875-1914* (London, 1987).
10. Benjamin Madley, 'From Terror to Genocide: Britain's Tasmanian Penal Colony and Australia's History Wars', *Journal of British Studies*, 47:1 (January 2008), 77–106; Lyndall Ryan, 'Abduction and Multiple Killings of Aborigines in Tasmania: 1804–1835', Yale Genocide Studies Program Working Paper no.35 (2007), 9, 13, 19.
11. Perhaps 150,000 Indians populated California when the United States took control while the Aboriginal population did not exceed 15,000 when Britain began colonizing Tasmania. See Sherburne Cook, *The Population of California Indians, 1769-1970* (Berkeley, 1976), 44 and Madley, 'From Terror to Genocide', 78.

12. Benjamin Madley, *'American Genocide: The California Indian Catastrophe, 1846-1873'* (New Haven, forthcoming).
13. Justice Crawford, et al. (eds.), *The Diaries of John Helder Wedge, 1824–1835* (Devonport, 1962), 44.
14. James Ross, *The Settler in Van Diemen's Land* (Melbourne, 1836; 1975), 26.
15. Hobart, *Colonial Times*, 18 September 1829, 4.
16. California, *Journal of the Third Session of the Legislature...at the Cities of Vallejo and Sacramento* (San Francisco, 1852), 720.
17. Carl von Clausewitz discussed the problems and rarity of early nineteenth-century night marches toward enemies. Clausewitz, James Graham and Frederic Maude, trans., *On War* (London, 1918; 1832), 308–14.
18. Lyndall Ryan, 'Chronological Index: List of Multiple Killings of Aborigines in Tasmania: 1804–1835', 3, www.massviolence.org (viewed 10 April 2009)
19. George Robinson, *Friendly Mission: The Tasmanian Journal and Papers of George Augustus Robinson, 1829-1843* (Kingsgrove, 1966), 219.
20. George Hobler, *The Diaries of Pioneer George Hobler, October 6 1800-December 13 1882*, 5 vols. (California, 1992), 1:40.
21. Henry Melville, *The History of Van Diemens Land, From the Year 1824 to 1835* (1836; Hobart, 1965), 30, 71. Emphasis original.
22. Ernest de Massey, Marguerite Wilbur, trans., 'A Frenchman in the Gold Rush', *California Historical Society Quarterly*, 5:3 (September 1926), 231, 234.
23. Joseph Revere. Album, 1870, Huntington Library, 29–30, 35, 43–46. In 1831 French Foreign Minister Horace Sébastiani probably coined the phrase 'Order reigns in Warsaw' to refer to Russia's suppression of the 1830–1831 Polish Uprising.
24. N.J.B. Plomley (ed.), *Jorgen Jorgenson and the Aborigines of Van Diemen's Land* (Hobart, 1991), 98.
25. *Sacramento Daily Union*, 26 August 1859, 2.
26. Keith Windschuttle described William Tibbs's 1824 trial and conviction for the manslaughter of '"an Aborigine"' in Tasmania (Windschuttle, *The Fabrication of Aboriginal History: Volume One, Van Diemen's Land, 1803-1847* [Sydney, 2002], 191). However, James Boyce argued that the victim was likely a visiting ship's non-white crewmember (Boyce, 'Fantasy Island' in Robert Manne (ed.), *Whitewash* [Melbourne, 2003], 36–37). Whatever the truth, Tibbs's 'sentence was later reversed and he was discharged' (N.J.B. Plomley, ed., *Weep in Silence: A History of the Flinders Island Aboriginal Settlement* [Hobart, 1987], 43, n.42).
27. *Colonial Times*, 6 July 1827, 4.
28. Colonial Secretary's Office, Hobart, 1/320:7578, 23; hereafter CSOH.
29. *Hobart Town Courier*, 13 December 1828, 2.
30. Ryan, 'Chronological Index',' 3.
31. Herman Altschule, 'Exploring the Coast Range in 1850', *Overland Monthly*, 11:63 (March 1888), 322.
32. *Daily Alta California*, 4 May 1852, 2.
33. Robert Anderson, *Fighting the Mill Creeks* (Chico, 1909), 21–24.
34. House of Commons Parliamentary Papers (1831) 259, XIX, 49; hereafter HCPP.
35. *Hobart Town Courier*, 24 November 1827, 2. The Field Police were apparently 'not certain whether any of the natives were hurt' in this incident.
36. CSOH 1/330:7578, 109; CSOH 1/316:323, 152, emphasis original; CSOH 1/330:7578, 109. All sixteen may have been 'bayoneted' to death.
37. Madley, 'American Genocide', Chapter 2. Victims may have included Wappo Indians.
38. *Daily Alta California*, 4 May 1852, 2.
39. Melville, *History of Van Diemen's Land*, 71–72.
40. Alastair Campbell, *John Batman and the Aborigines* (Melbourne, 1987), 31–32. The *Colonial Times* reported: 'about 15 ... killed and wounded' (8 September 1829, 3).
41. Plomley, *Weep in Silence*, 325.

42. HCPP, 48. This likely occurred before 1830. Ryan believes that this is a retelling of the April 1827 massacre 'near the River Macquarie'.

43. *Daily Alta California*, 26 January 1860, 1.

44. George Stuart, *Bret Harte, Argonaut and Exile* (Boston, 1931), 85–86.

45. HCPP, 53; Bonwick, *Last of the Tasmanians*, 67. Lang may have described two incidents; in 1831 a colonist told Robinson that stockmen 'killed seventeen natives ... first ... seven and [at] the lagoon ... ten more' (Robinson, *Friendly Mission*, 503).

46. *Humboldt Times*, 30 August 1862, 2; *Sacramento Daily Union*, 18 September 1862, 1; *The War of the Rebellion: A Compilation of the Official Records of the Union and Confederate Armies*, 1:50:1 (Washington, 1897), 66; hereafter *WOR*; A.J. Bledsoe, *Indian Wars of the Northwest* (San Francisco, 1885), 227–28.

47. HCPP, 37, 51; Henry Reynolds, *Fate of a Free People: A Radical Reexamination of the Tasmanian Wars* (Ringwood, 1995), 88; Robinson, *Friendly Mission*, 197–98.

48. *Humboldt Times*, 16 January 1864, 3; Keith Murray, *The Modocs and their War* (Norman, 1959), 211–12.

49. *WOR*, 1:50:1, 391.

50. John Connor, *The Australian Frontier Wars*, 1788–1838 (Sydney, 2002), 51.

51. *Colonial Times*, 2 August 1836, 262.

52. Jon Montagu to Col. Sec., 18 August 1836 in Ian Macfarlane (ed.), *Historical Records of Victoria, Volume 2A: The Aborigines of Port Philip, 1835–1839* (Melbourne, 1982), 41–42.

53. Tony Roberts, *Frontier Justice: A History of the Gulf Country to 1900* (St. Lucia, 2005), 170–77.

54. Jonathan Richards, 'The Native Police of Queensland', *History Compass*, 6:4 (May 2008), 1025, 1024.

55. Elwood Evans, et al., *History of the Pacific Northwest* (Portland, Oregon, 1889), 444; Nathan Douthit, *Uncertain Encounters: Indians and Whites at Peace and War in Southern Oregon, 1820s–1860s* (Corvallis, 2002), 134.

56. Stan Hoig, *The Sand Creek Massacre* (Norman, 1961), 177–87, Appendix.

57. John Gibbon, 'The Pursuit of Joseph', *American Catholic Quarterly Review*, 4:14 (April 1879), 335–37, 343; John Gibbon, 'The Battle of the Big Hole', *Harper's Weekly*, 21 December 1895, 1215–16; and 28 December 1895, 1235–36.

58. Jeffrey Ostler, *The Plains Sioux and U.S. Colonialism from Lewis and Clark to Wounded Knee* (Cambridge, 2004), 335–37, 339, 343.

59. Richard Jensen, 'Big Foot's Followers at Wounded Knee', *Nebraska History*, 71:4 (Winter 1990), 198.

60. Paul Kennedy and George Andreopoulos, 'The Laws of War: Some Concluding Reflections', in Michael Howard, George Andreopoulos and Mark Shulman (eds), *The Laws of War: Constraints on Warfare in the Western World* (New Haven, 1994), 215.

61. Michael Howard, 'Constraints on Warfare', in *Laws of War*, 1.

62. Kennedy and Andreopoulos, 'Laws of War', in *Laws of War*, 215.

CHAPTER 10

A BLUEPRINT FOR MASSACRE: THE UNITED STATES ARMY AND THE 1870 BLACKFEET MASSACRE[1]

Blanca Tovías

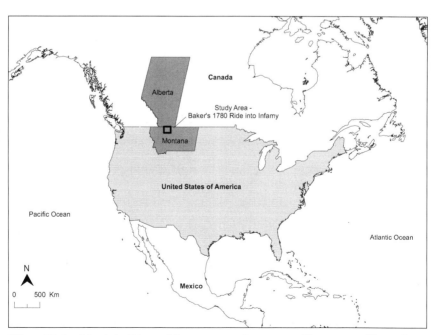

Map 10.1   Maria's River, Montana, and surrounding areas. Base data: U.S. National Atlas (USGS). © Robert J. Anders.

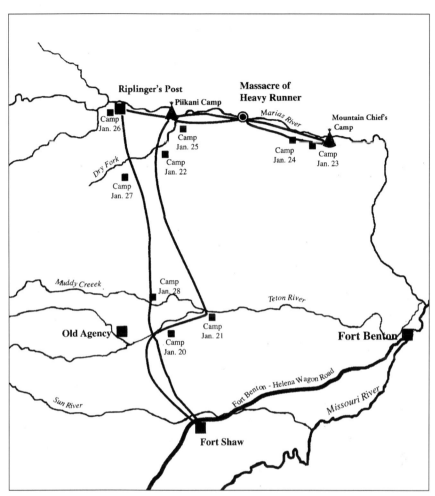

Map 10.2   Baker's 1870 ride into infamy: the massacre of the Black-foot on Maria's River, Montana. Compiled by John G. Lepley.

As the sun rose on 23 January 1870, an expedition of some 200 mounted men, commanded by Colonel Eugene Baker, prepared to attack a Pikuni (Blackfeet) band under the leadership of Heavy Runner, camped for the winter on a spot on the Marias River known as the Big Bend.[2] Heavy Runner and his followers, some of whom were afflicted by smallpox, woke to find themselves surrounded by soldiers, who had marched by night and camped by day, with temperatures hovering well below freezing, to avoid detection. Heavy Runner came forward to meet the soldiers 'holding up his [treaty] medal and his papers', which proved that he was not 'hostile'. He was the first to fall dead. The soldiers fired into the thirty-seven lodges that made up the camp, killing 173 men, women, and children. Pikuni survivors reported that ninety women and fifty children under twelve years of age were among the victims. A civilian witness accompanying the army claimed that Baker had been drunk at the time.[3]

This chapter seeks to increase our understanding of the mechanics of massacres. To this end, it analyses the combination of circumstances that paved the way for the attack on Heavy Runner's village at the very time when Ulysses S. Grant's government was advocating a Peace Policy. It draws links between the United States army's deployment of total war during the Civil War and the military strategies that led to the massacre of Heavy Runner and his followers. The violence that characterized the Montana frontier during the 1860s, when gold discoveries attracted thousands of prospectors and settlers to the West, provides the backdrop for the army's campaign against the Pikuni on the Marias. Until 1869, such violence had resulted in a series of payback killings in which the Blackfoot bands – especially the Pikuni and the Kainai – and Montanans alternated as victims and perpetrators. Acknowledging the extent of white violence against Indians, however, may not have been as high a government priority as documenting so-called 'Indian depredations'. That year, under the leadership of two victorious Civil War generals, Philip Henry Sheridan and William Tecumseh Sherman, this frontier conflict was to be ended once and for all with a carefully planned and executed campaign to 'chastise' the Pikuni. Sheridan's and Sherman's respective roles in planning and authorizing the expedition against the Pikuni, and their subsequent defence of Baker's actions, preclude us from viewing the eventual outcome merely as the blunder of a drunken Baker.

The Precedents of Total War

The concept of total war deployed by Union generals during the Civil War also had an effect on the conduct of the army's campaigns against Indians. Grant's instructions to Sheridan to turn the Shenandoah Valley in Virginia into a 'barren waste' may not compare in scale to the destruction of an Indian camp, but similar principles applied.[4] During the Civil War, total war blurred the line between combatants and civilians; it meant the utter destruction of enemy supply lines, including burning farms and farm equipment. Sheridan's actions at the Shenandoah Valley were gratefully recognized by the President, Congress, and by the civilian population. The need for total war against the Confederates, General Sherman argued, arose because '[w]e are not only fighting hostile armies, but a hostile people, and must make old and young, rich and poor, feel the hard hand of war'.[5] When adapted against the Plains Indians, total war translated into attacks in winter, when the bands were most vulnerable; little distinction being made between combatants and non-combatants; and the utter destruction (by burning) of the bands' means of survival, including homes (lodges), blankets, clothing, and food stores. Horses were either impounded or destroyed, leaving the bands without the means for transportation and for hunting buffalo. With their food reserves destroyed, starvation became a real possibility. Indians' preparedness for war was at its peak during the warm season, when buffalo were plenty. The scarcity of this precious resource during winter brought hardship to their lodges. Sheridan and Sherman understood this cycle; they would also have been aware of the impact that the killing of women had upon their communities' capacity for survival. Indian women tanned skins to make their lodges, bedding, clothing, footwear, and to trade for white goods, including firearms and ammunition. Women gathered, dried, and preserved food (pemmican) that kept starvation at bay during lean times. Pemmican was also a prized commodity of exchange. Without women's labour, the bands' economy collapsed. For buffalo hunting bands such as the Pikuni, women were the supply lines that the farmers in the Shenandoah Valley were to the Confederates.

Without attempting to provide a totalizing perspective of the army's actions against Indians during the 1860s, which would go beyond the bounds of this chapter, it is sufficient for our purposes here to illustrate specific cases of the army's *modus operandi*. Several parallels can be drawn between the massacre of Pikuni in 1870, and the massacre of Black Kettle's Cheyenne camp at the Washita River Valley in November 1868. Sheridan, the hero of the Shenandoah Valley, planned and oversaw both campaigns. Against Black Kettle, Sheridan appointed Lt. Col. George A. Custer to lead the expedition, while Sheridan oversaw the campaign from Camp Supply, a few days' march from the Washita.[6] Against the Pikuni, Sheridan appointed Baker and briefed him in person in Chicago before Baker travelled to Montana. Both the attacks at Washita and on the Marias were executed at first light, during the coldest of winter. At the Marias, army casualties of one man killed, and one injured after falling off of his horse, justified the army's strategies. In the burning of the villages that followed both massacres, the smell of flesh mingled with the smell of burning lodges. There were no Pikuni male survivors in the camp, but some managed to escape. To prevent Indians from attempting to recover their horses, Custer had most of the horse herd killed at Washita, whereas Baker impounded three hundred horses at the Marias.[7] Another pattern can be discerned that provided the backdrop for the army's actions at Washita and the Marias. This pattern is one of settlers invading First Nations lands, killing Indians indiscriminately, attracting violent retribution, and then demanding the army's intervention against the 'hostiles'. When this point was reached, Washington's policy was to 'chastise' the 'hostiles' irrespective of the circumstances. Sherman's interpretation of Indian policy was unambiguous: '[w]e have now selected and provided reservations for all, off the great roads. All who cling to their old hunting-grounds are hostile and will remain so till killed off … we must take chances and clean out Indians as we encounter them.'[8] Sherman's cleaning metaphor echoes what Jacques Semelin calls 'political practices of "purification" and destruction of the "social body"'.[9] This policy, and not a blundering Baker, paved the way for the massacre of Heavy Runner's band. Sheridan planned it, Sherman approved it, and Baker executed it. Sheridan had the experience, the authority, and the boldness to mount an operation of the magnitude of Baker's expedition to the Marias, where a number of Pikuni and Kainai bands were camped for the winter in January 1870.

Sheridan became directly involved in planning the expedition against the Pikuni, even though the superior officer in charge of Montana was Major General W.S. Hancock, the Commander in Dakota. Hancock agreed with and supported Sheridan's decisions. In late December 1869, with the army preparing to strike, Sheridan sent Inspector General James A. Hardie to Montana. He arrived at Fort Shaw on 7 January. Hardie reported a 'too long catalogue of crime, and the continued stealing of stock in nearly all counties of the territory'. He also noted what officials in Montana had reported previously: that violence was often associated with settlers' abuses. Moreover there were 'plenty of lawless and unprincipled men upon the border who supply Indians with whiskey surreptitiously, if not openly, in defiance of the law'.[10] As General Alfred Sully, the Montana Indian Superintendent, claimed, violence was associated with a '"white element" … which, from its rowdy and lawless character, [could not] be excelled in any section'.[11] After the Civil War, however, the army's brief was not to address white trespasses. As Sheridan argued in March 1970, his 'chief and only duty' was to give protection to families residing on the frontier settlements 'against the outrages of Indians'. From its inception, Sheridan's plan against the Pikuni was to strike 'a good strong blow', his final instructions being '[i]f the lives and property of the citizens of Montana can best be protected by striking Mountain Chief's band, I want them struck. Tell Baker to strike them hard.'[12]

Grant's Peace Policy

The massacre on the Marias occurred after a decade in which, as Robert Utley notes, Washington had been divided in its attitude toward Indians. The victorious Civil War generals, Grant, Sherman, and Sheridan, collectively wielded considerable influence in Indian affairs. Grant was sworn in as President in 1869; Sherman became Chief Commander of the Army; and Sheridan filled Sherman's old post as Commander of the Great Plains, with headquarters in Chicago. Grant's Peace Policy was meant to rid Indian affairs of endemic corruption, and to promote peaceful relations. To this end, the President oversaw the formation of a Board of Indian Commissioners in 1869. Grant's Peace Policy, however, reserved 'a sharp and severe war policy' for those who did not conform.[13] In 1868, Grant had declared to the press his determination to protect settlers and emigrants 'even if it meant the extermination of every Indian tribe'.[14] Vocal humanitarian reformers in Washington agreed in principle with the need to place Indians on reservations, but believed in civil, rather than military control. They pointed out the obvious, that soldiers were not trained for peace.[15] It was often noted that it would be cheaper to feed the Indians than to fight them. However, the wellsprings of First Nations' discontent, which often underlay attacks against settlers and the stealing of livestock, were not all of the army's making. Violent resistance against settlers was often linked to Washington's non-compliance with the stipulations of peace treaties; its failure to ratify treaties signed in good faith; and settlers' encroachment on First Nations lands without due compensation being forthcoming.

The link between non-compliance with treaties and the violence that led to the massacre of Pikuni in 1870 can be found in the annual reports to Washington from Blackfeet agents.[16] Apart from the officially recognized problem of corruption in the delivery of treaty goods, and the logistical problems that had to be surmounted in order to transport annuities to far-flung territories, settlers in Montana disregarded the boundaries of the Blackfeet Reservation as defined by the 1855 Blackfeet Treaty.[17] Gold discoveries in 1862 and 1863 attracted to Montana 'not a few men' who would not 'be tolerated in any civilized society'.[18] A drought in 1863 caused buffalo to be scarce, increasing hardship in the territory; and a Sioux uprising in Minnesota compounded the insecurity of Montana, as Sioux bands moved into the territory to avoid the army.[19] Concerned with his own safety, Henry Reed, the Blackfeet Indian agent, abandoned his post at this critical time, leaving his charges without treaty benefits for eighteen months. In the meantime, the extent to which settlers had encroached upon the boundaries of the 1855 treaty became evident when a new Blackfeet treaty was negotiated in 1865. In this new treaty, the Blackfeet 'ceded' part of their territory where the towns of Helena, Virginia City, and Bannack now stood. The new boundaries, boasted an article in the *Montana Post*, contained 'all our rich mines, our best agricultural lands, some of our largest rivers and, in fact, all those portions of our Territory that have proved to be of any worth'.[20]

Blackfoot discontent with increased numbers of settlers on their territory and Washington's refusal to compensate them found expression in isolated killings of settlers. Violence begat violence, and this revenge cycle also saw the 'driving off of horses', a compensatory practice that had entered the Blackfoot's repertoire of contention against whites in the early fur trade days.[21] Horse stealing was a time-honoured occupation among the First Nations of the Plains. When treaties were signed with Washington, stopping this practice was one of the agreed conditions. In practice, horse raiding, albeit sporadic, survived until the 1890s. Sully had prepared a list of 'animals stolen by Indians' during 1869, totalling 197. However, Marshall William F. Wheeler told a grand jury that during 1869 the Blackfeet had stolen one thousand horses.[22] It is not clear if any evidence, other than a settler's word, was required to justify such claims, but given that the United States compensated settlers for horses stolen by Indians to the tune of 150 dollars each, the number could well have been exaggerated.[23]

Washington's reservation policy sought to separate settlers from First Nations peoples. Indians who refused to go onto reservations were declared 'hostile'. However, in 1869 the Blackfoot had 'no reservation to go to'.[24] Neither did they have a valid treaty. Congress had not ratified successive treaties negotiated with the Pikuni, Kainai and Siksika in 1865 and 1868. Redress was not in sight because in 1868, with Grant yet to be elected but already wielding influence, the Taylor Peace Commission voted to 'quit recognizing Indian tribes as "domestic" dependent nations', except as necessitated by existing treaties. Despite these anomalies, Blackfeet agents continued to be nominated and, according to their reports, they continued to distribute goods among their charges, although the extent or rationale of these deliveries is not clear. In 1869, aware of the discontent created by these irregularities, Commissioner of Indian Affairs, Ely Parker, warned the War Department of a possible outbreak by the 'Piegans, Blood, and Blackfeet'.[25] However, this much touted general war did not materialize. It is notable that throughout the 1860s, and even when Montana had few troops to maintain order (before 1866), the Blackfoot alliance never declared open war against the Americans. Undeterred, vocal Montanans raised the alarm of a 'Blackfeet war' several times. Blackfoot lands were much coveted, and those settlers who stood to benefit would have liked to see the former removed from their path. Indeed, they were prepared to remove them themselves. While in the East reformers advocated peaceful means to deal with the Indians, citizens in Montana petitioned their Governor in 1866 to form a militia force of five hundred men 'to chastise [the Piegans] so severely that they will never be any more trouble'.[26] In 1869 pressure was exerted again to form a volunteer force of citizens to 'chase and fight the Indians wherever they might find them' for no other reward than 'whatever captures they could make from the enemy'.[27] Contradicting the 1866 claim of a Blackfeet war, Augustus Chapman, the Flathead agent, having recently crossed Montana, wrote to the Commissioner on July 1867 as follows: 'Governor Meagher's Indian war in Montana is the biggest humbug of the age'.[28] Likewise, in 1869, the Montana Commander, General Philippe Regis De Trobriand, stressed that there was *'no Indian war'* (his emphasis) in Montana.[29] De Trobriand provided a fairly balanced view of violence in the territory, which he attributed to a small number of Indians and whites. He identified among Mountain Chief's Pikuni band 'a certain number of ill-disposed and positively hostile young men which must be punished', and whose 'capture or death' would restore peace.[30] This became more imperative in August 1869, when a band of Pikuni murdered Malcolm Clarke, a prominent ex-trader turned rancher, and injured his son, Horace, leaving him for dead. Malcolm Clarke was married to Kahkokimah Ahki (a.k.a. Cutting-off-Head Woman), a Pikuni woman from Mountain Chief's band. His killer, Pete Owl Child, was a relative of his wife, with whom Malcolm and Horace had had a dispute two years earlier. The Clarkes had publicly humiliated Owl Child, an offence he was bound to revenge in order to regain his honour, but the domestic character of the dispute mattered little.[31] What mattered was that, subsequent to the attack on the Clarkes, Mountain Chief's band was identified as being collectively responsible for most of the crimes committed in the territory during the previous year.

Paving the Road to Chastise Mountain Chief

The murder of Clarke at his ranch in the Prickly Pear Valley galvanized Montanans to clamour for army intervention. The Clarke family identified among the perpetrators men of Mountain Chief's band, who were indicted by a grand jury: Pete Owl Child or Ne-tus-che-o, Eagle's Rib, Bear Chief (a son of Mountain Chief, who shot Horace), Black Weasel, and Black Bear.[32] By then, Mountain Chief's band had crossed the boundary line into the British possessions. Sheridan decided to 'chastise' the Pikuni, and proposed to 'find out where these Indians are going to spend the winter, and about the time of a good heavy snow … give them a good hard blow, which will make peace a desirable object'.[33] Sherman approved the plan. As well as stealing one thousand horses, the Blackfeet were collectively accused of fifty-six murders in 1869.[34] The bulk of these crimes were blamed on Mountain Chief's followers. When Baker set out to punish the Pikuni in January 1870, his orders were 'to chastise that portion of the Indian tribe of Piegan, which, under Mountain Chief or his sons, committed the greater part of the murders and depredations of the last summer and last month, in this district.'[35]

While Mountain Chief was portrayed as the leader of a murderous band, the venerable leader himself had been at the receiving end of white violence. In 1868, after signing the new treaty as Pikuni Head Chief, Mountain Chief 'was insulted and abused in an outrageous manner by some whites', who were angered that 'this chief, in council, had asked the commissioner to have certain men sent out of the Indian Country, and all good citizens agree that these men are *not* fit to be in an Indian country'.[36] A more damning report by the Special Commissioner, W.J. Cullen, claimed that Mountain Chief 'was without cause struck and shot at by two white men, citizens of Benton'. When Cullen tried to obtain a warrant for the arrest of the two men, 'rather than have a white man punished for assaulting an Indian, the justice of the peace and sheriff resigned their offices'.[37] In August 1869, General Sully reported the cowardly murder by whites of two Pikuni men (an old man and his fourteen year old companion) on the streets of Fort Benton.

They were shot 'in broad daylight in revenge for the Indian killing of two white cattle herders'. The old man was Heavy Charging in the Brush, Mountain Chief's brother; neither he nor his companion was connected to the attack on the herders. Although Sully could arrest the murderers, he could not 'convict them in any court'.[38] Whites in Benton also hanged three men from Mountain Chief's band.[39] In terms of the mechanics of massacre, this series of crimes against Mountain Chief and his followers was ignored in order to cast Mountain Chief in the role of perpetrator. This process of discrediting the intended victim could only occur within a context of racial hatred in which settlers enjoyed impunity, and the army generals saw their chief duty as being the protection of settlers 'against the outrages of Indians'.[40] Baker's superiors may have questioned the attack against Heavy Runner, in contradiction of Baker's orders, which were to leave this band 'unmolested'.[41] Instead, they supported Baker unanimously. According to Sheridan 'if a village is attacked, and women and children killed, the responsibility is not with the soldier, but with the people whose crimes necessitate the attack'.[42] De Trobriand recommended Baker for promotion by brevet. Such unwavering approval indicates that Baker's annihilation of a Pikuni band, whether it was Mountain Chief's band or not, was a satisfactory outcome in the eyes of the army generals. Sheridan was staunch in defending his subordinate against public condemnation when news of the massacre made headlines in the Eastern press. Sherman likewise told Sheridan: '[y]ou may assure Colonel Baker that no amount of clamor has shaken our confidence in him and his officers'.[43]

Shifting Blame: The Paper War against 'Indians'

While official reports of Baker's campaign hailed it as a complete success, and the Montana press as cause for celebration, the Eastern press damned Baker's actions. Based on Pikuni reports collected by the Blackfeet agent, Vincent Colyer, of the Board of Indian Commissioners, released details indicating that there were ninety women and fifty children under twelve years of age among those killed on the Marias.[44] In damage control mode, Sherman wrote to the Secretary of War: '[Baker] does not report in detail, as is proper ... the sex and kind of Indians actually left dead at the camp on the Marias'. In order to respond to the public charge that those killed were mostly 'squaws and children',[45] Sherman demanded that Baker report the 'number, sex, and kind of Indians killed', in view of 'the severe strictures in Congress on this act as one of horrible cruelty to women and children'.[46] Sherman's concern emerged nearly two months after the massacre, and a month after receiving Baker's report dated 18 February.

Sheridan defended Baker's actions by going on the offensive. He accused Colyer of writing in the interests of the 'old Indian ring', which was eager to 'get possession of Indian affairs, so that the treasury can be more successfully plundered'. Next to come within Sheridan's sights were 'Indians', and his attack made no tribal distinctions. He challenged that '[s]o far as the wild Indians are concerned ... the good people of the country must decide ... , who shall be killed, the whites or the Indians'. He claimed that 'at least eight hundred [white] men, women, and children' had been murdered within the limits of his command since 1862. He provided gruesome details of mutilations and rapes, but made no connection between these atrocities and Blackfeet culpability.[47] Sherman forwarded Sheridan's letter to the Secretary of War, who read it to Cabinet and approved its publication.[48] On 18 March, with Baker's supplementary report yet to arrive, Sheridan fired another salvo. He claimed that settler families were in constant fear 'of being murdered in the most fiendish manner – the men scalped, the women ravished, and the brains of the children dashed out'. Soldiers, Sheridan bemoaned, were in the middle of two opposing sides, and were abused by both: 'If we allow the defenseless people of the frontier to be scalped and ravished, we are burnt in effigy and execrated as soulless monsters, insensible to the suffering of humanity. If the Indian is punished to give security to these people, we are the same soulless monsters from the other side.' Sheridan expressed regret that 'the women and children of the Piegans' had no refuge where they could have been protected. But even if they did, he argued, they would have not availed themselves of such refuge, 'for they fight with more fury than the men'.[49] In response to his friend and subordinate, Sherman confided that he 'deplored that some of our people prefer to believe the story of the Piegan massacre, as trumped up by interested parties in Benton, more than a hundred miles off [the site of the massacre], rather than the official report of Colonel Baker who was on the spot.' Sherman was confident that the conduct of the campaign raised 'no question at all of [army] responsibility, save and except only as to whether Colonel Baker wantonly and cruelly killed women and children unresistingly, and this [he] never believed'.[50]

The army generals' emphatic defence of the massacre exposes the way in which internal loyalty triumphed over evidence of Baker's massacre of the wrong band, which was conveniently ignored in Baker's defence. It is notable that neither Sherman nor Sheridan commented on the release of prisoners – 'over one hundred squaws'[51] – in the middle of one of the coldest winters known to Montanans, without food, shelter or transportation. Nor did Baker's superiors remark upon the significance of freeing them to spread smallpox among other bands. Traders reported that many women and children who tried to cross the line into the British possessions died.[52] De Trobriand's explanation for Baker's release of the prisoners indicated that 'it would have been extremely inconvenient in several ways to keep them' at the army's post. Sheridan claimed that Baker had no transportation for the prisoners, ignoring the fact that Baker had impounded three hundred horses.[53]

To judge Baker's expedition a success ignores the salient fact that he attacked the very camp he was ordered to leave unmolested, and failed to strike at Mountain Chief. Yet De Trobriand, referring to Heavy Runner's village as 'the hostile camp', reported:

> my previsions were fully realized, and complete success was attained, not only in the severe punishment of the Piegans, but in the telling effect of that manifestation of our power on the whole of the Blackfeet nation, Bloods and Blackfeet proper, who henceforth will carefully avoid bringing upon themselves a similar retribution by murders of white men and depredations on the settlement.[54]

He averred that Baker had 'conducted the operations, conforming himself, in every respect to his instructions'. This remark could only be accurate if Baker was instructed to seek out and annihilate any Pikuni camp, whether friendly or hostile.

Massacre as a Means to a Peaceful Future

Labelling the expedition a complete success indicates that Sheridan's plan was not primarily concerned with punishing criminals. Ensuring future peace emerges as a predicate both of the planning of Baker's expedition and the generals' subsequent defence of Baker's actions. The ideology of inflicting terror as a means to ensure future peace infused the attitudes of Montanans who had earlier demanded permission to punish the Pikuni 'so severely that they will never be any more trouble'. The same link to a peaceful future for settlers that could only be ensured through the killing of Indians (as per Sherman's 'cleaning' metaphor) finds expression in the reports of Inspector Hardie, Sheridan's envoy to Montana during the last stages of planning the attack against the Pikuni. Adding his support to the call to chastise the Pikuni, Hardie argued that 'to shrink from doing what the occasion called for as necessary, no matter how severe, is to incur responsibility for future massacres of men, women and children, for the destruction of homes and the plunder and ruin of the settlements'. Nowhere else is the policy of deploying total war in order to ensure a peaceful future more explicit than in Hardie's telling remark, which many historians have overlooked: 'it is to be remembered that the object is to stop aggressions for the future, not to punish for the past'.[55] Indeed, it appears that what mattered most to the army generals was to make a show of force. When Sheridan notified Sherman of Baker's success, his closing remarks highlighted his main concern: 'I think this will end Indian troubles in Montana, and will do away with the necessity of sending additional troops there in the spring as contemplated'.[56] De Trobriand seems to have been alone in evaluating Baker's success in terms of the punishment of criminals, but in so doing he sacrificed accuracy in the interests of self-congratulation: 'most of the murders [sic] and marauders of last summer are killed. Pal and Mountain Chief escaped with a few followers, leaving everything but horses they were on'.[57] Those reading his report would not have guessed that while a friendly village was destroyed, Mountain Chief and his followers had eluded Baker.

On the basis of the foregoing, it would appear that when Baker marched against the Pikuni, the ground was already prepared for indiscriminate killing. On 17 January, Hardie wrote a note to General George L. Hartsuff, the Assistant Adjutant General in Chicago, to inform him that 'chastisement' was necessary. He had earlier recommended to Hartsuff that Baker 'should be allowed to proceed generally according to the circumstances under which he finds himself in his operations'.[58] According to Hardie, 'horses and mules stolen from citizens' had been seen in various camps on the Marias. Moreover, 'murderers' were present 'among them camps of Indians pretending to be innocent ... Colonel Baker may be relied on to do all that the General [Sheridan] would wish in the way of vigorous and sufficient action ... In any case good, and no harm, will be done.'[59]

Asserting that Baker's campaign was an exercise of chastisement begs the question of how guilt was apportioned to Heavy Runner's band, if their massacre was touted as a successful outcome. Crude notions of 'us' and 'them' and dire predictions of future massacres of settlers by the Indians struck a chord with the Montana colonists in the 1860s. In making reprisals, one Indian was much like another. From its inception, Sheridan's plan was calculated to make the greatest possible impact, such that the annihilation of one group would serve as a potent demonstration of American power – a clear signal of the fate awaiting those who resisted settlers' encroachment in the frontier territories.

Among the historians who have turned their attention to the massacre of Pikuni, John Ewers remarked that Sheridan's 'philosophy of warfare differed little from the primitive Blackfoot one – that losses suffered from enemy raiders should be vigorously avenged by attacking any members of the enemy tribe'.[60] As the history of massacre demonstrates, conflict for territorial control laid the foundation for frontier violence. However, a campaign of the proportions of that executed by Baker requires manpower and equipment to ensure overwhelming victory. Such military capacity seems to have belonged to the army alone in 1870, and the army generals were willing to deploy it in the settlers' cause. In seeking to add to our understanding of the mechanics of massacre, this chapter's exploration of the U.S. Army's adaptation of total war in their campaigns against First Nations has necessarily concentrated on the planning and execution of Baker's attack against the Pikuni on the Marias. Blackfoot history demonstrates that they themselves were capable of massacre, but such actions need to be studied in context, and should not prevent us from examining the army's actions in January 1870.

It would be wrong to suggest that a majority of Americans advocated the extermination of First Nations peoples in the late nineteenth century. Public opinion was divided; so too was Washington, as became clear in congressional debates after the massacre. During Grant's presidency, Sherman and Sheridan had both the power and the inclination to pursue 'peace' by strategically deploying total war. They were of one mind with their President: protect settlers at all costs. There was, however, one signal consequence of the Baker massacre: the negative reaction it provoked in the public sphere and government circles in Washington derailed plans to transfer Indian Affairs to the War Department.[61] In the final analysis, however, the generals' calculations proved accurate. After the massacre, the Blackfoot chiefs unanimously sued for peace, believing that further provocations would bring about their eventual extermination.[62] This would have satisfied the generals, even though their success was predicated upon the open abrogation of military protocols distinguishing between combatants and non-combatants. In 1870, no peace reformer or press furore could alter the army's brief and their strategies. In the final analysis, from the perspective of the generals, the campaign against the Pikuni had produced the desired result.

Notes

1. This chapter was written thanks to a University of Sydney Postdoctoral Fellowship. I also acknowledge the Faculty of Arts and Social Sciences, University of New South Wales, for providing me with a grant to research materials utilized here. I am indebted to the Librarians at the Medicine Springs Library, Blackfeet Community College, Browning, and the Montana Historical Society, Helena, for allowing access to documents pertaining to the massacre of Pikuni.

2. The Pikuni, Pikani, Piegan (Peigan in Canada) is the southernmost division of the alliance of Blackfoot-speaking Nitsitapiksi (Blackfoot, The Real People), who currently occupy the Blackfeet Reservation in Montana and three reserves in Alberta (the Peigan [Pikuni], Blood [Kainai], and Blackfoot [Siksika] reserves). In the late nineteenth century George Bird Grinnell, *Blackfoot Lodge Tales: The Story of a Prairie People* (Lincoln, 2003), 208–10, listed twenty-four Pikuni bands, which he defines as 'gentes, a gens being a body of consanguineal kindred in the male line'. James Willard Schultz, *Blackfeet and Buffalo: Memories of Life among the Indians*, ed. Keith C. Seele (Norman, 1962 [c.1878–1915]), 302–4, notes that the massacre site is located north of Goosebill Butte.

3. Brian Reeves, 'The Marias Massacre Site: A Progress Report': Blackfeet Tribe, December 1995, Blackfeet Community College Library, Browning, citing Horace Clarke, who accompanied Baker's men; and Ewers, *The Blackfeet: Raiders on the Northwestern Plains* (Norman, 1958), 250–51.

4. Christon I. Archer, et al., *World History of Warfare* (Lincoln, 2002), 414.

5. Christon I. Archer, et al., *World History of Warfare*, 416.

6. Richard G. Hardorff (ed.), *Washita Memories: Eyewitness Views of Custer's Attack on Black Kettle's Village* (Norman, 2006).

7. *Piegan Indians*, 16–17, Baker's Report, 18 February 1870.

8. Emerson Hough, 'The Passing of the Frontier: A Chronicle of the Old West', in Allen Johnson (ed.), *The Chronicles of America Series* (New Haven, 1918), 125–26.

9. Jacques Semelin, *Purify and Destroy: The Political Uses of Massacre and Genocide,* trans. Cynthia Schoch (New York, 2007), 6.

10. *Piegan Indians,* 19–34, 20, Hardie to Hartsuff, 29 January 1870.

11. *Piegan Indians,* 2, Sully to Parker, 3 August 1869.

12. *Piegan Indians,* 32, Sheridan to Hardie, 15 January 1870.

13. Robert M. Utley, *The Indian Frontier of the American West 1846–1890* (Albuquerque, 1984), 130.

14. Utley, *The Indian Frontier,* 125, citing *New York Times,* 16 October 1868.

15. Utley, *The Indian Frontier,* 106.

16. *Annual Reports of the Commissioner of Indian Affairs* (henceforth *Annual Reports*), 1863 and 1864 (Washington, Government Printing Office).

17. See http://digital.library.okstate.edu/kappler/vol2/pgimages/Bla0736.jpg, accessed 30 January 2009, for *Treaty with the Blackfeet, 1855.*

18. Ewers, *The Blackfeet,* 237, citing *Annual Reports,* 1862, 180; and Hough, *Passing of the Frontier,* 57–82.

19. *Annual Reports,* 1863, 169–71.

20. Montana Historical Society, *Montana Post,* Virginia City, 9 December 1865.

21. James H. Bradley, 'The Bradley Manuscript', *Contributions to the Historical Society of Montana,* 9 vols. (Boston, Mass., 1966), 8:147.

22. *Piegan Indians,* 7, and 45–46; and Ewers, *The Blackfeet,* 238–39, and 247.

23. Of the three hundred horses Baker impounded from Heavy Runner's village, settlers claimed back thirty-four horses and one mule, and 230 horses were 'Indian ponies, in a poor condition, and of but little value'. *Piegan Indians,* 13–14, De Trobriand to Green, 18 February 1870. For the amount of compensation, see *Piegan Indians,* 7.

24. *Annual Reports,* 1869; and Sully to Parker, 293.

25. *Piegan Indians,* 1–2, Parker to Acting Secretary of the Interior, 16 August 1869. Parker was a Seneca, and through his loyalty to Grant during the Civil War became the first Indian Commissioner of Indian Affairs. For his views on treaties see Herman J. Viola, *After Columbus: The Smithsonian Chronicle of the North American Indians* (Washington, DC, 1990), 164.

26. Hugh A. Dempsey, *Firewater: The Impact of the Whiskey Trade on the Blackfoot Nation* (Calgary, 2002), 19 and 226, n. 6, citing Petition, 10 January 1866.

27. *Piegan Indians,* 55–59, De Trobriand to Greene, 9 September 1869.

28. *Annual Reports,* 1868, 259.

29. *Piegan Indians,* 60–62, De Trobriand to Montana Citizens Committee, 6 October 1869.

30. *Piegan Indians,* 61, De Trobriand to Greene, 6 October 1869.

31. For the dispute, see Schultz, *Blackfeet and Buffalo,* 298; and Leslie Wischmann, *Frontier Diplomats: The Life and Times of Alexander Culbertson and Natoyist-Siksina' Among the Blackfeet* (Norman, 2000), 324–26.

32. *Piegan Indians,* 60–62, De Trobriand to Montana Citizens Committee, 6 October 1869, lists also 'the half-breed Star'. An additional list was circulated of fourteen hostiles, 'all deemed guilty'. Robert J. Ege, *Tell Baker to Strike Them Hard!: Incident on the Marias, 23 Jan. 1870* (Bellevue, Nebraska, 1970), 24 and 39.

33. *Piegan Indians,* 7, Sheridan to Army Headquarters, Washington, 21 October 1969.

34. *Piegan Indians,* 7, Sully to Parker; and Ewers, *The Blackfeet,* 247.

35. *Piegan Indians,* De Trobriand to Baker, 16 January 1870. Baker was ordered to leave unmolested other bands of Piegans 'as they have uniformly remained friendly: the bands of *Heavy Runner* and Big Lake.'

36. *Annual Reports,* 1868, 215–16. Emphasis in original.

37. *Annual Reports,* 1868, 221–22.

38. *Piegan Indians,* 2, Sully to Parker, 3 August 1869.

39. Schultz, *Blackfeet and Buffalo,* 299; and Dempsey, *Firewater,* 34–35.

40. *Piegan Indians,* 70, Sheridan to Sherman, 18 March 1870.

41. *Piegan Indians,* De Trobriand to Baker, 16 January 1870.

42. *Piegan Indians*, 70, Sheridan to Sherman, 18 March 1870.
43. *Piegan Indians*, 73–74, Sherman to Sheridan, 28 March 1870.
44. Ewers, *The Blackfeet*, 251.
45. *Piegan Indians*, 17–18, Sherman to Secretary of War, 12 March 1870.
46. *Piegan Indians*, 70, Sherman to Sheridan, 12 March 1870.
47. *Piegan Indians*, 9–10, Sheridan to Sherman, 28 February 1870.
48. *Piegan Indians*, 10, Sherman to Sheridan, 5 March 1870.
49. *Piegan Indians*, 70–71, Sheridan to Sherman, 18 March 1870.
50. *Piegan Indians*, 72, Sherman to Sheridan, 24 March 1870.
51. *Piegan Indians*, 9, Sheridan to Sherman, 31 January 1870.
52. Dempsey, *Firewater*, 49–50.
53. *Piegan Indians*, 9, Sheridan to Sherman, 31 January 1870.
54. *Piegan Indians*, 13–14, De Trobriand to Green, 18 February 1870.
55. *Piegan Indians*, 19–34, 23, Hardie to Hartsuff, 29 January 1870.
56. *Piegan Indians*, 13, Sheridan to Sherman, 29 January 1870.
57. *Piegan Indians*, 8, Sheridan to Sherman, 29 January 1870, transmitting message from De Trobriand.
58. *Piegan Indians*, 47, Hardie to Hartsuff, 13 January 1870.
59. *Piegan Indians*, 49, Hardie to Hartsuff, 17 January 1870.
60. Ewers, *The Blackfeet*, 252.
61. Ewers, *The Blackfeet*, 252.
62. Father Camillus Imoda, a Jesuit priest, informed Sully of their decision. Dempsey, *Firewater*, 52, citing a letter of 11 April 1870; and Ewers, *Blackfeet*, 252.

CHAPTER 11

WHEN MASSACRE APPEARS: REPRESENTATIONS OF AUSTRALIAN INDIGENOUS MASSACRES IN FICTION

Katrina Schlunke

Massacres that have occurred in the past are still present in the form of historical record, oral history and most popularly in film and novels. This chapter is concerned with the ways in which knowledge of past massacres are transmitted in fictional form, through novels and films. It looks at two particular examples of scenes of past massacres of Indigenous Australians as they appear in the international award-winning novel *Secret River* by Kate Grenville and the internationally acclaimed feature film *Tracker* directed by Rolf de Heer.[1] The novel is set in the early Australian colonial period near the settlement of Sydney, and the film is set in Central Australia at the end of the colonial period. In this way the two texts span the period of overt Australian colonization between 1788 and 1930, in which most massacres of Indigenous Australians occurred. The texts are used in support of the argument that how we write historical massacre matters, whether it be in fictional or non-fictional form. Not only must we write of massacre as an event that sits within a recognizable and possible past but as an event that is accountable to the 'miracle of survival' that is ongoing Indigenous presence and cultural practice. At the same time writing on massacre should continue to evoke the ineffable experience of those who suffered within that massacre which cannot be entirely written or wholly known but the attempt to make that suffering known still must be continually made.

The representation of Indigenous massacre in fiction and film is complicated by at least two issues. While a particular massacre may have occurred over one hundred years ago, the memory and effects of that massacre can still constitute a key part of an Indigenous group's living, contemporary, culture. In such cases massacre is much better understood as being about survival rather than an 'historical' event from the past. This reality means that a 'fictional' representation is to be judged not simply on its historical accuracy (could such a thing reasonably have happened in this time and place?) but on the possibilities that the representation evokes in the present.

These elements are particularly important to consider because of the often isolated nature or hidden geography of the occurrence of massacre and the often extreme ferocity of the violence used. Both mark the massacre as 'outside' of or beyond that knowledge which is readily assimilated into ideas of national history. Depicting massacre in fiction can help to establish these often hidden histories as an accepted part of the violent colonial encounter through which the nation was established. But that very depiction in fiction can at the same time remove the necessary specificity and truthfulness that will properly mark the many different massacres 'historically'.

In discussing the massacres of Indigenous Australians that occurred throughout the first 130 years of the British colonial occupation of Australia, I am focusing on one particular part of a takeover that also included the tactics of disease, removal from place, removal of children, incarceration, denial of education, refusal of participation in government, and individual as well as group murder. Most of this violence was organized through an emerging and then established governing order and much of the unofficial violence can also be understood as the actions of non-Indigenous individuals emboldened to act violently because they believed they were carrying out the intention if not the letter of the existing law.

Sketching the earlier period of Australian colonialism in this way introduces a peculiar kind of historical kilter. It sounds a little like the strategies used by the Nazi regime and a compliant German population, in a place far away and a time long after, these events in Australia. But if it was the vast scale, the camps and the gas chambers that finally remain as the evidence, forever, of what occurred in Europe, in Australia it is the still emerging bureaucratic trail of those who were removed and the cultural and social effect of the small and large massacres that remain within the cultural memory of both Indigenous and non-Indigenous Australians.

I am not simply referring to those few, and very far between, massacre sites which are actively commemorated, but also to the knowledge held by both Indigenous and non-Indigenous Australians that those massacres took place. Unlike the exclusion of Indigenous peoples from national processes such as land ownership, education, health and governance itself, massacres show the violence of the state and its disseminated practices on the body and help to reveal the particular blend of modern and pre-modern authority that was imposed directly onto and through Indigenous bodies. This combination of pre-modern and governmental power made for a distinctive order of terror that is partly explored by anthropologist Barry Morris in his work on the colonial frontier.[2] But to effectively 'remember' massacre now we need to be 'jolted': an affective and often locative strike that reveals massacre not only through material evidence but through the triumvirate of enduring Indigenous presence, historical record and the experience of self in Australian space. This is to extend the project that Sontag saw photographs undertaking of, 'continually renewing, of creating, memories'.[3] So must we write.

A discussion of the massacres of Indigenous Australians requires an appreciation of the fact that we will also be looking at the corporeal eruption of violence that was also occurring in other forms (removal of children, forced migration to missions and reserves) – and which might indeed be hidden by the much more visible and remembered violence of massacre.

Having said that massacre foregrounds particular hurt and maimed bodies, massacre of Indigenous Australians is also one of the more invisible acts of violence. The paper trail left behind is only slight, unless the massacre in question underwent some kind of legal recognition, as in the case of the Myall Creek Massacre in 1838.[4] Officially, massacre required nothing more than a policeman's report that a 'punishment' had occurred. And only the literate squatter or selector ever wrote about what they did, while the physical scars of fires or the exposed corpses do not endure. There are strong and weak oral histories and local stories that continue to circulate but there will never be anything like the order of numeration that the Holocaust produced, which, it should be noted, still gives rise to bizarre attempts at denial and obfuscation. Something more than just careful and truthful numeration is at stake in the communication of the event of massacre – massacre is always a politically alive event with local, national and international cultures impacting on its representations and the readings of those representations.

What should remain beyond (or really exist within) any representation of massacre is what Lyotard calls the remainder: 'But it is one thing to do it (*represent*) in view of saving the memory, and quite another to try to preserve the remainder, the unforgettable forgotten, in writing.'[5] This is a call to be both political and stylistically aware of the particular burden of recording and communicating traumatic events. Many people, Indigenous and non-Indigenous, have attempted to do exactly that in quite different ways. Some have numerated exactly the deaths of Indigenous peoples but have shown that they know those deaths are of particular people, many of whom will still have living relatives who need to know about these deaths in order to keep alive the stories that enable cultures to rebuild themselves and remain strong. Others know that the fetishlike national importance placed on the number of those who died may not be a mathematics of survival but calculations of colonialism that make numbers the strangest translation yet, of that experience we inadequately call death.[6]

But the political, ethical and indeed poetical care that Lyotard suggests we should take when working with the deaths of others gets quickly ignored when faced with national denial. Throughout many years of Australian history, and again within the period of the conservative government of John Howard (1996–2007), a particular cultural and political environment was created, known as the History Wars, that sought to accentuate only the positive achievements of Australia's history. This was maintained through the claiming of a rational, 'middle of the road' position which used rhetoric such as: 'I believe the balance sheet of Australian history is a very generous and benign one. I believe that, like any other nation, we have black marks upon our history but among the nations of the world we have a remarkably positive history. ... I think we have been too apologetic about our history in the past.'[7]

One of the events of the past that was subject to this ideological rethink was the massacre of Indigenous Australians, most particularly through the public performances of polemicist Keith Windschuttle. While his particular focus were the numbers of Indigenous peoples killed during the extended period of colonization, from 1788 to 1930, he was only one part of a public/political movement that celebrated the image of an Australian past claimed by Windschuttle to be 'the least violent of all Europe's encounters with the New World'.[8] This public rhetoric and its popular dissemination made any mention of massacre a national political act of treason. To write about massacre as an academic was to continually risk dismissal as a 'black armband' historian and to be seen simply as a 'left' rather than a critical Australian thinker; and including the massacre of Indigenous peoples in novels and films implied that one was already on one side or another. As Windschuttle reportedly said of Grenville's novel in *The Age* newspaper: 'He hasn't read Grenville's book, but "I think the topic itself sounds strange. The issue has gone beyond a case where a fictionalized account is going to make any impact. Those people who now believe the story of guns and violence against Aborigines will be comforted by a book like that. Not one mind will be changed".'[9]

In this way the fictional accounts I will be looking at were responses to both the Howard years and the History Wars but were also limited by the politics of massacre which raged at the time. As Collins and Davis suggested of *The Tracker*, 'On one level *The Tracker's* mythic tale of massacre and other colonial atrocities arrives too late in the history wars, in that it is behind the times in its thinking about how best to remember traumatic colonial events ... On another level ... *The Tracker* comes too soon'.[10]

In the face of this climate of denial that any massacres of Indigenous peoples had occurred, it is a simple matter to claim that in such a situation any representation of massacre is better than none. This thinking arises from seeing what one government could do to produce so quickly an environment where one had a simple choice of whether to 'believe' in a violent past or not, and where the choices of what one could be were reduced to two: either a black armband or a white blindfold follower of a particular historical orthodoxy, as if such simple summations of any national past were possible. The Australian people were then encouraged to have the courage to forget the violence of settlement, as something that we had all 'moved on from'. This atmosphere of there being only one supported version of Australian history also gave rise to a new 'forgetting' so that the Australian people could say (again) 'we were never told' or 'we have been told for the first time' when details of a massacre were disclosed.

In such a political environment, even a broad journalistic catalogue of massacre sites (here I am thinking of the enduring popularity of Bruce Elder's *Blood on the Wattle*) or the fictional inclusion of massacre in a best-selling and much awarded literary novel (such as Kate Grenville's *Secret River*) at least kept the record and reality of Indigenous massacre alive in the popular imagination.[11] And as a political point, as a means of establishing a new 'common sense' within the broad Australian community this may be true.

But we must always return to the point that the histories and stories that are passed on, where stories exist, belong to the people whose lives were lost. When we write about massacre, we should bear in mind three aspects: the recognition of enduring Indigenous presence, historical record and experience of self in place. Each effort – whether clumsy or elegant, effective or obscure – should work toward the 'unforgettable forgotten', always striving towards something more, that cannot be articulated or represented, remembered or memorialized but which none the less motivates efforts to commemorate and recall each massacre. Work on massacre that creates conclusions rather than connections, that promises, a final truth by complete denial that the massacre ever occurred or through its complete exposure, in the end runs counter to what grants massacre its constant need to keep coming into the present and that is that which cannot be said, that which necessarily remains unsayable – the suffering of those who died.

Saturation

When massacre is written in the mistaken belief that an author can know exactly what happened, something goes wrong but we do not always know what. When I read Kate Grenville's *Secret River*, particularly the massacre sequence, I felt sick, not as I suspect I was meant to, at the violence depicted but at the heavy-handed way in which 'the massacre' appeared on the pages as a final climactic act and was then abandoned. *The Secret River* received much critical acclaim and its author some minor notoriety for her claims about the historical qualities of her novel. In particular the historian, Inga Clendinnen carefully pointed out the problems with Grenville's claim that novelists, unlike historians, 'can actually get inside the experience'.[12] The idea that the past can be accessed through a mixture of research and imagination and then re-presented so that the reader will in turn experience that past is an old one and is taken thoroughly to task by Clendinnen. But my argument is that when an author presumes that the fact of the multiple deaths of others is entirely knowable, then a massacre, as just one more 'imaginative experience' that can be written 'in character' 'within the plot', fails as fiction and writing because it fails writing itself.[13] There is no longer a point of alterity, a place where what is happening cannot be reduced to the predictable narrative drive or characters that we know, and so this massacre of Indigenous people becomes one more novelistic device. Without any space for the difference of the past nor the deaths of many, this writing tells us of massacre in such a way that we can forget massacre because we know it all. This fails the imaginative and ethical possibility of writing to evoke the unrepresentable.

Anecdotally, this novel was reported to be one where we who 'weren't told'[14] or did not know, learnt the truth about Australian history in early colonial times. One of the 'truths' presented within this work of fiction is the massacre of an Indigenous group of men, women and children on the Hawkesbury River. This was an area where recorded massacres of Indigenous Australians did take place. Popular historian Keith Willey portrays it as 'a centre of conflict from the time European settlers arrived there' and describes some of the individual acts of great cruelty that were carried out there, as well as the periods of resistance, open war and regular deployment of troops.[15] Grenville, constrained by the traditional narrative form of her novel, needs 'her' massacre to be distinct and to result from the particular moves and counter-moves of her key characters. It does not make for a good novel if the story strays into the realm of colonial strategy or incomprehensible cruelties that might threaten the relationship between reader and character. But in depicting a massacre, Grenville is clearly writing about an event that could plausibly have happened in at least something like the way in which she describes it, even if her version is more contained and personality-driven than the history of ongoing warfare along the Hawkesbury might suggest.

The twelve pages that deal with the massacre comprise the penultimate section of the book. A blank page follows the massacre scene and the next chapter, 'Thornhill's Place', is set some ten years after the massacre. The massacre is, therefore, really the climax of the book. In it the transformation of the Thornhills – from transported convicts to well-to-do gentleman and woman – is depicted. The final chapter spells out the established success of Thornhill, who is still haunted by the violence he and his fellow settlers committed (although he appears to be the exception in feeling that way) even though the massacre has been in every other sense beneficial for him. Thus the book concludes on the worst possible note of what reconciliation could mean. The Indigenous people of the area have entirely disappeared and the whites prosper on the stolen land but they *feel* something that a contemporary audience can read as regret and sadness for what could have been. But it is a regret that is based on the condition that the non-Indigenous people have complete control of the land – there is nothing here of the legal realities of ongoing Indigenous Australian sovereignty, simply that this now sensitized white feels bad.

The description of attack is cinematic in its detail. A mother is struck through with a sword, her baby's head is cut off and a dog is shot in the mouth. Knees become 'flowers of blood', 'blood pumps' from a throat, there is much 'bright blood' and shoulders are opened in a 'long red strip'.[16] Each phrase moves our watching eyes from one explicit detail to the next, as a camera might. As readers we are witnessing this event from Thornhill's point of view plus some more. The violence depicted here is familiar in its actions and rhythm from television and cinema, and from other horror stories. It is almost a cliché. Does this matter? Is one of the possible purposes of the historical novel to make fictional violence – with its real antecedents – produce real effects? It has 'worked' if it makes people react like they do when they see television violence or when they read of international violence. This could be understood as the fictional invention of a past that we are then able to feel in our present. All the time knowing that that past was imagined within the constraints of the novel form and what can be published and sold. We will not forget that a massacre happened in this book. But then what? Nothing. The final lines of this chapter are: 'And a great shocked silence hanging over everything'.[17] As mentioned above, there then follows a blank page, and a new chapter entitled 'Thornhill's Place'. Ten years have passed. We discover that the scar in the earth made by attempts to burn the murdered can still be seen but we learn nothing of how the white and black silence in such a small community has been maintained. Instead we are presented with a twentieth-century white Australian dream that there were Indigenous Australians and they have now gone, forever, leaving only silence. We can compare this with the fictional re-telling of the Myall Creek Massacre from the perspective of an Indigenous woman character, Ginny, in Phillip McLaren's novel *Sweet Water-Stolen Land*. In this novel, the violence is equally dreadful but it is felt violence, it is happening to Ginny. And the first shock is not that of pain but of the broken friendship ties of one of the killers, Kilmeister, a white stockman, who only the night before was dancing with them all. Perhaps most tellingly, this fictional account is told from a survivor's perspective and that survivor is cared for after the attack by a white family.

In providing a more complex sense of the textured alliances between black and white sharing the same place, this massacre scene is able to show the ways in which Indigenous survival can be evoked through the depiction of destruction.[18]

In *The Secret River* there are no survivors and only minor references to any surviving Indigenous Australians anywhere. There is mention of a group of Indigenous Australians who have been moved to the local reserve and of one old man who, clutching some earth, reminds Thornhill that he will never have a relationship with the land like this old Indigenous man. But the massacre challenges and changes nothing. It merely confirms a past that looks just like the one imagined by so many contemporary non-Indigenous Australians. The crude elements of this fantasy are: the absence of Indigenous people, (except for the occasional individual who is ill or dying and in need of white help and other Indigenous Australians who are far away from the centre of the action of the novel) and a present, prosperous white population who are, at most simply asked to care in the abstract – to have 'bad feelings'. As cultural historian Chris Healy says of other examples, but which fits the case here: 'What's striking in these examples of "feeling bad" is a narcissist shift from Aboriginality as a space of potential negotiation to a focus on "we" who have won and are the model for all people. This is less forgetting Aborigines than a complete displacement of Aboriginality.'[19] That this displacement should occur through massacre seems particularly 'obscene'.[20]

This fictional massacre is merely a narrative prop. It provides a necessary climax, an action scene which in no way challenges the convention of a 'good' novel, the assumptions of teleological history or the idea that relations could be negotiated differently now. The white figure is left with a feeling of limited melancholia but also with an idea that most of his children will have forgotten. The erasure is almost complete except for that 'bad feeling' which in its own way is another erasure, of something that happened – it is a political schema reduced to a private act, a silent feeling. There is no space here for what will always be unknowable about massacre, for what should always remain in any effort to represent mass death in fiction or non-fiction. What made those deaths unique is here erased through the novelistic details, the seduction of narrative, which renders all, all knowable and therefore forgettable.

Preservation

In *The Tracker,* something quite different occurs. Throughout this film both the difference of the past and the 'remainder' of massacre is sustained through the management of a point of view that cannot be reduced to the same as ourselves or to a familiar, knowable history.[21]

The Tracker is the story of three white men in Central Australia in 1922 who are searching for an Aboriginal escapee from white justice and who are guided by a black tracker (played by David Gulpilil). The Tracker of the title has the job of tracking the Aboriginal who is suspected of murdering a white woman. In following the tracks he leads the police officer (the Fanatic, played by Gary Sweet), his offsider (the Follower) and a seconded assistant (the Veteran) across the very difficult outback terrain. During that journey the men test and tease each other, revealing and hiding their intentions and dispositions as Indigenous Australians are murdered without compunction by the Fanatic and as the Tracker's role shifts and turns with each move.

The initial capture, chaining and interrogation of an Indigenous group of men, women and children begins with the three white men riding forward with guns drawn while a contemporary tune in an Indigenous language, sung by well-known Indigenous performer, Archie Roach, is overlaid with the sounds of the white men's yahooing. There follows a still shot of a painting showing the actual massacre, including the clubbing of the Indigenous Australians with rifles. The next scene is of a chained Indigenous man and the group being interrogated by the three white men while Archie Roach still sings quietly 'we are no longer free, we are dispossessed'. Archie Roach's voice continues to drown out the ranting of The Fanatic, the leader of the party. The song picks up and we hear the lyrics clearly – 'My people, my people', and then see a painting of the Fanatic putting a gun to a man's tongue. This is followed by the sound of shooting and cries and the scene then cuts to the next still painting, showing us that the man has been shot in the mouth and the woman next to him shot by the other policeman. The sounds of shooting only, are heard as we watch the painting, and then the camera pans round to the crying young Follower, the Tracker pacing around a tree, the Fanatic triumphantly cleaning his gun and then a wider shot of the entire group of Aboriginal people dead before them.

At no point in any of this, could we as viewers be unaware of contemporary Indigenous political and cultural production nor that the massacre cannot be (entirely) shown. The triple technique of contemporary Indigenous Australian music, still painting amid film, and black and white actors gives this depiction both stillness and action, historic situatedness and contemporary commentary – this is an act of both the past and the present.

The use of Archie Roach's music works in multiple ways. Best known for his moving song about the 'Stolen Generations', called 'Took the Children Away', he sings in a way that teaches and moves an audience at the same time. He is probably the best known Indigenous singer today and his own life has been one of survival in the face of a range of government policies aimed at the disruption of Indigenous communal life. He sings for his people as they are killed; his voice is therefore both lament and testimony. Massacre was not the only way in which his people were dispersed and yet it remains one of the least acknowledged in any sustained way.

At the end of the film, relations between the Tracker and the Follower are reversed and supplemented. By the end the Tracker is openly in charge. The Tracker rides off once they arrive at a place where the young policeman can find his way and the film ends with the Tracker riding into the hills. This scene is then overlaid by another still painting over which the credits roll.

The actual painting of the massacre shows stark trees – a deliberate choice by the white artist Peter Coad – set against an ochre walled backdrop, with a shock of white in the hair of the Indigenous woman and man who are being shot, and the overlarge eyes and white lips of everyone else. It is animated and yet still. It seems to fall somewhere between the paintings of Fred Williams or Charles Blackman and a graphic novel.[22] Yet they also evoke certain Indigenous Australian motifs through the paintings' use of dots and simple stark figures. In particular, the bend and shape of the figures recalls the painting by Indigenous artist, Queenie McKenzie, titled *The White Bull with Black & White people,* one part of a series from 1996 that includes *The White Bull and Massacre Site.*[23] So even as we are watching potent white power in action, we are looking through white forms that evoke the pervasiveness of Indigenous Australian representations via Indigenous art. In this way we 'see' the continuity of Indigenous culture while witnessing part of its destruction. The director Rolf de Heer speaks of the way in which 'it gets harder and harder to have any real effect with violence on the screen. So to go the other way, to make it representational rather than actual seemed to be an interesting thing to do.' He also acknowledges the fact that one of his commissioning agents was an arts festival which gave him more freedom to try new things.[24] The stillness of the paintings reminds us that massacre remains, that it will not move on like the rest of the movie – it is a reminder of what cannot be shown or entirely known. It is also the marker of the presence of the past in the present – that which is not merely 'representation' but the mark of the 'catastrophe' of the frontier and enduring Indigenous survival.

This re-enactment/representation/evocation of massacre is never stabilized to mean only one thing and neither is it passed through and the people disappeared forever as in Grenville's novel. As a plot device the massacre weakens rather than strengthens the relations between the white men. One cries, one is triumphant and one resigns. The Tracker begins his path to hanging the Fanatic using the same explanation the Fanatic used to justify the massacre he carried out – 'as a warning'. The viewer is never quite certain what will happen next as the story becomes one of being in Aboriginal hands, of shutting up, listening and obeying an Aboriginal man, the Tracker. The survival of the remaining white man depends upon the Tracker's careful negotiations with the larger Indigenous groups they encounter, the Tracker's knowledge of the country and the Tracker's willingness to go on guiding the Follower to a place from which he can find his own way home. Then the Tracker rides away.

Although the film achieved critical acclaim, one criticism came from film reviewer Julie Rigg, who said of the script: 'There are pompous, unbelievable speeches these men deliver at certain times which undercut credibility'.[25] This would be quite true if credibility were judged in terms of whether a contemporary audience would believe that anyone would speak like that. But the language used by the Fanatic in particular, will be very familiar to those who have read the written pronouncements upon Aboriginal people that emerged in the colonial period from 1788 to 1930. The words do sound pompous and unbelievable but certainly, 'historically' believable. Seeing those wooden pronouncements emerging from a 'real' figure dressed as a colonial policeman who likes to shoot is unsettling, and represents a conflation of Hollywood convention and historical sources. Something that is not credible to a contemporary audience is, I think, a useful mechanism to remind everyone that the past cannot always be fitted easily into a pre-digested present.

Saturation and Preservation

As my critique of the two fictional texts has demonstrated, remembering massacre in the contemporary moment entails a certain degree of struggle with representation itself. Words and images have multiplied themselves throughout geographies but also throughout genres and disciplines. This has resulted in an instability of meaning and often only a fleeting recall of an event, particularly an historical one. To preserve the remainder of massacre now requires the preservation of a mode of inquiry that sustains the possibility of knowing the past in the present in this multi modal environment of simulation and endless replacement. This means that we need to find new ways of making memory – of writing these traumatic pasts. The task would seem to be one of maintaining an awareness of how massacre as an event in history, is always an act of translation that carries with it a particular need to attempt to say – through affect, through image, through style of circulation, through being open to what may or may not work – what cannot be said. And yet we must go on trying to say the unsayable of Indigenous massacre in a context of ongoing, contemporary Indigenous presence and culture making.

This demand is particularly acute with regard to the visual representations of massacre in history where massacre becomes linked with the well-established experience of seeing and hearing traumatic events. Given the ubiquity of violence on screen many believe they have 'seen it all' and in one way they may have. But to 'see' generic violence is not to remember historical massacre. Can we work harder to ensure that the memory of massacre continues as an historical truth and as a reminder of an enduring Indigenous presence? How could we achieve this? What medium may better attempt to recall and record the unforgettable, not simply in the massacre itself but the images, sounds and texts that come to represent it?

We continue to read and write about massacre as just one act in Australian history but we also need to recognize that massacre is a process of meaning making in the Australian present. We live through massacre not beyond or past massacre. Massacre is with us always. As writers of 'histories' of massacres, we are challenged to not only write in ways which might stretch the historical form but also in ways which consider the multiple modes in which histories are told. What can we learn from the visual modes of film and painting? What can we learn from the genres of fiction? How can we continue to show that we know (but not everything, not know so completely as to forget) within history while recogniszing that the past always appears to us in the present? Massacre entails knowing the past in three ways: as a reminder of Indigenous presence; as an exploration and invocation of the historical record; and as an experience of self in place. This creates an ongoing challenge to what we think the past is and how we represent it and who we are and where we are, who write it.

Notes

1. Kate Grenville, *The Secret River* (Melbourne, 2005); Rolf de Heer, *The Tracker* (Melbourne, 2002).
2. Barry Morris, 'Frontier Colonialism as a Culture of Terror', in Bain Attwood and John Arnolds (eds), *Power, Knowledge and Aborigines*. Special issue, *Journal of Australian Studies*, 35 (Melbourne, 1992), 72–87.
3. Sontag, *Regarding the Pain of Others,* 78.
4. For an account of the trials of the Myall Creek Massacre, see R.H.W. Reece, *Aborigines and Colonists: Aborigines and Colonial Society in New South Wales in the 1830s and 1840s* (Sydney, 1974).
5. J.F. Lyotard, *Heidegger and the 'Jews'*, trans. Andreas Michel and Mark S. Roberts (Minneapolis, 1990), 26.
6. For a discussion of Aboriginal population decline and violence, see Richard Broome, *The Aboriginal Victorians* (Melbourne, 2005), 91.
7. John Howard, *House of Representatives, Weekly Hansard* (Canberra, 1996), 30 October 1996, 4. See also Stuart Macintyre and Anna Clark, *The History Wars* (Melbourne, 2003).
8. See also Macintyre and Clark, *The History Wars.*
9. Keith Windschuttle, quoted in Macintyre and Clark, *The History Wars*, 165.
10. Felicity Collins and Therese Davis, *Australian Cinema After Mabo* (Melbourne, 2004), 6, 17.
11. Bruce Elder, *Blood on the Wattle: Massacres and the Maltreatment of Australian Aborigines since 1788* (French's Forest, New South Wales, 1988).
12. Inga Clendinnen, *The History Question: Who Owns the Past?* (Melbourne, 2006), 20.
13. Clendinnen, *The History Question*, 21.
14. Henry Reynolds, *Why Weren't We Told?: A Personal Search for the Truth about Our History* (Melbourne, 2000).
15. Keith Willey, *When the Sky Fell Down: The Destruction of the Tribes of the Sydney Region* (Sydney, 1979), 173–80.
16. Grenville, *The Secret River*, 303–306.
17. Grenville, *The Secret River*, 309.
18. Philip McLaren, *Sweet Water-Stolen Land* (Brisbane, 1993), 116–30.

19. Chris Healy, *Forgetting Aborigines* (Melbourne, 2008), 218.

20. Lyotard, *Heidegger and the Jews*, 210.

21. This assumes an acceptance of Levinas's notion that the ethical is that point of alterity or 'exteriority' that cannot be reduced to the same as ourselves, to the already known or knowable. See Emmanuel Levinas, *Totality and Infinity*, trans. A. Lingis (Pittsburgh, 1969), 43–45 and Simon Critchley, *Ethics of Deconstruction: Derrida and Levinas* (Oxford, 1992), 5–7.

22. See http://www.nga.gov.au/williams/ for an example of Williams' thick paint which is used to evoke various stark Australian landscapes and peoples. See also James Mollison, *A Singular Vision: The Art of Fred Williams* (Canberra, 1989). See also http://qag.qld.gov.au/collection/australian_art_to_1970/charles_blackman for an example of Blackman's paint use. Blackman is well known for his haunted 'Alice' figures, but it is also his chunky style that Coads paintings remind us of. (http://www.ngv.vic.gov.au/whats-on/exhibitions/exhibitions/charles-blackman)

23. For images of the massacre sites referred to in Queenie McKenzie, see (http://www.aboriginalartcoop.com.au/aboriginal-art/gallery/cooee-aboriginal-art/queenie-mckenzie/slideshow.php). A publication about McKenzie's life and work was put together by the community, 'Written in the Land', see http://writtenintheland.com/index.php?page=book.

24. Interview by David Stratton with Director Rolf de Heer, in DVD version of *The Tracker* (Melbourne, 2002).

25   Julie Rigg, *Film Review– Sunday Morning*, ABC Radio National, http://www.abc.net.au/rn/arts/nclub/stories/s646510.htm (last accessed 15 February 2009).

PART III

CONTESTED NARRATIVES: MEMORY, ATROCITY AND MASSACRE

Chapter 12

Memories of Massacres and Atrocities during the Revolutionary and Napoleonic Wars

Philip G. Dwyer

On 3 March 1799, the French army arrived before the walls of Jaffa in what was then known as Syria (now just outside Tel Aviv) and started to lay siege to the town. Four days later, after a breach in the wall had been made, Napoleon sent two emissaries to negotiate the surrender; the reply was the appearance of their heads on pikes behind the walls. That same day, the town fell and the troops gave themselves up to pillage, rape and murder for two, possibly four whole days (witnesses diverge on this point), indiscriminately killing anyone that fell in their way, regardless of sex or age, stopping only when exhausted.[1] Etienne-Louis Malus, a doctor who had accompanied the army, recalled what he saw many years later:

> The soldiers cut the throats of men and women, the old and the young, Christians and Turks, anyone that had a human face fell victim to their [that is, the soldiers'] fury. The noise of the massacre, smashed doors, ruined houses, the sounds of shots and of the cleaning of swords, the shrieks of women, father and son one on top of the other (on the same pile of bodies), a daughter being raped on the cadaver of her mother, the smoke from the burnt clothes of the dead, the smell of blood, the groans of the wounded, the shouts of the victors who were quarrelling about the loot taken from a dying victim, angry soldiers who redoubled their blows the more their victim cried out in order

to finally sink, satiated by blood and gold, without further feeling, on top of a heap of dead.[2]

Once the sack of the town was over, the killing did not stop there. Over a three-day period, from 8 to 10 March, between 2,400 and 3,000 prisoners were marched to a beach a little over a kilometre south of the city and slaughtered.[3] On the second day, the soldiers were instructed not to waste ammunition, and to bayonet to death their victims.[4] The troops, it seems, only reluctantly obeyed the order – 'extreme repugnance' is the phrase used by one witness – but obey they did.[5]

* * *

Most historians of the Revolutionary and Napoleonic Wars consider this type of massacre to be an aberration. One historian has recently argued, for example, that the two regions most renowned for their extreme violence, the Vendée and Spain, 'are noteworthy because their atrocities were not typical of warfare in the period'.[6] The observation is shared by a French specialist of the civil war in the Vendée who believes that during the fighting there the 'normal rules of war disappeared' for some political and military authorities as well as for soldiers and rebels.[7] There appears to be a commonly held view that, with few exceptions, the wars were relatively civilized and that there is 'little evidence that soldiers attacked civilians'.[8] But this is certainly not the impression one gets from a reading of the memoirs, journals and letters of the period. It is clear from the sources that massacres were not only widespread, but that they were an integral and possibly an accepted part of eighteenth-century warfare.

Most of what we know about Jaffa, and about massacres and atrocities in general,[9] is almost entirely due to the accounts found in memoirs, journals and letters, not entirely reliable and often considered by historians to be less than truthful. Memoirists in particular weave oral folktales into their anecdotes, and they distort and fictionalize events.[10] This chapter is not, however, particularly concerned with the accuracy or inaccuracy of specific atrocity stories, nor is it an attempt to categorize and explain the different types of massacres committed during the wars. Rather, it is an attempt to understand, from the French perspective, the manner in which massacres and atrocities were recollected and portrayed, as well as the reasons put forward by veterans to justify them. It also explores the reasons why veterans felt it necessary to mention particular atrocities at all, often many years after the event, and why they did so in a medium that was not always meant for public consumption, that is through private writings that took the form of memoirs and diaries. By focusing on the types of stories that are told, some light is thrown on the mechanisms behind the killings and the state of mind of the men who ordered and committed them.

The Frequency of Massacre during the Revolutionary and Napoleonic Wars

The sacking of towns, during which soldiers committed murder and rape in what is often described as an uncontrolled 'frenzy', was part and parcel of eighteenth-century warfare.[11] It had indeed been that way for many centuries, although there is surprisingly little literature on the subject.[12] It was based on an unspoken understanding, namely, that the troops would be rewarded for the hardships, and often the lack of pay, they had endured during a campaign by being given possession of the town they were laying siege to. Jaffa therefore conforms in many respects to the sacking of countless numbers of towns in the seventeenth, eighteenth and early nineteenth centuries. And some were carried out on a vast scale, such as the sack of Magdeburg by Imperial troops in May 1631, which supposedly resulted in about twenty thousand deaths; or the fall of Warsaw in November 1794 to Russian troops, which reportedly resulted in between twelve and twenty thousand deaths in the space of a few hours;[13] the French storming of Tarragona in June 1811, which resulted in the deaths of around fifteen thousand civilians;[14] or the British capture of the Spanish city of San Sebastián in 1812, which saw half the population killed.[15]

But this is only part of the picture. Massacres and atrocities took place on a large scale outside of the sacking of towns when, for example, villages were occupied and looted by troops on the hunt for provisions,[16] or simply in reprisal against casualties incurred by local rebels. And those are just the massacres committed by armed troops against noncombatants. Without wanting to go into a taxonomy of massacre for the period, there is little in common, except the end result, between the execution (by guillotine and shooting) of five hundred-odd men and women who had fought with the British against French Republican forces in Guadeloupe in December 1794;[17] the burning alive of three thousand wounded Austrian soldiers in the village of Ebersberg in Germany in 1809 by troops of the Grande Armée;[18] and the massacre of around 320 French men, women and children in Valencia in 1808 by a small band of men led by a friar called Baltasar Calvo.[19]

Each massacre, in other words, is surrounded by a particular set of circumstances, and the perpetrators are driven by different reasons that have to do with the place and timing of the killings. Some of the most notorious massacres committed during the wars were carried out by republican troops in the Vendée – the so-called 'infernal columns' – that left a swathe of destruction as they marched through the French countryside.[20] But a similar tactic was used in southern Italy, if on a smaller scale, where in the summer of 1806 the French army killed hundreds if not thousands of locals and devastated dozens of villages in an attempt to wipe out local resistance.[21]

In these instances, the order to kill came from above, in this case, the general on the ground, but Napoleon was also known to urge the eradication of villages which resisted.[22] These brutal and openly public killings served a purpose – to reduce areas of resistance and to strike fear into the hearts of neighbouring populations in the hope that opposition would melt away. This did indeed occur on occasion. After the village of Longo-Bucco in Calabria, for example, was pitilessly sacked, the neighbouring town of Bochigliero opened its doors without resistance.[23] More often than not, however, the harsh repression instigated against local populations was justified by the fact that the inhabitants had resisted or that they had committed atrocities against the occupying army. One often comes across accounts in the memoirs of comrades ambushed and killed by rebels, their bodies violated, as a justification for the killings that ensued. 'Murdered [French] prisoners', wrote an Italian officer serving in the Grande Armée in Spain, 'were found torn to pieces with the most inhuman cruelty, their hearts, bowels, and brains gorged out, their private members stuffed into their mouths … there was no form of cruelty that the insurgents did not perpetrate against our men who fell into their hands, even when they were already dying.'[24] Massacre as reprisal.

Other memoirists attempted to explain the excessive brutality with which resistance was put down by the fact that the locals had been 'worked up into a religious frenzy' by priests and monks who had convinced their people that they were fighting the forces of Satan, that is, the French.[25] Priests were classically described as holding bibles in one hand and weapons in the other.[26] Captain François entered the town of Manzaneres in Spain in June 1808 to find that over twelve hundred sick and wounded left behind had been killed by the inhabitants of the town and the neighbouring villages and their bodies cut into pieces and dispersed around the town and the surrounding fields. They were told by a number of Spanish that priests had counselled the inhabitants to commit the crimes. 'One word from those ghosts [that is, the priests] with which the country is infested and all sorts of cruelties are committed by the people towards their enemies.'[27]

Of course, there is some truth in all of this, as the clergy often did play a role in stirring up if not leading the revolt against the French, but what is important is how those who resisted occupation were portrayed. Any form of violent resistance immediately led to those people being categorized as enemies of the Revolution, and as either counter-revolutionary and/or in the pay of the enemy. If rebels were anti-revolutionary, then the brutal suppression of regional populations in revolt was justified by that fact alone. Indeed, there appears to have been a concerted effort to portray some massacres not as the result of French repression but rather as an episode, difficult but necessary, on the road to bringing the Revolution to the peoples of Europe.[28]

Recalling Massacres

If references to massacre, murder and rape are common enough throughout the contemporary sources, as a rule veterans tend to limit themselves to describing in the broadest possible terms the circumstances surrounding a particular atrocity. The memoirs dealing with the Spanish campaign, for example, are replete with (generally brief) descriptions of what Spanish guerrillas, invariably dubbed 'brigands', did to captured French soldiers – tongues torn out, ears and noses cut off, eyes and nails plucked out, captives slowly burnt alive, genitalia stuffed in men's mouths, victims sawn in half, limbs nailed to trees[29] – although there is far less detail when the French describe how they were given orders to sack villages and to spare no-one. François Lavaux recalled how 'We succeeded in entering the village [...]. We burnt [it down] and killed everyone we found there'.[30] Joseph de Naylies mentions, almost in passing, that two Spanish villages were burnt to the ground and hundreds of their inhabitants killed.[31] Charles-Pierre-Lubin Griois refers to the sacking of the town of Corigliano in Calabria in which 'soldiers smashed in doors, pillaged houses, killed and threw people out the windows, and the cries of the men who were being pursued and the women who were being raped was mixed with the noise of shots being fired from all sides'.[32]

The interesting point about these descriptions – any number of examples could be given – is that the act of recalling past campaigns and the horrors that went with them almost never equated to an individual admittance of having taken part in massacres, atrocities or rape. One veteran insisted, after talking about the frenzied killing of the inhabitants of a southern Italian town, that 'he had never killed anyone in that manner'.[33] Indeed, there are few direct references to killing in memoirs of the period, even in the course of battle.[34] This may have been a question of guilt and shame on the part of some, or it may have been because massacres and atrocities were such a common feature of eighteenth- and early nineteenth-century warfare, and were therefore so accepted, that they had to be particularly horrific to merit a mention at all. To cite one memoirist, 'If I were to list all the villages that we pillaged and burnt, I would never finish'.[35] Propriety no doubt played a role here too. Joseph de Naylies, a veteran of the Spanish campaign whose memoirs touch on the horrors committed by both sides in the conflict, nevertheless refused at one point to enter into the details of the exactions committed by some Spanish peasant women against the body of a French officer.[36]

Evident too is the difficulty many veterans experienced in writing about what they had witnessed.[37] General Bigarré served in Saint-Domingue in 1792. Writing about his experiences almost four decades later, he admitted being witness to an 'infinity of horrors' whose memory still afflicted him.[38] General Lejeune, who was captured by the *guerrilla* in Spain in 1810 and who witnessed the brutal killing of three French prisoners in front of him, was still haunted thirty-five years later by the noise of sabres hacking into their heads and shoulders, '[it] has not ceased to reverberate in my ears and still makes me shudder with horror'.[39] Colonel Jean Trefcon described the retreat from Oporto in Portugal in 1809: 'We were obliged to abandon our artillery and the baggage train. The wounded, the women and children had to stay behind and were pitilessly murdered by the Spanish less than two minutes later, and God knows with what refined cruelty. It still makes me shudder.'[40]

One can assume that, for some at least, the act of writing, the translation of their experiences and emotions into some kind of comprehensible account, was a personal catharsis that may have helped them to exorcize their fears and anxieties.[41] This was the case for Sergeant Bourgogne, who declared in his memoirs that 'I should not, out of respect for the human race, write about all the scenes of horror, but I have made it a point of honour to describe all that I saw. It would be impossible for me to do otherwise, and as all of this would unsettle my mind, it seems to me that once I have put them on paper, I will no longer think of them.'[42] Others simply preferred silence, being unable or unwilling to dwell at any length on their experiences, or perhaps simply unable to put them into words. It is not uncommon therefore to find explanations such as 'It is impossible to give an account of all the atrocities to which they [he is referring to the Spanish] had resorted to in those mountains. It would make the hardiest tremble. I would rather just leave it at that.'[43] 'I won't go into the details of the terrible event,' wrote one civilian witness of the sack of Soissons by Russian troops in 1814: 'I will simply say that the massacre of our poor soldiers and the pillage of the town lasted for a full hour.'[44]

Mutilation and Atrocities

Writing as catharsis can only go so far and never entirely dissipates the trauma involved in witnessing massacres and atrocities. In Spain, captured rebels and soldiers alike were invariably tortured to death and their bodies mutilated. It is difficult to explain this particular 'logic of violence' and why the humiliation of the body was so widely practiced. One can speculate whether there was a hierarchy of cruelty, that is, whether the desecration of a particular body part was considered to be more frightful than another, whether some tortures were considered worse than others, or whether the types of mutilations carried out may have been tied to local custom and practices, not to mention religious culture as well as political and socio-economic factors. Let me give a few examples before talking about possible explanations.

The Grande Armée in Spain was composed of, among others, three Italian divisions. In one instance, Piedmontese troops exacted vengeance against monks caught after the capture of St Jacques of Compostella, accusing them of inciting the people against them. It has to be said that French prisoners had been tortured and mutilated during the siege. On capturing two monks, described as 'among the fattest', the Piedmontese tied them back to back against a young oak which was then used as a skewer with which they were placed over a fire and roasted alive. The Italians called it an *auto-da-fé à la piémontaise*.[45] General Renée was captured in the gorges of Sierra Morena with his wife and child. He was supposedly sawn in half in front of his wife, who was first 'dishonoured' in front of him, after which the child was sawn in half in front of the mother before she too endured the same fate.[46] There were even reports of cannibalism. In one particular incident, ten Polish prisoners were found by the French after they had taken the town of Strongoli in Calabria in July 1806. According to the surviving Poles, each day one prisoner was taken to the town square, tortured to death, cut up and fed to the remaining prisoners.[47] On another occasion, a somewhat more symbolic form of cannibalism occurred in the village of Acri in Calabria when a brigand chief by the name of Spaccapitta is supposed to have roasted a number of pro-French officials in the public square. He is said to have taken a piece of bread and placed it on the body of one of the victims and then, to the delight of the assembled crowd, eaten it.[48]

In the past, ritualistic killings that involved acts of mutilation, disembowelling, and cannibalism have been interpreted as having religious overtones, so that if tongues were torn out it was an attempt to render mute the blasphemer, if hands and limbs were cut off it was an attempt to render inactive the desecrator, or if genitalia were cut off it was because the victim was perceived as being sexually aberrant.[49] Removal of the offending part is thus seen to be a symbolic purging of the (social) body.[50] The extent to which monks and priests were an integral if not inspirational part of the *guerrilla* in Spain lends some weight to the possibility that the repertory of atrocities committed by the Spanish against members of the Grande Armée could have been inspired by either the clergy or the Bible; however, this approach is rather restrictive and does not take into account local traditions of popular folk justice (intended to purify local communities and humiliate the enemy), or the extent to which these atrocities often involved public performances. It is, moreover, highly unlikely that the atrocities carried out by the French revolutionary and imperial armies, staunchly republican and secular, can be interpreted in this manner. One should not read too much into the killing by bayonet of fifty monks cornered in a church in Spain.[51] There was probably nothing symbolic or metaphorical about that incident; the monks were simply killed where they were found, no doubt held responsible, as we have seen, for inspiring the neighbouring villages to revolt.

Nor does this explain the extreme violence perpetrated by both regular soldiers and armed insurgents in certain theatres of war. In some respects, all torture and mutilation are public acts. They are performed in front of a group of witnesses (even if only other perpetrators), or the corpse or body part is subsequently exposed in a public space, either attached to or hung from a tree, placed along the roadside, or displayed in a public square. Indeed, as we have seen in the case of the victims tortured in the village of Acri in Calabria, it occurred in the public square – the centre of all cultural and economic activity – in front of an approving crowd.[52] In some instances, the victims were left with a warning note or a placard was hung around their necks.[53] This type of 'public presentational torture' was meant as a warning to those that might contemplate collaboration with the enemy, or possibly to communicate to the enemy the extraordinary lengths they were prepared to go to prosecute the war to a successful conclusion.[54] In these instances, the mutilated body was meant to elicit shock and horror and serve as a warning.

The Plight of Women

Another theme present among accounts of the wars is the excesses committed against women.[55] It was not unusual for men even outside of the 'normal' atrocities that took place during the storming of towns and the systematized marauding of villages to assault women, including pre-pubescent girls. Some of the accounts found in the memoirs of the period were no doubt meant to titillate or to strike horror and loathing into the reader,[56] and hence were possibly exaggerated, but there is no doubt that assaults took place with monotonous regularity (although there is no evidence that rape was carried out in any systematic way, or indeed that it was used by the French imperial regime as a tool of terror to subdue recalcitrant populations). Indeed, it appears to have been so prevalent during this period that it was probably considered a 'right of conquest', a 'reward' of sorts, and should thus be considered a random act of (sexual) violence. This sort of behaviour was sometimes endorsed by the army. Some of the ditties distributed and sung by soldiers, for example, were virtual invitations to rape.[57] Rape nevertheless underlined the powerlessness of the communities concerned and the superiority, both physical and cultural, of the conqueror. The following passage from an anonymous book on the first Italian campaign gives an indication of just how widespread the practice was: 'Debauchery is the epidemic evil of all armies. In that of Buonaparté, it was carried to excess. Almost every honest family has had to lament its dishonour. Age, state, condition, education, nobility, nothing guarantees the honour of the sex from the lust of the soldier. Altars, even sanctuaries, have not sheltered those who have devoted their lives to God. The examples have been frequent and horrible. I have even seen a number of these cannibals cruelly massacre those that had been abducted and dishonoured'.[58]

Similarly, the sack of Jaffa led to a 'traffic of young women' being exchanged for other objects looted in the town. When fighting broke out over them, Napoleon ordered his men to bring all the women back to town, 'on pain of a severe punishment', where they were promptly executed by a company of chasseurs.[59] While campaigning in Portugal, Pierre Guingret described how women of all classes were abducted, bought and sold, or exchanged during card games for luxury items. Other, less fortunate women were obliged to 'satisfy the most unbridled passions' in order to avoid death, but were often killed anyway.[60] Sergeant Lavaux writes of several soldiers entering a convent in Spain where an unspecified number of nuns were raped and murdered; the whole incident is described in a few lines.[61] In a remarkably frank admission, Esprit Castellane, an officer of the general staff, described entering a house after the storming of Burgos in Spain to find a woman 'in the midst of fifty soldiers. Each one was waiting his turn'.[62] He says he went on to save her.

If rape committed by others was often described, it was much more frequent for officers to portray themselves as helping defenceless women, or taking steps to limit excesses and even to prevent massacres being committed. Jean Trefcon entered the Spanish town of Medina del Rio Secco shortly after it was stormed by the French and witnessed 'revolting scenes that he could not prevent because of the small number of men' he had with him.[63] He nevertheless managed to save a 'young person' who, without his intervention, would invariably have been raped. Georges Bangofsky describes fighting off soldiers in a house in order to protect a woman and her daughters.[64] Joseph de Naylies intervened to protect a young woman in Portugal who was about to become the victim of a number of drunken soldiers.[65] Charles-Pierre Griois supposedly intervened to prevent a group of nuns from being raped by Polish soldiers in Corigliano.[66]

These anecdotes are no doubt meant to offset the accounts of rape and murder with which they are often interspersed, as though officers were pointing the finger at the lower ranks, underlining just how horrible war was but at the same time intimating that this particular type of atrocity was common among the lower orders; it was not the kind of thing that a gentleman did. Captain Routier admitted that saving one peasant woman amid the general carnage that was taking place around him 'fed his heart for a long time with a sweet satisfaction', as though the one good deed helped to offset the atrocities he had been witness to.[67]

Some Preliminary Conclusions

This chapter has focused on the French perspective, even though massacres cut across national armies. We know that they often occurred as a result of enforced hardships and privations; that they sometimes involved the loss of comrades before the killings took place; that they were often characterized by a 'frenzied' killing of the inhabitants without distinction of age or sex; that they often involved communities that had risen in revolt against an army of occupation; that they generally involved a certain cultural disdain for the victims in question; that they demonstrated a certain lack of control by officers over the troops; and that they were an accepted if not expected part of the conduct of the soldier. It is safe to say there was not a region or country invaded by the French in which massacres did not occur, although they were more frequent in some areas than in others.

If this chapter is in part a reflection on the nature of (revolutionary and Napoleonic) warfare, it is also one from the perspective of the veteran, who sometimes assumes the voice of the perpetrator, consequently describing the horrors committed against others, combatants and non-combatants alike, but who more often than not assumes the voice of the victim, describing the horrors inflicted on French troops by rebels resisting the invading armies. It is possible that in doing so, French veterans were underlining just how difficult it was to campaign in these countries and the adversities they faced in bringing the benefits of the Revolution to the 'ignorant' peoples of Europe. A passage in the memoirs of Denis Charles Parquin underlined how thankful some Spaniards were, despite the horrors the French had brought in their wake, for putting an end to the Inquisition.[68] The message is clear; even when suffering was incurred the end goal was a noble one. If some veterans dwelt now and then on the crimes committed by their own side it served to underscore the horror of war. What is clear is that many had difficulty recalling what they had lived through even if there does not appear to have been any shame involved in recounting what they had witnessed. What is also clear is that the hatred in which the French were held by many occupied peoples and the narratives of the latter surrounding massacres and atrocities are entirely different from those of the French, that is, massacres are a much more contested history than is portrayed here. But that is an altogether different study.

Notes

1. Pierre-Jean-Baptiste Millet, *Souvenirs de la campagne d'Egypte* (1798–1801) (Paris, 1903), 82; Charles François, *Journal du capitaine François* (Paris, 2003), 275 (7 March 1799).
2. Etienne-Louis Malus de Mitry, *L'Agenda de Malus. Souvenirs de l'expédition d'Egypte, 1798–1801* (Paris, 1892), 135–36.
3. According to Detroye, the number massacred over the three days came to 2,441 (S[ervice] H[istorique de l']A[rmée de] T[erre], Mémoires et Reconnaissances, Journal de Detroye, M1 527, f. 54 (20 ventôse an VII)). Bonaparte boasted of four thousand executions in a letter to the Directory (*Correspondance de Napoléon I*, 32 vols. (Paris, 1858–1870), vol. 5, n. 4035 (13 March 1798)).
4. Cited in Clément de La Jonquière, *L'Expédition d'Egypte*, 5 vols. (Paris, 1899–1907), iv. 271–72; Vigo-Roussillon, *Journal*, 83.
5. Jaques-François Miot, *Mémoires pour servir à l'histoire des expéditions en Egypte et en Syrie pendant les années VI, VII et VIII de la République française* (Paris, 1814), 145–48.

6. Howard Brown, 'Napoleon Bonaparte, Political Prodigy', *History Compass*, 5 (2007), 1392.

7. Jean-Clément Martin, *Violence et Révolution. Essai sur la naissance d'un mythe national* (Paris, 2006), 205.

8. Peter Browning, *The Changing Nature of Warfare: The Development of Land Warfare from 1792 to 1945* (Cambridge, 2002), 47.

9. For the purposes of this essay, an atrocity is characterized by the exactions committed against the victim's body, living or dead, such as torture or the hacking off of body parts, by the perpetrator. Rape also falls within this category.

10. On this point see David Hopkin, *Soldier and Peasant in French Popular Culture, 1766–1870* (Suffolk, 2003), 100; and idem., 'Storytelling, Fairytales and Autobiography: Some Observations on Eighteenth- and Nineteenth-century French Soldiers' and Sailors' Memoirs', *Social History*, 29 (2004), 186–98, which traces the influence of oral storytelling on French military and naval memoirs.

11. See, for example, Franco della Peruta, 'War and Society in Napoleonic Italy: The Armies of the Kingdom of Italy at Home and Abroad', in John Davis and Paul Ginsborg (eds), *Society and Politics in the Age of the Risorgimento. Essays in Honour of Denis Mack Smith* (Cambridge, 1991), 43.

12. For an earlier period, one can consult Elena Benzoni, 'Les sacs des villes à l'époque des guerres d'Italie (1494–1530): les contemporains face au massacre', in David El Kenz (ed.), *Le massacre, objet d'histoire* (Paris, 2005), 157–70.

13. Adam Zamoyski, *Holy Madness. Romantics, Patriots and Revolutionaries, 1776–1871* (London, 1999), 93; idem., *The Last King of Poland* (London, 1992), 429–30.

14. Rothenberg, 'The Age of Napoleon', 93.

15. Not to mention the British storming of the Spanish cities of Ciudad Rodrigo and Badajoz. See Charles Esdaile, *The Peninsular War: A New History* (London, 2002), 386–87; Jack A. Meyer, 'Wellington and the Sack of Badajoz: A "Beastly Mutiny" or a Deliberate Policy?', *Proceedings of the Consortium on Revolutionary Europe, 1750–1850* (1991), 251–57; Pat Hayward (ed.), *Surgeon Henry's Trifles: Events of a Military Life* (London, 1970), 43–44; Antony Brett-James (ed.), *Edward Costello. The Peninsular and Waterloo Campaigns* (London, 1967), 97–98; Louis-Gabriel Suchet, *Memoirs of the War in Spain, from 1808 to 1814*, 2 vols. (London, 1829), ii: 99–105.

16. A common occurrence during the wars and which often led to clashes and violence between civilians and the military. On this point see, T.C.W. Blanning, 'Liberation or Occupation? Theory and Practice in the French Revolutionaries' Treatment of Civilians outside France', in Mark Grimsely and Clifford J. Rogers (eds), *Civilians in the Path of War* (Lincoln, 2002), 111–35; and idem., *The French Revolution in Germany: Occupation and Resistance in the Rhineland, 1792–1802* (Oxford, 1983), 83–98.

17. Laurent Dubois, *A Colony of Citizens: Revolution and Slave Emancipation in the French Caribbean, 1787–1804* (Williamsburg, Va., 2004), 201.

18. Reported in Georges Bangofsky, 'Les Etapes de Georges Bangofsky, officier lorrain. Extraits de son journal de campagnes (1797–1815)', *Mémoires de l'Académie de Stanislas* (1905), ii.291.

19. Esdaile, *Fighting Napoleon*, 64. It seems that Calvo incited the crowd in order to further his own political ambitions. He was refused a position on the local Junta; the massacre was a means of persuading the authorities to change their minds. An English account of this event is in Enos Bronson (ed.), *Select Reviews of Literature, and Spirit of Foreign Magazines* (Philadelphia, 1812), ii.262–63.

20. The literature on the Vendée is too large to cite extensively here. One can consult: Jean-Clément Martin, *La Vendée et la France* (Paris, 1986).

21. Report by Berthier in S[ervice] H[istorique de l']A[armée de] Terre, Correspondence, Armée de Naples, carton C-5, 4, 15 August 1806. See also Léon-Michel Routier, *Récits d'un soldat de la République et de l'Empire* (Paris, 2004), 87; Milton Finley, *The Most Monstrous of Wars: The Napoleonic Guerrilla War in Southern Italy, 1806–1811* (Columbia, S.C., 1994), 64–65; David A. Bell, *The First Total War: Napoleon's Europe and the Birth of Warfare as We Know It* (Boston, 2007), 273–74.

22. Maximilien Vox, *Correspondance de Napoléon. Six cents Lettres de Travail (1806–1810)* (Paris, 1943), 312–14 (7 February 1806).

23. Duret de Tavel, *Séjour d'un officier français en Calabre* (Rouen, 1820), 173–76.

24. Cited in della Peruta, 'War and Society in Napoleonic Italy', 43.

25. SHAT, Corr. Armée de Naples, carton C-5, 4.

26. The image dominated portrayals of the Spanish clergy. Examples can be found in della Peruta, 'War and Society in Napoleonic Italy', 40.

27. François, *Journal*, 570.

28. Annie Duprat, 'La construction de la mémoire par les gravures: Carle Vernet et les *Tableaux historiques des campagnes d'Italie*', in Jean-Paul Barbe and Roland Bernecker (eds), *Les intellectuels européens et la campagne d'Italie, 1796–1798* (Münster, 1999), 202–203.

29. Lavaux, *Mémoires de Campagne*, 137, 150–51; François, *Journal*, 567, 569.

30. Lavaux, *Mémoires de Campagnes*, 151, 152–55.

31. Naylies, *Mémoires sur la guerre d'Espagne*, 64–65.

32. Charles-Pierre-Lubin Griois, *Mémoires du général Griois, 1792–1822*, 2 vols. (Paris, 1909), i:326–27.

33. Routier, *Récits d'un soldat*, 87.

34. The same phenomenon has been remarked upon in First World War narratives (Hynes, *The Soldier's Tale*, 66). There are, however, exceptions to the rule. Captain François freely admits to killing and wounding enemy soldiers and peasants (*Journal*, 567, 568, 572).

35. Sergeant Lavaux, *Mémoires de Campagne* (Paris, 2004), 159.

36. Naylies, *Mémoires sur la guerre d'Espagne*, 94.

37. One can note a similar phenomenon with battlefield experiences in Alan Forrest, *Napoleon's Men. The Soldiers of the Revolution and Empire* (London, 2002), 112–17.

38. Auguste-Julien Bigarré, *Mémoires du Général Bigarré, 1775–1813* (Paris, 2002), 42. He went on to recount one incident in which two black rebels were caught by a black 'general', Couacou, aligned with the French, who pulled out their teeth and eyes, had them tarred, impaled with stakes and then set alight.

39. Louis-François Lejeune, *Mémoires du général Lejeune, 1792–1813* (Paris, 2001), 329.

40. Toussaint-Jean Trefcon, *Carnets de campagne du colonel Trefcon, 1793–1815* (Paris, 1914), 71.

41. Hynes, *The Soldier's Tale*, 16; Montroussier, *Ethique et commandement*, 147.

42. Bourgogne, *Mémoires*, 84.

43. Lavaux, *Mémoires de Campagnes*, 155.

44. Louise B. de Saint-Léon, *Mémoires et souvenirs de Charles de Pougens* (Paris, 1834), 262.

45. Thirion, *Souvenirs militaires*, 40.

46. François, *Journal*, 567.

47. Finley, *Most Monstrous of Wars*, 52–53.

48. Cited in Finley, *Most Monstrous of Wars*, 49.

49. Natalie Zemon Davis, 'The Rites of Violence: Religious Riot in Sixteenth-Century France', *Past and Present*, 59 (1973), 51–91. In an analysis of a massacre which took place at Machecoul in 1793, Jean-Clément Martin, *Révolution et contre-révolution en France de 1789 à 1995* (Rennes, 1996), 41, 47–50, looks at how peasants carried out 'vengeance fantasies' on the bodies of their victims. See also Edward J. Woell, *Small-Town Martyrs and Murderers: Religious Revolution and Counterrevolution in Western France, 1774–1914* (Milwaukee, Wis., 2006), 145–86. It is also possible that the infamous 'noyades' (drownings) that took place in the Loire, at Nantes, Angers and Saumur, can be interpreted in semi-religious terms; there is an obvious connection between water and the cleansing of the body, and revolutionary zealots used the metaphor with horrific consequences (Woell, *Small-Town Martyrs and Murderers*, 161).

50. Davis, 'Rites of Violence', 57–65.

51. Jean Duhut to his father, 16 July 1808, cited in Forrest, *Napoleon's Men*, 93.

52. An element underscored by Michel Foucault, *Discipline and Punish. The Birth of the Prison* (Harmondsworth, 1979), 59–60. See also Michael Humphrey, *The Politics of Atrocity and Reconciliation: From Terror to Trauma* (London, 2002), 1–10, 91–104.

53. If Goya's engravings on the subject are to be believed. On Goya see Robert Hughes, *Goya* (London, 2003), 261–319.

54. The phrase is from Daniel Rothenberg, '"What We Have Seen Has Been Terrible". Public Presentational Torture and the Communicative Logic of State Terror', *Albany Law Review*, 67 (2003–2004), 465–99, although he examines torture as an element in contemporary governmental policy. A similar experience can be found in the public lynchings that took place in the United States, a kind of 'racial terrorism'. On this point see Christine Harold and Kevin Michael DeLuca, 'Behold the Corpse: Violent Images and the Case of Emmet Till', *Rhetoric & Public Affairs*, 8 (2005), 263–86; and Kirk W. Fuoss, 'Lynching Performances, Theatres of Violence', *Text and Performance Quarterly*, 19 (1999), 1–27.

55. There are no figures, and indeed no studies on the numbers of women that may have been raped during the wars. On legal attitudes towards rape in France at the end of the eighteenth century, see Georges Vigarello, *A History of Rape: Sexual Violence in France from the 16th to the 20th Century* (Malden, Mass., 2001), 87–102.

56. Some German examples are cited in Blanning, *The French Revolution in Germany*, 91, n. 27, and 98.

57. Michael J. Hughes, 'Making Frenchmen into Warriors: Martial Masculinity in Napoleonic France', in Christopher E. Forth and Bernard Taithe (eds), *French Masculinities: History, Culture and Politics* (Basingstoke, 2007), 62; and idem., '"Vive la Republique, Vive l'Empereur!": Military Culture and Motivation in the Armies of Napoleon, 1803–1808' (Ph.D. thesis, University of Illinois at Urbana-Champaign, 2005), 229–31.

58. *Examen de la campagne de Buonaparte en Italie par un témoin oculaire* (Paris, 1814), 82–83.

59. Bernoyer, *Avec Bonaparte en Egypte* (19 April 1799), 147–48. We do not know how many were killed on this occasion.

60. Pierre Guingret, *Relation historique et militaire de la campagne de Portugal sous le maréchal Masséna* (Limoges, 1817), 123–27. The only explanation he could give for this was that there were a few 'wretches' (*misérables*) drawn by lot that had been introduced into the ranks from towns.

61. Lavaux, *Mémoires de Campagnes*, 152–53.

62. Esprit Victor Elisabeth Boniface Castellane, *Journal du maréchal Castellane, 1804–1862*, 5 vols. (Paris, 1895–1897), iv:33.

63. Trefcon, *Carnets de campagne*, 50.

64. Georges Bangofsky, 'Les Étapes de Georges Bangofsky, officier lorrain. Extraits de son journal de campagnes (1797–1815)', *Mémoires de l'Académie de Stanislas* (1905), ii.17.

65. Joseph-Jacques de Naylies, *Mémoires sur la guerre d'Espagne, pendant les années 1808, 1809, 1810 et 1811* (Paris, 1817), 99–100.

66. Griois, *Mémoires*, i.327. Other examples can be found in Lejeune, *Mémoires*, 144 and 146–47; and Routier, *Récits d'un soldat*, 87–88.

67. Routier, *Récits d'un soldat*, 88.

68. Denis Charles Parquin, *Souvenirs de commandant Parquin* (Paris, 2003), 257.

CHAPTER 13

STALIN'S TRAP: THE KATYN FOREST MASSACRE BETWEEN PROPAGANDA AND TABOO

Claudia Weber

In March 1940, the Soviet NKVD killed about fifteen thousand Polish prisoners of war who had been captured by the Red Army in the wake of the invasion of Poland in September 1939. When German troops discovered the mass graves three years later, the so-called Katyn Forest massacres became the focus of war propaganda and politics. This chapter analyses the history of the Katyn massacres in the context of Allied policy on the treatment of war crimes during and immediately after the Second World War. In doing so, it concentrates on Soviet war crimes policy, often neglected by the academic literature due to difficulties in accessing archival sources. This chapter also considers the impact of Soviet war crimes policy on the Allies' handling of the Katyn massacre after the war and, in particular, how Soviet policy shaped the beginnings of the Cold War. The failures and achievements of Allied policy on war crimes not only formed and influenced legal prosecution of war crimes but also shaped postwar narratives and myths on both sides of the Iron Curtain.

Joseph Goebbels' Propaganda Machine

In April 1943, the German *Reichspropagandaministerium* launched a propaganda campaign about the recently discovered mass graves at the Kosogory [Ziegenberg] area near the small village of Katyn. Joseph Goebbels had accidentally learned of the graves and the exhumations that had been initiated by the High Command of the Wehrmacht on 29 March 1943. The importance of the mass graves was first recognized by an editor from the German News Office [*Deutsches Nachrichten-büro*], Hans Meyer, who was assigned to a propaganda unit in Smolensk. Sometime between late March and 1 April, Meyer informed *Ministe-rialrat* Werner Stephan in Berlin about the exhumations. Meyer told him about his concern that 'the whole thing hadn't been approached in the right way and the military hadn't grasped the significance of the matter'.[1] On Stephan's recommendation, Goebbels met with Meyer on 1 or 2 April.[2] The minister and his staff began to discuss the Katyn issue at their daily conferences at the ministry no earlier than 7 April. At that meeting, the decision was reached to use Katyn in propaganda disseminated outside of Germany, while avoiding public attention at home. Goebbels declared at the conference on 7 April that 'he would defer using this material for domestic purposes, since the population might draw conclusions about the treatment of German prisoners of war by the Bolshevists. As far as [use] abroad was concerned, that was to be completely free of restriction.'[3] On 11 April 1943, the first public mention of the Katyn graves was made by the German news agency Trans-Ocean, which reported on the discovery of the corpses of some three thousand Polish officers killed by the Soviet state security organization, the GPU, in the spring of 1940.[4] During this early stage, German propaganda targeted the Polish population in the occupied territories, especially in the *Generalgouvernement*. In order to promote support for its own occupation regime and to discredit the Soviets, the German ministry even planned a Remembrance Day as well as the creation of Katyn monuments in Lublin, Warsaw, and Krakow.[5]

After an official announcement by Radio Berlin on 13 April, German propaganda about Katyn gained momentum. The objective of this next stage in Goebbels' plan was to promote a split in the wartime alliance by revealing the 'real face of barbarous Bolshevism'. As Goebbels noted in his diary, Katyn served as an 'excellent opportunity ... to refute most drastically the attempts undertaken in England and the USA to whitewash Bolshevism'.[6] To this end, the ministry organized visits to Katyn by British and US prisoners of war and published photographs of the exhumation for the international press. Goebbels even thought about sending a high-ranking European writer to Katyn.[7] But despite all these initiatives, Goebbels ordered the ministry to 'act in an apolitical fashion and avoid the impression that it is deliberately sowing seeds of discord among the Allies'. The campaign should be limited to 'emphasizing the pure facts, which will reveal the unchangeable nature of Bolshevism as well as the humanitarian aspect of the case'.[8] The latter aspect prompted the ministry to call on the International Red Cross in Geneva to send an independent, international commission to investigate the case on site.[9] Under pressure from the Western Allies, as well as the Soviets, who threatened to cancel ongoing negotiations about the situation of prisoners of war in Soviet camps, the International Red Cross eventually decided not to get involved. Perhaps because it anticipated that the Red Cross would reject this request, the German ministry installed its own international commission, which began work in Katyn on 28 April.

Apparently intoxicated by the success of his first efforts, Goebbels changed course and abandoned all restraint with regard to using Katyn to promote the regime's domestic goals.[10] At a staff conference, Goebbels declared that the aim was now to have all photographs and film footage from the mass graves and the exhumations presented not only by the media abroad but also in the German media and newsreels 'notwithstanding the danger that thousands of women will see these horrifying pictures and will be plunged into awful anxiety with respect to the fate of their family members at the front. If higher national interests are at stake, then they must take precedence; indeed, everything pertaining to warfare must follow this principle.' And, Goebbels went on, 'I consider it necessary to show these pictures, so that all this jabbering among the German people will stop: Well, maybe things won't be so bad with Bolshevism after all.'[11] In the weeks that followed, domestic propaganda about Katyn became part of the new propaganda campaign based on the notion of 'strength through fear'.[12]

'Strength through fear' signified the end of the propaganda myth of German invincibility; a myth that had lost its persuasiveness after Stalingrad. Working with terrifying images of the barbarous Bolsheviks, the new strategy aimed to persuade the German people that it was better to bear the hardships of 'total war', which Goebbels had declared on 18 February, than to fall prey to Bolshevist tyranny. Official propaganda changed from the forecast of a glorious victory to exhortations to persevere in order to prevent Germany and the world from being overrun by barbarous Jewish Bolshevism.[13] In this context, Katyn was the most convincing proof of the accuracy of Goebbels' warnings. Speaking at one of the daily staff conferences in his ministry, he remarked, 'In the entire history of the war, there has been no such ideal case of Jewish bestiality together with the most infamous Jewish mendacity; therefore, it must be taken up again and again on a large scale in the coming days and weeks'.[14]

An understanding of German propaganda is a prerequisite to understanding the Western Allies' political response to Katyn. Germany's propaganda campaign in the spring of 1943 was part of German occupation politics in the *Generalgouvernement* aimed at strengthening anti-Semitism and anti-Soviet attitudes among the Polish population. It also represented an attempt to split the anti-Hitler coalition and to reinforce the image of barbarous Jewish Bolshevism. Katyn was also used to deflect attention away from atrocities and war crimes perpetrated by the Germans. When, in the midst of the Katyn affair, the Soviet press informed the international public about mass shootings committed by German soldiers, Goebbels' staff decided at the daily meeting that 'we will not react to the Soviets' attempts, ... the dissemination of reports about purported German atrocities – the Soviet information bureau has reported, for example, that supposedly 4,000 peaceful inhabitants of the Rostov region have been killed by the Germans – ; it is better if we respond to such reports with silence'.[15]

Between Realpolitik and Morality?

Stalin and his Western Allies seemed somewhat surprised by the German revelations. Goebbels noted smugly that it took 'the enemy three days ... to even collect itself and now they have just begun stammering their excuses, which are as to be expected'.[16] The Soviet leadership was forced to offer some explanation. On 15 April, the Sovinformburo [Soviet Bureau of Information] issued an official communiqué that was read on Radio Moscow, and published in *Pravda* the following day, sharply refuting the German allegations. According to the communiqué, the Polish prisoners were engaged in railroad construction work in the area around Katyn in the autumn of 1941. Like countless ordinary Soviet citizens, so the story went, they were shot by 'German fascist hangmen' after the Red Army withdrew from this area in the summer of 1941.[17] Moreover, instead of refuting German accusations by presenting medical or forensic evidence, Stalin exploited the Katyn issue to settle political scores with the Poles. The German revelations placed the Polish government-in-exile in London in a difficult situation. Although it had no intention of supporting Goebbels' campaign, its members were well aware of the identity of the true murderers. When the government-in-exile asked the International Red Cross to install an independent investigation, echoing the Germans' suggestion, Stalin recognized a long-awaited chance to outmanoeuvre his rivals in London and secure control over postwar developments in Poland. On 19 April, *Pravda* accused the Polish government-in-exile of being 'Hitler's Polish collaborators'.[18] The Soviet Union broke off diplomatic relations, confident that this move would be backed by the Allies. What had at first represented a threat for Stalin – Goebbels' campaign had after all been designed to challenge and perhaps even create a rupture among the alliance – instead eventually bound the West closer to Stalin and secured the Allies' almost unconditional loyalty to the Soviet leader.

By the spring of 1943, the German discovery of the mass graves, Goebbels' propaganda, Stalin's attacks on the Polish government-in-exile and support for Stalin from the Western Allies, together with the reluctance to investigate the case, came together to form what we today call the Katyn case. At the time, Katyn attracted attention around the world. International newspapers – from the *New York Times* to small papers like the *Göteborgs Handels- und Schiffahrtszeitung* – discussed the issue of guilt and weighed the accusations and evidence.[19] The situation in the spring of 1943 seemed paradoxical. The more the world debated the massacres, the more communiqués were issued and diplomatic notes exchanged, the more Katyn became politically taboo. Surely, nobody expected Stalin to solve the mystery and admit responsibility for the crime. The West's silence opened the door for speculation, fabrications, and forgeries that marked the history of Katyn during the Cold War.

Most historians explain the West's silence by pointing to the urgent need to maintain the wartime alliance with Stalin.[20] Indeed, neither Churchill nor Roosevelt was willing to risk endangering the pact with Stalin, although both knew very early on who the true culprits were. As early as 15 April 1943, Churchill told Wladyslaw Sikorski, the head of the Polish government-in-exile in London, 'Unfortunately, the German accusations are probably true. The Bolsheviks are capable of the worst atrocities.'[21] We are familiar with Churchill's often quoted answer to Sikorski, when the latter asked for support in investigating the case. Churchill declined, saying, 'If they are dead, there is nothing that will bring them back to life.' At the same time he reassured the Soviet ambassador to London, Ivan Majski, 'We must beat Hitler, this is not the right time for bickering and accusations.'[22] How far President Roosevelt went in ignoring all information on the Katyn massacres is illustrated by a conversation he had with the special envoy to the Balkans, George Earle. Forbidding further investigations by Earle, who wanted to publish self-collected material on Katyn, Roosevelt tried to assure him that the crime was 'entirely German propaganda and a German plot.' And Roosevelt went on, 'I am absolutely convinced the Russians did not do this.'[23]

There is no reason to doubt that Churchill and Roosevelt considered preservation of the wartime alliance to be of the highest priority. However, the accepted interpretation of the Allies' behaviour is worth questioning. Overwhelmingly, the academic literature explains the decision not to openly assert the Soviets' guilt as a victory of Realpolitik over morality. This interpretation dates from the early works on Katyn, most of which were written by Polish émigrés to the West. Janusz K. Zawodny, for example, a former member of the *Armia Krajowa* (Home Army) who immigrated to the United States after the communist takeover, published in 1962 an account of the massacre that remained the most reliable until the 1990s when new documents became available thanks to the work of Russian historian Natalja Lebedeva.[24] Most publications about Katyn that appeared during and even after the Cold War adopted Zawodny's assessment of Western behaviour. Zawodny asserted that 'when forced to face ethical aspects and power considerations as alternatives, they [the Western Allies] chose the latter'.[25] More than forty years later, British historian George Sanford reaffirmed this evaluation by calling the Western reaction 'a triumph of Allied self-interest and realistic statecraft over abstract truth', a triumph 'that challenges the alleged moral and principled bases of democratic societies'.[26]

This reductionist view of Western behaviour as a choice between Realpolitik and morality, if such a choice ever really drove Western decision-making, adds little to our understanding of the history of propaganda surrounding Katyn. It appears to be an interpretation reached through hindsight and based on the myth of democratic politics as the embodiment of political morality. To a large extent, this image grew out of the Cold War ideology that shaped the contrast between morality = democratic versus immorality = undemocratic or totalitarian. Not surprisingly, from the perspective of democratic politics as the embodiment of political morality, the West's silence on Katyn appears to be a betrayal of its own self-commitment. This is not the place to undertake a broader discussion of democracy, morality, and politics; the point to be made here is that the Western decision to remain silent can indeed be regarded as a moral decision. In the spring of 1943, the decision to remain silent about Katyn was not only influenced by the necessity of preserving the alliance, it was also influenced by the knowledge of the barbaric nature of the Third Reich. Weighing the crimes of Stalin and Hitler against each other was not so much a decision between morality and Realpolitik as between two murderous and violent systems. The Western Allies decided to back one in order to fight against the other. The alliance with Stalin was no love match, but it was necessary to end the war and the Germans' ongoing crimes. In that sense, Churchill's famous phrase – 'If they are dead, there is nothing that will bring them back to life' – should not only be interpreted as another cynical statement by the British prime minister. In the context of the state of the Second World War in the spring of 1943, it should be read as both a realistic and a moral decision.

Despite various political and public initiatives such as the establishment of the US-Congressional (Madden) Commission in 1952 or the erection of a Katyn monument in London – which caused a veritable diplomatic conflict between the Soviet Union and Great Britain in the 1970s – the official position of the West did not change until Mikhail Gorbachov's admission of responsibility in 1990. Both the United States and Great Britain avoided the issue and continued to assert that there was insufficient evidence to blame the Soviet Union. 'Whether due to bureaucratic lethargy or cynical pragmatism,' Zaslavsky explains, 'in the decades that followed British governments continued to sacrifice the truth about Katyn in order to avoid offending the Soviet superpower and endangering the advantages of economic relations with the Soviet Union.'[27] Again, although these arguments, together with the political will to foster Cold War appeasement, are plausible, they nonetheless leave the picture incomplete. Would an open discussion about Katyn really have jeopardized economic relations with the Soviet Union? Moreover, would such a discussion have endangered the Cold War order and the Soviet empire? To be sure, any official accusation against the Soviets would have resulted in a diplomatic conflict, but it would have also meant significant support for the dissident movements within the Eastern bloc, especially in Poland, and caused trouble within the Soviet empire. In short, abandoning the wartime stance on Katyn would have caused neither a serious economic nor a political crisis, much less posed a threat to the Cold War order.

The decision of the West not to hold the Soviet Union responsible for the Katyn massacre was, instead, a long-term consequence of the Allied policy on war crimes during the Second World War. It was also linked to the Cold War narrative on the Second World War created in the East and in the West after 1945. In order to explain the silence over Katyn during the Cold War, we need to come back to the paradoxical situation in 1943. Let me shift the focus away from Goebbels' propaganda to the Allied policy on war crimes.

Stalin's Trap: Katyn and the Allied Policy on War Crimes

In his book on Allied war crimes policy, Arieh Kochavi writes that 'the issue of punishing war criminals was widely discussed throughout most of the war years'.[28] And yet the question led to serious disagreements between the Soviet Union and the Western Allies. The states involved favoured different positions, and until Nuremberg they failed to negotiate a common war crimes policy.[29] Whereas the Unites States and Britain did not give this question high priority until the end of war, the Soviet Union did, mainly because its population was directly exposed to the horrors of German occupation. Since June 1941, the German 'war of extermination' (*Vernichtungskrieg*) had been implemented in the Soviet Union. Any promise made by the Soviet leadership to severely punish German war criminals was more than mere lip service in the interests of propaganda. Such pronouncements were essential in order to heighten and secure the fighting spirit of the Soviet population and to preserve their unshakeable ties to their Soviet leaders. They assured the Soviet people that they would have the right to take revenge against the Germans and their collaborators who were, as a result, warned in the process. For the Soviet leadership, the importance of the war crimes issue went beyond the actual wartime situation; it became a crucial element in Stalin's war myth and in his postwar image, designed to downplay some 'inconvenient' truths about the Soviet past. That is, Stalin's role as the uncompromising prosecutor of fascism was meant to supplant any memories of the Hitler-Stalin Pact and the joint occupation of Poland in 1939. Moreover, the war crimes issue legitimized the Soviet plan for the postwar development of Eastern Europe. This constellation led Stalin, in contrast to the Western Allies, to single out war crimes as a high priority political issue. It was indeed so high that the Soviets could not allow it to become a topic for international negotiation.

Consequently, on 2 November 1942, the Presidium of the Supreme Soviet, chaired by Mikhail I. Kalinin, signed a decree that created the 'Extraordinary State Commission for the Establishment and Investigation of the Crimes of the Fascist German Invaders and Their Accomplices, and of the Damage They Caused to Citizens, Collective Farms, Public Organizations, State Enterprises, and Institutions of the USSR' (ChGK). The date was no accident. The next day, 3 November, the Soviet Union officially refused to participate in negotiations on the establishment of a United Nations War Crimes Commission (UNWCC).[30] In part, the Soviet response was a reaction to the British who, since they were not terribly interested in Soviet participation, had invited Moscow at the last moment. The Soviets regarded this as an affront and indeed the British foreign minister, Sir Anthony Eden, had anticipated the reaction.[31] On 14 October, two weeks after the Allied invitation, the Soviet government made its views on the treatment of war crimes officially known to the public. Moscow declared its will to 'severely punish the Hitlerite government and all its accomplices for the infamies committed by them against all freedom-loving peoples' and to cooperate 'in searching for, turning over to the authorities, bringing to trial and severely punishing [those] guilty of organizing, abetting or committing crimes on occupied territories'.[32]

The Soviet refusal to participate in the UNWCC, together with an attack in *Pravda* accusing Britain of giving asylum to Nazi leaders such as Rudolf Hess, paved the way for the establishment of the ChGK. The history of this internal Soviet war crimes commission demonstrates how consciously and purposefully the Soviet leadership followed its own war crimes policy, which was linked to political goals and myth-building. In the eyes of Stalin and his henchmen, the ChGK was a success story. For the Western Allies, in contrast, it was to pose a dilemma, because it gave the Soviet government a nearly complete monopoly on the investigation and publication of war crimes in the occupied territories in the East.

Although the decision to establish the ChGK in November 1942 can be read as a direct response to the UNWCC, internal discussions on a special commission and the Soviet treatment of war crimes and war criminals had started well before the creation of the UNWCC, that is, by the summer of 1942, when the Western Allies were just beginning to discuss the basics of creating an international commission.[33] Indeed, the first idea for the creation of a Soviet commission dated back to August 1941 although it was not officially created until November.

Officially, the commission had broad powers, among them the right to conduct investigations of Hitler's war crimes, to collect material from the provinces, to question witnesses and reveal the names of war criminals, and to publish official reports on their findings.[34] Since it was free to investigate, collect evidence, and publish, the purpose of the commission went beyond propaganda. Consciously created as a public commission, the ChGK answered to Western standards of public discourse. Yet its main purpose was to give international legal legitimacy to material that was prepared without international intervention or control. Created as a parallel institution or even an alternative to the UNWCC, the ChGK provided the Soviet leadership, quite successfully, with a broad 'freedom of action'. The huge body of material collected by its more than one hundred regional commissions was widely used in diplomatic notes issued by the Soviet People's Commissariat of Foreign Affairs and at the various Allied peace conferences conducted during the war years. It is moreover important to note that, in accordance with Article 21 of the Charter of the International Military Tribunal at Nuremberg, all ChGK material, just like official government documents and United Nations reports, had the status of incontrovertible evidence and was accepted by the tribunal without additional confirmation. Indeed, the evidence collected by the ChGK constituted the most reliable legal basis for the prosecution of German war crimes in Eastern Europe. It also remains one of the most valuable sources on the Holocaust in that part of the continent. Some of the material, which is still unpublished and housed at the State Archive of the Russian Federation (GARF), only recently became the subject of historical research.[35] However, as will be shown below, the same commission that provided first-hand evidence on German war crimes and the Holocaust also falsified and fabricated evidence. It was hard to avoid Stalin's trap.

The material published by the ChGK was controlled by the NKVD and carefully edited by Stalin's loyal henchman, Andrey Vyshinskiy. Every regional or auxiliary commission was headed by a 'troika' – a structure that was strikingly reminiscent of the investigation teams of the Great Terror. Each troika consisted of the first secretary of the regional party committee, the head of the corresponding local Council of People's Commissars and the local head of the NKVD. The NKVD also recruited 'public representatives' for work on the commissions.[36] In Moscow, Andrey Vyshinskiy, the Deputy People's Commissar of Foreign Affairs and Chairman of the Council of People's Commissars, controlled the internal work of the ChGK and edited its public reports. This was the same Vyshinskiy who, as general prosecutor, was the legal mastermind behind the political show trials during the 1930s and the same individual who would soon head up the Soviet commission at the Nuremberg trials, and later, in the 1950s, become the Soviet Union's permanent representative to the United Nations.

Vyshinskiy was the key figure in the process of preparing the material for the public. Unconditionally fulfilling Stalin's orders, he edited the reports for propaganda purposes, making the statements strong and clear. Any doubt or indecisiveness had to disappear; phrases such as 'with a high decree of probability and plausibility' were replaced by 'it can be confirmed.'[37] The members of the Central Commission of the ChGK fell into line with Vyshinskyi's standards of editing, as evidenced for example by the following statement made during a discussion of some changes in the commission's working procedures in the autumn of 1943. Evgenyi Tarle, a commission member and an historian with a focus on French history, international relations, and Russian foreign policy, noted that 'We do not need to worry about anyone arguing or legally debating with us ... If we say there were three chickens instead of two, nobody will be able to tell the difference.'[38]

Different factors contributed to the manipulation of reports by the Moscow based Central Commission. Practical difficulties and the extremely adverse conditions under which the local commissions were forced to work during the war, as well as the Stalinist politics of deportation and war migration, meant that the information collected was false and imprecise. These deficits in the reports submitted by local commissions were glossed over by members of the Central Commission like Tarle or Vyshinskiy. When, for instance, the work of the local (oblast) commission in Voronezh, which had five offices, was about to start, communication between the branches became almost impossible due to the lack of electricity. In the Kursk area, the commission suffered a paper shortage and thus no written eye witness testimony could be taken. But the absence of witness statements was not always due to a lack of material. The work of the Kalmykian commission was severely hampered when wholesale deportation of the Kalmyk population to Astrakhan oblast took place in late 1943. Thus, the Astrakhan oblast attempted to reorganize the registration process, but these efforts evaporated without results. However, in the Voronezh region (oblast), most of the former population had died or fled during the war, a fact that rendered it virtually impossible to find witnesses and to name the perpetrators.[39]

The Burdenko Commission

As well as the difficulties of investigating German war crimes under wartime conditions in Stalinist society, which lead to inaccuracies in many ChGK reports, there was also 'considerable effort to cover up own crimes'.[40] As the Danish historian Niels Bo Poulsen has convincingly demonstrated in his detailed study, the reports of the ChGK were used to counter German propaganda and accusations on several occasions; the Katyn case is just the best-known example.[41]

Until today, the majority of literature on Katyn describes the Soviet handling of the affair without considering the influence of the ChGK. This neglect is an impediment to our understanding of Allied policy on Katyn and on the prosecution of war crimes during and after the Second World War. It is important to note that the well-known Burdenko commission, which established the official Soviet version of Katyn, was a special commission of the ChGK. The overlap in personnel alone is striking. The prominent Kremlin physician and president of the USSR Academy of Medical Sciences, Nikolai Burdenko, after whom the commission was named, worked simultaneously in the central commission of the ChGK, as did the writer Aleksei Tolstoi and Metropolitan Nikolai.

On 25 September 1943, the Red Army liberated Smolensk. On 22 September, Georgi Aleksandrov, the head of the propaganda department of the Central Committee, had already noted in a letter to Aleksandr S. Shcherbakov, deputy politburo member and head of the Sovinformburo, that preparations should be made 'to unmask the German provocation regarding Katyn'.[42] Aleksandrov proposed the establishment of a special commission consisting of members of the ChGK, supplemented by staff from the intelligence service. About the same time, a special NKVD group took up its work at the Katyn graves. The group manipulated the human remains at the site prior to further investigations in order to camouflage obvious contradictions with the Sovinformburo's April communiqué regarding the purported time of death of the Polish officers. As Natalja Lebedeva has pointed out, the NKVD working group planted forged documents and newspapers with dates later than May 1940 at the site and 'encouraged' local Russians to testify as witnesses before the commission, whose impending arrival had been announced.[43] By the time the so-called Burdenko commission was about to be established, the graves were ready to deliver the expected results.

On 12 January 1944, the central ChGK proposed the establishment of the 'Special State Commission for Ascertaining and Investigating the Circumstances of the Shooting of the Polish Prisoners of War by the German Fascist Invaders in the Katyn Forest'. It ultimately consisted entirely of loyal, Stalinist functionaries who were associated with the ChGk or who were dependent on its members. The Special State Commission worked in Katyn from 18 to 23 January 1944, issuing its final report in Smolensk on 24 January 1944. Not surprisingly, the report confirmed the Soviet version that had been stated in the Sovinformburo communiqué in April 1943. The forensic medical investigation stated that the Poles had been killed between September and December 1941. The conclusion was based on the expert forensic medical analysis pertaining, for example, to the state of the officers' clothing and the degree to which it had rotted. Second, it established that the methods used to execute the Polish POWs and the methods used to execute Soviet citizens were 'completely identical'. And third, special attention was paid to the documents found at the site, which the NKVD had secretly planted and then 'discovered', as well as to the witness testimony gathered by the NKVD among the local population.[44]

Upon publication of the final report of the Burdenko commission in January 1944, three reports on investigations into the Katyn massacres existed: one composed by the German International commission; one by the Polish Red Cross Technical Commission; and the third by the Soviet

Burdenko Commission. Whereas the third stated the time of death as the autumn/winter of 1941, the two others concluded that the murders took place in the spring of 1940. It goes without saying that the process of fabricating and editing the report of the Burdenko Commission was carefully orchestrated and guided by Moscow. Even Burdenko admitted, shortly before his death in 1946, that as medical expert he knew the graves were four years old.[45] Yet it was the Burdenko report that, as part of the material collected by the ChGK, was officially submitted to the Nuremberg Court. The fact that the Soviets were formally acting in accordance with the Court's procedures by submitting the report under Article 21 of the IMT illustrates the dilemma the Western Allies had helped to create. Stalin's trap snapped shut.

In order to get Nuremberg to work, the West had to accept the Burdenko version. Seen from this perspective, the British and the American silence over Katyn and the decision to allow it to vanish from the trial's agenda had less to do with loyalty towards their former wartime ally and more to do with a policy of damage control. Any official challenge of the veracity of the Burdenko report would have been a challenge to the authority of the Allied system of providing legal and reliable information on German war crimes, thus undermining the Nuremberg system; this was a risk the Western Allies were not willing to take. The Allies had already risked too many undesirable revelations by admitting the request of Goering's defender, Otto Stahmer, to call German witnesses for the defence in the case and by considering Katyn in sessions in February, March, and July 1946. The decision to pass over any mention of Katyn in the final verdict saved the fragile system of international prosecution of war crimes that had been installed in Nuremberg after a troubled history of hard negotiations, misunderstandings, and failures.

War Myths and the Erasure of Katyn

In order to understand the Allied silence over the Katyn massacres, we need to analyse the system of war crimes policy and punishment. This holds especially true for the Stalinist system of special commissions and personal networks. It goes without saying that the Soviet ChGK was one of the immediate participants in the creation of the Stalinist war myth.[46] The careful selection of the published material, the editing by Vyshinskyi, as well as the careful composition of the commission's personnel clearly served Stalin's goal of strongly separating between the 'good' and the 'evil', 'us' and 'them'. The ChGK helped to wash away the wartime shades of grey. What remained was the mythical dichotomy of heroes and victims versus war criminals and perpetrators. The sensitive history of the Hitler-Stalin pact, a period during which both dictators acted in concord as mass murders and war criminals in Poland, was erased from memory and history. After the ChGK had been formally dismantled by

the Soviet Council of Ministers on 9 June 1951, the vast body of material
it had collected continued to be used. It was deployed in trials against
Soviet collaborators or in propaganda campaigns to unmask Nazi criminals, especially those living in West Germany. The question as to what
extent the ChGK material was used in the GDR, either to strengthen
the myth of the 'other' antifascist Germany, to prosecute German war
criminals, or to cover up for others, many of whom were members of
the East German elite, warrants further research, although documents
from the archives of the BStU in Berlin and the Russian State Archive
of Contemporary History (RGANI) in Moscow suggest an active cooperation for propaganda purposes as well as for legal prosecution and trials.
Yet in sharp contrast to its propaganda value during the Cold War, the
ChGK material itself was subject to the highest level of security restric-
tions and was not accessible to the public nor to researchers. Historians
like Lev Bezymenski, Marina Sorokina, and Pavel Knyshevski explain
this secrecy by pointing to the ChGK's fabrications, manipulations, and
forgeries, which reached their peak on the Katyn issue.[47] This explanation seems quite plausible, since the official Soviet propaganda material
on Katyn was the first set of documents to disappear after the war.

Instead of propagating its version, the Soviet leadership preferred
to suppress the issue internally, only using it – if necessary – in foreign propaganda. The moment the Burdenko commission report was
presented at the Nuremberg trial, it disappeared from book shops and
libraries in the Soviet Union and Poland. The reference to Katyn and
the short summary of the Burdenko report that had survived in the
1953 edition of the Soviet Encyclopedia were deleted in 1957. And, as
another example for Stalin's perfidious double-crossing, people who
knew about the forgeries in the ChGK and Burdenko reports, were
detained or killed by the NKVD on the basis of ChGK evidence. One
instance of this is the former mayor of Smolensk, Boris G. Menshagin,
who had been appointed by the Germans and knew about the guilt of
the NKVD, and who spent twenty-five years in KGB prisons.

The history of forgetting and suppressing Katyn during the Cold War
peaked in the late 1960s when the Brezhnev administration ordered
the erection of a monumental memorial complex at the small village
of Khatyn near Minsk. The Belorussian Khatyn was one of around
136 Belorussian villages in which SS-Sonderbataillons slaughtered all
inhabitants.[48] It is no coincidence that the village of Khatyn was chosen
to become the central site for commemorating German mass crimes in
Belorussia. It reflects Brezhnev's policy of erasing Katyn completely
from history and memory by replacing it with Khatyn. On the surface,
the Soviet attempt to sow confusion was successful.

During the Cold War, both Great Britain and the United States
avoided any involvement in the Katyn issue, not to mention the notion
of initiating a new propaganda campaign. For them, as well as for the
Soviet Union, talking about Katyn meant talking about the wartime

shadows of grey, the fragility of the wartime alliance, and the Nuremberg system. In any case, the history of the Katyn massacres was incompatible with postwar narratives. Both sides presented the outcome of the war as their victory, a victory either for democracy or for communism. In both cases this narrative was linked to hopes and stories of progress and modernity, from which the dark shadows had to be excluded. It seems to be no accident that the complex interdependencies between the Second World War and the Cold War have only recently become the focus of historical research. During the Cold War itself, the world of war criminals, mass killings, propaganda, and prosecution looked like a dark and dirty but now closed chapter of the past. It is in this context that the reaction of the British Foreign Office to requests for an international commission to investigate Katyn becomes plausible. In 1950 the Foreign Office refused such a request brought forward by the Scottish-Polish Society and Wladyslaw Anders, the prominent Polish general-in-exile, arguing that even 'as a propaganda stunt Katyn is too closely identified with Dr. Goebbels'.[49] A short time later, internal Foreign Office annotations to a report from the British embassy in Washington concerning the establishment of the so-called Maiden Congressional Commission stated, 'There seems no useful purpose in raising these ghosts now'.[50]

Notes

1. John Fox, 'Der Fall Katyn und die Propaganda des NS-Regimes', *Vierteljahreshefte für Zeitgeschichte*, 30 (1982), 465.
2. Fox, 'Der Fall Katyn', 465.
3. Russian State Military Archive (RGVA), Special Archive, fond 1363k (Reichsministerium für Volksaufklärung und Propaganda), opis 4, delo 26, list 10f; Sitzungsprotokoll vom 7. April 1943.
4. Anna M. Cienciala, Natalja Lebedeva and Vojtech Materski (eds), *Katyn. A Crime without Punishment* (New Haven, 2007), 216.
5. Fox, 'Der Fall Katyn', 474.
6. *Die Tagebücher von Joseph Goebbels*, ed. Elke Fröhlich, 15 vols. (Munich, 1987–1995), vol. 8, part 2, dictation 1941–1945; April–Juni 1943; München 1993, 104.
7. RGVA, Special Archive, fond 1363k, opis 4, delo 26, list 10f. Sitzungsprotokoll vom 7. April 1943.
8. See Fox, 'Der Fall Katyn', 480.
9. See Thymian Bussemer, 'Das Internationale Rote Kreuz und die NS-Kriegspropaganda. Der Fall Katyn', *Vorgänge*, 3 (2000), 83ff.
10. RGVA, Special Archive, fond 1363k, opis 4, delo 27. list 18.
11. RGVA, Special Archive, fond 1363k, opis 4, delo 27. list 18.
12. David Welch, *The Third Reich. Politics and Propaganda* (London and New York, 2002), 142.
13. Ernest K. Bramstedt, *Goebbels and Nationalist Propaganda 1925–1945* (Michigan, 1965), 263.
14. RGVA, Special Archive, fond 1363k, opis 4, delo 27. list 11.
15. RGVA, Special Archive, fond 1363k, opis 4, delo 27, list 13. Stenogramm/Konferenzprotokoll April 1943, no day.
16. RGVA, Special Archive, fond 1363k, opis 4, delo 27, list 26, Ministeranweisung, no date.

17. Cienciala, Lebedeva, and Materski (eds), *Katyn*, 306f.
18. Cienciala, Lebedeva, and Materski (eds), *Katyn*, 218.
19. RGVA, Special Archive, fond 1363k, opis 4, delo 27, list 11, Konferenzprotokoll, no date.
20. For instance, George Sanford, *Katyn and the Soviet Massacre of 1940. Truth, Justice and Memory* (London and New York, 2005), 124ff; Victor Zaslavsky, *Klassensäuberung. Das Massaker von Katyn* (Berlin, 2007), 69ff, 116.
21. Fox, 'Der Fall Katyn', 490.
22. Winston Churchill, *The Second World War, vol. IV; The Hinge of Fate* (London 1951), 679–81.
23. Zaslavsky, *Klassensäuberung*, 71.
24. See Natalja Lebedeva, *Katyn: prestuplenie protiv chelovechestva* (Moscow, 1994). As the original Soviet sources confirmed, Zawodny's detailed description of the massacre came close to what had happened in the winter and spring of 1940.
25. Janusz K. Zawodny, *Death in the Forest. The Story of the Katyn Forest Massacre* (Notre Dame, 1962), 190.
26. Sanford, *Katyn*, 157.
27. Zaslavsky, *Klassensäuberung*, 116.
28. Arieh Kochavi, *Prelude to Nuremberg. Allied War Crimes Policy and the Question of Punishment* (Chapel Hill and London, 1998), 1.
29. Kochavi, *Prelude to Nuremberg*, 1.
30. Kochavi, *Prelude to Nuremberg*, 27ff; Martin Kitchen, *British Policy towards the Soviet Union during the Second World War* (London, 1986), 132–45.
31. Kochavi, *Prelude to Nuremberg*, 36. Eventually, the UNWCC was inaugurated on 20 October 1943 in London by representatives of seventeen Allied nations.
32. 'Zajavlenie Sovetskogo pravitelstva ob otvetstvennosti gitlerovskich zachvatchikov i ich soobshtnikov za zlogejanija, sovepshennye imi v okkypirovannich stranach Evropy',' in *Vneshnaja politika Sovetskogo Sojuza v period Otechestvennoj vojny* (Moscow, 1944), 273–78.
33. Marina Sorokina, 'People and Procedures. Toward a History of the Investigation of Nazi Crimes in the USSR', *Kritika: Explorations in Russian and Eurasian History*, 6 (2005), 811.
34. Sorokina, 'People and Procedures', 801.
35. It is noteworthy that the ChGK fond R-7021 was closed to researchers during the Cold War, although some material was published or even given to other states in the Eastern bloc, for example to the German Democratic Republic in 1965, to use as propaganda against the Federal Republic of Germany.
36. Sorokina, 'People and Procedures', 813.
37. Sorokina, 'People and Procedures', 829.
38. Sorokina, 'People and Procedures', 829.
39. For more information on the working conditions of local commissions and the methods of manipulating local reports, see Niels Bo Poulsen, 'The Soviet Extraordinary State Commission on War Crimes. An Analysis of the Commission's Investigative Work in War and Post War Stalinist Society' (Ph.D, Copenhagen University, 2004).
40. Poulsen, 'The Soviet Extraordinary State Commission', 137.
41. Besides Katyn, Poulsen describes the cover up of the NKVD killings of several thousand prisoners in Lvov's Brygidki prison in the last days of June 1941, the NKVD mass executions in Vinnitsa as well as in the village of Bukivnia near Kiev. Ebenda.
42. Russian State Archive of Social and Political History (RGASPI), fond 17, o125, delo 170, list 103; letter from Aleksandrov to A.S. Sherbakov dated 22 September 1943.
43. Cienciala, Lebedeva, and Materski (eds), *Katyn*, 226ff, 318f.
44. The Burdenko Commission Report (excerpts), printed in Ciencala, Lebedeva, and Materski (eds), *Katyn*, 319ff. Besides the statement of the forensic medical appraisal, the report contained an extra paragraph on the 'Documents Found on the Corpses', 323ff.
45. Zawodny, *Death in the Forest*, 158.

46. Sorokina, 'People and Procedures', 801.
47. See Sorokina, 'People and Procedures', 804, also on Bezymenski and Knyshevski.
48. For a short summary see Bernd Boll, 'Chatyn 1943', in Gerd R. Ueberschär (ed.), *Orte des Grauens. Verbrechen im Zweiten Weltkrieg* (Darmstadt, 2003), 19–29.
49. Sanford, *Katyn*, 178.
50. Sanford, *Katyn*, 191.

CHAPTER 14

THE GREAT SECRET: SITES OF MASS KILLINGS IN STALINIST RUSSIA

François-Xavier Nérard

On 25 July 1937, the heads of the Western Siberia regional operational sectors of the NKVD, the political police in Stalin's USSR, were gathered in Novosibirsk by Sergei Mironov, their regional leader. The agenda of this meeting was very simple: the implementation of the forthcoming operational order n. 00447, to be issued by Nikolai Ezhov, the people's commissar for internal affairs.[1] This order had been prepared by the highest authorities in the USSR during the month of July 1937.[2] Its aim was to 'crush mercilessly this entire gang of anti-Soviet elements, to defend the working Soviet people from their counterrevolutionary machinations and finally to put an end, once and for all (*raz i navsegda*), to their base undermining the foundations of the Soviet state'.

The order described very precisely how it was to be implemented and provided quotas of arrests to be filled for all the administrative parts of the Soviet Union. The people concerned by this action were to be divided in two groups. Those who were included in the first category were supposed to be shot immediately; people included in the second category were to be sent to camps or prison. The quotas gave a total estimate of 75,950 for the first category and 193,000 for the second. This operation was to be completed by a series of so-called 'national operations' against national minorities in the USSR (Poles, Latvians, Germans and so on). However, the number of people killed as a direct result of the order is estimated to be much higher, approximately 700,000 between August 1937 and November 1938.

Secrecy was an important part of this plan, as was so often the case in the Soviet Union. Particular attention was drawn to the sites where the executions were going to be conducted. The order explicitly mentioned that 'the time and the place of the execution of the verdicts had to be kept in a compulsory total secret'. As we can learn from the stenographic account of the Novosibirsk meeting miraculously kept in the archives, Serguei N. Mironov was even more straightforward and spoke with his subordinates of these 'technical questions' with stunning frankness:

> [You have to] find a place, where the verdicts are going to be implemented and a place where the corpses are going to be buried. If it is going to be in a forest, the turf has to be cut in advance, and then you will have to use these pieces of turf in order to conceal in every possible way the place where the sentences were executed. That's because all these places may become a site where the counterrevolutionaries [he uses a slang word or a diminutive of it, something like the 'contras'], the religious bigots [the Holy Joes] are going to express their religious fanaticism. Your staff must in no way be aware of either the place of execution of the verdicts, neither of the quantity of persons executed. They must know absolutely nothing as it is our own staff, who may spread this information.[3]

The Russian Great Terror strongly differs from the French Revolution's Terror in 1793 or even, up to a certain point, the Red Terror during the Russian civil war. In 1918, when Lenin called for executions, his aims were explicit: 'people for hundreds of miles around will see, tremble, know and scream out: let's choke and strangle those blood-sucking kulaks'.[4] In 1937–1938, the terror was ambivalent: it was a two-sided phenomenon. There was of course the public face of the Terror, constituted by the Moscow show trials, workers' meetings during which resolutions calling for a merciless verdict were voted in, and the dismissal and subsequent elimination of political, economic, military and administrative officials (for example, almost eighty per cent of the delegates to the 17th congress of the Communist Party in 1934 were executed before the next congress in 1939).[5] For years, the expression, 'The Great Terror', forged by Robert Conquest (1968), was mainly (if not only) used to refer to this part of the terror. But this 'staged' terror was only the upper stratum of a wider process. In its popular and massive dimension, the Stalinist terror remained hidden and unseen, almost invisible. It was made up of nightly arrests and executions. Its victims were former peasants and Soviet national minorities, more often than not inconsequential innocents. In addition, secrecy surrounding the places of execution was closely maintained. The State did not speak about them, and people directly concerned with them were not able to speak about them. Even historians forgot about them as they focused on the public face of the Terror.

The orders of Serguei Mironov were understood perfectly and the orders of the NKVD were carried out to the letter. Mass graves were carefully hidden. In the south of Moscow, or north of Leningrad, these sites were protected from alien eyes by high wooden fences, which were erected before the executions or burials took place, and well maintained afterwards. If people living nearby knew that something happened, they kept silent for many years. When the terror stopped, these events disappeared behind a wall of silence. Even the XXth congress of the CPSU, and Khrushev's 'secret speech' once again stressed solely the visible face of terror, even if it was this time to condemn it.

Re-discovering the Sites

As a result, from the end of the Terror until the end of the 1980s and the beginning of the 1990s, there were no known sites of Stalinist mass murder and no graves for the dead, as though no massacres had taken place. There are very few exceptions to this rule, and those that exist are usually the consequence of extraordinary circumstances. The mass graves of Vinnitsa in the Ukraine, for example, were discovered and exhumed by the Nazis when they occupied the city during the Second World War.[6] Germans used them as proof of the so-called 'Judeo-Masonic plot against the Ukraine'. These mass graves thus became a tool in the conflict between the Nazis and the Soviets, and were subsequently even used during the Cold War when the House Committee on Un-American Activities investigated the case in September 1959.[7] These ideological frameworks of interpretation have deeply confounded the issue and made even more impossible the disclosure of truth. Another mass grave was accidentally unearthed at Kolpachevski Yar in the Siberian province of Tomsk. A few days before the May Celebrations of 1979 – the 1 and 9 May were holidays in the USSR – the river Ob washed away part of its bank, 270 kilometres north of the city of Tomsk. Corpses of Stalinist victims were thereby revealed, sometimes mummified thanks to the peculiarities of the local climate. For some time the leaders of the region and of the country, busy with the preparations of the forthcoming celebrations, did not react, but rumours of the appearance of the bodies spread and people came to see them. However, cases such as these, even if they were not easily erased from public memory, were the exception.

As Mikhail Gorbachev's *perestroika* brought the Stalinist past back to the front of the social and political debate at the end of the 1980s, public interest in the repression reached its peak. In response, two texts were published, on 5 January 1989 by the Politburo of the Central Committee of the Communist Party of the USSR, and then on 16 January 1989 by the Presidium of the Supreme Soviet of the USSR; they were entitled 'On additional means of restoration of fairness to the victims of repression that took place during the 1930s, the 1940s and the beginning of the 1950s'.[8] The texts stipulate that the local councils of people's deputies were 'to assist the victims in the process of rehabilitation' and had to 'create monuments to the dead and to maintain the burial sites in good state'.

This was the beginning of the official re-discovery of Stalinist sites of mass murder. The secrecy surrounding these sites was, however, so absolute that when officials started to look for them their task was made extremely difficult if not impossible. The history of the discovery of the Butovo mass graves near Moscow is a good example. In a memorandum dated from the 14 April 1993,[9] two regional officials of the then Ministry of security of the Russian Federation explained how they conducted their research.[10] At first, they were unable to find anything; none of the acts of execution referred to in the archives of the security organs mentions the sites where the mass killings had been implemented. The two officials consequently attempted to find some collaborators of the then NKVD who had been alive at the time, but those who played a direct part in the executions proved to be just as hard to find. Most of them had been executed themselves in 1938 and 1939 during the post-Ezhov purges conducted by Beria, or they had died afterward. The two regional officials then had to work through the data files of NKVD retirees where they finally succeeded in finding a former head of the administrative and financial services of the NKVD in the Moscow region, as well as two members of the technical services (actually, two drivers). They had to meet these people at least three times to gain their trust and obtain information.[11] In the 1993 memorandum, their names are not even revealed (they are only mentioned as S, I and T). The three former NKVD members confirmed that the shooting range at Butovo was the site where the executions occurred and where the bodies were buried. It is only thanks to their testimonies that the site was ever found and that Butovo became known as a place of mass shootings and burials.[12]

The stories surrounding the rediscoveries of sites of mass murder naturally vary, but they all have in common a mixture of reluctance on the part of the perpetrators to come forward and a complete lack of knowledge of the whereabouts of the killing sites. In Leningrad, for example, the cemetery of Levashovo was already well-known to the KGB; the fence and the entrance gate of the zone were repaired in 1975–1976.[13] But when activists from the Memorial Society began to look for mass graves in the Leningrad region in the spring of 1989 and approached the local KGB for information, they were told that it was impossible to determine such a place.[14] It was only thanks to the political decision of the Leningrad municipal council, then headed by the reformist leader Anatoli Sobchak, that a site of mass burial was made public – a glade north of the city.

In most cases, the 're-appearance' of the massacres may be attributed to the convergent efforts of four main actors: the State and the Party; the KGB; Soviet society; and the involvement of political activists. The decisions of January 1989 were of course essential, but they were only performative; they did not provide any means (in particular financial) for their implementation. In the case of Butovo, pressure was brought to bear by journalists and activists. Two men stand out as key personalities: Mihail Borisovitch Mindlin, a former prisoner of the Gulag camps in Kolyma;[15] and Alexandrovitch Mil'tchakov, the son of a former official of the Komsomol. Mindlin headed a group campaigning on behalf of the memory of the victims of political repression. The constant pressure he put upon the authorities played a crucial part in the process leading to the re-appearance of Butovo. Even today, he is referred to as the man 'thanks to whom Butovo became known'. The role of the journalist Alexandr Mil'chakov was equally important. He published numerous articles in the newspaper *Komsomolskaja Pravda* and even made a television film ('Rastannaja doroga', taken from the name of a street leading to a cemetery in Saint Petersburg) on the places of mass terror in the Moscow region, which was shown during Vladimir Moltchanov's very popular TV show ('Before and after Midnight'). At the beginning of the 1990s, Mil'chakov was appointed head of the commission of the Moscow city council (Mossovet) for the search for secret sites of mass burial of the victims of Stalinist repression. In Levashovo, a similar role was played by Valentin Muravsky and Anatoli Razumov, who is still working to recover the memory of these massacres.[16]

These concerted efforts brought the massacres of the Great Terror back onto the stage of late Soviet and post-Soviet Russian history. Suddenly, the sites of mass burials were discovered and lists of victims of state repression found (their names, and often their photographs have since been published).[17] A new history of the Great Terror appeared,[18] and the text of the operational order 00447 was first published in the newspaper *Trud* on 4 June 1992 during the preparations for the trial of the Communist Party of the Soviet Union after the failed coup of August 1991. It is important to understand that although the significance of the operations that began during the summer of 1937 is now better understood and emphasized by most scholars, this is a still a relatively recent phenomenon in the historical field and in the politico-memorial field of Russia and the former Soviet republics.[19] The irruption of these massacres onto the Russian political, historical, social scenes was crucial, but nevertheless was only one stage in the process of reintegrating Stalinist massacres into Russian history. It confronted Russian society with a new question: what is to be done with these sites? The answer was not so obvious.

The Memorialization of Mass Executions

The mass graves were put at the centre of a web of memories: the massacres gave rise to books, websites, and scientific research, all produced in an attempt to give the massacres meaning. This production is, however, in no way homogeneous. The main result of these efforts was the compiling of lists of victims, the so-called 'books of memories' that can be found either in printed form or on the web. The archival works used for these projects offered the possibility for scientific research: in the eight volumes of books on Butovo, lists of names are followed by numerous brilliant historical articles by Alexandr Vatlin (a professor at Moscow University). Relatively free access to archival sources has also allowed him to publish a small monograph on the terror in one district of Moscow.[20] But this scientific approach is only one of the methods chosen in Russia. In the same books of memory, other articles opt for a discourse approaching that of a funeral oration; the language used contains a mixture of religious and scientific terms and expressions. All of these works are, however, closely linked to the concrete scene of the massacres. The way in which these places have been set up is therefore a crucial part of the discourse on the Stalinist terror.

When Levashovo was discovered and officially recognized as a 'memorial cemetery' (18 July 1989) during *perestroika*, interest in Stalin's crimes and political repression was at its climax in Soviet society.[21] This may explain why the appropriation of the site was above all popular and spontaneous. Relatives of the victims came there and decorated the trees or ground with small ribbons, small plaques on which the name of their loved ones were engraved. The first religious services (*panikhidi*) took place as early as 21 October 1989. The 'Levashovo wilderness', as it was called, became a popular memorial of the repression, but its spontaneous nature clashed with the Soviet political traditions of control and memorialization. A committee was charged with planning the organization of the cemetery by the political authorities in May 1990, but lack of funding, closely linked with the country's economic situation, meant that nothing was ever done.[22]

Until 1992, the cemetery remained the same. According to some activists, it was the risk that the cemetery might change under the influence of popular pressure that led to the erection of the first community monument, dedicated to victims from Belarus and Lithuania, on 8 May 1992.[23] The man behind the creation of this monument, Anatoly Razumov, was convinced that these 'official' monuments would make it impossible (or at least very difficult) for people to make any subsequent changes in the appearance of the cemetery. These monuments were certainly more difficult (physically, practically and politically) to remove than the small popular signs of grief. Over the subsequent years, the number of these monuments increased so that there are now twenty. The last one erected, dedicated to the Italian victims of repression, was inaugurated by the Italian ambassador in July 2007.

The religious dimension has not been forgotten. Most of the monuments bear religious symbols and in June 1993 a bell was erected at the entrance to the Levashovo cemetery. The result is a polysemous space in which everybody has an input. The only monumental sculpture, in the Soviet style, can be seen outside the cemetery. Called the 'Moloch of totalitarianism', it was erected by the city of St Petersburg in 1996. The last extensive works on the Levashovo cemetery were carried out in 1996 thanks to Lidia Tchoukovskaja. An important writer and Soviet dissident, daughter of the well-known Soviet writer Kornej Tchoukovski, she received a State prize in 1995 for her work on Anna Akhmatova and donated the prize money to the workers of Levashovo for the maintenance of the cemetery.

At the beginning of the 1990s, Russian society, barely coping with the difficulties brought about by *perestroika* and the subsequent liberal 'shock therapy', increasingly lost interest in uncovering the past and learning about Soviet history. It was in that very different context that a small group of people, made up of activists, officials and some relatives of the victims, first visited Butovo on 7 June 1993. Some months later, on 10 October 1993, a sober plaque of rose granite, prepared by activists with the help of sponsors and authorized by a formal decision of the Moscow city government, was inaugurated. The text on the plaque was neutral: 'In this zone of the Butovo shooting range, several thousand people were, in 1937–1938, shot in secret and buried. May their memory be eternal.' This kind of plaque can be found at many different sites of Stalinist massacres in Russia, such as at Debin, not far from Magadan or Pivovarikha, in the vicinity of Irkutsk.

Nevertheless, as a result of an underlying lack of interest, the discovery of Butovo was not as heralded in Russian society as it might have been a few years earlier and consequently it did not make such a large impact as Levashovo. There was in fact no popular appropriation. However, when activists got involved in archival work in order to establish the names and identities of the Butovo victims, they happened to learn that a senior figure of the Orthodox Church, Serafim, the Metropolitan of Leningrad, was killed and buried there. When Alexei II, the then patriarch of the Russian Orthodox Church was informed of this in the winter of 1993, he decided to go to Butovo. In honour of his visit, which was to take place in May 1994, a cross, especially designed by the son of a Butovo victim, D. Chakhovskoj, was erected on the terrain of the former shooting range. In the foundation of the cross, a sealed inscription was inserted on behalf of the Patriarch in which he promised the construction of a church.

The terrain of Butovo and of Kommunarka, another execution site close by, were transferred to the Orthodox Church in 1995 for 'exploitation without time limit' by Russian security agencies. The explanation commonly put forward for such a decision is that at the time nobody else wanted to take charge of them, which is likely to have been the case.[24] In 1995, there were virtually no other institutional structures other than the Church that could afford to take care of such a place. A few months later, on 16 June 1996, a small wooden church was inaugurated. The Church has also been influential in governing and regulating the site. In 1996, for example, as a result of plans worked out at the end of the

1980s, the construction of a number of apartment blocks a few metres from the graves had been envisaged, and indeed building on the site had begun as though the administrative authorities had no inkling of the significance of the graves. Reactions from activists, the Memorial Society and the Church were immediately forthcoming. As the building was financed by the city of Moscow, the Patriarch intervened with the then mayor of the Russian capital, Juri Luzhkov. His intervention proved to be decisive and the works were stopped.

From that moment on, the Russian Orthodox Church attached more and more importance to the site of the former shooting range. Butovo achieved, for example, the statute of historical site (*pamiatnik istorii*) in July 1997. A number of projects to build a memorial at Butovo were worked out, but probably as a result of a lack of funds and of the competition between different administrative and political areas (Butovo is on the territory of the *oblast* [region] of Moscow, an administrative unit different from the city of Moscow), nothing was really done before 2004. Nevertheless, the city of Moscow financed most of the infrastructure for the development of the memorial (such as a new road and a bus line from the nearest metro station, also opened in 1998). It also financially backed the publication of the books of memory. Finally, important sums of money were granted by the city and the region of Moscow in 2005 to allow for a new layout of the former shooting range: the lawns were cleaned, tumuli were built on the location of the mass graves to make them apparent, and paths were laid to allow visitors to walk around. The result of the ever-increasing involvement of the Church is a site that is very different from that of Levashovo, with almost no visible signs of commemoration other than the original monument, a cross, a church, and a list of the Orthodox victims. With the help of private funding, a large church was also opened on land next to the mass graves. The domination of the memory of Butovo by Orthodox Church has nevertheless been the source of conflict.

The Meaning of Stalinist Massacres

The resolve of Levashovo activists to keep the cemetery in its original form, to avoid Soviet monumentalism, and to insist on individual rather than institutional mourning suggests an interpretation of the repression and the Terror itself. It insists on the plurality of broken destinies and avoids the rivalry between victims that seems to be at the centre of Butovo's problem. It insists on the personal side of the tragedy.

The Orthodox Church (the patriarchate), the community of Butovo, and the Butovo Centre, a 'centre for scientific memory and popularization' founded in 2002, have proposed a very different and a very structured discourse on Butovo.[25] It is a double-sided discourse, well maintained and within an Orthodox framework (and therefore which emphasizes the essential role played by the Church in the creation and organization of the Butovo memorial), that wants to be universal and is directed at the whole Russian-Soviet population, not just at Orthodox followers. In a journal published by the parish of Butovo in 2006, the terror of 1937–1938 is referred to as a 'national catastrophe' and the memorial is dedicated to 'the memory of the victims of the shooting range of Butovo of whatever ethnic or confessional origin'.[26] The Orthodox organizers of the Butovo memorial constantly remind their interlocutors of the presence of Jewish or Muslim victims. This dual discourse can even be found in the organization of the space. Butovo might be seen as a homogenous space in which almost all the exterior signs are Orthodox, but a whole discourse is produced to attenuate this impression. The presence of a church on the gravesite is thus presented not as a symbol of the Orthodox confiscation of the site, but rather as a long-lived Russian tradition. The head of the Butovo Centre wrote an article on the 'churches-on-the-blood' that links Butovo with the martyrdom of Boris and Gleb in 1015.[27] Several churches of this type, he reminds us, were built in Russia on the sites of the murder of 'innocent victims who did not resist death' One of the most famous is the church built in Uglich on the site of the murder of the son of Ivan the Terrible, the Tsarevich Dmitri. Given the rhetoric used in the article and the name of the rubric under which it appeared ('Russian traditions'), Garkavy insists on the idea that this is a specifically Russian tradition. The tumuli that are now covering the mass graves are also linked – in the press, on the web, and in personal interviews – to the Russian traditions of the *bratskie mogily*, mass graves from the Middle Ages.[28] Several scientific and denominational conferences (with the participation of other religious leaders) have even been organized on this theme since 2005.

These general ideas are nevertheless completed by a specific religious discourse which stresses the ideas of sacrifice and martyrdom and which presents Butovo as a Russian Golgotha. Among the 20,761 victims buried at Butovo, 935 were killed for their religious faith, 304 of whom had already been sanctified by the Russian Orthodox Church. The discourse surrounding the Russian Golgotha strives to pass from the particular to the universal: Butovo is thus supposed to be the symbol of the tragic history of the Church during the twentieth century in Russia.[29]

This predominance of the religious discourse in Butovo was a source of violent conflicts in particular between the Church and the first activists at the origin of the re-discovery of Butovo. Mindlin, in particular, was very upset by the Church's control of the site. He tried to break the monopoly by inviting different religious leaders to pray at Butovo on the Radonica (the day of mourning in the Orthodox Church). Years later, Kirill Kaleda, the priest at the Orthodox community, still criticized the initiative in an interview published by the Patriarchate.[30] If Kaleda spoke positively about Mindlin, he nevertheless qualified the ceremony as 'an absurd incident'. Although Kaleda's discourse is relatively open-minded, it remains strictly religious; Kaleda may consider the rights of other confessions but never thinks of Butovo as a site of national, a-confessional memory. Other associations, such as the Memorial Society, have still not accepted the Church's control. One of its harshest critics is Natalia Ogorodnik, a member of the 'Memoria Pamjat' association. She strongly contests the idea of a Russian Golgotha, and denies the right of the Orthodox Church to speak in the name of all.[31]

Conclusion: What Are Massacres?

The history of the foundation of the Levashovo and Butovo memorials tells us a lot about Russian society and its complex relationship with its Stalinist past. It also gives us the opportunity for a better understanding of the social meaning of a massacre. Can the killings that took place during the Stalinist 'Great Terror' be called 'massacre'? There seems to be three crucial stages that have to take place before an event can qualify as a 'massacre'. The first stage is, of course, the killing of defenceless people, a necessary pre-condition but not a sufficient one in and of itself: a slaughter committed but kept hidden will not exist for the rest of the world. The 700,000 victims of the Great Terror were ignored by historians and remained unknown to Soviet populations for many years. In order for a 'massacre' to be recognized – and this is the second stage – it is important that it is disclosed. The events of the Great terror became fully known only sixty years after they were committed. A massacre that has been made public may nevertheless be forgotten and consequently stop 'existing'. In short, a massacre only definitively exists if it is acknowledged and remembered. Therefore, the discourses that may arise around a massacre, produced by different actors (including historians), represent another, third crucial stage. The mass killings, committed and disclosed, must have a 'scandalous' dimension, they must shock society into calling the killings a 'massacre'. In contemporary Russia, this qualification of the Stalinist terror, obvious for the Western reader, becomes blurred. Stalin is increasingly remembered as the great *vozhd'* (guide) who led the country through industrialization and brought it to victory during the Great Patriotic War. The status of the victims of the Great terror is therefore unclear. The knowledge of these three stages allows us to understand a massacre in all its dimensions and teaches us about societies in which the massacres are committed, revealed and interpreted. Massacre is therefore more than a subject of history; it is also a tool for historians to understand societies.

The Stalinist terror, in all its complexity, its national, popular and even personal dimensions, is now far better known. Contemporary Russian society, however, hardly knows how to deal with all these representations of Stalinist violence. None of them really finds an echo in contemporary society. Butovo is all too often empty,[32] whereas Levashovo seems to be frequented mostly by relatives of victims. The federal state is strangely silent about these massacres. The visit of Vladimir Putin to Butovo on 30 October 2007, accompanied by the Patriarch, was thus highly significant. He gave his own interpretation of the massacres, an alternative to the suggestions made in this chapter. Wondering 'how all this could happen', the then President of the Russian federation and the first elected Russian official to pay a tribute to Butovo attributed the deaths of so many people to the 'excesses of the political conflict'.[33] This surprising interpretation was widely accepted. The Stalinist terror of 1937 was nevertheless hardly a consequence of a political fight as there remained almost no opposition to Stalinism. Most of the victims lying in the mass graves of Butovo were not the political foes of Stalinism; they were shot because of their nationalities, or just because they were caught in the 'Red Wheel' of the Terror. Putin's remarks were actually linked to the then political situation of Russia and his conception of n unified society where political fights were to be avoided. This confusion is probably another example of the difficulty of the New Russia to understand and to know its past, and therefore to give meaning to the Stalinist massacres of 1937–1938.

Notes

1. Marc Junge and Rolf and Stepanov A. Binner, *Kak terror stal 'bol'shim': sekretnyj prikaz no. 00447 i tekhnologija ego ispolnenenija* (How the Terror became 'Great': The Secret Operational Order n. 00447 and the Technology of Its Implementation) (Moscow, 2003), 81–83. A partial English translation of this now well–known order may be found in J. Arch Getty and Oleg V. Naumov, *The Road to Terror: Stalin and the Self-Destruction of the Bolsheviks, 1932–1939* (New Haven, Conn., 1999), 473–80.
2. For a good description of the process, see Junge and Binner, *Kak terror stal 'bol'shim'*, 17–77; and Nicolas Werth, *L'ivrogne et la marchande de fleurs: autopsie d'un meurtre de masse* (Paris, 2009).
3. This text was published for the first time in Russia in V.N Uimanov and Ju. A. Petrukhin (eds), *Bol' ljudskaja : kniga pamjati tomichej repressirovannykh v 30-40-e i nachale 50-kh godov* (Tomsk, 1999), 102–11. An excerpt of the stenographic account is also published in Junge and Binner, *Kak terror stal 'bol'shim'*, 81–83.
4. RGASPI [Russian State Archive for Social and Political History], fund 2, inventory 1, file 6, 898. English translation of the Library of Congress.
5. The literature on this elite terror is abundant. Most criticized, but still paradigmatic, is Robert Conquest, *The Great Terror; Stalin's Purge of the Thirties* (New York, 1968). There are also numerous testimonies, such as that by Nikolaï Bukharin's wife Anna Larina, *This I Cannot Forget: The Memoirs of Nikolai Bukharin's Widow* (New York, 1993).
6. Irina Paperno, 'Exhuming the Bodies of Soviet Terror', *Representations*, 75 (2001), 89–118.
7. Paperno, 'Exhuming the Bodies of Soviet Terror', 97–98.
8. The original texts are kept in the archives RGANI (Russian State Archive for Contemporary History), fund 3, inv. 103, file 103, 22–23 and 218–19. They were published in the *Izvestija CK KPSS*, 2 (1989), 22–23, and in the *Vedomosti Verhovnogo soveta SSSR*, 3 (1989), 19. They may be found online at http://www.alexanderyakovlev.org/fond/issues-doc/66198.

9. A text on the memorandum was published in *Memorial Aspect* in 1993. The original memorandum can be found in the first volume of the Book of memory of Butovo, in 1997. A transcript may be found online at http://www.martyr.ru/content/view/48/41/.

10. The KGB (Committee for the State Security) was suppressed by B. Eltsin at the end of 1991. The Ministry of Security was its successor from 24 January 1992 to 21 December 1993. The predecessors of the KGB were the Tcheka, the OGPU and the NKVD.

11. L. Golovkova, 'Specobekt "Butovskij poligon": Istorija, dokumenty, vospominanija' ('The Special Place "Butovo Shooting Range": History, Documents, Memories'), in L. Golovkova (ed.), *Butovskij Poligon, 1937–1938. Kniga pamjati žertv političeskih repressij* (The Butovo Shooting Range, 1937–1938. Book of Memory of the Victims of Political Repression) vol. 1 (Moscow, 1999).

12. François-Xavier Nérard, 'Case Study: The Butovo Shooting Range', in Jacques Semelin (ed.), *Online Encyclopedia of Mass Violence*, http://www.massviolence.org/Article?id_article=277 (retrieved February 2009).

13. Anatolij Jakovlevič Razumov, *Levašovskoe memorial'noe kladibšče* (The Memorial Cemetery of Levashovo) (Saint-Petersburg, 2006), 7.

14. Razumov, *Levašovskoe memorial'noe kladibšče*, 9.

15. M.B. Mindlin was born in 1909 and arrested for the first time in 1937. He spent most of his life in banishment and in camps. From the end of the 1980s, he fought for the discovery of places of mass burials, until his death in 1998. See Mikhail Mindlin, *Anfas i profil': 58.10* ('Full Face and in Profile: Article 58:10') (Moscow, 1999).

16. See his project http://visz.nlr.ru/project/index.html.

17. The Memorial Society has made an impressive inventory (in Russian) that can be seen at http://www.sakharov-center.ru/asfcd/pam/default.htm (Sakharov Centre in Moscow) or the less precise http://www.memo.ru/memory/martirol/index.htm (Memorial Society).

18. For a good review of the latest works on Stalin's Soviet Union, see Sheila Fitzpatrick, 'The Soviet Union in the Twenty-first Century', *Journal of European Studies*, 37 (2007), 51–71.

19. Junge and Binner, *Kak terror stal 'bol'shim'*; Getty and Naumov, *The Road to Terror*; and Werth, *L'ivrogne et la marchande de fleurs*.

20. Aleksandr Vatlin, *Terror rajonnogo maštaba* (Terror at the District Level) (Moscow, 2004).

21. The other 'memorial cemetery' of the Leningrad region, Piskarevka, was opened in 1960 and contains the dead of the Leningrad blockade during the war. It is a perfect example of Soviet monumentalism. The choice of the name 'memorial cemetery' by the municipal administration is therefore politically highly significant, and makes the dead of the Great Terror appear as important as the dead of the blockade.

22. A. Razumov, 'Memorialization of Places of Mass Massacres', Paris, December 2007 (unpublished paper).

23. Interview with Alexei Razumov, Levashovo, 7 June 2008.

24. Interview with Father Kaleda, Butovo, 11 April 2008.

25. François-Xavier Nérard, 'La mémoire de Boutovo, massacres de masse des années trente en Russie soviétique', in Luc Buchet and Isabelle Segu (eds), *Vers une anthropologie des catastrophes: Actes des 9e journées d'anthropologie de Valbonne* (Antibes, 2008), 143–59; Kathy Rousselet, 'Butovo: La création d'un lieu de pèlerinages sur une terre de massacres', *Politix*, 20 (2007), 55–78; idem., 'Les mémoires de la Grande Terreur: Butovo', in M.-C. Maurel and F. Mayer (eds), *L'Europe et ses représentations du passé. Les tourments de la mémoire* (Paris, 2008), 131–46.

26. This expression may be found in a box in the journal *Nyne i prisno* (2006), 200, that reminds readers of the massacre site and which gives instructions for getting there.

27. Igor' Garkavy, 'Hramy na Krovi v tradicijah drevnerusskoj memorial'noj kul'tury XI–XVII vekov', ['The Churches on the Blood in the Traditions of the Old-Russian Culture of Remembrance, XI–XVII Centuries'], *Nyne i prisno*, 3 (2006), 201–16.

28. Interview with Igor Garkavy, Butovo, August 2006.

29. Rousselet, 'Les mémoires de la Grande Terreur'.

30. http://www.patriarchia.ru/db/text/194486.html

31. Rousselet, 'Les mémoires de la Grande Terreur'; See their website, http://www. memoria-pamyat.ru/

32. There are no statistics on the frequentation of these places. The main affluence in Butovo is linked with religious celebrations and particularly with the presence of the Patriarch. But despite a new road and a bus route, paid for by the municipality, the site does not seem to be well-known to the Russian people.

33. See *Kommersant*, 31 October 2007.

CHAPTER 15

SPECTACULAR ATROCITIES: MAKING ENEMIES DURING THE 1965–1966 MASSACRES IN INDONESIA

Annie Pohlman

Following a military coup on 1 October 1965, an estimated 500,000 Communists and their sympathizers were murdered and a further one and a half million detained at the beginning of General Suharto's 'New Order' regime (1966–1998). What incited these crimes was a pervasive propaganda campaign staged immediately after the coup by the Indonesian military. The propaganda blamed the coup on the military's mass-supported political rival, the Indonesian Communist Party (PKI), and presented the party together with its supporters as an evil, atheist and treacherous influence that had to be eradicated in order to save the nation.[1] The killings and mass arrests that followed were perpetrated by the Indonesian military with the cooperation of civilian militia, mostly drawn from the youth membership of religious groups and political parties opposed to the PKI.[2] The result was the creation of new internal enemies – the PKI and their supporters – who had always been part of local communities. Party members and cadres, their families and friends, and even occasionally those wholly unconnected to the PKI but who were labelled as such because they were in the wrong place at the wrong time, subsequently became victims of the massacres and arrests.[3]

The majority of those murdered were first captured then taken to remote locations and executed. Their bodies were disposed of in mass graves, thrown into the ocean and rivers, or hidden in caves.[4] The focus of this chapter, however, is on a far less common though widespread form of violence perpetrated during the massacres, 'spectacularized atrocities' – the intentional display of dead, mutilated bodies or body parts in public areas and the performative structures of these acts. It is also about how bodies are staged instrumentally at the centre of mass violence and how the deformation of bodies is commodified and consumed as part of conflict. As such, reports by witnesses and stories about spectacularized violence during the 1965–1966 massacres are analysed in order to reveal crucial elements of these atrocities.

The argument is that mutilation was a way of identifying the 'PKI and their sympathizers' during a period of great social uncertainty. During the massacres perpetrators mutilated their victims in order to uncover or expose their 'real' identities. To explain this, the first half of this chapter discusses how violence transforms individual victims into artefacts for the victim group and investigates the connection between mutilation and the verification of identity. In the second half, it briefly charts the development of politicized identities in the late 1950s and early 1960s in Indonesia and discusses how victims' bodies were the stage upon which these identities were revealed.

This argument connects the formative practices of spectacularized violence with the cumulative effect of the 1965–1966 massacres. In essence, the mass killings and arrests laid the foundations of the New Order's authoritarian rule. The terror of those months following the 1 October 1965 coup played a determining role in establishing and perpetuating the New Order's state terrorism, that manifested itself in the militarization of public institutions, the depoliticization of civil society and the intermittent displays of the regime's willingness to use suppression, coercion and violence to retain power.[5] Spectacularized atrocities were fundamental to both the killings themselves as well as to their overall impact. As such, the chapter deconstructs this violence and argues that these atrocities must be examined within the context of both the impact and legacy of the massacres in Indonesia.

The Dismemberment and Making of Bodies, the Creation and Detection of Enemies

N___, daughter of M___, aged 17. From the town of T___.

In 1965, N__ was captured by a gang of *Pemuda Pancasila* youth militia in the middle of the night, gang raped and killed by being *dicucuk* (stabbed, stuck through) with a piece of iron from her middle through to her genitals. While still *dicucuk*, she was hung upside down and left on the road near the town mosque.[6]

This description of a young woman's torture, mutilation and murder at the hands of one of the youth vigilante groups involved in the massacres is brief, the details succinct and sickening. N__ may (or may not) have been a member of or associated with the (allegedly atheist) PKI. However, how she was murdered, how her body was mutilated and where she was displayed are significant. Her body was inverted, a piece of iron used to pierce her reproductive organs and her corpse staged as spectacle in a highly visible and public area near the town's central place of religious observance. This atrocity transformed a person and a place into horrifying alterity; what was normally up was down and a place was marked by a body so wholly out-of-place, a transgression that was perhaps meant to warn others of the atheist, treacherous offense for which this girl had needed to be punished.

The violence itself is similar to that perpetrated in conflicts across the world, the atrocities repeated in different times and places. And yet each case is contextual to the place and time in which it occurs. Each case cannot be abstracted too far from its local field of significance and meaning. As Neil Whitehead argues, these acts are 'specific forms of violence [that] are not produced by the febrile excess of savage or pathological minds but are cultural performances whose poetics derive from the history and sociocultural relationships of the locale'.[7] Nevertheless, the violent acts mirror those of countless others.[8] Conflicts in the twentieth century alone have produced a long list of cases of human dismemberment and display, of lynching, of trophy taking, of severed body parts and mutilated corpses.

It is this human dismemberment and display occurring during larger scale conflicts that is analysed here within the context of the 1965–1966 massacres. These acts, while often ritualized in their performance, are not taken to be part of rituals *per se*.[9] Nor can they be conflated with singular acts of sadistic crime perpetrated by mentally disordered individuals that take place external to conflict zones,[10] although it is evident from various accounts about 1965 that some perpetrators of these atrocities exhibited strong asocial tendencies.[11] Much research into various conflicts mentions, often only in passing, atrocities committed as part of these conflicts; however, there have been very few studies that discuss the phenomenon of intentional mutilation and display during mass violence.

Each of these previous studies contributes to an understanding of these atrocities in 1965–1966 in Indonesia, and all engage at some level with how uncertain or unstable bodies and the material practices of violence on these bodies play a role in the production and commodification of atrocities as part of conflict. This argument is greatly influenced by the anthropologist Arjun Appadurai's more recent works on mass interethnic violence and modernity.[12] For Appadurai, uncertainty is a fundamental condition of mass violence. This uncertainty results from what he views as the impact of large-scale modern forces on social group identities.[13] How social uncertainties played out in the case of mid-1960s Indonesia will be addressed in the second half of this chapter, but what Appadurai shows is how these factors coalesce to generate uncertainty which, in turn, leads to suspicion and the attempt to remove these uncertainties and suspect Others through violence.[14]

For Appadurai, social uncertainty is inscribed on victims' bodies. The unmaking of bodies through mutilation during conflict is, therefore, a creative process; it is done in order to produce or make 'real' uncertain Others. At the end of this section, I will outline how these forms of vivi-sectionist identification were used to identify the 'PKI betrayers' during the massacres in Indonesia. First, however, I will explain Appadurai's concept of making bodies through violence by drawing on the works of Allen Feldman and Liisa H. Malkki – each of whom provide crucial insights into the way in which bodies are transformed into material signifiers as part of conflict – before returning to Appadurai, whose work builds upon these insights, and who argues that it is the very instability or uncertainty of these bodies that leads perpetrators in conflicts to mutilate them in order to ascertain their victims' 'true' identities, to make 'real' or 'certain' persons out of bodies.[15]

Allen Feldman's study of political violence in Northern Ireland during the 1970s and 1980s provides three crucial points which elucidate the atrocities committed in 1965–1966: (a) the body is both commodified by and becomes a stage for political violence; (b) to become this commodity, the self is detached from the body and transformed into signifier, that is, they are staged as political texts; and (c) the production of this signification occurs in the rationalization and fictionalization of the reason for the act of violence. To understand the first part of this process – the commodification of the body – we can draw on Feldman's discussion of 'stiffing', a politically motivated murder, although the corpse is not necessarily displayed. The political violence enacted on the body serves to not only transform a body and a place; it is also an effort to make that body into a substitution for the larger conflict.[16] For Feldman, the body is the stage for the production and possession of political power. Both the body and the space in which an atrocity is performed are deformed, made horrifyingly Other by the act of violence. This deformation is fundamentally about commodification. Deformation makes both the body and place become a stage for a 'transaction' between the different sides of the conflict.

This leads to the second element of Feldman's argument – how violence also disconnects the body from the self and transforms it into a political commodity and signifier so that it may be consumed ideologically by different sides of the conflict. With the torture and murder of N___, it is the spectacle of her mutilated remains on the road near the mosque and not her self as individual that is consumed by the local population. The violence carried out by the *Pemuda Pancasila* youth militia gang who murdered her was an act that created a body that 'emerges as a political construct and the self as apolitical residue, an excess left over from the process that transforms the body into a political form'.[17] N___ is no longer a seventeen-year-old girl from the town of T__, daughter of M___; she is made into an artefact for the PKI.

Finally, Feldman explains the third crucial element in this process which is that this violence is deterministic; it invests the body of the victim with a phantasmal search for and identification of what that body is. The fact that N__ has been mutilated and displayed removes uncertainty over who she is or how she came to be there. She is (must be) a member of the enemy PKI. This transfer of meaning occurs in the way that the torture and mutilation both rationalizes and creates the reason for this violence.[18] This is a process of false motives, ends absorbed by means, self-mimesis, and of 'how the ritualized and the symbolic provide the foundations for the rationalization of power and thus the fictionalization of its violence'.[19] Again, the fact that N__ has been murdered and mutilated means that she must be a member of the PKI, because her murder and mutilation make it so. These atrocities are consequently their own explanation. The process of self-rationalizing violence and its connection with the search to identify the 'real' identity of the victim will be revisited below. However, the aspects of Feldman's study about how the body is commodified, transformed into artefact, and made to signify for an enemy 'other' leads in turn to the work of anthropologist Liisa Malkki.

Malkki's study of memories of violence against Hutus in Burundi perpetrated in the early 1970s also engages with the issues of how violence inflicted on bodies is used in an effort to demarcate and in turn make (again, in this case, ethnic) others. Malkki, strongly influenced by Mary Douglas' *Purity and Danger*,[20] engages with how violence is intimately tied to the classification of persons, with the need to establish the identities of others, and with the search for purity. As Malkki shows, physiognomy became the direct marker for ethnicity during the genocide against the Hutus. Who was 'Tutsi' and who 'Hutu' was determined by what she terms the 'necrographic maps' that grew out of colonial efforts to solidify complex socio-economic strata into the different 'ethnic' groups in the region, Hutu, Tutsi and Twa.[21] In essence, it was these maps, these created and invented differences in height, nose size and other phenotypic interpretations that 'construct and imagine ethnic difference. ... Through violence, bodies of individual persons become metamorphosed into *specimens* of the ethnic category for which they are supposed to stand.'[22] As with Feldman, the significance of Malkki's work lies in explaining how bodies become signifiers and that, during mass violence, the search for identity is staged on these bodies through violence. These bodily inscriptions of difference – the difference between Hutu and Tutsi, between Catholic and Protestant or, as I will show below, between Communist and non-Communist – are the necrographic maps by which people are identified. These maps, these ways of identifying others, come into play during periods of mass violence because they mediate between what is known (i.e. Tutsis are tall) and what can be detected (he is tall, therefore he must be Tutsi). Yet, as Appadurai explains in relation to Mallki's work, '[T]he body is both a source and a target of violence. The categorical uncertainty about Hutu and Tutsi is played out not in the security of the "body maps" shared by both sides but by the instability of the signs of bodily difference: Not all Tutsis are tall; not all Hutu have red gums. ... In a word, real bodies in history betray the very cosmologies they are meant to encode. So the ethnic body, both of victim and of killer, is itself potentially *deceptive*.'[23]

Both Feldman and Malkki show how bodies become signifiers – the necrographic maps are there to determine who the 'others' are that need to be destroyed. Appadurai, however, makes it clear that these signifiers are inherently unstable, uncertain, deceptive and therefore unreliable. For Appadurai, this is the reason mutilation is instrumental during conflicts. Mutilation is 'an effort to stabilize the body of the ethnic other... It literally turns a body inside out and finds the proof of its betrayal, its deceptions, its definitive otherness, in a sort of premortem autopsy ... which, rather than achieving death because of prior uncertainty, achieves categorical certainty through death and dismemberment.'[24]

Although Appadurai, Malkki and Feldman address primarily 'ethnicized' bodies, this chapter is about the destruction of a political/social group, the PKI and those associated with the party. But to say that the same argument does not apply to politicide simply because the necrographic maps for destruction are not based on historical phenotypic constructions (as is Malkki's argument in ethnocized violence) is to miss Appadurai's essential point. The vivisectionist logic of mutilation as verification is not dependent upon phenotypic difference as the cause for uncertainty but rather upon social uncertainty as the cause for anxiety. That anxiety is constructed through an imagined phenotypic difference, especially in the case of 'racial' or 'ethnic' violence. To put it simply, the macabre logic of dismembering bodies to uncover their 'real' identities constructs and reinforces difference as self-rationalizing justification.[25] The imagined differences of race or ethnicity that hold such significance during 'ethnic' or 'racial' violence are just as much historiographic constructions as those created to imagine difference between religious, socio-economic and political groups.[26] It is therefore not the forms of difference themselves but the categorical uncertainty that arises from their construction that leads to this 'verificationist' mutilation in conflict.

Unmaking and Making the PKI

Appadurai's type of verificationist mutilation and display seen during the 1965–1966 massacres was caused, in part, by uncertainty over identifying 'PKI members and sympathizers'. The weeks and months that followed the 1 October 1965 coup were a time of great fear and uncertainty. It was a reactionary fear against the PKI and its members who, according to the military's propaganda, were planning a bloodbath against non-Communist supporters. There was also a fear of not being involved with anti-Communist forces. The PKI were considered evil, treacherous and dangerous and so it was an unpleasant but necessary duty to destroy them. Non-involvement could be interpreted as support for the PKI, a theme which is common in stories by perpetrators to justify their participation (or at least collaboration) in the violence. One woman who was imprisoned in the mass arrests described the fear of the months after the coup: 'If you spoke up, then the same thing would happen to you. That's what it was like. Be careful, because if you spoke up [in defence of someone], they'd do the same thing to you. So everyone was afraid... So if someone seemed guilty, well then, you let it happen.'[27]

This fear was also, however, caused by social uncertainty over how to identify the PKI. Suddenly, people who had been part of their communities their entire lives were revealed as enemies who had not only plotted to overthrow the government but who were planning to kill their non-Communist neighbours. The speed and intensity with which the PKI and its supporters were politically isolated and demonized left people wondering how many PKI there were, and how far their influence had spread. In the climate of inculcated fear following the coup, former social intimates could no longer be sure of their neighbours, associates and even family members. On occasion, murder, torture and mutilation against suspected PKI was therefore not only a way to eradicate them, as Appadurai argues, but it was also a way to use 'the body to establish the parameters of this otherness, taking the body apart, so to speak, to divine the enemy within.'[28]

This uncertainty is reflected in stories about the killings, both in the very small number of literary accounts ever published which mention the violence of 1965–1966 and in the anecdotes told somewhat reluctantly by Indonesians old enough to remember these events.[29] The victims in these stories are, for the most part, deliberately depersonalized and remain nameless; they are tropes for the PKI and the violence done to their bodies is the violence that could be perpetrated against any Communist. The fact that the victims are assumed to be members of the PKI justifies their treatment. Sometimes the victims are depicted as evil or disruptive enemies who deserve their punishment; sometimes they are described with pity because of their inevitable but justifiable fate. Moreover, stories that include incidents of spectacularized atrocities are rare and often vague. They recall images of heads on posts and the stench of bodies left to decay, but not victims as individuals. Once again, victims are depersonalized. One of the more well-known stories about the killings is a short autobiographical account by Pipit Rochijat (who

refers to himself as 'Kartawidjaja's Son No. 2') in which he recounts his
childhood memories of seeing and later participating in the massacres.

> Each day, as Kartawidjaja's Son No. 2 went to, or returned from, State Sen-
> ior High School No. 1, he always saw corpses of Communists floating in
> the River Brantas. The thing was that the school was located to the 'kulon'
> (west) of the river. And usually the corpses were no longer recognizable as
> human. Headless. Stomachs torn open. The smell was unbelievable. To make
> sure they didn't sink, the carcasses were deliberately tied to, or impaled on,
> bamboo stakes... Kartawidjaja's Son No. 2 often stole out of the house... to
> watch the despatch of human souls. This too made sleeping difficult. Remem-
> bering the moans of the victims as they begged for mercy, the sound of the
> blood bursting from the victims' bodies, or the spouting of fresh blood when
> a victim was beheaded. All of this pretty much made one's hair stand on end.
> To say nothing of the screams of a Gerwani [communist women's movement]
> leader as her vagina was pierced with a sharpened bamboo pole. Many of the
> corpses lay sprawled like chickens after decapitation.[30]

Evidence of social uncertainty as to how to identify the 'PKI' is also
reflected strongly in the wide range of stories about those who became
victims of the massacres and mass arrests. In essence, the majority of
those who became victims were associated with the PKI. This included
members of the party itself, members of the PKI's associated organizations, such as the youth wing, *Pemuda Rakyat*, the women's organization, *Gerwani*,[31] or the farmers' association, *Barisan Tani Indonesia,
BTI*, or their families and friends. Yet there were also other victims
caught up in the killings and arrests. There was for example, the occasional revenge or opportunistic killing over land, possessions or wives,[32]
as well as cases of mistaken identity and those involving individuals who
were in the wrong place at the wrong time. As time went on, there were
also drives under Suharto's New Order to 'cleanse' the public service,
government, political parties and military of 'PKI elements'.' In reality,
these purges were a chance for General Suharto's new government to
be rid of supporters of those who had previously been in power under
President Sukarno.[33] Thus not only those directly associated with the
PKI became victims.

One of the reasons that these diverse groups of people became victims
was the uncertainty over identities following the coup. This uncertainty
was the result of a complex combination of factors, three of which are
briefly outlined here. First, it can be traced to how the 'political' group
destroyed in 1965–1966 (that is, 'suspected Communists and their sympathizers') was a political, cultural, socio-economic and historical construct which developed during a period which Robert Cribb describes as
political pillarization during the 1950s and 1960s in Indonesia. It was
this 'group' which, after the 1965 coup, became the primary (though not
sole) category for persecution during the massacres and mass arrests.[34]
This political pillarization can be traced to the later colonial period

during which three possible ideals or 'nations' emerged amongst the emerging nationalist elites in the contested vision for what the post-Independent Indonesia could become. Cribb has labelled these three streams of ideals as Islamic, Communist and developmentalist.[35] While it cannot be argued that Cribb's three streams were stable or discrete groups or even that similar groups existed across the diverse contexts of the various regions of Indonesia, it is fair to say that these groups were identifiable insomuch as Indonesians both identified themselves with these streams and that there was clear organizational and institutional membership with them. Furthermore, this identification with the different groups could stretch beyond individuals with particular allegiances to include family members or even entire communities.[36] A passage in one story about the killings set in East Java gives a brief insight into this process. In the story, 'Dark Night', a young man travels to a village to marry his fiancée, Partini, whose father was killed because he was a communist. On the way to the village, he finds out that she and her family have also been killed. 'They were all killed. Partini, her mother, the other children... The families of communists in other areas have disappeared as well, you know. The fact that Mrs. Mulyo (Partini's mother) couldn't read and that her children knew nothing about politics made no difference. Politics is blind. They all went into the river.'[37] In essence, the political pillarization created agile socio-political identities while also investing them with great social and political significance. It was this fluidity of group categorization, the infective quality of the label 'PKI' to spread from family member to family member, or from acquaintance to acquaintance, that was one of the factors which contributed to untenable categorical uncertainty during the massacres.

Second, the social uncertainty following the coup also arose from the fact that the killings and arrests were localized to a certain extent, in the sense that, in each region where the killings occurred, the influence of national politics always combined with regional developments and local factors. There are larger patterns of the massacres that are traceable, that is, in most cases, the killings and arrests would begin following the arrival of the armed forces to a particular area. However, these patterns were subject to individual, regional variation. As Kenneth Young has convincingly argued in his discussion of the killings in the Kediri region of East Java, the violence was shaped inevitably by a combination of national and local factors and 'by 1965 at least, the working out of national conflicts was still very variable from region to region. These regional patterns were not wholly separate, autonomous processes, but neither are these easily assimilable in analysis into a uniform national pattern.'[38] The significance for this localized nature of the killings for understanding social uncertainty following the coup lies in acknowledging the fact that national events and forces can never be disentangled from local conditions or vice versa. Local antagonisms between PKI and non-PKI supporters were exacerbated by the larger trends in social pillarization across the main islands of Indonesia. This meant that social uncertainty over who the 'PKI' or 'PKI sympathizers' could be was compounded by local antagonisms.[39] Within each region where the killings occurred, issues at the national level and the military's propaganda were transformed and articulated at the local level. As Michael Taussig has shown, larger genocidal processes are played out within specific locales and, in the case of the Indonesian massacres, national and local antagonisms were both instrumental in provoking and intensifying the killings.[40]

Finally, what incited the killings was the Indonesian military's anti-Communist propaganda campaign which began almost immediately following the 1 October 1965 coup and which depicted the PKI and anyone associated with it as evil, atheist, treacherous and, most importantly, in need of eradication. In addition to creating a terrifying enemy in the PKI, the military's propaganda also deliberately engineered a climate of impending danger. This included reports about how the PKI and their supporters had been preparing for the destruction of their enemies. Among these reports were revelations that pits had been dug in which the PKI were to bury their enemies, that death-lists had been drawn up, and that innocuous pieces of farm equipment were cleverly disguised eye-gouging tools.[41] As Cribb asserts, within 'a matter of weeks, by skilful exploitation of rumor and propaganda in an environment of enormous uncertainty and tensions, the opponents of the Communist Party were able to turn it ... into a pariah'.[42]

It was these three factors that combined to create an untenable social uncertainty. But why did this social uncertainty lead to cases of such violence as dismemberment and bodily mutilation? How did this social uncertainty lead to the murder and mutilation of individuals by unknown military personnel and also by those known to their victims, their neighbours, relatives and other community members? How did dismembering bodies work to allay these uncertainties by verifying their identities as 'PK ' or 'PKI sympathize'?

To explain this and the way in whicw it played out in terms of spectacularized violence, let me return to the points made at the beginning of this chapter. After the coup, within a matter of weeks, several things changed. The reification of group difference — that is, between being 'PK' and non-PKI — took on a new, more deadly meaning. In the highly charged atmosphere of mid-1960s Indonesia, extant social and political antagonisms between communists and non-communists at the national, regional and local levels, together with the military's deeply dehumanizing and demonizing propaganda, created a new, more dangerous PKI enemy. The danger posed by the PKI was reinforced by the depiction of communists as internal enemies. As internal enemies, members of the PKI were an infectious and poisonous influence that, unless cleansed, would be a continuing danger. This is evidenced, for example, in the military's propaganda which described the PKI as 'poisonous stabbers in the back [who] must be eliminate' and admonished people to '[c]ast out this spawn of hell root and branch, tear down the walls of their ideological edifices, plow the salt into the sterile sands of their alien mental beachhead, let Communism nevermore sojourn in this Nation'.[43]

This process of removing categorical uncertainty over who the PKI and its supporters were through spectacularized atrocities was heavily reinforced in survivors' stories about the detention camps and interrogation facilities. These stories recount a similar pattern: capture by the military, police or civilian vigilantes; being taken to an over-crowded detention facility; interrogation which frequently involved torture and, very often, confession. The latter included confessions, to absurd charges ranging from direct involvement in the coup, to storing weapons and digging pits in which to bury Muslims, to being forced to 'give up' other Communist traitors. It was in these interrogation rooms, as it was in the dismemberment and display of victims in public areas, that uncertainties over political identity were detected and stabilized. In story after story by those who survived the interrogations and torture in 1965–1966, the pattern is set. An individual is brought in for interrogation, tortured and ordered to confess. Once again, it creates a system of false motives, a self-rationalization and fictionalization for the violence against victims' bodies.[44] Verification of the victims' uncertain, hidden identities is found in inflicting pain and destroying bodies. The testimony of Ibu Sulami, one of the former leaders of the communist women's movement, *Gerwani*, reveals this process of interrogation as well as her defiance of her torturers.

> I arrived at the [military] post where all the detainees were being heavily tortured... There were people being tortured in the yard behind the building — completely naked, blood flowing from their heads and other parts of their bodies, forced to walk around the yard, men and women. Whatever the soldiers wanted, they did while they watched and laughed... I was stripped naked... I could not count the number of hits I received all over my body from the rattan canes. The cane left cuts on my breasts, arms and torso. My whole body was beaten black and blue. But that was not enough, for I would not confess that I had been involved in the 30 September Movement [1965 Coup...] I stood completely naked before the bloodthirsty and harsh [interrogators]. I stayed like that for about an hour... A number of finger-length pieces of rattan were thrown down on the table in front of me. Why? Not long after two... torturers came in. I was threatened in order that I would confess. I refused to do so. With a nod of [the commander's] head, he gave an order to the two torturers who were standing either side of me. My arms were extended. The rattan pieces were put in between my index, middle and little fingers. Four pieces of rattan for two hands. Then [the torturers...] pushed hard upon [the pieces of rattan]. Pain wracked my body, right down to my bones. The sweat poured off me. My two eyes were shut, and my teeth crackled. The pain caused me to involuntarily urinate, but I did not cry out... Finally they stopped. My fingers wouldn't move and I couldn't even feel them. The skin turned blue. Perhaps the bones were fractured. I was ordered

to stand by the wall. Once again I was ordered to confess. I did not answer. Without warning, a knife was stabbed in behind each of my ears and on the top of my head… and I fell to the floor in pain.[45]

Conclusion

Verificationist mutilation was not the only cause for human dismember-ment and display during the 1965–1966 massacres in Indonesia. As with all violence, there were multiple causes and there are multiple explana-tions, all of which add to our understanding of this deeply dehumanizing form of violence. It is my contention that the material forms of violence perpetrated against victims' bodies during conflicts must be examined *per se* because they reveal more fully the poetics of violent practices in the contexts where they occur. Evidence that the terror of those months following the 1965 coup deeply affected communities and civil society in Indonesia is well documented.[46] Spectacularized atrocities, so often mentioned in interviews with eyewitnesses and survivors of the mas-sacres, were central to the terror of 1965–1966. Therefore, in order to try to understand these atrocities, we must go back and examine the essential site where violence gains its socio-cultural meanings, that is, to the bodies of victims.

Notes

1. See Saskia E. Wieringa, 'Sexual Metaphors in the Change from Soekarno's Old Order to Soeharto's New Order in Indonesia', *Review of Indonesian and Malaysian Affairs*, 32 (1998), 143–78.
2. See Rex Mortimer, *The Indonesian Communist Party and Land Reform, 1959–1965* (Clayton, Victoria, 1972).
3. I discuss those who became victims of the killings and mass arrests in my thesis, A. Pohlman, 'Ashes in My Mouth: Women, Testimony and violence during the Indo-nesian Massacres of 1965–1966' (Ph.D. Thesis, University of Queensland, 2011).
4. See Robert Cribb, 'The Indonesian Massacres', in Samuel Totten, William S. Parsons and Israel W. Charny (eds), *Century of Genocide: Eyewitness Accounts and Critical Views* (New York, 1997), 233–60.
5. See Ariel Heryanto, *State Terrorism and Political Identity in Indonesia: Fatally Belonging* (New York, 2006), 3.
6. Institute for the Rehabilitation of the New Order Regime's Victims, 'List: People Raped and Killed in the 30 September 1965 Event in the North Sumatra Area which have been Verified', photocopied partial document, passed to me by Ibu Wanti, Jakarta, October 2005. Please note that all names have been obscured by the use of pseudonyms.
7. Neil L. Whitehead, 'On the Poetics of Violence', in Neil L. Whitehead (ed.), *Violence* (Santa Fe, 2004), 74.
8. For a recent example, see 'Sowing Terror: Atrocities against Civilians in Sierra Leone', *Human Rights Watch*, 10 (A) (1998), http://www.hrw.org/reports98/sierra.

9. See Richard J. Chacon and David H. Dye, 'Introduction to Human Trophy Taking: An Ancient and Widespread Practice', in Richard J. Chacon and David H. Dye (eds), *The Taking and Displaying of Human Body Parts as Trophies by Amerindians* (New York, 2007), 8–21.
10. Here I mean sadistic crimes more often committed by individuals with antisocial personality disorders (section 301.7), but also psychotic disorders (including those induced by substances) as well as the paraphiliac focus of sexual sadists (302.84) as defined by the American Psychiatric Association, *Diagnostic and Statistical Manual of Mental Disorders, Text Revision* (DSM-IV-TR), 4th edn (Washington, DC, 2000).
11. In some interviews with survivors of the killings, informants talked about particular male perpetrators being 'expert' or 'the worst' killers.
12. See Arjun Appadurai, *Fear of Small Numbers: An Essay on the Geography of Anger* (Durham and London, 2006); and idem., 'Dead Certainty: Ethnic Violence in the Era of Globalization', *Public Culture*, 10 (1998), 225–47.
13. See Appadurai, *Fear of Small Numbers*, 4–13.
14. Appadurai, 'Dead Certainty', 229–39.
15. Appadurai, 'Dead Certainty', 225–47.
16. Allen Feldman, *Formations of Violence: The Narrative of the Body and Political Terror in Northern Ireland* (Chicago, 1991), 63–64.
17. Feldman, *Formations of Violence*, 64.
18. Elaine Scarry explores a similar process by which state torture transforms the pain of the victim into fictionalized political power. See Elaine Scarry, *The Body in Pain: The Making and Unmaking of the World* (New York, 1985), 56–59.
19. Feldman, *Formations of Violence*, 114–15.
20. Mary Douglas, *Purity and Danger: An Analysis of Concepts of Pollution and Taboo* (London, 1966).
21. Malkki, *Purity and Exile*, 56–90.
22. Malkki, *Purity and Exile*, 88. Italics in original.
23. Appadurai, 'Dead Certainty', 231–32. Italics in original.
24. Appadurai, 'Dead Certainty', 232.
25. This point again returns to Feldman's understanding of violence as self-rationalizing. See note 19 above.
26. More recent works in the areas of ethnic/race studies and critical whiteness studies have elucidated the very shallow roots and constructed nature of 'ethnicity' and 'race'. See, for example, Stephen Spencer, *Race and Ethnicity: Culture, Identity and Representation* (London and New York, 2006).
27. Interview with Ibu Nana, Sumatra, September 2005.
28. Appadurai, 'Dead Certainty', 233–34.
29. The best known collection of some of these literary accounts is *Gestapu: Indonesian Short Stories on the Abortive Communist Coup of 30th September 1965*, edited and translated by Harry Aveling (Honolulu, 1975).
30. Pipit Rochijat, 'Am I PKI or Non-PKI?', trans. Ben Anderson, *Indonesia*, 40 (1985), 44–45.
31. *Gerwani* was not officially part of the PKI at the time of the coup, though it aligned itself and was seen to be closely aligned with the party.
32. See note 3 above.
33. See, for example, Harold Crouch, *The Army and Politics in Indonesia* (Ithaca and London, 1978), 197–244; and Amnesty International, *Indonesia: An Amnesty International Report* (London, 1977), 20–25.
34. Robert Cribb, 'Genocide in Indonesia, 1965–1966', *Journal of Genocide Research*, 3 (2001), 219–39. Clifford Geertz's model of *aliran*, roughly translated as 'streams' of political, social and religious strata, is another way of thinking about this political pillarization in 1950s Indonesia. See Geertz, *The Religion of Java* (London and Chicago, 1960); and *The Social History of an Indonesian Town* (Cambridge, 1965), 127–29.
35. Cribb, 'Genocide in Indonesia', 219–39.

36. See note 3 above.

37. Martin Aleida, 'Dark Night', in *Gestapu: Indonesian Short Stories on the Abortive Communist Coup of 30th September 1965*, edited and translated by Harry Aveling (Honolulu, 1975), 92.

38. Kenneth R. Young, 'Local and National Influences in the Violence of 1965', in Robert Cribb (ed.), *The Indonesian Killings of 1965–1966: Studies from Java and Bali* (Clayton, Victoria, 1990), 66.

39. Robert Cribb, 'Introduction: Problems in the Historiography of the Killings in Indonesia', in idem., *The Indonesian Killings*, 26.

40. See Michael Taussig, 'Culture of Terror – Space of Death. Roger Casements Putumayo Report and the Explanation of Torture', *Comparative Studies in Society and History*, 26 (1984), 467–97.

41. For an analysis of some of these reports, see Steven Drakeley, 'Lubang Buaya: Myth, Misogyny, and Massacre', Working Paper 108 (Clayton, Victoria, 2000), 5.

42. Robert Cribb, 'Genocide in Indonesia', 232.

43. The two headlines come from *Djakarta Daily Mail*, 16 November 1965 and 11 December 1965 respectively. Cited in Drakeley, 'Lubang Buaya', 9.

44. This returns to the discussion of Feldman's work, see note 19 above.

45. Ibu Sulami, *Perempuan – Kebenaran dan Penjara* [Women – The Truth and Prison] (Jakarta, 1999). Please note that Ibu Sulami published this account under her true name, so I have not used a pseudonym in this case.

46. See, for example, Heryanto, *State Terrorism*, and Michael van Langenberg, 'Gestapu and State Power in Indonesia', in Cribb (ed.), *The Indonesian Killings*, 45–61.

CHAPTER 16

A NECESSARY SALVE: THE 'HUE MASSACRE' IN HISTORY AND MEMORY

Scott Laderman

When Richard Nixon appeared before a national television audience on 3 November 1969, he had before him an unenviable task. Having been elected by a citizenry increasingly anxious to bring American involvement in the Vietnam war to an end, the president found himself confronting the twin, and seemingly contradictory, goals of appeasing this growing sentiment while, at the same time, maintaining the American military commitment and thus the 'credibility' of American power. To achieve the former objective, Nixon proposed 'Vietnamization', a gradual withdrawal of US combat troops coupled with heightened aerial bombardment and an intensified effort to train the Republic of Vietnam's (R.V.N.) armed forces. To legitimize the latter, he appealed to those he called the 'silent majority', the tens of millions of Americans that, the president claimed, supported US policy in Southeast Asia but, unlike members of the antiwar movement, did not take to the streets in demonstration. Nixon framed his appeal in simple moral terms. Pleading with his compatriots to appreciate the implications of a 'precipitate [American] withdrawal', the president hearkened what became known as the 'bloodbath theory'. A justification for continued intervention, the bloodbath theory posited that a US withdrawal from Southeast Asia would lead to such widespread massacres of Vietnamese sympathetic to the American presence that the United States was morally obligated to maintain its military commitment.

At the heart of the theory lay the so-called 'Hue Massacre', a series
of alleged atrocities undertaken by the Vietnamese revolutionary forces
throughout their weeks-long capture of Hue, the central Vietnamese city
that once served as a seat of royal power, during the 1968 Tet Offensive.
Although it faced serious evidentiary challenges, a basic narrative of the
massacre soon developed. Entering the city with lists identifying American and R.V.N. sympathizers, it began, the revolutionaries immediately
began rounding them up. What followed was 'a bloody reign of terror',
according to Nixon's November 1969 speech, 'in which 3,000 civilians
were clubbed, shot to death, and buried in mass graves'. The narrative's
symbolic power was obvious. A 'sudden collapse' of American support,
Nixon cautioned his countrymen, and 'these atrocities of Hue would
become the nightmare of the entire nation'.[1] The message resonated.
Following the speech – an event viewed by over 72 million people, a
figure three times greater than those who had watched the president's
inauguration just ten months earlier – approximately 400,000 letters,
telegrams, and postcards poured into the White House, ninety per cent
of which favoured Nixon's plea for continued intervention.[2]

While not all of the missives addressed, let alone accepted, the bloodbath scenario, a number of them – from one governor's warning that
'our immediate capitulation' in Vietnam would 'scar our souls with the
remorse of a people who, wearily after 200 years, first stamped their
approval on genocide' to the head of the Retired Officers Association's
applause for Nixon's 'enduring efforts' to end American participation in
the war 'in a manner that will not only illiminate [sic] American casualties but prevent wholesale slotter [sic] of the Vietnamese...' – expressed
not even the slightest reservation about the theory's legitimacy.[3] Neither
did a number of editorial writers. Those at the *Orlando Sentinel*, for
example, soberly predicted massacres following an American withdrawal
that 'might approach the genocide of Hitler's Germany in the 1940s'.[4]

While the Hue atrocities thus served to substantiate the bloodbath
hypothesis during a moment in which US policy was undergoing serious
challenges, the atrocities would also soon be exploited for another political purpose: to 'balance' the emerging stories of the US-perpetrated
massacre at Son My (My Lai). And their utility did not end with the
war's conclusion. After 1975, memory of the executions would help to
restore moral integrity to the American campaign and, among overseas Vietnamese, legitimacy to the exiles' earlier support for the Saigon
regime. Given that government's brutality and corruption, as well as
the conflict's widespread remembrance as a 'bad' war, this was no incon-
siderable achievement.

A Contested Narrative

Forty years after the Tet Offensive, precisely what happened in Hue
remains uncertain. The postwar Vietnamese government, anchoring

its legitimacy in the revolutionaries' earlier resistance to France and the United States, has not been eager to reopen the wounds of the past, while antiwar scholars, no longer feeling compelled to puncture the bloodbath hypothesis, have moved on to more immediately pressing concerns. Yet it would be a mistake to dismiss the incident as merely a distant chapter of Vietnamese and American history. Its significance – not to mention its perceived utility at a time of 'revisionist' proliferation – persists. For right-wing academics seeking to restore nobility to the American cause, the Hue executions remain an article of faith. For the historian Mark Moyar, for example, they are a 'massively documented fact', though one for which he has failed to cite any credible documentation.[5] Among likeminded pundits, the massacre, insisted one such commentator, represents an 'embarrassment' for 'the left' that has been 'swill[ed] … down their collective memory hole where it now largely remains, a grim testimony to their immorality, hypocrisy, blind political bigotry, and capacity for hatred'.[6] And within the Vietnamese diaspora, the Hue atrocities have been adjudged, according to one published account, 'the most barbaric and worst crime of all in our country's historical tragedies' – and, importantly, one about which younger generations 'need to know'.[7]

Yet while the conventional narrative serves a useful function to celebrants of American global power, its basic outline enjoys little support among scholars who have closely examined it. It is true that uncertainty exists about the precise details of what occurred in Hue. But this uncertainty should not be confused with affirmation of the claim – one that has been popularly enshrined as truth – that some three thousand civilians were methodically executed by the Vietnamese insurgents. There is no credible evidentiary basis for this version of events. Even the traditional narrative's foremost architect had, by 1988, retreated from his wartime allegations about the scale of the atrocities. Nevertheless, the dubiousness of the Hue Massacre – by which, through the use of capital letters, I am referring to the conventional narrative of what transpired – has not tarnished its reliability in popular memory or elements of the scholarly literature.

The story of how this basic narrative achieved popular currency is ultimately a story of Cold War propaganda. Originally a discursive construction of an Army of the Republic of Vietnam (A.R.V.N.) political warfare battalion, the Hue Massacre was given its respectable veneer in a controversial 1970 document authored by Douglas Pike for the United States Mission in Saigon. According to Pike, an employee of the United States Information Agency and a staunch proponent of the bloodbath theory, the 'meaning of the Hue Massacre' seemed 'clear'. If the insurgents were to 'win decisively in South Viet-Nam (and the key word is decisively)', a succession of events would follow. 'First, all foreigners would be cleared out of the South, especially the hundreds of foreign newsmen who are in and out of Saigon. A curtain of ignorance would

descend. Then' – and here Pike conjured an explicit allusion to Nazi
Germany – 'would begin a night of long knives. There would be a new
order to build. The war was long and so are memories of old scores to
be settled. All political opposition, actual or potential, would be systematically eliminated.' Communist justice, he asserted, would be 'meted
out to the "tyrants and lackeys..." The communists in Viet-Nam would
create a silence. The world would call it peace.'[8] Given the undeniable
force of the author's language and its utility to pro-war partisans, the
report seemed destined to reach an audience far broader than diplomats
and military planners. It soon did. Perhaps most significantly, *Reader's
Digest* excerpted the study just months after the American invasion of
Cambodia – and the explosion of antiwar agitation it sparked – in its
September 1970 issue.[9]

Yet if the conventional narrative was welcomed within some quarters at a time of tremendous national polarization, its verisimilitude
did not go unchallenged. Countering those who viewed the episode as
a harbinger of what might follow a revolutionary victory, a number of
scholars, many of them active in the antiwar movement, believed the
official account to be a largely unsupported instance of pro-war propaganda. Foremost among these critics was the political scientist Gareth
Porter. In outlets ranging from the *Indochina Chronicle* to the *New
York Times*, Porter challenged the Nixon administration's bloodbath
hypothesis, demonstrating its reliance on problematical evidence, faulty
translations, and inconsistent logic. For the Cornell-trained political
scientist, whose published 1974 dissection of the atrocities narrative
has influenced much postwar scholarship, the 'enduring myth' of the
Hue Massacre 'bore little resemblance to the truth, but was, on the
contrary, the result of a political warfare campaign by the Saigon government, embellished by the [United States] government, and accepted
uncritically by the US press'.[10] Decades later, Vietnam specialists would
concur. The historian David Hunt, for instance, noted the logical inconsistencies in the conventional accounts and concluded that Pike's study
for the United States Mission was, 'by any definition, a work of propaganda'.[11] Indeed, in 1988 Pike readily conceded that he had earlier been
engaged in a conscious 'effort to discredit the Viet Cong'.[12] Yet given the
politics and perceived credibility of the narrative's foremost wartime
critic – Gareth Porter was an outspoken opponent of American policy in
Southeast Asia and, before 1978, one of the principal sceptics concerning the earliest evidence of the Khmer Rouge genocide in Cambodia
– the tenability of the Hue Massacre has remained a matter of bitter
contestation.[13] This is in spite of what has amounted to, in essence, a
nearly wholesale scholarly rejection of Pike's study and the emergence
of further support for Porter's wartime critique through the postwar
research of Ngo Vinh Long.[14]

To be sure, the question of whether or not there were executions in
Hue is not in dispute. Porter and other scholars agree that members of

the National Liberation Front (N.L.F.) killed non-combatants during the Tet Offensive, and these certainly merit our collective attention. However, the most reliable enumerations of those killed range from 300 or 400 to a more precise 710, estimates that constitute from ten to twenty-five per cent of the approximate figure of 3,000 typically cited in support of the conventional narrative, which is a figure from which even Douglas Pike had distanced himself by the late 1980s.[15] Yet problems with the traditional narrative go far beyond an inflation of its scale. The available evidence suggests that the atrocities were, in fact, nothing like the indiscriminate slaughter presented by Pike, Nixon, and other champions of US militarism. This is, historically speaking, not surprising, as all accounts concur that the executions represented a stark departure from N.L.F. policy – a point, conceded by Pike, that would be ignored in later statements on the potential for a postwar bloodbath.[16]

While there undoubtedly were a number of individuals killed immediately after the insurgents' capture of Hue, scholarship on the issue has provided a very different portrait from that reported by proponents of the conventional narrative. According to Porter, the N.L.F., which sought to create a revolutionary administration in the city, entered Hue with lists containing certain residents' names and dividing them into several categories. These included persons who had worked for the R.V.N.'s secret police apparatus, those who were high civilian or military officials, and those who were ordinary or low-level civil servants in the R.V.N. government. Many of these individuals were slated for temporary imprisonment outside the city or for 'reeducation' under the revolutionary authorities, although others – in particular those from the first category, who were personally involved in the repression of the resistance movement – were summarily executed.[17] But citing interviews with 'most of the people involved', Ngo Vinh Long concluded that most of the killings occurred 'at the last minute' as the insurgents found themselves forced by an American offensive to abandon the city. '[T]hey were afraid their organizations in Hue were exposed, he explained, and if the captives were allowed to live, the guerrillas believed, they would have sought vengeance against the clandestine revolutionaries remaining in Hue.[18] Somewhat similarly, Porter and Len Ackland claimed in 1969, in the first study to be critical of the conventional massacre narrative, that the bulk of the executions 'were not the result of a policy on the part of a victorious government but rather the revenge of an army in retreat', referring to the disposition of persons originally identified for 'reeducation' but executed when, following US attacks, it became 'increasingly apparent that the [National Liberation] Front would not be able to stay in Hue indefinitely'.[19]

A prominent feature in many accounts of the Hue Massacre is the 'shallow mass graves' said to contain the revolutionaries' victims – an image that penetrated US popular consciousness in the 1980s in Stanley Kubrick's *Full Metal Jacket* (1987). In the film, the uncovering of the Vietnamese corpses offered one of the few moments in which the protagonist, Joker, appeared truly repulsed by the bloodshed in Vietnam. A lieutenant on the scene explained to him, 'Well, it seems the N.V.A. came in with a list of gook names. Government officials, policemen, A.R.V.N. officers, schoolteachers. They went around their houses real polite and asked them to report the next day for political re-education. Everybody who turned up got shot. Some they buried alive.' Yet this Hollywood vision presented a stark departure from reality. Whereas civilian reporters were shown to be examining a mass grave in Kubrick's production, Gareth Porter found that investigation of the sites by independent journalists was in fact strictly prohibited and that official claims about the graves were often contradicted by the available evidence. The only Western physician known to have been given access to the sites, for example, wrote that the number of bodies in the graves he examined was inflated sevenfold by the United States and the Saigon authorities. Most of the victims, he added, appeared to have been killed as a result of the combat in Hue, with many of the corpses clothed in the threads of military uniforms. Even the R.V.N. government's minister of health expressed scepticism about A.R.V.N.'s claims. '[T]he inconsistencies and other weaknesses of the various official documents, the lack of confirming evidence, and the evidence contradicting the official explanation, Porter wrote, 'all suggest that the overwhelming majority of the bodies discovered in 1969 were in fact the victims of American air power and of the ground fighting that raged in the hamlets, rather than of N.L.F. execution.' The 'undeniable fact', the political scientist asserted, 'was that American rockets and bombs, not communist assassination, caused the greatest carnage in Hue'.[20]

Embracing the Conventional Account

Perhaps because of the greater confusion in 1968 about exactly what transpired in Hue, the Johnson administration was less aggressive than its successor in highlighting the atrocities' propaganda value to American and R.V.N. officials. Nevertheless, before the fighting in the former imperial capital had even ended, the State Department drafted a presidential statement for southern Vietnamese dissemination that celebrated the 'military valor' of the US and R.V.N. forces while decrying the revolutionaries' 'incredible brutality and terror against civilian officials and an innocent populace which accompanied their attack on a sacred city at a sacred time'.[21] For months afterward the events were addressed by the White House unit responsible for making 'the most effective use of the information coming in from Vietnam to put out our position over here at home', whether in presidential speeches, press briefings and leaks, or in 'background material' for Johnson's 'use on the Hill'.[22] However, it was not until late in 1969, months after Richard

Nixon assumed the presidency and when reports of the Son My (My Lai) massacre first began to appear in the American press, that the atrocities in Hue achieved considerable political currency.

From that time until shortly after the war officially drew to a close, the Hue Massacre – together with exaggerated accounts of the land reform executions in northern Vietnam in the mid-1950s – was cited repeatedly in Congress, in the media, and among pro-war activists in an effort to bolster support for an increasingly embattled US foreign policy.[23] 'While US leftists shout and proclaim a gospel of dissent against all throughout our land, Representative John Rarick proclaimed in a typical statement, 'their counterpart, the Communist Vietcong, slaughter thousands of innocent men, women, and children in South Vietnam, if for no other reason than the victims reject communism and are not yet under party control.'[24] The interventionists' goal was simple: to make continued warfare, rather than its cessation, the morally imperative choice. Redirecting charges of criminality and immorality levelled at the conflict's American architects, the logic of the bloodbath theory rendered opposition to the official US position an effective endorsement of the mass slaughter of thousands or even millions of Vietnamese.[25] 'That there would be a massive bloodletting is something that is taken for granted by virtually every serious student of Vietnamese affairs, Senator James Eastland maintained in 1972.[26] The debate was simply over numbers.[27]

In addition to bolstering support for continued US intervention, the Hue Massacre played a crucial ideological role when, months after the March 1968 event itself, reports began to appear in the United States about the Son My atrocities perpetrated by American troops. National Security Adviser Henry Kissinger, recognizing the threat this posed to US assertions of moral superiority, suggested to Richard Nixon that the White House should remind Americans about 'Communist terror tactics in South Vietnam', including the executions in Hue.[28] The basic framework US officials should employ was summarized by Nixon speechwriter Pat Buchanan. Atrocities such as those at Son My were 'done *against* the policy of the American government', Buchanan counselled the president. Conversely, a '*policy of atrocity is the policy of the enemy* we confront in Vietnam... Any individual who cannot see the difference between the isolated acts of members of the American army, and the premeditated and systematic atrocities of its Communist enemy in the field, he continued, 'does not know what this war is about – or what his society is about.'[29] The message was replicated widely. Whereas the massacre at Son My, 'if true', was 'committed against all instructions of the American [g]overnment', Senator George Murphy maintained in a representative example, the atrocities at Hue 'were carried out as part of the officially ordered plan and design to establish a Communist government in South Vietnam'.[30] For champions of continued intervention, the Hue Massacre could thus be used to remind Americans that the

Vietnamese revolutionaries, unlike US officials, had no concern for the sanctity of human life.

Among the Vietnamese the Hue atrocities performed a similarly ideological function. Visual imagery of bodies being excavated from mass graves, and the devastated relatives of these victims mourning their heartfelt losses, was circulated in a brief film presented by the psychological warfare unit of the R.V.N. armed forces.[31] (The film appeared before an American audience years later in a 1987 exhibition organized by the Washington Project for the Arts.)[32] Also employing print, the R.V.N.'s American embassy published a special issue of *Viet-Nam Bulletin* dedicated to the 'red mass murder' in Hue, as well as the sympathetic counsel offered to relatives of the 'red victim[s]' by the R.V.N. president, Nguyen Van Thieu. 'Look at these sad faces, then look at these coffins, Thieu pleaded in a eulogy for the deceased. 'Is this the final freedom offered by the Communists – to lie in a coffin in the ground?'[33]

The Hue Massacre – as a potent symbol and rhetorical device – did not disappear once its interventionist utility dissipated in 1975. In 1988, for instance, Representative Newt Gingrich, the Georgia Republican who, six years later, would emerge as speaker of the House of Representatives, pointed to 'the human cost of Democratic failures', chastising a member of the opposition who had earlier 'engaged in self-deception' by suggesting that 'some of the people buried in the trenches at Hue may have been killed by American bombs'.' Gingrich professed disgust. '[T]his particular liberal Democrat, he fulminated, 'had to blame America for the bodies which virtually every historian agreed were the deliberate acts of the Communists in Hue.'[34]

Right-wing activists and authors have likewise drawn on the Hue executions to criticize the left, the mainstream press, and the antiwar movement – which are synonymous, according to many of these critics – for their alleged inattention to revolutionary terror while focusing on atrocities perpetrated by American troops. According to Gerard Jackson, for example, what transpired in Hue was not unusual but was merely 'the most shocking example of the North's barbaric policy' of 'terrorism by mutilation and massacre'; the 'cold-blooded business of calculated mass murder' in Hue, Jackson's headline writer concluded, was 'the massacre the left wants us to forget'.[35] In the midst of the 2004 presidential contest, writers from the *National Review*, the *Washington Dispatch*, and other outlets employed John Kerry's silence on the Hue executions when testifying before Congress in 1971 to portray the Democratic contender as, at best, a Communist dupe or, at worst, a dishonest propagandist.[36] At the very least, he was unfit for command.

Among elements of the Vietnamese diaspora, the Hue Massacre has come to symbolize the genocidal threat of the wartime revolutionary movement, in effect justifying the exiles' earlier support for the R.V.N. regime. For many members of the overseas community, the factual basis of the atrocities narrative is beyond reproach; the critical scholarship refuting it is either unknown to them or has been ignored or dismissed. The editors of a book published by the Vietnamese Laity Movement in the Diaspora, for instance, sought to 'collect fragments of the truths available to remind one another and to advise the younger generations that the 1968 massacre at Hue is the most barbaric and worst crime of all in our country's historical tragedies'. The editors did not address studies challenging the conventional account. Their principal concern was the education of those too young to have experienced the war at first hand; the atrocities provided a crucial lesson. 'The facts in this book are not unfamiliar [to] most Vietnamese who kept themselves abreast of the situation when the war was going on,' they wrote. 'But for those who live under the communist rule and are affected by the communist propaganda, especially the younger generations, and for a vast majority of foreigners who, for a time, could only have access to secondhand sources of information that were brutally tampered and distorted by the anti-war reporters and journalists, these are the truths that they need to know.'[37] The exiled Buddhist activist Le Huu Dan agreed. Drawing for support on a documentary film produced by the right-wing outfit Accuracy in Media, Dan published a volume in 1998 that in considerable part focused on the 'savage killing of thousands of Hue's civilians with tremendous cruelty'. The Hue Massacre, he wrote, was a crime 'unprecedented in the history of human kind' that exceeded even 'Pol Pot's crime[s]', for the N.L.F., according to Dan, killed a Buddhist monk, a transgression for which, he said, not even Pol Pot and the Khmer Rouge had been accused.[38]

The atrocities emerged as a contentious public issue in 2003 with a dispute between elements of the overseas community and the curatorial staff at the Oakland Museum of California. During that Bay Area institution's preparations for a historical exhibit on California and the Vietnam war, Mimi Nguyen, a Vietnamese-American staff researcher at the museum, was dismissed days after her submission of a memo complaining about various shortcomings she perceived in the exhibition's initial organization. Among these was insufficient attention to the Hue executions.[39] Nguyen's termination – which museum officials denied was related to the memo but declined to explain, telling reporters they could not discuss personnel matters – led to outrage within the Vietnamese diaspora.[40] Letters were sent to the museum, and within days an online petition criticizing the exhibition and Nguyen's dismissal had gathered hundreds of signatures. While most signatories simply lent their names to the document without providing additional comments, among the minority who did offer their remarks were two individuals who specifically referred to the need for the museum to publicly memorialize the Hue Massacre.[41]

* * *

The atrocities in Hue hold an important position in the study of war and massacre. Unlike well-documented events whose memory is suppressed for reasons of political convenience, the conventional story of the Hue executions is, at base, a poorly documented narrative that has nevertheless been popularized so as to achieve convenient political ends. The reasons are not difficult to discern. For American policymakers and politicians, belief in the atrocities provided a moral basis for prolonging a devastating intervention whose objectives were largely geopolitical. For overseas Vietnamese, traditional accounts of the executions justified their collaboration with a corrupt wartime regime. And for the broader American populace, the Hue Massacre has, then and since, allowed the nation to redirect guilt over its own wartime criminality onto the elusive Other it failed to subdue in Indochina. In this respect, the narrative has provided a necessary salve for America's wounded collective conscience. Over thirty years after the inglorious American withdrawal, stories persist of a gruesome and premeditated slaughter of thousands of civilians at the hands of the Vietnamese revolutionaries. In this respect, the Hue Massacre continues to serve as a neutralizing agent, reminding Americans that as horribly as 'we' acted during the war, 'they' most certainly were worse.

Notes

1. Richard Nixon, 'Address to the Nation on the War in Vietnam,' 3 November 1969, *Public Papers of the Presidents of the United States: Richard Nixon, 1969* (Washington, DC: Government Printing Office, 1971), 902.
2. On the A.C. Nielsen figures, see Henry Rahmel to Herbert Klein, 20 November 1969; Nixon Presidential Materials Staff [hereafter N.P.M.S.]; White House Central Files [hereafter W.H.C.F.]; Subject Files: Speeches (Ex); Box 106; Folder: SP 3-56/Nationwide T.V. and Radio Address re: Vietnam at Wash. Hilton Hotel, November 3, 1969 (3 of 3); National Archives II, College Park, Maryland [hereafter N.A. II]. On the hundreds of thousands of letters, telegrams, and postcards to the White House, see Herbert G. Klein to Pope Hill, 24 January 1970; N.P.M.S.; W.H.C.F.; Subject Files: Speeches (Gen); Box 106; Folder: SP 3-56/Nationwide T.V. and Radio Address re: Vietnam at Wash. Hilton Hotel, November 3, 1969 (2 of 2); N.A. II. Klein added that in addition to the 400,000 individual correspondents, 'hundreds of thousands of names were signed to petitions'.
3. Tom McCall to Richard Nixon, 12 November 1969, and 'Governor McCall's Statement on President Nixon's Vietnam Message', 3 November 1969; N.P.M.S.; W.H.C.F.; Subject Files: Speeches (Ex); Box 107; Folder: SP 3-56/PRO, [11/4/69]-11/13/69; N.A. II; and W.R. Smedberg III to Richard Nixon, 4 November 1969; N.P.M.S.; W.H.C.F.; Subject Files: Speeches (Ex); Box 107; Folder: SP 3-56/PRO, [11/4/69]-11/13/69; N.A. II.
4. 'President on Solid Ground in Search for Vietnam Peace', Editorial, *Orlando Sentinel*, 5 November 1969; N.P.M.S.; W.H.C.F.; Subject Files: Speeches (Ex); Box 106; Folder: SP 3-56/Nationwide T.V. and Radio Address re: Vietnam at Wash. Hilton Hotel, November 3, 1969 (1 of 3); N.A. II.

5. Mark Moyar, 'A Call to Arms', *Passport: The Newsletter of the Society for Historians of American Foreign Relations* 38, no. 3 (December 2007), 17.

6. Gerard Jackson, 'The Media, Abu Ghraib, and the Forgotten Massacres', *BrookesNews*.com (24 May 2004), www.newaus.com.au/042305_Abu_Ghraib.html (accessed 23 September 2004).

7. Phong Trao Giao Dan Viet Nam Hai Ngoai [Vietnamese Laity Movement in the Diaspora], *Tham Sat Mau Than o Hue: Tuyen Tap Tai Lieu / The '68 Massacre at Hue: Documentation* (Reischstett, France: Dinh Huong Tung Thu, 1998), xi.

8. Douglas Pike, *The Viet-Cong Strategy of Terror* (Saigon: United States Mission, Viet-Nam, 1970), 42.

9. Douglas Pike, 'The Bitter Story of Hue', *Reader's Digest* 97 (September 1970), 105–9.

10. D. Gareth Porter, 'The 1968 "Hue Massacre,"', *Indochina Chronicle* 33 (24 June 1974), 2.

11. David Hunt, 'Images of the Viet Cong', in Robert M. Slabey (ed.), *The United States and Viet Nam from War to Peace: Papers from an Interdisciplinary Conference on Reconciliation* (Jefferson, North Carolina: McFarland & Company, 1996), 56.

12. Douglas Pike to Patricia Way, 11 November 1988. I am grateful to Grover Furr of Montclair State University for furnishing me with this document.

13. On Porter and the Khmer Rouge, see George C. Hildebrand and Gareth Porter, *Cambodia: Starvation and Revolution* (New York: Monthly Review Press, 1976); and Subcommittee on International Organizations of the Committee on International Relations, United States House of Representatives, *Human Rights in Cambodia*, 95th Congress, 1st Session (Washington, DC: Government Printing Office, 1977), 34–53. By 1978, as the evidence of widespread atrocities grew more compelling, Porter retreated from his initial scepticism and accepted Khmer Rouge responsibility for the horrific human rights situation in Cambodia.

14. For historians' rejection of Pike yet curious embrace of the conventional narrative, see Hunt, 'Images of the Viet Cong', 56–57. Ngo Vinh Long's research on the Hue executions has not yet been published, but he summarized his findings in Ngo Vinh Long, 'Vietnam Today', *Critical Asian Studies*, 34, no. 3 (2002), 459–64. He also discussed his research with me in a private conversation at the 2004 annual meeting of the American Historical Association in Washington, DC.

15. Pike acknowledged in 1988 that '[t]here are differences of interpretation as to the number,' and that he 'think[s] about 1,200 [were executed] but it could be less, for there are many [residents of Hue] who simply vanished'. Pike to Way, 11 November 1988. On the figure of 300 to 400 executions, see Marilyn B. Young, *The Vietnam Wars, 1945–1990* (New York: HarperPerennial, 1991), 217, who cited the contemporaneous research of Len Ackland. Young was presumably referring to the interviews reported in D. Gareth Porter and Len E. Ackland, 'Vietnam: The Bloodbath Argument', *Christian Century*, 86, no. 45 (5 November 1969), 1414–17. But elsewhere, citing an unpublished study, Ackland was reported to have learned from US and Vietnamese officials that approximately seven hundred Vietnamese were killed by the insurgents, and that this figure was generally consistent with Ackland's own investigations into the matter; Noam Chomsky and Edward S. Herman, *The Washington Connection and Third World Fascism* (Boston: South End Press, 1979), 346–47. More recently, Ngo Vinh Long concluded that 710 persons were executed in Hue; Ngo Vinh Long, 'Vietnam Today', 464.

16. Pike, *The Viet-Cong Strategy of Terror*, 31. See also Stephen T. Hosmer, *Viet Cong Repression and Its Implications for the Future*, R-475/1-ARPA (Santa Monica, Calif.: RAND Corporation, 1970), 76.

17. Porter, 'The 1968 "Hue Massacre,"', 8–9.

18. Ngo Vinh Long, 'Vietnam Today', 464.

19. Porter and Ackland, 'Vietnam', 1415–16.

20. Porter, 'The 1968 "Hue Massacre,"', 3–5, 6, 8.

21. Walt Rostow to Lyndon Johnson, 25 February 1968; Papers of Lyndon Baines Johnson, President, 1963–1969 [hereafter L.B.J. Papers]; National Security File [hereafter N.S.F.]; Country File – Vietnam [hereafter C.F. – Vietnam]; Box 70; Folder: General Military Activity, 2 C (7), 2/21–29/68; Lyndon Baines Johnson Library, Austin, Texas [hereafter L.B.J.L.]. It is unclear whether the statement was ever released.

22. George Christian to Lyndon Johnson, 22 August 1967; Office Files of Fred Panzer; Box 427; Folder: Viet-Nam Information Group; L.B.J.L. I am indebted to John Wilson of the Lyndon Baines Johnson Library for locating and providing me with a copy of this document. On the attention of the Vietnam Information Group to the Hue executions, see Talking Notes [hereafter T.N.] No. 7, 29 February 1968; T.N. No. 8, 6 March 1968; T.N. No. 11, 19 March 1968; and T.N. No. 16, 30 April 1968; L.B.J. Papers; N.S.F.; C.F. – Vietnam; Box 100; Folder: Public Relations Activities, 7 E (4)b, 2/68–4/68; L.B.J.L.; T.N. No. 17, 6 May 1968; L.B.J. Papers; N.S.F.; C.F. – Vietnam;Box 101; Folder: Public Relations Activities, 7 E (5), 5/68–6/68; L.B.J.L.; and T.N. No. 25, 30 July 1968; L.B.J. Papers; N.S.F.; C.F. – Vietnam; Box 101; Folder: Public Relations Activities, 7 E (6), 7/68–8/68; L.B.J.L.

23. On the land reform executions, see Edwin E. Moïse, *Land Reform in China and North Vietnam: Consolidating the Revolution at the Village Level* (Chapel Hill: University of North Carolina Press, 1983), 216–22.

24. *Congressional Record*, 91st Congress, 1st Session, 21 April 1969, 9826.

25. Indeed, the United States ambassador to Indonesia, Francis J. Galbraith, placed those calling for an American withdrawal from Vietnam in the same moral universe as 'those who are guilty of the atrocity at My Lai' in that both were 'afflicted by the same inability to feel the plight of the people of South Vietnam'. Francis Galbraith to Richard Nixon, 8 December 1969; N.P.M.S.; W.H.C.F.; Subject Files: Speeches (Ex); Box 106; Folder: SP 3-56/Nationwide T.V. and Radio Address re: Vietnam at Wash. Hilton Hotel, November 3, 1969 (3 of 3); N.A. II.

26. Subcommittee to Investigate the Administration of the Internal Security Act and Other Internal Security Laws of the Committee on the Judiciary, United States Senate, *The Human Cost of Communism in Vietnam*, 92nd Congress, 2nd Session (Washington, DC: Government Printing Office, 1972), 2–3.

27. For his part, Richard Nixon went back and forth over whether he should identify the total as being in the 'millions' or merely the 'hundreds of thousands'. Conversation No. 333–21, Executive Office Building, 26 April 1972, Nixon White House Tapes, N.P.M.S., N.A. II.

28. Henry Kissinger to Richard Nixon with attachment ['Communist Terror Tactics in South Vietnam'], 4 December 1969; N.P.M.S.; National Security Council Files [hereafter N.S.C.F.]; Alexander M. Haig Special File [hereafter A.M.H.S.F.]; Box 1004; Folder: My Lai Incident (2 of 2); N.A. II.

29. Patrick Buchanan to Henry Kissinger with 'Questions and Answers' for Richard Nixon, 5 December 1969; N.P.M.S.; N.S.C.F.; A.M.H.S.F.; Box 1004; Folder: My Lai Incident (1 of 2); N.A. II. Emphases in the original. See also 'Questions on My Lai', no date; N.P.M.S.; N.S.C.F.; A.M.H.S.F.; Box 1004; Folder: My Lai Incident (1 of 2); N.A. II.

30. *Congressional Record*, 91st Congress, 1st Session, 10 December 1969, 38223.

31. Video Recording 342-USAF-48733, 'Viet Cong Massacre in Hue, Vietnam, 1968', Record Group 342, N.A. II.

32. Program Notes for 'War and Memory: In the Aftermath of Vietnam', Washington Project for the Arts, 15 September–19 December 1987, Clippings File: Vietnam War Films, Pacific Film Archive, University of California, Berkeley.

33. 'In Memory of Hue, Tet 1968', *Viet-Nam Bulletin*, Viet-Nam Info Series No. 28 (Washington, DC: Embassy of Viet-Nam, April 1970), 2, 4, 7.

34. *Congressional Record*, 100th Congress, 2nd Session, 1 August 1988, 19685.

35. Gerard Jackson, 'Hue: The Massacre the Left Wants Us to Forget', *New Australian* 66 (16–22 February 1998), pandora.nla.gov.au/pan/10189/20021026/www.newaus. com.au/news29b.html (accessed 28 February 2004).

36. See, for example, Mackubin Thomas Owens, 'Vetting the Vet Record', *National Review Online* (27 January 2004), www.nationalreview.com/script/printpage. asp?ref=/owens/owens200401270825.asp (accessed 12 March 2004); Hugh Hewitt, 'The Kerry Files, Volume II', *Daily Standard* (19 February 2004), www.weeklys-tandard.com/Content/Public/Articles/000/000/003/751gbmvt.asp (accessed 29 August 2004); and Greg Lewis, 'A Quarter Century of Disinformation', *Washington Dispatch* (2 March 2004), www.washingtondispatch.com/article_8208.shtml (accessed 29 August 2004).

37. Phong Trao Giao Dan Viet Nam Hai Ngoai, *Tham Sat Mau Than o Hue*, xi–xii.

38. Le Huu Dan, *Tuyen Tap Su That / Accounts of the Truth* (Fremont, Calif.: Xuat Ban Publishing Co., 1998), 7. For a refutation of the author's charge about monks under the Pol Pot regime, see Chanthou Boua, 'Genocide of a Religious Group: Pol Pot and Cambodia's Buddhist Monks', in P. Timothy Bushnell, Vladimir Shlapentokh, Christopher K. Vanderpool, and Jeyaratnam Sundram (eds), *State-Organized Terror: The Case of Violent Internal Repression* (Boulder, Co.: Westview Press, 1991), 227–40.

39. For press coverage of the affair, see Pueng Vongs, 'Vietnamese Slighted in Vietnam War Exhibit', *CaliToday* (4 November 2003), news.ncmonline.com/news/view_article. html?article_id=5cd7175cb57b97fb83228d2c2b286a1a (accessed 27 February 2004); Joyce Nishioka, 'Inclusive or Exclusive?' *AsianWeek* (21 November 2003), news. asianweek.com/news/view_article.html?article_id=a5d28df0f1f884b0bd046c14f1ad bfc2 (accessed 3 March 2004); Vanessa Hua, 'Oakland Museum Show Stirs Trouble', *San Francisco Chronicle*, 19 December 2003; and Carol Pogash, 'In Imperfect Compromise, Exhibit Tells of Vietnam Era', *New York Times*, 7 September 2004. The exhibition and the case of Mimi Nguyen are also treated in Loan Dao, 'What's Going On with the Oakland Museum's "California and the Vietnam Era" Exhibit?' *Amerasia Journal* 31, no. 2 (2005), 88–106.

40. On the museum's response to the protest over Nguyen's dismissal, see Nishioka, 'Inclusive or Exclusive?'; Hua, 'Oakland Museum Show Stirs Trouble'; and Pogash, 'In Imperfect Compromise, Exhibit Tells of Vietnam Era'.

41. The text of the petition, the signatures, and the comments, including those of Que H. Le (No. 101) and Lien Ton That (No. 200) discussing the Hue Massacre, were at www. petitiononline.com/111403/petition.html (accessed 13 March 2004). The petition can now be found online at the Internet Archive (though without the signatures and comments); http://web.archive.org/web/20040329154925/http://www.petitiononline. com/111403/petition.html (accessed 22 July 2011).

CHAPTER 17

A BATTLE FOR PERCEPTIONS: REVISITING THE CASSINGA CONTROVERSY IN SOUTHERN AFRICA

Gary Baines

The name Cassinga (or Kassinga) came to the attention of the world a little more than thirty years ago. At the time it evoked a range of responses, from outrage to grief to the celebration of military bravado. The name still provokes strong reactions among those who have a stake in a particular version of the Cassinga story. According to the South African Defence Force (SADF), it launched a cross-border strike against a South West Africa People's Organization (SWAPO) training base in Angola. The strike targetted 'terrorists' and the success of the mission was measured in terms of its achieving strategic military goals. If there were civilian casualties this did not detract from the success of the mission. SWAPO's account is altogether different. According to the liberation movement's version, those killed were innocent women and children, and Cassinga was a 'massacre' on a par with atrocities such as Guernica, Nanking and My Lai.

This chapter will examine how the events of 4 May 1978 have been narrated by the SADF and SWAPO respectively. Narratives use not only words but frequently employ images (or visual language) to convey their meanings. They are generated in order to explain, rationalize, and frame events. Participants in the operation have a vested interest in preserving the story that it was a daring exploit without parallel in the annals of South African military history whereas survivors of the 'massacre' have adopted SWAPO's narrative that holds that the deaths of those in the camp was a necessary sacrifice for the making of the new nation of Namibia. Members of these opposing interest or warring groups have attempted to appropriate Cassinga for their own purposes. The struggle to fix the meaning of Cassinga extends into the (overlapping) spheres of political polemics, public discourse, and scholarly debate. The Cassinga controversy is the South African/Namibian equivalent of Australia's 'history wars'[1] or a 'battle for perceptions' in which an ideological contest between competing versions of (past) events is waged.[2]

In his introduction to *The Massacre in History*, Mark Levene asked (rhetorically?) whether it is the historian's role to adjudicate between competing versions of the truth. He further asked whether the historian is capable of cutting through the mythic accretions that attach themselves to massacres and provide a thorough and comprehensive investigation of the event itself.[3] I think that rather than attempting to establish the veracity of historical facts, a more productive approach is to interrogate competing narratives about past events in order to understand how history is used (and abused). The past, especially when it comes to controversial episodes such as massacres, is highly contested. So it is incumbent upon the historian to try to understand how history and memory are used or manipulated by stakeholders, opposing groups and even enemies when they seek to construct their versions of the past and to discredit the stories of others.

The contestation over meaning and memory thus amounts to a battle *for* Cassinga. The name Cassinga is a floating signifier (in the Barthesian sense) that attaches itself to a chain of meanings. Meanings are partly determined by other words with which it is associated. So when Cassinga is used in conjunction with 'battle', it suggests an engagement between two (roughly equal) armed forces. This phrase is usually employed by SADF apologists. Other military terms that are frequently used in conjunction with Cassinga include 'assault', 'attack' and 'raid'. Such terms imply that the operation was a strike on an enemy base and, as such, a legitimate act of warfare. The use of these terms implies no moral judgment of SADF actions because (so the argument goes) in a war situation it is not always possible to distinguish between civilians and combatants, and civilian casualties are regarded as an unfortunate but unavoidable by-product of military operations – what the Americans euphemistically call 'collateral damage'.[4] Conversely, Cassinga is invariably coupled with the emotive term 'massacre' by SWAPO and its sympathizers. This term implies the purposeful killing of innocent civilians, especially unarmed women and children. It also implies moral condemnation.

The SADF Story

The SADF version of events goes something like this. On 4 May 1978, it launched Operation Reindeer, a three-pronged attack on targets in southern Angola from Namibia. The town of Cassinga, situated 250 km north of the Namibian border, was the primary target as it was the main operational base of SWAPO in the region. SADF aerial reconnaissance photographs suggested that it was a well-fortified regional HQ (known as 'Moscow') from which PLAN (People's Liberation Army of Namibia, SWAPO's armed wing) soldiers infiltrated Namibia. The objective was to destroy this base and capture PLAN commander Dimo Hamaambo, as well as to disrupt SWAPO's supply lines to the Namibian border. Cassinga was strafed by Alpha anti-personnel bombs and 30mm cannons. This was followed by an airborne assault that resembled a standard vertical envelopment operation without armoured support.[5] Transport planes dropped 370 paratroopers in the vicinity of the target. The drop went slightly awry with some troops landing in the SWAPO camp and others landing in and across the Cubango river to the west of the town and then having to regroup for the attack on the base. The main assault group encountered fierce resistance from SWAPO cadres who employed anti-aircraft (AA) guns (visual and anecdotal evidence suggests that two AA guns were incapacitated by the initial SAAF bombing of the camp), machine guns and small arms. Following a protracted firefight the objective was secured, documents seized, munitions destroyed, and some SWAPO prisoners rounded up. But before evacuation could proceed, a combined Cuban-FAPLA (Popular Armed Forces for the Liberation of Angola) force of armoured cars and tanks from the nearby base of Techumatete approached. Fighter jets were recalled to blunt the counter-attack and their timely intervention enabled the paratroopers to hastily board helicopters. Casualties amounted to approximately 600 dead and many more wounded among the inhabitants of Cassinga, eighteen Cuban/FAPLA soldiers killed and sixty-three wounded, and four of their own paratroopers killed and eleven wounded.[6] The SADF claimed its pre-emptive strike against 'terrorists' was justified on account of SWAPO's increased border violations and the assassination of Herero chief Clemens Kapuuo.[7] It had dealt SWAPO a mortal blow

There is no official history of Cassinga but an account by Willem Steenkamp amounts to a semi-official or SADF-sanctioned chronicle of the event.[8] A former military correspondent, sometime national serviceman and citizen force reservist, Steenkamp can be regarded as an embedded journalist. He glamorizes the Cassinga story as an exceptional military endeavour by citizen force soldiers and reservists. He is effusive in his praise for the paratroopers' contingent planning after the chaotic drop, which meant that they had to change their axis of attack. Steenkamp's account is peppered with descriptions of acts of heroism befitting the conduct of the paratroopers, as well as gallantry of the pilots of fighter planes and helicopters. His triumphalist narrative is essentially a tribute to South Africa's military capabilities. Steenkamp does not ask difficult questions about the timing of Operation Reindeer nor of the motives of the Minister of Defence, P.W. Botha and the SADF leadership in scuttling the negotiations sponsored by the Western Five to secure an internationally acceptable solution of the Namibian issue. He is content to repeat Pretoria's official explanations for the Cassinga attack.

Many accounts of Cassinga on the internet have been written by former SADF personnel who offer little or no contextualization of their stories. A good example is an anonymous and fairly detailed entry in Wikipedia which displays insider knowledge of SADF planning and obvious familiarity with Operation Reindeer; it can be safely deduced that this piece is the work of a SADF paratrooper.[9] It proclaims the result of the Battle of Cassinga a 'decisive victory for South Africa'. The outcome is measured by means of a body count ratio of 4:600. These casualty figures suggest a one-sided or unequal engagement notwithstanding the acknowledgment of the bravery of the SWAPO and Cuban soldiers. Such accounts emphasize that Cassinga was a battle that was waged by two armed forces, and does not entertain the idea that the SADF might have killed civilians, let alone committed war crimes. Many veterans continue to believe that the SADF was somehow above politics and beyond reproach for its conduct, and that they were simply doing their duty.

Colonel Jan Breytenbach, who commanded the troops on the ground during Operation Reindeer, insists that most of the SWAPO dead were killed during trench-clearing. He points to SADF photographic evidence to back up this claim.[10] He asserts that combatants outnumbered civilians in Casssinga and that they put up a spirited resistance against his men. In Breytenbach's published account, though, PLAN cadres are simultaneously applauded for their bravery and maligned as cowards for using civilians as human shields to protect themselves. Breytenbach believes that the civilians (including schoolchildren) were abductees rather than refugees, having been force-marched or transported against their will from Namibia to the SWAPO base in southern Angola. He observes sarcastically that the 'refugees' were well armed with a variety of weapons, including 14.5mm AA guns, 12.7mm heavy machine guns, 82mm mortars, RPG-7s and AK-47s. He also notes that Cassinga housed an arsenal of weapons of almost every calibre that he instructed should be blown up. The cumulative weight of such claims lends credence to the argument that Cassinga was an operational military base and not a camp for refugees. This implies that the inhabitants of Cassinga were neither unarmed nor defenceless. In fact, Breytenbach has no qualms about his participation in the operation and his exhaustive account savages his detractors and dismisses as unashamed propaganda SWAPO's depiction of Cassinga as a 'massacre'.[11]

Retired SADF generals have acknowledged that civilians may have been killed at Cassinga but reject with contempt SWAPO allegations of a 'gross massacre of innocents'.[12] They refused to cooperate with the Truth & Reconciliation Commission (TRC) in its efforts to document this and other operations in which the SADF were involved. Most refused to testify for fear of implicating themselves in human rights violations. Certain former generals also acted as gatekeepers for SADF soldiers who might have testified before the TRC. In the event, the only soldier who testified about Cassinga was Sergeant 'Rig' Verster, an ex-SADF Special Forces officer who participated in the assault. His testimony was undoubtedly solipsistic and self-serving as it was designed to elicit sympathy from the commissioners by depicting himself as a victim of circumstances: 'I don't know if I must apply for amnesty for Kassinga. It was probably the most bloody exercise that we ever launched... It was a terrible thing. I saw many things that happened there but I don't want to talk about it now because I always start crying about it. It's damaged my life.'[13]

Verster declined to elaborate on what he had witnessed or participated in on that fateful day, nor did he incriminate himself or implicate his fellow troops in atrocities. But previously he had confessed to executing wounded survivors at the behest of his superiors.[14] His statement is as close as any of the paratroopers have come to an admission of culpability for the wanton murder of civilians (or POWs) at Cassinga,[15] but it has not been independently verified. And because Verster was known to have participated in 'third force' and criminal activities such as political assassinations, extortion and drug smuggling, and to have been convicted for murder, his record tends to cast doubt on his bona fides. His erstwhile comrades are unanimous in denouncing Verster (rather than his testimony). Whilst they have clearly closed ranks against a 'renegade', this does not necessarily prove that a code of silence prevails among them.

Apologists for the SADF are also to be found among conservative historians. Leo Barnard of the History Department at the University of the Free State has published a number of articles on Cassinga.[16] Barnard is sceptical of SWAPO accounts because they make no mention of military installations, and the presence of PLAN combatants notwithstanding evidence to the contrary. He is equally suspicious of Cuban accounts that ignore their engagement with SADF forces at Cassinga and disclaim knowledge of any losses. He is more inclined to believe SADF accounts that tally with the documents he has consulted and the stories of participants whom he has interviewed. But Barnard's faith in his sources rests on his naïve invocation of 'scientific objectivity'. When he argues that articles such as his own are 'based on highly academic reasoning with full reference to the sources used' by a professional historian who has conducted years of research on the subject, then the reader is supposed to accept that expertise qualifies him to provide a definitive account of events. And when Barnard asks readers to accept that the 'personal experience of people who were involved in the war effort' provides such accounts with the credibility accorded to witnesses, then they are supposed to accept this formulation at face value. But these assumptions are flawed and have been thoroughly discredited. There is now widespread recognition in the profession that historical knowledge is constructed and that neither expertise nor closeness to the events necessarily guarantees an authoritative account of the past. The veracity of the SADF's version of events can be no more vouchsafed than that of SWAPO or Cuban narrators by appealing to objectivity.

McGill Alexander's dissertation on Cassinga has caused a considerable furore in the ranks of retired SADF paratroopers. As a former paratrooper himself, his opinions have been more closely studied than pronouncements by SWAPO spokespersons. Whilst wishing to focus on strategic and tactical aspects of the military operation, he found it impossible to disengage from the controversy that followed the events of 4 May 1978. He notes numerous inconsistencies in the standard SWAPO version that was disseminated by the international media. However, his effort to achieve balance is compromised by a failure to locate and interview survivors, as well as an inability to secure the cooperation of SWAPO military personnel to answer his queries. On the other hand, Alexander had access to declassified SADF documents that accorded him a privileged insight into the SADF's logistical planning of the operation. However, he does point out certain anomalies in the SADF story and is occasionally critical of the conduct of the paratroopers. Consequently, he has been taken to task by self-styled 'Cassinga veterans'. Retired SADF captain, Tommie Lamprecht, accused Alexander of betraying his fellow parabats,[17] and members of the Legion of Associated Airborne R.S.A. (LAARSA) condemned his dissertation 'as it cast aspersions on the good name and character of the South African paratrooper'.[18] Whilst LAARSA could hardly claim to speak on behalf of the country's elite fighting force, the mere fact that its members declared a former commanding officer persona non grata is an indicator of how much they had vested in their reputation as soldiers and the integrity of their Cassinga story.

Alexander also contends that most of casualties were caused by the bombing and strafing of Cassinga rather than the ground fighting. The air strike was apparently timed to coincide with the early morning parade when inhabitants of the camp assembled in order to be assigned their daily tasks. The death toll caused by the air strike is a matter of dispute. Alexander (presumably drawing inferences from published eyewitness accounts) suggests that a considerable number of schoolchildren and cadres were killed. He seeks to explain this indiscriminate killing by arguing that the SADF grossly underestimated the number of women and children in the camp and that they had no intention of killing them.[19] Alexander concedes that the technology of mass destruction is likely to cause unavoidable casualties among civilians but he is not prepared to call the act a 'massacre' – especially as the scale of the killing was unintended. In fact, Alexander studiously avoids using the term 'massacre' (except when directly quoting SWAPO sources) and prefers to speak of the 'raid'. However, this is not acceptable to LAARSA members who complain that they have been effectively portrayed as 'mass murderers'. Paratroopers involved in Operation Reindeer certainly do not regard it as an atrocity.[20] This means either that they concocted a story that has remained intact for more than thirty years or that they are telling the truth. However, their version has not gone unchallenged.

The SWAPO Story

After initially claiming to have successfully repulsed the SADF attack and inflicted heavy casualties on the invaders,[21] SWAPO changed its tune and emphasized that the dastardly deed was not a reprisal but aimed at scuppering an imminent political settlement. Subsequent statements issued by SWAPO spokespersons accused the SADF of the 'cold-blooded murder of innocent and unarmed refugees', and 'of massacring the terror stricken population in cold blood'. SWAPO sources stress that the enormity of the death toll shows that the SADF acted with excessive force and unrestrained brutality against 'soft' targets. Claims were made that SAAF planes dispensed poisonous gas and biological weapons prior to the ground attack by the paratroopers, and that once on the ground the paratroopers shot and bayoneted non-combatants. There were also claims that the paratroopers raped some of their victims.[22] Furthermore, it was suggested that the SADF soldiers systematically rounded up and killed all those who had not managed to flee the camp before their arrival and, somewhat contradictorily, it was also said that they took prisoners.[23] Essentially, the SWAPO version of events is that the SADF killed Namibian refugees who had fled their country to escape an illegal and repressive military occupation.

Although SWAPO described Cassinga as a refugee camp and not a military base, the evidence is not clear-cut. Relatively impartial sources suggest that it served a dual rather than an exclusive purpose; that it was a refugee camp-cum-military base.[24] A report of the United Nations International Children's Emergency Fund (UNICEF) published in *The Namibian* newspaper before the SADF raid stated that: 'Although it [Cassinga] housed a considerable number of combatants, including senior officers, it also housed considerable numbers of civilians'.[25] Even partial sources attest to this. SWAPO reported the presence of a three hundred-strong camp defence unit that manned two AA guns.[26] Yet it made no mention elsewhere of these PLAN members. To do so would have rendered Cassinga a site of battle rather than sacrifice.[27] Accordingly, the focus of attention was placed squarely on the defenceless children, women and the elderly who were victims of the SADF attack. By constructing a tale of sacrifice, SWAPO turned its story of Cassinga into a moral – as opposed to a military – one. A narrative coalesced around tropes of the innocence of the Cassinga casualties who became martyrs of the Namibian nation in the making.

The visit of international journalists to Cassinga seemed to confirm the massacre and give credence to SWAPO's version of events. On 8 May, they were shown two mass graves – one an open trench in which 582 victims were awaiting burial and the other covered up and apparently containing the bodies of 122 children.[28] The party of journalists included Gaetano Pagano who photographed the open mass grave. The images of corpses, some of whom are women, some young, and some wearing civilian clothing, are evident to viewers. The most widely disseminated photograph [Illustration 17.1] is a black and white print showing the body of a woman in a dress prominently visible in the foreground and lying on top of a pile of bodies.[29]

Illustration 17.1   Mass grave, Cassinga. Photograph by Gaetano Pagano. Used with the permission of the Basler Afrika Bibliographien. Every effort has been made to trace the copyright holder and to obtain permission for this image.

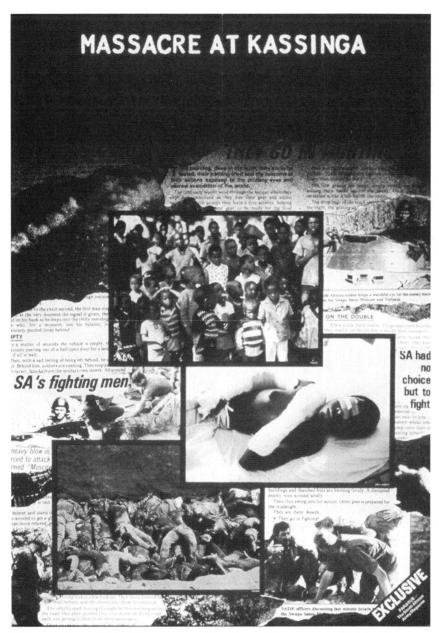

Illustration 17.2   Massacre at Kassinga. Poster compiled by Gaetano Pagano and Sven Asberg for the International University Exchange Fund. Used with the permission of the Basler Afrika Bibliographien. Every effort has been made to trace the copyright holder and to obtain permission for this image.

It was widely syndicated and published by newspapers throughout the world.[30] In June 1978, SWAPO issued a bulletin with the Pagano image on the cover with the byline 'Massacre at Kassinga: climax of Pretoria's all-out campaign against the Namibian resistance'.[31] The picture was also included in the Kassinga File, a collection of images compiled by Pagano and Swedish filmmaker Sven Asberg.[32] The file was distributed to the network of agencies and organizations affiliated to the international anti-apartheid movement. These organizations distributed and displayed the image of the mass grave at public exhibitions and included it in publications. The shot became emblematic of the Cassinga massacre.

The Pagano image was also reproduced on a number of posters commemorating Kassinga Day produced by solidarity organizations such as the International University Exchange Fund (IUEF) and SWAPO's own Department of Information and Publicity. Illustration 17.2, entitled 'Massacre at Kassinga', comprises a montage that foregrounds three colour images presumably of survivors and victims of the massacre.[33] These include the photograph of the mass grave, overlaid on black and white images reproduced from the SADF magazine *Paratus*. The superimposition of the colour images of Cassinga victims and survivors over the black and white images of text and South African soldiers seeks to focus the viewer's attention on the tragic loss of lives. The poster also seems to suggest that the victims were deemed expendable by the South African state intent on imposing the apartheid system on Namibians irrespective of the (human) costs.

On the strength of this imagery of Cassinga and what he has been able to access in archives, Alexander argues that the available visual evidence does not seem to support the contention that 'photographs and videos of the mass graves at Cassinga show almost exclusively corpses of women and children'.[34] This might be so, but it is hardly the point. In propaganda, it is perception rather than reality that matters, and public perceptions of Cassinga were shaped not by the referential but the symbolic value of the mass graves imagery. The graphic nature of the subject matter meant that it resonated with the imagery of mass killing such as the Nazi genocide (or Holocaust). The horrendous sight of a pit piled high with grotesquely twisted bodies in a state of rigor mortis is reminiscent of the images of death camps such as Belsen and Dachau after their liberation by the Allies in 1945. Images of piles of corpses – whether or not women and children were visible – conjured up atrocities or war crimes in the public mind. It was arguably this 'icon of outrage'[35] that 'had a marked effect on public opinion in Western countries' and turned Cassinga into a propaganda coup for SWAPO. And its widespread dissemination demonstrated that Cassinga became synonymous with the murder of innocent victims.

Recollections of survivors have been instrumental in reconstructing the SWAPO story of Cassinga. One such survivor is Ellen Namhila, who in 1978 was a fourteen-year old trainee nurse who happened to be visiting Cassinga at the time of the assault. She describes how she fled the camp during the bombardment and (mysteriously) fell asleep. She gives no indication that she personally witnessed the paratroopers' actions and is altogether vague on the details of the episode except to say that she was helped across the [Cubango?] river by a captain Kanhana.[36] The mention of the man's rank would seem to suggest that he was a PLAN cadre who also sought to escape during the confusion caused by the SADF assault in Cassinga. He was presumably armed. But in a recent letter to *The Sunday Independent*, Namhila categorically denies that Cassinga was a military base or that camp personnel carried weapons.[37] Like many of the Cassinga survivors, Namhila became a political activist who owes her education and job security to SWAPO. Survivors' stories have been appropriated by the ruling party in the construction of the nationalist narrative of martyrdom. And survivors themselves have a reciprocal interest in perpetuating SWAPO's Cassinga story.

A study published in 1994 under the auspices of the Namibian National Archives uses the ostensibly neutral term 'event' rather than 'massacre' in relation to Cassinga.[38] Annemarie Heywood's language is more restrained in its treatment of the topic than most previous publications by SWAPO apologists.[39] She wishes to avoid being regarded as biased or partial by virtue of her commitment to tried and tested methods of primary research. But her interrogation of extant evidence seeks to confirm that SWAPO's story is, for the most part, incontrovertible. What Heywood's work really lacks, though, is an appreciation of what Cassinga has come to mean for Namibia's narrative of nationhood, an appreciation that for SWAPO its symbolic value outweighs the organization's endorsement of her historical project committed to establishing the 'full and sober truth'. As far as SWAPO is concerned, political expediency trumps truth as what actually happened is often of less significance than how it is remembered.

After independence SWAPO proclaimed 4 May a public holiday and Namibians were prevailed upon to 'Remember Kassinga'. Along with Independence Day (21 March) and Heroes Day (26 August), Cassinga Day is part of a ritualized political re-enactment of the postcolonial Namibian liturgical year.[40] Cassinga Day is staged to commemorate the victims who have come to epitomize martyrs of the liberation struggle who made the sacrifices necessary to build a new nation. Indeed, Cassinga has become part of the founding myth of the Namibian nation. Its officially-designated founding father, President Sam Nujoma, repeatedly reinforced the idea that victims of the national liberation struggle embodied the supreme sacrifice for the nation in public speeches given on Cassinga Day and other occasions. Nujoma's rhetorical flourishes and (error-prone) descriptions of events set the tone by according due deference to those killed by 'the Boers' (read 'racist white Afrikaners').[41] Given that SWAPO exercizes extensive control of the media and there are no other groups competing for ownership of the Cassinga story, there is not much space to challenge the hegemonic version that prevails in Namibian public discourse.

However, the ruling party still deems it necessary to counter what Nujoma described as the enemy's 'disinformation campaign aimed at convincing world public opinion that Cassinga served as PLAN's military headquarters and that the victims were armed combatants'.[42] This statement appeared in a foreword to a booklet with a cover portrait that shows Nujoma holding a child, purportedly an orphan and one of the survivors of the massacre. Nujoma does not actually identify 'the enemy' but indicts the racist South African colonial army for its indiscriminate killing of women and children. The text was co-authored by a Namibian journalist and a Swedish political scientist, the latter having served on the UNHCR/WHO delegation that had visited the Cassinga site shortly after the attack. The 'untold story' of the sub-title presumably refers to the voices of the survivors – the testimonies of sixteen victims of the massacre. Although the booklet's blurb makes much of the fact that the stories are first-hand accounts of the survivors' experiences, they give the impression of being well-rehearsed stories that reiterate certain themes such as the brutality of the SADF soldiers who bayoneted and shot wounded refugees at close quarters. Certain of the stories repeat Nujoma's (unsubstantiated) claim that the SAAF planes emitted poisonous gas or chemical agent priors to the airborne assault. The repetition of such themes in survivors' stories might suggest a desire to embrace SWAPO's version of events. On the other hand, their contradictions and inaccuracies might be attributed to their experience of a traumatic life-threatening situation. Survivors are likely to remember the events of 4 May 1978 differently from perpetrators. Memory is, after all, selective and fashioned by personal and political agendas.

Conclusion: Complicating the Issue

Alexander believes that (apartheid) South Africa won the military battle for Cassinga but lost the propaganda war to the ANC and SWAPO. He laments the way in which the liberation movements have come to exercise a monopoly over the Cassinga story. He holds that: 'The victors of the liberation struggle, whose refrain is now the official voice, appear to have triumphed in their version of events. Those who espouse the SADF version are largely seen as discredited adherents of a regime based on lies.'[43] Alexander's assertion is presumably based on the adage that winners write the history books. In fact, the struggle over who gets to rewrite history is far more complicated.[44] Most contemporary transitions to democracy do not have clear winners and losers.[45] In southern Africa the liberation armies emerged as 'victors' but this has not necessarily meant that the 'vanquished' have been altogether silenced – something attested to by their access to the public sphere and cyberspace. Moreover, the story of Cassinga as related by combat veterans, retired SADF generals or military aficionados still appears in local bookstores. And as long as the SADF story is able to compete with the official Namibian narrative of the war of liberation, the battle *for* Cassinga will continue.

Whilst SWAPO may have successfully prevented Cassinga counter-narratives which challenged its hegemony in Namibia, it has been unable to do so beyond the country. For instance, South African para-troopers celebrated the Cassinga raid until 1996 when the ANC government put paid to that practice.[46] Although the ANC felt obliged to apologize to Namibia for the conduct of its soldiers, the ruling party has not managed to prevent organizations such as LAARSA from celebrating 'Cassinga Day'. Nor does it have quite the same vested interest as SWAPO in establishing a master narrative of the Namibian war of liberation. The solidarity between the (former) liberation movements does not necessarily extend to constructing a shared version of the past. This much is evident from the work of the TRC. Overall, the report paid relatively little attention to the apartheid regime's war of destabilization against the frontline states. Nonetheless, it singled out Cassinga as the most controversial external military operation undertaken by the SADF during the period covered by its brief.[47] The report condemned Operation Reindeer as a violation of Angolan territorial integrity launched from illegally-occupied Namibia and a gross violation of human rights. It added that the raid 'violated international humanitarian law on other counts, one of which was the failure to take adequate steps to protect the lives of civilians'. It asserted that the SADF took no heed of the doctrine of non-combatant immunity and by its actions on this and other occasions breached its own protocols. However, former generals insist that they observed the rules of engagement despite not officially being at war with SWAPO and that the SADF's code of conduct was strictly enforced in the ranks – notwithstanding the fact that South Africa did not ratify the 1977 addition to the Geneva Protocol that accorded captured 'freedom fighters' the status of POWs. Although members of the SADF occasionally abused and tortured those described as 'terrorists', there was only a solitary dubious admission of culpability for wrongdoing by a SADF paratrooper at Cassinga.

Cassinga will continue to elicit varied responses as long as participants and survivors are alive and the events remain part of living memory. This much is abundantly clear from the conflicting accounts of Cassinga that have been constructed by the SADF and SWAPO. Whilst the writer of a report headlined 'Battle of Cassinga still rages' published on the twenty-ninth anniversary might have used an incorrect preposition, there can be no doubt that he was correct to suggest that the events are still mired in controversy.[48] The battle *for* Cassinga has been complicated by the intersections and intricacies of the political transitions in South Africa and its neighbouring states (especially in Namibia and Angola). Is this battle likely to have a winner and a loser?

If so, will the winner determine the manner in which the event is to be narrated? Will the outcome of this battle shape the rhetoric of the dominant culture? Kali Tel holds that if the dominant culture manages to appropriate the story and can codify it in its own terms, the status quo will remain unchanged.[49] But this begs the question, what is the dominant culture in postcolonial southern Africa? If this were apparent would we be in a better position to determine whether Cassinga will be remembered as a massacre or a military operation?

Notes

1. Stuart Macintyre and Anna Clark (eds), *The History Wars* (Melbourne, 2003).
2. Deborah Posel, 'Symbolizing Violence: State and Media Discourse in Television Coverage of Township Protest, 1985-87', in N. Chabani Manganyi and Andre du Toit (eds), *Political Violence and the Struggle in South Africa* (Basingstoke, 1990), 154.
3. Mark Levene, 'Introduction', in Mark Levene and Penny Roberts (eds), *The Massacre in History* (Oxford, 1999), 3.
4. For expositions of the derivation and morality of this notion, see Sahr Conway-Lanz, *Collateral Damage: Americans, Noncombatant Immunity, and Atrocity after World War II* (New York, 2006); William Andrew Myers, 'How Civilians Became Targets: The Moral Catastrophe of "Collateral Damage"', http://www.inter-disciplinary.net/ati/Evil/Evil%207/myers%20paper.pdf
5. Edward George McGill Alexander, 'The Cassinga Raid' (MA Thesis, UNISA, 2003).
6. These figures vary considerably according to their sources. The SADF based its figures of enemy losses on intercepted and monitored communications. SWAPO statements inflated the number of casualties in order to emphasize the enormity of the slaughter. Cuban sources initially denied any involvement and later downplayed their losses. The TRC estimated a death toll of at least a thousand, a figure that includes 150 Cubans. See *Truth and Reconciliation Commission of South Africa Report* (Cape Town, 1998), 51. Piero Gleijeses, 'The Massacre of Cassinga', who has had access to Cuban sources, confirms the extent of their losses. See http://amadlandawonye.wikispaces.com/The+Massacre+of+Cassinga,+Piero+Gleijeses (accessed 26 November 2007).
7. Documentary evidence reveals that the South African security forces created incidents to justify the operation. See Jan-Bart Gewald, 'Who Killed Clemens Kapuuo?', *Journal of Southern African Studies*, 30 (2004), 571–73.
8. Willem Steenkamp, *Borderstrike! South Africa into Angola* (Durban, 1983), 15–141.
9. 'Battle of Cassinga', http://en.wikipedia.org/wiki/battle_of_Cassinga (accessed 18 September 2007).
10. Interview with Colonel (ret) Jan Breytenbach, Sedgefield, 30 April 2008. The photographs were taken by Mike McWilliams.
11. Jan Breytenbach, *Eagle Strike! The Story of the Controversial Airborne Assault on Cassinga 1978* (Sandton, 2008), passim. It should be noted that his real target is not SWAPO but Alexander who is accused of betraying his brothers in arms. See below.
12. See, for instance, Jannie Geldenhuys, *A General's Story: From an Era of War and Peace* (Johannesburg, 1995), 72; Magnus Malan, *My Life with the SA Defence Force* (Protoria, 2006), 193.
13. Testimony of Lieutenant Johan Frederick Verster to the TRC, 4 July 1977.
14. *The Star*, 8 May 1993 ('Haunted by a Mother's Look'), cited in Annemarie Heywood, *The Cassinga Event* (Windhoek, 1994), 34–35.
15. *TRC Report*, V.2, 44.
16. Leo Barnard, 'Die Gebeurte by Cassinga, 4 Mei 1978 – 'n Gevallestudie van die Probleme van 'n Militêre Historikus', *Historia* (May 1996), 88–99; 'The Battle of Cassinga,

4 May 1978: A Historical Reassessment Part 1: The Course of the Battle and Ensuing Controversy', *Journal for Contemporary History*, 31 (December 2006), 131–46; 'The Battle of Cassinga, 4 May 1978: A Historical Reassessment Part 2: Interviews with Two SADF Soldiers', *Journal for Contemporary History*, 31 (2006), 147–60.

17. Tommie Lamprecht to McGill Alexander on Cassinga, 4 June 2007.

18. Unsigned letter from LAARSA to Brig. Gen. (ret) McGill Alexander, 1 December 2007.

19. Alexander, 'The Cassinga Raid', 186.

20. Edward George, *The Cuban Intervention in Angola, 1965–1991: From Che Guevera to Cuito Cuanavale* (London, 2005), 135.

21. SWAPO spokesman Peter Katjavivi cited in *The Cape Times*, 6 May 1978 ('5 Die as SA Hits Swapo Bases').

22. Such claims were first made in SWAPO's Special Bulletin, *Massacre at Kassinga, – Climax of Pretoria's All-Out Campaign against the Namibian Resistance* (Stockholm, 1978), 17. The reference to a 'sticky inflammable phosphate liquid' placed on the ground sounds like napalm, but Alexander ('The Cassinga Raid', 150) discounts this. I have found reference to the use of napalm in sitreps (situation reports) documenting later SAAF air strikes in Angola but nothing to suggest its use during Operation Reindeer. Some survivors recount that they were rendered unconscious by a poisonous gas but the use of a substance that immobilized people has been dismissed as pure fiction by SADF paratroopers who were not issued with gas masks. Such tactics would also have delayed their own deployment in Cassinga. The SADF's own evidence regarding the use of bayonets is contradictory.

23. Those captured at Cassinga were left behind but the SADF raids on Chetequera and Dombondola netted over one hundred prisoners who erroneously became known as the 'Kassinga detainees'. Despite being relocated to camps where supervised Red Cross inspections were carried out, many of these prisoners were reportedly subjected to torture during lengthy incarceration. There were also reports of the bodies of victims being dumped into the sea from helicopters. The 'Kassinga detainees' became a matter of grave concern for the international community. See *International Development Aid Fund (IDAF) Focus*, 23 July–August 1978, 16 ('Cassinga Raid'), *IDAF Focus* 28, May–June 1980, 10 ('Kassinga Detainees'), *IDAF Focus* 29, July–August 1980, 8 ('Detainees Visited').

24. *TRC Report*, v. 2, 50.

25. *The Namibian*, 2 May 1978.

26. *Massacre at Kassinga*, 20.

27. For obvious reasons there are no accounts of the fateful day by SWAPO combatants. There is, however, an account by a 'dissident' – some might say 'renegade' – member of Umkhonto we Sizwe (MK), the ANC's armed wing, whose visit coincided with the SADF assault. He describes Cassinga as a military base where Cuban instructors were training SWAPO guerrillas. See Joseph Kobo, *Waiting in the Wing* (Milton Keynes, 1994), 134.

28. Breytenbach, *Eagle Strike!*, 564, reckons that the covered grave might have been an elaborate con trick. He inquires why SWAPO covered this grave rather than the one with the bodies of combatants when it was seeking to score as much sympathetic publicity as possible.

29. This image appears in Pagano's publication *The Kassinga File* but the East German news agency, AND, claimed that it had been taken by one of their photographers. See Alexander, 'The Cassinga Raid', 170.

30. Basler Afrika Bibliographien (BAB), A.A3, Swapo Collection, 78aSPR2, 16 May 1978.

31. BAB, A.A3, Swapo Collection, 78fSLkPb1, Special Bulletin of SWAPO, Lusaka, June 1978.

32. Published and produced by the IUEF, an NGO that had provided assistance to Namibian refugees and SWAPO since 1963. See BAB, Swapo Collection, 78aSpb7, The Kassinga File.

33. BAB Poster Collection, X 445 'Massacre at Kassinga' which is part of the Kassinga File photographic exhibition, 1978.
34. Alexander, 'The Cassinga Raid', 170 note # 832.
35. David Perlmutter, *Photojournalism and Foreign Policy: Icons of Outrage in International Crises* (Westport, Conn., 1998).
36. Ellen Ndeshi Namhila, *The Price of Freedom* (Windhoek, 1997), 40–41.
37. *The Sunday Independent*, 9 March 2008 ('I Was at Cassinga and it Was Not a Military Base').
38. Heywood, *The Cassinga Event*.
39. See, for instance, D. Herbstein and J. Evenson, *The Devils are Among Us: The War for Namibia* (London, 1989) who are unequivocal in condemning Cassinga as the 'bloodiest massacre of the war'.
40. Heike Becker, '"We Remember Cassinga": Political Ritual, Memory, and Citizenship in Northern Namibia', Unpublished paper, 2008.
41. Nujoma interview in 'Namibia Special Report', *New African*, 423 (November 2003), 8, cited in H. Melber, 'Namibia's Past in the Present: Colonial Genocide and Liberation Struggle in Commemorative Narratives', *South African Historical Journal*, 54 (2005), 102.
42. Foreword to Mvula ya Nangolo and Tor Sellström, *Kassinga: A Story Untold* (Windhoek, 2005), vi.
43. Alexander, 'The Cassinga Raid', 5.
44. See Wolfgang Schivelbusch, *The Culture of Defeat: On National Trauma, Mourning, and Recovery* (London, 2004).
45. Teresa Phelps, *Shattered Voices: Language, Violence and the Work of Truth Commissions* (Philadelphia, 2004), 78.
46. *The Star*, 6 June 1996 ('SA to Say Sorry for Celebrating Defence Force Raid').
47. *TRC Report*, v. 2, 46.
48. *The Star*, 19 May 2007 ('The Battle of Cassinga Still Rages'), http://www.iol.co.za/news/south-africa/battle-of-cassinga-still-rages-1.353716 (accessed 28 September 2007).
49. Kalí Tal, *Worlds of Hurt: Reading the Literatures of Trauma* (Cambridge, 1996), 7, 18–19.

Part IV

The Dynamics of Modern Massacre and Mass Killings

CHAPTER 18

METHOD IN THEIR MADNESS: UNDERSTANDING THE DYNAMICS OF THE ITALIAN MASSACRE OF ETHIOPIAN CIVILIANS, FEBRUARY–MAY 1937

Giuseppe Finaldi

The Massacres of February–May 1937

On 19 February 1937 a ceremony was held outside the seat of the Italian government in Addis Ababa, capital of the newly conquered colony of Ethiopia. It honoured the birth of the first son of Italian heir to the throne Humbert of Savoy; the Viceroy of Ethiopia Marshall Rodolfo Graziani presided. The highest authorities of the new Italian Government handed out small gifts to various Ethiopian dignitaries and petitioners and made the usual speeches. The atmosphere and the activities of the day, as well as the ceremony itself, were not unusual; all colonial governments gave great importance to these small but significant reminders of the official connection between metropolis and far-flung colonial outpost. Graziani and his staff, however, were unaware that that morning security had already broken down. Two men hailing from the territory Italy had designated as Eritrea in 1890 had earlier stolen into what had been former Ethiopian Emperor Haile Sellassie's palace, concealing eight Italian made Breda hand grenades. They had succeeded in mingling with the crowd and climbing up to the first floor balcony overlooking the stairs and platform on which the Italian dignitaries had located their chairs. From here, at around midday, it was child's play to arm and drop the grenades on the tightly packed bigwigs seated below.

As might be imagined, the result was mayhem. Seven people were killed and more than fifty wounded. Graziani himself was painfully peppered with shrapnel, and various other dignitaries, including the Vice-Governor of the colony, three generals, two colonels, the governor of Addis Ababa, and a visiting Italian Member of Parliament were rushed to hospital. Italian soldiers caught unawares, without orders and panicking, began indiscriminately firing into the tightly massed crowd of Ethiopian onlookers, killing an unknown number. In the blood-soaked chaos the two bombers were able to escape to a waiting Opel car parked outside the palace compound and from there left Addis Ababa making their way to the Coptic monastery of Debra Libanos, about 100 kilometres from the Ethiopian capital.[1]

From his hospital bed Graziani unleashed a general 'reprisal' which took on the character of what was to occur on a regular basis in German-occupied Poland and Russia in the not too distant future.[2] Italian police, Blackshirts, soldiers and civilians rampaged through the city shooting, bombing or clubbing anyone they could get their hands on. No attempt to verify a relationship with the morning's act of terror was made; it was sufficient to belong to the same racial category as the 'terrorists' to become targets of homicide. The number of innocent Ethiopians murdered over the next few days is estimated to be as high as fifteen thousand. When the Italian blood lust died down a carefully planned project to liquidate the Ethiopian nobility, Coptic clergymen and even street storytellers (considered to be responsible for spreading anti-Italian sentiment among the populace at large) was implemented, leading to thousands of further killings. Graziani himself toyed with the idea of completely destroying the native quarters of Addis Ababa but stopped short for 'strategic' reasons. As the smoke of burning huts lifted and the bodies in the streets were cleared, the Ethiopians who had witnessed the Italian 'madness' must have realized that their newly acquired *padroni* (Italian troops had entered the Ethiopian capital less than a year before) were going to be harsh masters in fulfilling their promise to bring Civilization to the only part of Africa which had so far avoided any form of European tutelage. Some took to the hills, as so many Italians were to do after Germany occupied Italy in 1943, and joined the Ethiopian resistance movement; others, reluctantly or not, acquiesced to the new order.

In a seminal interpretation of the Addis Ababa massacre,[3] Giorgio Rochat emphasized the 'Fascist' character of what had occurred. Ian Campbell, who has certainly studied the events surrounding Italian atrocities in Ethiopia more thoroughly than anyone, has also published works on what he termed 'Fascist repression'.[4] Ken Kirby's noteworthy 1989 BBC documentary on Italian atrocities in Ethiopia and Yugoslavia (he also denounces the fact that no one, including Graziani, was ever

called to account for crimes perpetrated in Africa) also insisted on calling Italian brutality a 'Fascist Legacy'.[5] Angelo Del Boca has edited a
book, more ambiguously entitled 'Fascism's Colonial Wars',[6] in which
he makes it clear how he distinguishes Fascist from liberal-democratic
colonialism (before Mussolini's dictatorship began in 1922 Italy had
already been a minor colonial power for forty years). Del Boca suggests that the difference between the two lay not so much in the fact
that 'liberal' Italian colonizers tried to be good and Fascist ones did
not, but because the structures with the potential to bridle or mitigate
state sponsored violence in Fascist Italy had been silenced. There was
no opposition, no anti-government newspapers, and no questions could
be raised in parliament; hence, says Del Boca, 'Assured that they were
safe from all criticism and relying on the government's total silence, the
[Fascist] colonial military apparatus acted with extreme determination
and was prepared to use any means, legitimate or illegitimate, to obtain
its ends'.[7] Del Boca also stresses the importance of Mussolini himself
whom he sees as 'the supreme director'[8] of African policy, only rarely
asking for advice and always pushing for radical action on the part of his
representatives on the spot. No parallel to the personal (almost obses-
sive) control of the *Duce* is to be found in the colonialism of liberal Italy.

But was the February 1937 massacre really Fascism at work?
According to one Italian eyewitness it would appear that it did not take
much political conviction to get 'normal' Italians to incriminate themselves. But of course there was no incrimination: 'In general', this eyewitness recounts,

> they would set fire to a Tucul [Ethiopian house] with petrol and then throw
> hand grenades at the people trying to get out. I heard one man bragging
> that he had 'done ten Tuculs' with only one jerry can of petrol. Another
> complained how tired his right arm was with all the grenades he had thrown.
> I knew a lot of these men personally. They were shopkeepers, businessmen,
> drivers, and office workers; people who I considered to be completely respect-
> able; people who hadn't fired a single shot during the war and that were now
> full of rancour and capable of unsuspected violence. The fact is that they
> could do what they liked without risk of punishment. The only risk was being
> awarded a medal.

Another eyewitness, placing more emphasis on Fascism, described that
night thus:

> All the [Italian] civilians in Addis Ababa took on the role of avengers in the
> most authentic style of Fascist squadism. They roamed around the town
> armed with clubs or iron bars killing any Ethiopians to be found in the
> streets. I saw a driver who, having knocked down an old Negro, shoved a
> bayonet right through his head. It goes without saying that this was a mas-
> sacre of innocent people.[9]

'Squadism' refers to the origins of the Fascist movement in the early 1920s when motorized 'squads' of Blackshirts terrorized socialist peasants or Slav nationalists in Italy, providing the impetus for Mussolini's rise to power. One Fascist residing in Addis Ababa proudly announced that on the afternoon of 19 February 'they [the Fascists] had in an instant transformed the masses of [Italian] workers in armed squads ready for action'.[10] In this case had all the 'masses of workers' residing in Addis Ababa become Fascist or rather had they merely been organized by Fascists into squads? Either answer is of course plausible.

The culling of the Ethiopian clergy in the weeks that followed the attack on Graziani was of an altogether different character to the cudgelling and force-feeding with castor oil that had been the speciality of Fascist thugs in the early days. The occupants of the large convent of Debra Libanos were literally wiped out. In a similar story to that of the Italians who resisted the Germans on the island of Cephalonia in 1943 (around five thousand were, in what had become a German tradition, rounded up and machine gunned), the monks and their attendants, as well as a number of beggars and cripples who were hanging around the monastery, were brought out into the countryside and shot. Graziani had specifically ensured that the massacre (20–25 May) should take place when the convent was at its busiest, and the days celebrating Debra Libanos' thirteenth-century founder, Saint Tekle Haymanot, were considered the most appropriate. Many pilgrims witnessed the murders or were themselves swept into the orgy of bloodletting. A reprieve for clerical novices, herded into a makeshift camp, was rescinded after a few days and these boys, some little more than children, were also murdered and their bodies heaped in mass graves. Ian Campbell puts the total number of executed in the harrowing of Debra Libanos at close to two thousand.[11] Meanwhile any Ethiopians in Italian custody who had travelled abroad, deemed therefore to belong to a threatening intelligentsia, were also summarily executed.[12] The Amhara nobility, long the backbone of the Ethiopian ruling class, were culled as being irreconcilably inimical to the new Italian order.

In Addis Ababa on 21 February (so after two days of murderous havoc wreaked by 'maddened' Italians) the head of the Fascist party in Addis Ababa printed and distributed the following on a 'glossy' leaflet: 'Comrades! I order that at midday today the 21 February XV [year of Fascism] all acts of reprisal will cease... Extremely severe sanctions will be imposed on transgressors.'[13] On seeing these leaflets one Italian said he 'could not believe his eyes! After a massacre like that how could they put documents like that around? They were a clear admission of guilt.'[14] The 'Fascist' was clearly indifferent to the fact that he was printing a paper trail leading to his own men for their 'reprisals'; the other Italian was more perturbed, concerned that the massacre should not be remembered as a 'reprisal' on printed paper, although he may well have gone along with the idea that after the Graziani bombing the native population of Ethiopia should not celebrate having come so close to flouting Italian authority.

When things did calm down, the dead numbered in the region of twenty thousand, although there is some debate as to the exact figure. Considering that the bomb plot to murder Graziani had involved only two men plus another accomplice who had driven them to Debra Libanos (they had escaped well before the Italian round-up at the monastery began), this scale of violence needs explaining. Why were Italians prepared to perpetrate a bloodbath of such magnitude? What motivated their actions and allowed them to behave as they did? What were the dynamics involved? Can their actions be blamed on 'Fascism'?

The Conquest of Ethiopia: Last Gasp of the Scramble for Africa or First Shot in the European Second World War?

In order to answer such questions we should take up the story at the beginning. What were Italians doing in Addis Ababa in the first place? What justified and energized the madness on the streets of that city in February 1937? In 1935–1936, under Mussolini's guidance, Italy attacked and occupied Ethiopia, the last remaining independent African nation. If forty years earlier the liberal Italian government had had to put aside its ambitions of making the Ethiopian kingdom an Italian colony on the battlefield of Adowa, in May 1936 the *Duce* proclaimed to the Italian people that they were finally the possessors of a worthy Empire. Mussolini could hardly resist the temptation of linking his conquest to those of Italians' illustrious classical antecedents and his speech claimed Empire's 'reappearance' on the 'fatal hills of Rome'. It was a bit late compared to the other European powers, which some historians suggest were already envisaging a big colonial close-down, or at least were at the 'beginning of the end' of Empire[15], but Mussolini or 'his' people were as yet unaware that the historical tide had turned. Others have seen Italy's aggression against Ethiopia rather as the first hot conflict of the European Second World War;[16] following hard on its heels came the Spanish Civil War, then the Anschluss, Munich and of course the invasion of Poland in 1939. Head of the British Foreign office at the height of the Ethiopian crisis, Sir Robert Vannsittart later bewailed the fact that, as he put it: 'because a few Italian colonial troops had died by brackish water-holes in an African waste, was taken the first step to the second German holocaust. The pretext was more trivial than the murder of Franz Ferdinand.'[17]

Italy's invasion of Ethiopia might therefore be seen as the final chapter of the Scramble for Africa or the first episode in what was to unravel as the Second World War. If we categorize it as a last gasp of the European colonial project we must insert its correlated episodes of violence, its visions, its massacres with those of other European colonialisms; if, on the other hand, we see Italy's invasion as the first blow in the Second World War we would be tempted to compare Italian policies with Italian and or German practice in Second World War occupied Europe. The latter view would presuppose that ideology, and in particular 'Fascist' ideology really matters: that is, the violence meted out by Italians in Africa was specifically linked to the new way of thinking inculcated via the Fascist dictatorship at home; the former would perhaps be more keen to associate Italian violence in Africa with such 'normal' (however difficult using this term might be here) issues as European racism, the colonial context, etc.

So, was there anything specifically 'Fascist' about Italy's invasion and occupation of Ethiopia in the 1930s? Was there some substantial difference in the fact that the Italians conquering yet another colony for Europe were doing so under the banner of Fascism rather than some other flag, such as the liberal democratic one? As one famous song whistled by troops heading off to Africa put it: *si va per Mussolini, nell'Africa oriental* ['we're off to East Africa for Mussolini']; but the anonymous writer of this song must also have been hedging his bets because he added a stanza further into the ditty stating that Italians (like the colonial armies which had crossed the Mediterranean before 1922) were also going to the Dark Continent for 'Italy and the King'.[18] But the question remains: was the extraordinary violence of the Italian occupation of the 1930s due to the way in which the agendas and ideology of Fascism had introduced themselves into the mentality of Italians at work in Africa; or rather should we simply talk about colonial contexts, the banalities of evil, that European law was expendable in the tropics? Can we explain the horrific massacres and the killings of so many Ethiopians under Italian occupation as the product of a new 'ideological' way of thinking established in the minds of Italians over the fifteen years that Mussolini's regime had had to mould them, or was no such thing necessary?

The Nature of Fascism and the Invasion of Ethiopia

'Fascism Means War' was a slogan of the Left in the Europe of the 1930s. According to the older view, again of the Left, it had been Capitalism pure and simple which had 'meant war,' but after the coming to power of Hitler in 1933, there was a growing willingness to regard Fascism not simply as yet more capitalism in disguise but as a qualitatively different (and more pernicious) way in which the state exercised its dominion over society. The very existence of Fascism in one nation threatened neighbours and other territories as a given. For those who took this view there could therefore be no long-term co-existence with the Fascist states because it was only a matter of time before their will to conquer would rise inexorably to the surface.[19]

But did Fascism really mean automatic war? On the face of it the great conflict of 1939–1945 would seem to suggest that this is case. Yet Fascist Italy could hardly be accused of international hooliganism before 1935. Mussolini had come to power in 1922 but, barring an 'incident' in Corfu in 1923, had been very well behaved. He may have made those expansive gestures Italians are unable to repress when talking but he had in practice acquiesced to, indeed bolstered, the post First World War international order; Fascist Italy had been a dutiful member of the League of Nations and had signed, like everybody else, the Geneva Convention. So, why this sudden change: an attack on Ethiopia, a League of Nations member in 1935?

In the 1930s, according to some historians, Mussolini's dictatorship had reached a political cul-de-sac. The relative weakness of Fascism when it had come to power in 1922 had forced Mussolini into a series of compromises which limited what Fascism could actually do with the state and society it had inherited. Fascism was, as it were, superimposed on the old political and social order which had preceded it but had failed to radically transform the institutionalized powers which had in the first place called on Mussolini to form a government. The Church, the Italian monarchy, the state and bureaucracy, the armed forces and the old economic elites were still there and Mussolini had done little to dent their dominating presence in Italian society. For all his blustering, what was trumpeted as the 'Fascist Revolution' had ground to a halt, if it had ever really begun at all. Mussolini himself risked redundancy. In particular, with Hitler taking power in 1933 the stakes were suddenly raised. The *Duce* had the choice of presiding over a shoddy and half-hearted dictatorship (leaving the leadership of the 'Fascist' world to the mad man who had taken power over the Alps) or attempting something to enhance his position at home and to prove that his dictatorship was still in the business of 'not giving a damn!' [*me ne frego!* in the words of an old Fascist slogan].

Colonialism, or rather a glittering new Roman Empire, came to the rescue. According to a new spate of histories of Fascist Italian society and foreign policy written by historians such as Emilio Gentile, David Mallet, MacGregor Knox, John Gooch or Davide Rodogno,[20] the Italian shift to Empire in the 1930s was in fact, in the words of Rodogno, an 'essential component of a totalitarian project to transform society'.[21]In this version of the story the drive to Totalitarianism, its associated violence and will to succeed no matter what cost, was embedded in the very DNA of Fascism and, with the invasion of Ethiopia, bubbled to the surface. As John Gooch has recently put it, 'Mussolini was sure that the Fascist masses would back the war, and so would the young. The only people who feared the adventure were the remnants of "the old world" but ... politically and socially they counted for nothing.'[22] Fascism would come into its own at last, connecting to the young and the new and casting aside the old standards and morality of liberal Italy; Mussolini's colonialism was meant to be a new dynamo charging the Fascist revolution on to new heights. The war for the conquest and the transformation of Ethiopia would be different to the old colonialisms of the liberal democratic powers and would be produced by, as well as produce, the 'New Fascist Man'.

The opprobrium of the international community towards Italy's aggression on Ethiopia turned Mussolini's rather sordid and opportunistic Ethiopian campaign into what I like to call a *folie à deux*. Mussolini and the Italian people came together in the face of a perfidious Britain and France, who between them owned around half the globe, and who hypocritically pointed the finger because a small piece of it might do some good to Italy. The conquest of Ethiopia itself was portrayed as Mussolini and Fascism – notwithstanding foreign abhorrence and sabre-rattling – bending to the needs of the Italian people, or rather providing the leadership necessary to satisfy its long-held desires. One well-known image from the campaign, for example, showed Italian soldiers as the 'immigrants' who had in the past been forced to leave their beloved homes, clearly suggesting that the Fascist regime, in contrast to liberal and democratic Italy, was finally providing the living space necessary to contain the vigorous and virile manpower of which Italy abounded and which in the past had gone to enrich the economies of other countries. Indeed, this was to be an empire not just of a white elite (living off the labour of the natives) but a new society of worker-peasant-soldier-settlers, the product of the 'proletarian nation' in the ambiguous phrase coined well before Fascism.

Much was made of Italy's Roman past, supposedly now re-emerging. As Italian troops passed Adowa (and the scenes of the many defeats suffered at the hands of Ethiopia during the liberal period) the dishonour of that moment, what Mussolini had called 'the humiliation of belonging to a white nation that had allowed itself to be defeated by blacks', was finally and permanently ransomed. Ethiopia itself was pictured as a wasteland inhabited by a corrupted people, which awaited the European plough, Italian muscle and ingenuity. The construction of roads, railways and modern cities was to mark every footprint of these new Roman legionaries who, according to propaganda, could switch, like those soldiers of old, from fighting to building to fighting to building in a seamless fusion of the military and the civilizing virtues. The war was also meant to be one of liberation. The rulers of Ethiopia were depicted as slave holding despots and the Ethiopian population, above all the women, crushed by ignorance and poverty, were awaiting with bated breath the arrival of their white saviours: how thankful they would be and how willing to repay their Latin-lover liberators with sexual favours. The war was to be a kind of all-male hunting expedition; the lads going out together for a bit of a binge, taking time out from the tedium of the everyday. Indro Montanelli, a famous journalist in postwar Italy, would always remember the campaign in which he participated as 'a lovely and long holiday given to us by our great Daddy for having spent thirteen long years at school behind a desk'.[23]

The Logic of Massacre in the Italian Colonial Context

Such was one way of remembering instead what Ennio Flaiano, in a novel published in 1949, referred to as Italy's 'time to kill'.[24] For the regime, this conquest was a self-imposed test whose outcome would confirm or deny that Fascism was superior to that other Italy, the liberal one known contemptuously as *Italietta* or 'little Italy'. This was even more the case now that Fascism had been roundly condemned by the democratic powers. The possibility of defeat or that the colonial experiment should fail could simply not be contemplated. The methods used and the amount of wealth and manpower invested in Ethiopia's conquest were a direct consequence of this imperative. It was not so much about forming the Fascist New Man, but much more prosaically that defeat would have extreme consequences on how Fascism had insinuated itself in Italian society and how it was regarded abroad.

So began the 'time to kill,' As the 'civilized' world had already pronounced Italy's war to be illegal, there was little incentive to adhere to gentlemanly rules of conduct. Victory had to be obtained as quickly and as painlessly as possible for Italians. Much scandal was created by the Italian use of mustard gas bombs, which were banned by the Geneva Convention. But the latter, on which so much ink has been spilt over the years,[25] was only a symptom of the Italian attitude throughout the war which quite self-consciously rejected much of the politically correct phraseology of the times. Acquiring the right to rule by simple conquest was no longer the terminology accepted in the League of Nations world. Words and phrases such as 'mandates,' 'trusteeships,' pacifications, restoring the rule of law and such like (but not yet 'imposing democracy') would have been more attuned to the times. But Mussolini, and many Italians, rejected this kind of moral hypocrisy which had given in particular the British a vast empire and all in that 'fit of absence of mind' interpreted outside Britain as stiff-upper lipped perfidiousness. Pronouncing conquests to be 'illegal' after everything conquerable had already been taken was in the order of things as established by the 'haves' of the status quo. In reality this was glory at a bargain price: the Italians involved could fight for the greater glory of their country without much risk of dying themselves. The number of Italian casualties was so low (around four thousand) that they actually had to be falsified upwards to make the war seem worthy of being won. There is evidence that the pleasure of conquest and the gratification of domination were not emotions exclusively held by Mussolini or Fascist bigwigs. A trawl through the many diaries and memoirs of Italian Ethiopian war veterans will certainly provide a catch of phrases replete with Fascist triumphalism.[26]

As Italians marched into Menelik's capital city in 1936 in Rome, as ha been said, Mussolini pronounced one of his most famous speeches. The 'Empire has reappeared on the fatal hills of Rome', he announced to the oceanic crowds of the piazzas of the Eternal City. Historian Emilio Gentile describes that electrifying night in no uncertain terms:

> fourteen years of daily totalitarian propaganda, which had hammered and pervaded every corner of the Italian peninsula, had predisposed every social class, every generation of Italians to believe in the words of the *Duce* and to identify with his ambitions and to feel, that night, fused into one nation, possessed as in a powerful enchantment.[27]

According to this, the 'New Fascist Men' must have been the perpetrators of the killing of probably around 150,000 to 200,000 Ethiopians during the war and under Italian occupation, something that Alexander De Grand puts down to 'Fascist brutality [that] reflected the essential nature of the Fascist movement from its inception. It was no renegade aberration in the African "heart of darkness," but part of the bleakness at the centre of fascism itself.'[28]

However, this view ignores what went to make up the classic European colonial melange of uplifting ideals sordidly implemented. Italians, like most Europeans in the imperial context, concentrated on the former and closed their eyes to the latter, conscious that this was the price to pay for greatness, for the sweeping into modernity of indigenous peoples, or for the European claim on a piece of land that did not belong to it to be made permanent. Conquering Ethiopia's few, small cities was easy and achieved in a few months but effectively controlling this massive and mountainous African territory always eluded Italy in its brief tenure at Addis Ababa.[29] There was never 'peace' in Italy's new colony notwithstanding or perhaps because of the huge number of Ethiopians killed. What we are talking about is how far one should go in the struggle for the preservation of the colony itself. Widespread resistance to Italian rule was endemic over the whole period of the Italian occupation and, as for the French in Algeria and other colonial powers, Italy had to ask itself the simple question: what level of violence would be permitted in the preservation of a particular colony? For Fascist Italy the threshold was very high indeed because failure would in all likelihood have spelled the end of the regime, as the transformation of Ethiopia into Italian East Africa was very self-consciously posited as the great test of Fascism's achievements to date.

Yet in the long run, plans for Ethiopia were modelled on the colonies of settlement as pioneered by Britain in South Africa or France in Algeria. The Italians aimed to transform the colony into a racially segregated society where the top positions would be occupied by white

Italians and the mass of the black population would be forever separate and subservient. The struggle to achieve this was begun almost as soon as Mussolini had declared the Empire 'open' and laws passed to racially segregate the two populations were the natural offshoot of what was in reality a colony wracked by an ongoing civil war. The Italian government was unable to rely on its Italian population to show that effortless superiority which only long decades of colonial rule ensured. This lack of what was referred to as an 'imperial mentality' worried the authorities who felt, especially when it came to working-class Italians, that 'it was imperative to not give the native Ethiopians too much leeway; unfortunately with so many [Italian] workers required out there with their comic and easy manners, many natives would lift their crests and call the white man *arcu* i.e. friend. A few kicks in the right place and we will thankfully hear *goitana, goitana* [boss, boss].'

While it is of course nonsense that Italians were always nice and inherently un-racist, and therefore prepared to muck in with the natives, it is also true that there was a strong need to legislate and to educate Italians abroad into what might be called the colonial frame of mind. The 1937 racial legislation, the plans for a segregated city of Addis Ababa and the extraordinary architecture of colonial Asmara were all part of this overarching imperative.

Conclusion

I return now to the initial question posed at the beginning of this paper. At the turn of the twentieth century the British liberal thinker J.A. Hobson had denounced how the impulses of imperialism were like a dangerous disease that risked infecting the basically healthy body of a Europe struggling towards democratic civilization. 'Imperialism,' he wrote in his 1902 study,

> is a depraved choice of national life, imposed by self-seeking interests which appeal to the lusts of quantitative acquisitiveness and of forceful domination surviving in a nation from early centuries of animal struggle for existence. Its adoption as a policy implies a deliberate renunciation of that cultivation of the higher inner qualities which for a nation as for an individual constitutes the ascendancy of reason over brute impulse. It is the besetting sin of all successful States, and its penalty is unalterable in the order of nature.[30]

Half a century later, trying to understand where Europe had gone wrong in the wreckage of the Second World War, the historian Hanna Arendt diagnosed that unfortunately Hobson's cancer had indeed spread into the heartland of European civilization. She wrote:

> When the European mob discovered what a 'lovely virtue' a white skin could be in Africa, when the English conqueror in India, an administrator who no

longer believed in the universal validity of law, was convinced of his own innate capacity to rule and dominate, ... the stage seemed to be set for all possible horrors. Lying under anybody's nose were many of the elements which gathered together could create a totalitarian government on the basis of racism. 'Administrative massacres' were proposed by Indian bureaucrats while African officials declared that 'no ethical considerations such as the rights of man will be allowed to stand in the way' of white rule.[31]

The massacres perpetrated during Italy's brief tenure at Addis Ababa were not the result of a gut reaction or a moment of madness induced by fear; nor can they be seen merely as the offshoot of an Italian population imbued with the tenets and spirit of Fascist ideology; they were an essential ingredient in making Italy's colonial project actually work. The latter took place while Italy was ruled by Fascism and adopted this political ideology's phraseology, its style and possibly its particular ruthlessness. Yet one might just as easily argue that Italy's 'time to kill' was not so much 'part and parcel of the bleakness at the centre of Fascism' but part of the bleakness at the centre of the European colonial project itself. As such, I would argue, like Arendt, that the practice of massacre in the colonial context was linked directly with what became feasible in wartime Europe. Thus Italy's behaviour in Africa was both part of the Scramble for Africa and a harbinger of the horror of the Second World War, and provides a perfect example of how both locales of what has been called 'murder in our midst'[32] were intimately connected.

Notes

1. For more on these events see, for example, Angelo Del Boca, *Italiani Brava Gente* (Vicenza, 2005), 205–27.
2. So says Michael Mann in the *The Dark Side of Democracy: Explaining Ethnic Cleansing* (Cambridge, 2005), 309.
3. Giorgio Rochat, 'L'attentato a Graziani e la repressione italiana in Etiopia nel 1936–37', *Italia Contemporanea*, 118 (1975), 3–38.
4. For example Ian Campbell and Degife Gabre-Tsadik, 'La repressione fascista in Etiopia: la ricostruzione del massacro di Debra Libanos', *Studi Piacentini*, 21 (1997), 79–128.
5. *Fascist Legacy*, UK (BBC) 1989, directed by Ken Kirby.
6. Angelo Del Boca (ed.), *Le guerre coloniali del fascismo* (Bari, 1991).
7. Del Boca (ed.), *Le guerre coloniali*, 235.
8. Del Boca (ed.), *Le guerre coloniali*, 248.
9. Quoted in Angelo Del Boca, *Gli italiani in Africa orientale III. La caduta dell'impero* (Milan, 1992), 84–85.
10. Quoted in Romano Canosa, *Graziani* (Milan, 2004), 157.
11. Campbell and Gabre-Tsadik, 'La repressione fascista', 111.
12. Campbell and Gabre-Tsadik, 'La repressione fascista', 111.
13. Del Boca, *Italiani brava gente?*, 213.
14. Del Boca, *Italiani brava gente?*, 213.
15. For example Nicola Labanca in *Oltremare* (Bologna, 2004), 135.

16. See Zaude Hailemariam, 'La vera data d'inizio della seconda guerra mondiale', in Del Boca (ed.), *Le guerre coloniali*, 288–314. The article title translates as 'The True Beginning of the Second World War'.

17. Cited in Giuseppe Finaldi, 'The Italian Ethiopian War', in Martel Gordon (ed.), *A Companion to International History 1900–2001* (London, 2007).

18. For the text of the song visit http://it.wikisource.org/wiki/In_Africa_si_va.

19. See the chapter on the Popular Front in Geoff Eley, *Forging Democracy: The History of the Left in Europe 1850–2000* (New York, 2002).

20. D. Rodogno, *Fascism's European Empire: Italian Occupation During the Second World War* (Cambridge, 2006); R. Mallett, *Mussolini and the Origins of the Second World War, 1933–1940* (Basingstoke, 2003); M. Knox, *Common Destiny: Dictatorship, Foreign Policy, and War in Fascist Italy and Nazi Germany* (Cambridge, 2000); M. Knox, *Hitler's Italian Allies: Royal Armed Forces, Fascist Regime, and the War of 1940–1943* (Cambridge, 2000).

21. Rodogno, *Fascism's European Empire*, 466.

22. John Gooch, *Mussolini and His Generals: The Armed Forces and Fascist Foreign Policy, 1922–1940* (Cambridge, 2007), 251.

23. Angelo Del Boca (ed.), *I gas di Mussolini* (Rome, 1996), 29.

24. Ennio Flaiano, *Tempo di Uccidere* (Milan, 2000).

25. See especially Del Boca, *I gas di Mussolini*.

26. See on this especially Nicola Labanca, *Una Guerra per l'impero. Memorie della campagna d'Etiopia, 1935–6* (Bologna, 2005).

27. Emilio Gentile, *Fascismo di pietra* (Bari-Rome, 2007).

28. Alexander De Grand, 'Mussolini's Follies: Fascism in Its Imperial and Racist Phase 1935–1940', *Contemporary European History*, 13 (2004), 139.

29. See the chapter on the Ethiopian War in Giuseppe Finaldi, *Mussolini and Italian Fascism* (London, 2008).

30. J.A. Hobson, *Imperialism: A Study* (Cosimo, 2005), 368.

31. Hanna Arendt, *The Origins of Totalitarianism* (London, 1967), 221.

32. Omer Bartov, *Murder in our Midst: The Holocaust, Industrial Killing, and Representation* (Oxford, 1996).

CHAPTER 19

THE ALGERIAN WAR ON FRENCH SOIL: THE PARIS MASSACRE OF 17 OCTOBER 1961

Hélène Jaccomard

On the night of 17 October 1961, responding to calls by leaders of the French arm of the Federation of National Liberation (FLN),[1] about twenty thousand Algerian men, women and children converged on the centre of Paris in order to demonstrate peacefully against a racially discriminatory edict that imposed a curfew on Algerian workers, and obliged Algerian cafés to shut by 7 pm. The measure was meant to curb FLN operations against the police and non-FLN supporters.[2] Some workers were arrested even before they started marching and taken to police headquarters and detention centres in stadiums and other large public areas. Overreacting to the throngs of demonstrators coming out of metro stations or crossing bridges, the police – subjected to a string of daily attacks in the period leading up to the demonstration[3] – trapped and shot many demonstrators. Pro-independence activist and intellectual, Claude Lanzmann, witnessed 'with his own eyes how [the cops waiting at the metro exits] would smash Algerians' faces in ... Bodies were found hanging from trees in the Boulogne woods, and others, disfigured and mutilated, floating on the Seine.'[4] Thanks most probably to their *harki*[5] informers, the police were well prepared to stop the demonstrators[6] and turned the peaceful march into the so-called Battle of Paris. To this day the number of demonstrators actually killed remains a bone of contention and ranges from two to two hundred. Although not knowing the exact number of victims is probably a common denominator of all massacres, in this instance, the discrepancy is so wide that the magnitude of the massacre, and therefore its fundamental meaning, is at stake. On 18 October the police admitted to two dead, and thousands of arrests, maybe 11,500.[7] Later, according to Jean-Paul Brunet, around thirty-one deaths could be proven as being directly attributable to police brutality.[8] From a thorough examination of police archives only made available in the mid-1990s, it appears that the police were more interested in working out how many of the dead and the arrested were proven FLN supporters (3,729 minor and major cadres altogether, according to Brunet).[9]

Immediately after the incident, Paulette Péju, a journalist working for the then communist-backed *Libération*, and known for her pro-independence leanings, received evidence of that violent night in the form of photographs taken at great personal risk by Elie Kagan. They showed Algerian men with bloody faces and broken limbs, bodies lying on the ground, and police chasing fleeing, unarmed people. Unlike most massacres, the one that occurred on the night of 17 October 1961 was thoroughly documented in the heat of the moment. In her memoirs, Simone de Beauvoir states that the main national newspapers immediately denounced the 'police brutalities' and became a platform for the general public's indignant reactions. One member of parliament openly accused the minister of the Interior, Roger Frey, of condoning 'Nazism in France' and 'a police dictatorship'.[10]

From that point on Péju, driven by her own sympathy towards Algerian Independence and her views on the *harkis* of Paris, collected and gathered testimonies and complaints lodged by witnesses (some many pages long), as well as by victims of the repression and their families. A few weeks later, she published *Ratonnades à Paris*.[11] Forty or so pages long, it has the hallmark of a work carried out urgently. Although she included some replies from the police, judges and the Prefect of Paris, Maurice Papon, the bulk of *Ratonnades à Paris* is made up of victims' testimonies and reactions from lawyers, journalists, and even priests. Her own comments were sparse as if she intended the raw data to speak for itself, or as if the tremendous energy needed to clandestinely collect so many testimonies and cross reference them with articles and comments by outraged Parisians, journalists and intellectuals left little room for interpretation.

Like Simone de Beauvoir, Péju accused the French authorities of using methods and aims akin to those of the Nazis. For Péju, the ensuing cover up was not part of a bigger power game, such as bringing the French Federation of the FLN to their knees, but an attempt to hide from the French the fact that men were 'being tortured on their doorstep, with the same keenness as the Gestapo some time earlier'.[12] Twenty years after the Second World War, such parallels would endow her anti-colonialist stance with a good deal of 'symbolic capital'.[13]

Péju approached the left-wing Parisian publisher, François Maspéro, to publish her book. This was only a couple of months after the failed April 1961 putsch which, among other things, gave birth to the OAS,[14] and during which General de Gaulle escaped an assassination attempt. The year 1961 was shaping up to be a volatile and critical one. It was also the year Maspéro printed Frantz Fannon's *Wretched of the Earth*, only to have the essay immediately banned. A few months earlier Maspéro had tried to publish Paulette Péju's research on *Les harkis à Paris*, but the book was seized. In November 1961, shortly after *Ratonnades à Paris* had appeared, it too was impounded by the French police for reasons of State security, probably under pressure from the *Gouvernement provisoire de la République algérienne*.[15] Only about one hundred copies escaped the police and remained in circulation.

In 2000, Paulette Péju's book was reprinted together with *Les harkis à Paris*, a postscript by Maspéro, and a preface by Pierre Vidal-Naquet, a 'militant historian', as he used to define himself, and the author of a seminal book on torture during the Algerian War. Events at the dawn of the twenty-first century obviously acted as a trigger for the renewed relevance of Péju's books. A case in point is the public admission in 2000 by prominent General Aussaresses that torture was routinely practiced in Algeria. That torture was a common policing technique in Algeria had been public knowledge at least since Henri Alleg's *La Question* appeared in 1958, four years into the war, followed by Pierre Vidal-Naquet's *La torture dans la République* in 1972. Torture had indeed been practiced on all sides – by French soldiers, FLN fighters, and the OAS – but Aussaresses confirmed that it was condoned, indeed recommended, by the highest ranks of the French army and the French State. Up till then, the practice had been limited to Algeria. Péju demonstrated as early as 1961 that the use of torture was supported by the French authorities on French soil.

The 1998 Papon trial for Crimes against Humanity committed in 1942 and 1944, a period during which Papon was secretary general for police of the Prefecture of Bordeaux, was an even more direct motive for reprinting Péju's *Ratonnades*. The trial was the 'first legal intervention on the subject', that is, the night of 17 October.[16] It was then that Jean-Luc Einaudi, author of an authoritative document on the October massacre, was called as a witness against Papon, and publicly aired numerous facts surrounding the events that until then had been only the province of experts. And yet François Maspéro and Jean-Paul Brunet believe that it is simplistic and anti-historical to render one man responsible for the crimes committed that night since police repression has its own dynamic.[17] The pre-eminent French scholar on massacre studies, Jacques Semelin, also believes that state power perpetrates massacres.[18]

Vidal-Naquet's preface ends with the sad reminder that after Péju's thoroughly documented book, and after other courageous journalists conscientiously carried out their own investigative work, a long period of silence followed. Of all the bloody events of the Algerian War of Independence, and after being so extensively covered by the press and Paulette Péju, 17 October 1961 ended up being a massacre that remained forgotten for a long period of time. Subsequent tragic events erased the immediate memory of 17 October 1961, such as the 'Charonne killing' of nine people (eight of them communists) who had been demonstrating against the OAS in February 1962.[19] Again the police were caught in the act of murdering peaceful demonstrators just as the rally of around 50,000 was breaking up. More than half a million Parisians attended the funerals of the Charonne victims, all (non-Arabic) 'French',[20] in contrast with the hasty burial of the October victims and the dearth of public demonstrations – fifteen hundred courageous Algerians marched in Paris on 20 October 1961.

Due to the thirty-five year ban on some archives associated with the Algerian War in France, and the deep trauma associated with the war, it has taken twenty-five years for systematic research to be carried out, submitted to the public gaze, and integrated into France's collective memory.[21] The 'return of the repressed', as Henry Rousso famously labelled the Vichy Regime, and an expression also applied to the Algerian War, is a slow, staggered process with long periods of regression, denial, and finally acceptance.

And yet, the impression that the Algerian War was followed by a twenty-five year silence is a myth. If anything, Paulette Péju's thorough press review in *Ratonnades* and de Beauvoir's memoirs demonstrate that the lies of Papon and Roger Frey were immediately denounced not only by contemporaries, but also repeatedly since. Almost thirty years later, Einaudi reminds us of the numerous articles published in the 1970s and 1980s, some splashed on the front page of influential newspapers, such as *Libération* and *Le Monde*. Even the state-owned television opened its 8 pm news in 1981 with a report on the twentieth anniversary of 17 October 1961.[22] This myth of silence is part of a pattern that historian and sociologist Benjamin Stora eloquently describes on examining more than 2,500 books and hundreds of films on the Algerian War: '[I challenge] the legend of the "void" surrounding the Algerian War, this feeling of an absence of memory, when every year dozens and dozens of works dedicated to this burning period of French history were being published.'[23] Despite this, 'each film is hailed as the one that will at long last break the silence, only to become a commercial failure'.[24] A lot of work on 17 October 1961 has been, and is still being done and has now resulted in about forty books by historians, and half a dozen novels.[25]

It is remarkable then that none of the Algerian War's reputable scholars, even the ones who wrote after *Ratonnades* was reprinted in 2000, makes mention of Paulette Péju.[26] This is probably because of her alleged support of the FLN. In hindsight, her humanitarian sentiments and her struggle for justice appear to be stronger than her political views: 'In 1961 it was not a case of *writing* History, it was about *living* it, and if possible *making* it'.[27] This simple partition between actors and writers of history implies that, once events have passed, it is easy to entrust them to the history books. Yet the ups and downs of the 17 October 1961 historiography reveal an unresolved tension between ideology and neutrality. Liberated from solving some of the post-independence conflicts of identity politics, present-day historians are able to achieve a better measure of neutrality than a more contemporary historian like Péju. Or, post-modernists having warned us against absolutes, historians at the very least should now be able to attain a relative neutrality on the 17 October 1961 massacre.

Although not writing in the heat of the moment as did Péju, later scholars' relative neutrality nevertheless depends on the views they held prior to their writings, but also on the sources they have used. For instance, despite his own caveat that 'history is not built on an accumulation of information: it requires an always alert critical mind, and it requires that the historian shed all prior ideas and passionate views', Jean-Paul Brunet, who was able to access the archives of the police and the *préfecture*, was criticized for being too understanding of the police.[28] On the other hand, despite the magnitude and variety of sources used – the memoirs of FLN fighters, lawyers, survivors, and cemetery archives – Jean-Luc Einaudi is considered to be too sympathetic to the FLN.[29] Interestingly, despite using the same sources as these researchers, as well as oral testimonies, a French historian by the name of Linda Amiri comes to a different conclusion and does not exonerate either Papon or the police.[30]

Although these historians never refer to *Ratonnades,* Péju's revelation of torture carried out in Paris, even in the courtyard of the Prefecture of Police, as well as Papon's role during that time, has eventually become accepted knowledge. Her immediate history-writing revealed elements that could not be confronted in 1961 and which took some years to penetrate the French collective imagination, thereby allowing memory to become history.

There is one aspect of Péju's interpretation, however, that still runs counter to present-day views – the labelling of *harkis* as assassins. The 2000 edition of *Ratonnades à Paris* is preceded by the other book written by Péju and, as mentioned above, also banned at the time – *Les harkis à Paris*. The part played by the *harkis* in the October massacre seems to be incontrovertible although no other contemporary or later source grants the *harkis* any significant role. An examination of Péju's views on the *harkis*, actors she never directly approached or interviewed, will shed light on why she singled them out.

In June 1961, Paulette Péju was handed a collection of documents that had been gathered by an association of lawyers, headed by Jacques Vergès, who had made it their life's work to defend FLN militants. The file Péju received contained forty-four complaints from victims or their families, of French Muslim police brutalities, even murder, over the previous six or seven months. These form the second section of the book. The first (25–40) is a lengthy introduction contextualizing the complaints within the history of the *harkis*, starting in Algeria, and then moving to their integration into the French police as auxiliaries, the *supplétifs* of the French police, the so-called 'Blue caps'.[31]

Borrowed from the ethnologist Jean Servier in 1955, the word *harki* is synonymous with the Algerian auxiliaries incorporated into the French army, sometimes by force, sometimes by intimidation, and sometimes just as a means to earn an income and survive.[32] *Harkis* were used as informers, trackers, and soldiers in Algeria on the side of the French, and as policemen from December 1959 in Paris. Their duty was to infiltrate, arrest and even execute FLN fighters, and to wreck the *Fédération de France du FLN*. At the height of the system, in late 1960, about 120,000 *harkis* made up the auxiliary forces,[33] with about six hundred 'Blue caps' in the *Force de police auxiliaire* (FPA) in Paris. In effect there were a number of *supplétifs* units: *moghaznis*, mobile security groups, and self-defence groups, as well as 'white' *harkis*, all with very different roles.[34] The word *harki* subsumes those distinct units into one because, in essence, apart from the small number of 'white' *harkis*, they were Algerians fighting Algerians.[35]

Pierre Vidal-Naquet has asserted that some Muslim *supplétifs* were loyal to France, while others seized any opportunity to defect – with their weapons – to the FLN. Others were very much like the *miliciens* of 1942–1944, but 'their status was always ambiguous'.[36] In the final analysis, Vidal-Naquet believes that 'it is impossible to generalise' about their roles and behaviours.[37] Péju, on the other hand, does not entertain such nuances in her book, *Les harkis à Paris*. She and, much more recently historian Remy Valat, document how *harkis* imported into France repressive methods only used in Algeria at the time, including unjustified body searches watched by a gun toting *harki*, torture in the basements of quiet buildings, racketeering and the intimidation of Algerian shopowners, and the disposal of bodies in the Seine.

In the thirteenth *arrondissement* where they resided, *harkis* instituted a regime of terror against the Algerian workers living in and around Paris. Their role was an integral part of the ever tougher rules regulating Algerian migrants. As Remy Valat pithily puts it, 'The introduction of the Algerian conflict onto French soil increased the hardening of repressive methods'.[38] Whereas Valat underplays their systematic violence – and has been criticized for doing so – Péju condemns their 'gang mentality', their 'mafia-like' reign of terror.[39] Worse still, she describes them as 'mercenaries serving the occupier, they round up people, they rape, they pillage, they torture and they kill'.[40] According to Péju, *harkis* were recruited among hardened criminals 'whose sole recommendation [was] an extensive police record'; they were recidivists about to be caught, or else lost souls, and vagabonds.[41] She felt that the French police had uncomfortable memories of the Vichy regime and the purge (*épuration*), and so chose to have their dirty work done by people with few moral scruples, by French Muslims rather than police of French stock.[42] This exploitation of divisions between communities would provide the 'will and context' of a massacre.[43] Péju bitterly notes that paradoxically there had been less repression by the ordinary French police in the previous six months because the *harkis* were used as a substitute to actual justice, no more so, according to her, than during the night of the 17 October 1961.

In *Harkis à Paris* the background research gradually gives way to the documentation of the most significant complaints, written statements of unlawful arrest, detention and torture, interwoven with medical assessment reports which confirm or refute evidence of torture, and counterclaims by judicial or police authorities. Péju's point is to emphasize irregularities in the way in which authorities dealt with the complaints. Although lodged with lawyers or the police, the complaints were mostly ignored or resulted in no suits. Lawyers were often kept from visiting their clients. Although the perpetrators were often named, and sometimes meticulously described by different victims, the *harkis* were not called by the judicial authorities to answer for their crimes. In this, Péju mostly indicts the Prefect of Paris, Maurice Papon, and the President of the Commission for the Safeguard of Individuals' Rights and Freedom, M. Patin.[44]

Since Péju's discourse is, for at least half of *Les harkis à Paris,* one of 'copying complaints without comment', the thorny issue that is left unanswered is the connection or association of the victims to the FLN.[45] Most were requested by their interrogators to confess to being FLN activists, or at the very least to admit to paying FLN dues.[46] Only two victims admitted to being FLN activists, 'just like any other Algerian', Guessoum Brahim and Amirat Slimate, who, for his part, elaborated at length in his testimony. Before being beaten up he was given the option of joining the *harkis'* auxiliary police for a handsome salary. He replied, 'I refused and told them I was an FLN activist, and I couldn't betray my conscience. I must say that, upon arriving at the Harkis' place, I had admitted that I, like every Algerian, contributed to the organization, but that I had no responsibilities within it.'[47]

It is not known whether these victims were FLN members or not, but they were certainly some of the 130,000 migrant workers in Paris who fell prey to the *harkis'* abuse of power. Whether or not Péju is being naïve as to the victims' association with the FLN, it does not change the horror of the massacre and the ensuing cover up. It does, however, raise the issue of the hierarchy of responsibilities, which is often claimed as an extenuating circumstance by the rank and file of repressive organizations (Nazis or collaborators for instance). Péju takes for granted the divide between paying members who claim that they were forced to pay, but had no active role and therefore did not constitute an enemy to the French colonial power, and active FLN terrorist who did, and towards whom, like most anti-colonial intellectuals of the time, she felt some sympathy. Her purpose here was to air these complaints, thus far kept from public scrutiny, not to examine human rights abuses by the FLN that could vindicate the escalation of violence in France itself.

And yet, in recent years *harkis* have been re-fashioned as martyrs of the war, rather than perpetrators of crimes committed during the wars.[48] Furthermore, a careful examination of the archives and testimonies tend to underplay the efficacy of the *harkis'* actions: 'Harkis were suspected of contributing part or their wages to the FLN, of avoiding battle with FLN troops, and of showing insufficient zeal in rounding up FLN suspects.'[49] For example, Mohand Hamoumou, the son of a *harki*, only briefly mentions the *harkis* of Paris who were 'literally [involved] in urban guerrilla warfare that at times went too far'.[50] Brunet mentions one *harki* who might have been involved in the events of 17 October 1961, 'an allegation today strenuously denied'.[51] Most of the testimonies and books on the *supplétifs* relate to *harkis* from Algeria, their forced enrolment, their unjust treatment when repatriated – in the best case scenario, since many were not allowed to come to France and lost their lives at the hand of Algerians – and their struggles for recognition of their rights by the French authorities.[52] In France *harkis'* children suffer even more discrimination than the children of Maghreb immigrants.[53] In 1974, the year the French parliament recognized *harkis* as fully-fledged war veterans, *harkis* started to overcome their shame and launch awareness campaigns with hunger strikes, hostage taking, manifestos and interviews. One television programme in 1985 aired their claims of neglect, their 'drama', and their requests for compensation.[54] Indeed, over the following decade, indemnities, special loans and training programmes came their way. The *devoir de mémoire* (duty to remember) culminated in public commemorations in 1994 and 1996 with commemorative plaques and official monuments. This did not prevent one *harki* organization from suing the French government for crimes against humanity in 2001 – so far to no avail.

The momentum achieved by *harkis* associations remains strong, as is evidenced by recent accusations levelled at the respected historian Benjamin Stora for encouraging the 'FLNisation' of France.[55] A collective of *harkis* associations angrily refuted Stora's comments on the occasion of the release in 2005 of an old film of *harkis'* testimonies. The historian felt there were no grounds for indemnities to be granted to *harkis*, and that the Algerians, not the French, had been responsible for the massacre of *harkis* after the country gained independence in 1962, adding that 'The massacre of *harkis* comes from revenge and cruel reprisals from the population. However, it is certain that *harkis* were badly received in France.'[56] Despite this proviso, the very fact that those outside the memory group – *harkis* and their children – would express a judgement, re-ignites issues of legitimacy and claims of 'justifications for the *harkis'* massacre.'[57] The old divide between *harkis* and FLN inscribed in Péju's works is being reasserted by the keepers of *harkis'* memory. But in the case of Paulette Péju, this serves a purpose that has not been fully acknowledged to this day, her disregard for ethnicity.

Her most important contribution, and possibly the least conscious or recognized, beyond her incontrovertible evidence about the distribution of responsibilities in the 1961 events, is how she does not question the rights of Algerians to full protection under French law: to all intents and purposes, she produces proof of a massacre of French citizens by French citizens.[58] No victim, no perpetrator, is called French or Algerian in her books. The victims are rounded characters, with full names, families, jobs, emotions and rights. In short, she seems unaware of how Algerians represented the Others in the eyes of the general public and in particular the police, and that the process of othering was occurring almost unquestionably at the most basic level: 'Algerians in France [...] were not considered completely French even though they were nationals, nor were they considered Algerian, because their country was not recognized. They were called "Muslims" or "North Africans" and this juridical foreignness exacerbated the logic of suspicion that characterized police attitudes toward them.'[59]

Moreover, the French police 'in their majority did not distinguish between Algerians (and even North-Africans) and FLN..., a sly enemy, a killer, an assassin who would lie in wait for police colleagues in the dark'.[60] Othering out of 'French society (and universal history)' was also a common attitude amongst intellectuals, whether they were on the left or the right, a phenomenon historian James Le Sueur analyses as the intelligentsia's difficulty in conceptualizing 'violence, identity politics [and] the problem of reconciliation' between French and Algerians.[61] Definitions of French and Algerian identities as fundamentally incompatible render the mere concept of reconciliation null and void. The best-known proponent of the link between violence and identity politics is Frantz Fannon who hypothesized that 'it was possible to erase colonial identity through anticolonialist violence'. In other words, the process of decolonization would 'create a *tabula rasa* of human identity in Algeria' and would herald 'a veritable creation of new men'.[62] Paulette Péju, who did not have such a lofty aim, and who was a staunch opponent of the cleansing virtues of violence, based her plea for the victims neither on sameness nor on difference.

As is clear from this discussion, there is nonetheless an *Other* in her text: the *harki* of Paris. At a time of strong moral dictates the *harki* had no ideals. At a time when everyone had to choose their ideological camp, what Péju despises most in him is his lack of beliefs, and this fact alone seems to render him odious to society. Whoever protects the *harki* (Papon, the police, the Commission for the Safeguard of Individuals' Rights and Freedom) is tainted with the same brush. This has nothing to do with ethnicity or religion.

The reason why *harkis* have fascinated dozens of historians and actors of the war was possibly already present in Péju's texts and lay even deeper than national or ethnic identity politics or ideological stands. By taking up arms against their own kind, *harkis* enact a powerful taboo, that of fratricide: 'Betray one's brother: such is Moze's crime', writes Rahmani about her *harki* father. The social psychologist I. Mayeux, who interviewed about thirty *harkis* in France and in Germany, concluded that 'Both the individual and society as a whole subconsciously oscillate between brotherly love and murderous sibling impulses. Ethnicity constituted through collective identity works as a defense mechanism, muffling outright instinctual forces and enabling the development of a social belonging of the individual's identity.'[63]

Interestingly, in a rare instance of analysis of *harkis'* excessive violence, and straying from the usual role as a scribe of facts and figures entrusted to her by victims and survivors, Péju comes close to a similar psychological understanding of *harkis'* loss of identity: 'Despised by those who use them, rejected by the Algerian community, they're bent on tracking their compatriots, all the more so that they are murdering in themselves their own lost image: they try to erase what they can't be anymore, and flee desperately from what they have become: *faux-frères*.'[64]

Their self-hatred explains the escalation into violence against their coreligionists. 'Othering' is not always a sinister project: the concept can be used to 'foster' as well as to 'destroy tolerance'.[65] Othering *harkis* in Péju's case was meant to stop violence, overcome racism, and give birth to justice. In a sense Péju elected a scapegoat to be responsible for violence, and one against whom 'French' and 'Algerians' could unite, and even be reconciled. If today's project is to reconcile all memory groups in postcolonial France, Péju's scapegoating of *harkis* is neither historically viable nor desirable for the future. She is, however, delineating a form of closure with respect to 17 October 1961 with her clearly unsubstantiated, but highly significant exaggeration of the actual role of *harkis* in the massacre.

With Algeria nominating 17 October as its national Day of Emigration and France's official recognition only in 2001, the legacy of the events of 17 October 1961 has endured as a significant entry in the gory Algerian War of Independence. Whereas other horrific massacres – such as the crushing of the 1945 Sétif uprising (Planch , 2006), the reprisals of Philippeville, the 1962 slaughter of Europeans in Oran, or post-Independence killings of *harkis* – can be said to have now reached some kind of closure, research on 17 October 1961 seems to be revisiting over and over the existing material without ever reaching satisfactory conclusions on its true magnitude and meaning.

In October 2000, speaking as an authority on Algeria (1979, 2008), Pierre Bourdieu stated that 'the memories of these heinous crimes, a kind of concentrate of the horrors of the Algerian War' should be inscribed on all public places in France 'next to the official portrait of the President [...] as a solemn warning against any temptation of racist barbarity.'[66] It is not its extent then but its purported racist motives which give the night of 17 October 1961 a symbolic status and in effect now displace debates about 17 October 1961 into the thorny issue of the postcolonial reconciliation between French and Algerians. Re-visiting Péju's books is therefore an antidote to France's 'identity anxiety' caused by its colonial history and ethnic and religious diversity.[67]

Notes

1. *Le Front de libération nationale* (FLN) was established in 1954 to gain independence from the French. Previous independence movements, such as Messali Hadj's *Mouvement National Algérien* (MNA), favoured independence through peaceful means whereas the FLN used targeted bombings and assassinations, including against other pro-independence non-FLN members. In 1958, it formed a provisional government which became the interlocutors of the French authorities in peace negotiations.
2. J.-P. Brunet, 'Police Violence in Paris, October 1961: Historical Sources, Methods and Conclusions', *Historical Journal,* 51 (2008), 196.
3. Brunet, 'Police Violence in Paris', 195.
4. Simone de Beauvoir, *La force des choses* (Paris, 1963), 626. All French translations are mine.
5. *Harki* is the name given to Algerians who joined the French army or police, sometimes by force, sometimes willingly.
6. Philippe Bernard, 'An Interview with Benjamin Stora', in Richard J. Golsan, *Memory and Justice on Trial: The Papon Affair* (London, 2000), 234.
7. Jim House mentions 11,538 people arrested that night, 'Antiracist Memories: The Case of 17 October 1961 in Historical Perspective', *Modern and Contemporary France,* 9 (2001), 355.
8. J.-P. Brunet, *Police contre FLN* (Paris, 1999), 329. Jean-Luc Einaudi contests the findings of the 1998 Mandelkern report, based on official records of, in particular, the *Institut medico-légal,* that the number of protesters killed is 'very much smaller than the hundreds of victims claimed here and there'. At the Papon trial, Einaudi 'testified that there was a minimum of two hundred killed and probably as many as three hundred' (Einaudi, 'October 1961: For the Truth at Last', *Le Monde,* 20 May 1998, in Richard J. Golsan, *Memory and Justice on Trial: The Papon Affair* (London, 2000), 226–27). The controversy persists to this day with Jean-Paul Brunet responding to objections with his own figures (2008).
9. Brunet, *Police contre FLN,* 315.
10. Beauvoir, *La force des choses,* 627.
11. Paulette Péju, *Ratonnades à Paris* précédé de *Les Harkis à Paris* (Paris, 1961, 2000). *Ratonnade* was the term used for racist attacks against North Africans, usually perpetrated by the police.
12. Péju, *Ratonnades à Paris,* 107.
13. James D. Le Sueur, *Uncivil War. Intellectuals and Identity Politics during the Decolonization of Algeria* (Lincoln, 2001), 3.
14. *Organisation armée secrète,* established in February 1961 to resist Algerian Independence with a campaign of terror. Depending on sources, the OAS is responsible for between two and twelve thousand killings.
15. Pierre Vidal-Naquet, 'Préface', in Péju, *Ratonnades,* 11.
16. Philippe Bernard, 'The Magistrates' Court of Paris Acknowledges the "Extreme Violence" of the Police Crackdown of 17 October 1961', in Richard J. Golsan, *Memory and Justice on Trial: The Papon Affair* (London, 2000), 241.
17. François Maspéro, 'Postscript', in Péju, *Ratonnades,* 200; and Brunet, 'Police Violence in Paris', 195.

18. Jacques Semelin, 'Toward a Vocabulary of Massacre and Genocide', *Journal of Genocide Research*, 5 (2003), 194.
19. Jean-Luc Einaudi, *La Bataille de Paris. 17 octobre 1961* (Paris, 1991), 276. This event takes its name from the Charonne metro station in Paris where the killings took place.
20. Also described by de Beauvoir, *La force des choses*, 643–45, a participant in what she claimed was a 700,000-strong demonstration.
21. Brunet, *Police contre FLN*, 17.
22. Einaudi, *La Bataille de Paris*, 278–81.
23. Benjamin Stora, *Le livre, mémoire de l'histoire: réflexions sur le livre et la guerre d'Algérie* (Paris, 2005), 7.
24. Stora, *Le livre*, 17.
25. Nacer Kettane, *Le Sourire de Brahim* (Paris, 1985); Mehdi Lallaoui, *Les Beurs de Seine* (Paris, 1986); Tassadit Imache. *Une fille sans histoire* (Paris, 1989); Didier Daeninckx, *Meurtres pour Mémoire* (Paris, 1983, 1989); Anne Tristan, *Le Silence du fleuve* (Paris, 1991); Leïla Sebbar, *La Seine était rouge* (Paris, 1999); Lakhdar Belaïd, *Sérail killers* (Paris, 2000); Kathryn Jones, 'Le fantôme d'une mémoire meurtrie: Representing and Remembering La Bataille de Paris in the Novels of Nacer Kettane, Mehdi Lallaoui and Tassadit Imache', *Romance Studies*, 24 (2006), 91–104.
26. Brunet, 'Police Violence in Paris', 196, quotes Maspéro's postscript to *Ratonnades* but none of Paulette Péju's assertions.
27. Vidal-Naquet, 'Préface', in Péju, *Ratonnades*, 7.
28. Neil MacMaster, Jim House and Bruno Poncharal, 'La Fédération française du FLN et l'organisation du 17 octobre 1961', *Vingtième Siècle*, 83 (2004), 145–60; Vidal-Naquet, 'Préface', in Péju, *Ratonnades*, 8.
29. Brunet, 'Police Violence in Paris', 14–15.
30. Linda Amiri, *Les fantômes du 17 octobre 1961* (Paris, 2002).
31. See Rémy Valat, *Les Calots bleus, Histoire d'une police auxiliaire pendant la Guerre d'Algérie* (Paris, 2007).
32. François-Xavier Hautreux, 'L'engagement des Harkis (1954–1962): Essai de périodisation', *Vingtième Siècle*, 90 (2006), 33–45.
33. Charles-Robert Ageron, 'Le 'Drame des harkis': Mémoire ou histoire?', *Vingtième siècle*, 68 (2000), 3–15, explains that the numbers decreased in March 1962, on the eve of the Evian Accords. The other significant figure Ageron mentions is the number of *harkis* who took up the offer of remaining in the French army or the police at the time (only six per cent), whereas the others, preferring the offer of money, left. William Cohen, 'The Harkis. History and Memory', in Patricia M. Lorcin (ed), *Algeria 1800–2000: Identity, Memory and Nostalgia* (New York, 2006), 164, cites higher figures – '120,000 auxiliaries (and an additional 60,000 Muslims in the regular army)' – for the end of 1960, but the discrepancy is due to a 'lack of clarity on the status of these troops'. Finally, because *harkis* were contractual recruits and could leave after six months, the total number of men serving as *harkis* is much higher: Harkis are 'believed to be four hundred thousand strong in France' (Cohen, 'The Harkis', 179).
34. See the ANSSE (Association nationale des supplétifs de souche européenne) [*National Association of Supplementary Forces of European Origin*], http://www.babelouedstory.com/thema_les/harkis/04/04.html (accessed 8 March 2009).
35. Maurice Faivre, 'L'histoire des Harkis', *Guerres Mondiales et Conflits Contemporains*, 51 (2001), 55–63.
36. Vidal-Naquet, 'Préface', in Péju, *Ratonnades*, 9.
37. Ibid., 11.
38. It should be noted that Valat's book, published in 2007, was heralded as the first one on the subject, uncovering the 'gloomiest and least known hours of the Algerian War' (Rosa Moussaoui, 'Un éclairage discutable sur les polices supplétives dans la Bataille de Paris', *L'Humanité*, 12 January 2008).
39. Moussaoui, 'Un éclairage discutable'; Péju, *Ratonnades*, 40.
40. Péju, *Ratonnades.*, 25.

41. Péju, *Ratonnades.*, 41 and 30.

42. Péju, *Ratonnades.*, 29. This discourse about *harkis* is the one now adopted in Algerian history books (Benjamin Stora, *La guerre des mémoires: la France face à son passé colonial* (La Tour d'Aigues, 2007), 59).

43. Semelin, 'Toward a Vocabulary of Massacre', 202.

44. The *Commission de sauvegarde des droits et libertés individuelles* was created in 1957 by ex-*résistants* (Guy Mollet in particular) to take disciplinary actions against possible abuses by military or police personnel.

45. Péju, *Ratonnades*, 94.

46. Péju, *Ratonnades.*, 100.

47. Péju, *Ratonnades.*, 184.

48. Stora, *La guerre des mémoires*, 50.

49. Cohen, 'The Harkis', 165.

50. Mohand Hamoumou, *Et ils sont devenus harkis* (Paris, 1993), 117.

51. Brunet, 'Police Violence in Paris', 200.

52. For instance, Jean-Jacques Jordi, *Les harkis, une mémoire enfouie* (Paris, 1999); Zahia Rahmani, *Moze* (Paris, 2003); Fatima Besnaci-Lancou, Marie-Christine Ray, *Fille de harki: le bouleversant témoignage d'une enfant de la guerre d'Algérie* (Paris, 2005).

53. Cohen, 'The Harkis', 171–72.

54. Ageron, 'Le "Drame des harkis"'.

55. Khader Moulfi, 'Benjamin STORA (en noir et blanc), l'histoire travestie au service de la propagande', http://www.coalition-harkis.com/actualites/49-benjamin-stora-flnise-mais-ne-colorise-pas-lalgerie.html.

56. Falila Gbadamassi, 'Harkis: la France "reconnaissante" mais pas "responsable"', *Harkis.Info*, 15 February 2005, http://www.afrik.com/article8121.html.

57. Gbadamassi, 'Harkis'.

58. Since Algeria was a region of France, the word 'Algerians', although used in common speech and even in decrees, is legally improper. Algerians were French citizens until 5 July 1962. The same argument goes for *harkis*. A recent instance of a call for a proper labelling of *harkis* as French citizens was expressed by the spokesman for a collective of apolitical associations for *harkis'* memory. In his protest letter against Benjamin Stora's article, Kader Moulfi wrote: 'Harkis were neither traitors, nor despicable mercenaries, but French people enrolled in the French army... Therefore, the only parties in the conflict were French authorities and the FLN, a terrorist organization' (http://www.harkis.info/portail/article.php?sid=10924043).

59. Bernard, 'An Interview with Benjamin Stora', 234.

60. Brunet begins his 2008 refutation of House and McMasters' article with a reiteration of his views on the 'police savagery' at the time (Brunet, 'Police Violence in Paris', 195).

61. Le Sueur, *Uncivil War*, 11.

62. Le Sueur, *Uncivil War*, 243.

63. I. Mayeux, 'Harki, entre totem et tabou: Désastres et trouvailles d'une histoire collective refoulée et traumatique', *Pratiques Psychologiques*, 13 (2007), 443–57, here 445. After independence, four thousand *harkis* resettled in Germany; they are considered as models of the integration process. Mayeux does not delve into the fact that Germany might be a far more neutral terrain for *harkis* than former colonial France. Such an analysis of the explosion of deep-seated 'fratricide impulses' could also account for the suppression of memories in individuals as well as at the social level. For a thorough investigation of the interconnectedness of individual and collective memories, see Jo McCormack, *Collective Memory: France and the Algerian War (1954–1962)* (New York, 2007).

64. Péju, *Ratonnades*, 109. The term *faux-frères* (two-faced) literally means false brothers.

65. Le Sueur, *Uncivil War*, 215.

66. http://17octobre1961.free.fr/pages/Histoire.htm.

67. Stora, *La guerre des mémoires*, 50.

CHAPTER 20

WEDDING MASSACRES AND THE WAR IN AFGHANISTAN

Stephen J. Rockel

News reports filed in July 2002 tell a vivid and tragic story. Late in the evening of Monday 1 July, five hundred people were gathered in a remote village in Deh Rawud district, Uruzgan province, in central Afghanistan, celebrating a wedding. Chinara, an eighteen year old, was listening to songs on a cassette recorder with her girlfriends. Her sister was soon to marry a local tribal chief's son. All of a sudden, at around 11 pm, the roar of aircraft engines drowned out the music, and there was a huge explosion. At that moment and over the hours that followed, at least sixty-three people were killed and scores more were injured. Chinara did not see what happened – she woke up later in hospital in Kandahar where at least forty of the injured had been taken. Twenty-five members of the bridegroom's family were among the dead. Many of the casualties occurred in surrounding fields as fleeing men, women and children were 'chased' down by an AC-130 helicopter gunship. After destroying the house where the wedding party was concentrated, the AC-130 strafed the neighbouring villages over several hours with its 107mm cannon and machine guns. The Governor of Uruzgan province, Jan Mohammad, arrived at the scene the next day. He said that survivors 'were collecting body parts in a bucket'.

According to the US military, a patrol in the area had radioed for air support because it 'felt threatened by automatic gunfire'. A spokesman said that the AC-130 took fire from several locations around Deh Rawud, including from an anti-aircraft gun. As is normal in Afghan weddings, some of the wedding guests were firing their Kalashnikovs into the air. Others were sleeping. The US military refused to take responsibility. Spokesman Colonel Roger King said, 'The easiest and best way to avoid civilian casualties is to avoid firing at coalition forces in the proximity of innocent civilians'. Shah Wali, a local farmer, pointed out that if Taliban or al-Qa'eda forces had been present, no music, dancing and drumming would have been possible. No evidence of an anti-aircraft gun was found by any investigation.[1]

Was this a massacre? 'It was like an abattoir,' said one of the survivors. 'There was blood everywhere.'[2] The comment brings to mind the old French origins of the word 'massacre', with its original references to a butcher's chopping block and, by extension, to what butchers specialize in.[3] The answer from the perspective of those who experienced it is, yes. It was, moreover, just one of at least eight wedding massacres suffered by Afghanis and committed by coalition forces between 2001 and 2008. Similar cases have been documented in Iraq.[4] If we apply the definition and relevant analytical categories used by Jacques Semelin in his comparative study of massacre, we see a congruence. A massacre in empirical terms is 'a generally collective form of action, involving the destruction of non-combatants, men, women, children or disarmed soldiers'. Massacres vary enormously according to 'their scope, the possible distance between killers and victims, and the structure of the conflicts that these forms of extreme violence engender'. Most massacres involve one or a series of relatively small-scale incidents, but some massacres reach the degree of genocide.[5] Martin Shaw writes that, 'Western warfare shares the general tendency to produce massacres. However, it has a developed understanding of its own non-degeneracy: weapons are "precise", civilian targets are systematically "avoided", and deaths (let alone massacres) are "accidental".' He then posits the question: 'How plausible are the claims that the Western way has progressed from earlier degenerate warfare, and differs from the other contemporary ways of war?'[6] Air strikes clearly involve a high degree of detachment – the pilot and crew of an A-10 ground attack plane or AC-130 gunship are far above or beyond the targets they attack, and are insulated by their military culture and the legal framework under which it operates, the fiction of 'collateral damage', and technological domination. They are never faced with the direct consequences of their actions.[7] This very detachment and insulation contributes to the continual replication of similar massacres, or the 'organized process of destruction of civilians directed at persons and their property' (in Semelin's formulation).[8] After extensive analysis Shaw answers his own question: 'Civilian deaths are therefore normal in new Western wars, and typically take the form of *small massacres* ... most commonly of a handful of people, but in numerous cases of fifty to a hundred civilians at a time'.[9]

The earlier history of bombing in North and East Africa, British India, Afghanistan, and Iraq by Italy, France, Spain and Great Britain tells us something about imperial warfare in both the colonial and postcolonial eras, and massacres delivered out of the blue by the new technology of aerial bombardment. Italian pilots had wonderful opportunities for pioneering the new technology with the invasion of Tripoli in 1911. 'One of them mounted a camera in his airplane and took the first air photograph. Another made the first night raid, a third dropped the first firebomb, a fourth was the first to be shot down.'[10] In 1912, the French used six planes for 'police actions' in Morocco. 'The pilots chose large targets – villages, markets, grazing herds – otherwise their bombs would miss.' The following year Spain started bombing in its own Moroccan colony, using special German bombs that combined explosives and steel balls. The aim was to injure as many living targets over as wide an area as possible. Britain quickly saw the possibilities of using aircraft in its own colonies, first bombing the Pathans (Pashtuns) on the border between India and Afghanistan in 1915. The aim was not just to attack villages but, as in all colonial wars, to destroy the means of subsistence, the economy and the social structure. Thus, irrigation channels and water supplies were targeted.[11] During the Third Afghan War, in 1919, the British bombed Kabul and Jalalabad. The squadron's commanding officer, Arthur Harris, was to become infamous. In 1920 more British bombs fell on Enzeli, Iran, on Trans-Jordan, and on Somaliland.[12]

The best known of all of these colonial experiments was in early 1920s Iraq. Here the aim was to reduce the necessity of permanent military occupation, and to replace most of the 25,000 British and 80,000 Indian troops that controlled the territory with eight bomber squadrons of the Royal Air Force for 'air policing'. When bombing raids took place the local people were supposed to be warned first. In theory, the targets were to be armed men, houses and animals. The reality was different. An early official report from Iraq highlights the panic that an air raid caused amongst the inhabitants of the targeted village. 'Many of them jumped into a lake, making a good target for the machine guns.' Lionel Charlton, RAF staff officer in Iraq from 1923, was appalled by such matter-of-fact brutality and asked to be relieved of his position after an air raid killed twenty women and children. He was sent home and forced to retire in 1928. In the meantime, Squadron Leader Arthur Harris continued his career, bombing Arab and Kurd villages with incendiaries, and dreaming of bigger better bombers.[13] One of Harris's reports shows the indiscriminate nature of 'air policing': 'They now know what real bombing means, in casualties and damage; they now know that within 45 minutes a full sized village … can be practically wiped out and a third of its inhabitants killed or injured by four or five machines which offer them no real target … no effective means of escape … Night bombing is necessary to avoid a safe period intervening between daylight operations.' Harris proudly points out that bombing villages not only had a 'moral effect' but caused 'real casualties, and material damage'.[14] His commanding officer in Iraq, Air Marshall John Salmond, noted in a secret report that bombing civilians had further advantages for the British. It damaged houses causing problems during winter for house-holders, interfered with ploughing and harvesting, destroyed fuel stores and livestock, and could 'seriously interfere with the actual food source of the tribe'.[15]

In response to questions in parliament during the first Labour government concerning 'heavy casualties caused by air policing', the new Colonial Secretary, J.H. Thomas asked the High Commissioner for Iraq, Henry Dobbs, to report on RAF policy and practice. The result was the 1924 report, *Note on the Method of Employment of the Air Arm in Iraq*. It set out an elaborate three-stage procedure with reconnaissance, consultations, and required approval from the High Commissioner to prevent or limit civilian casualties. This was supposedly followed before any air raid was carried out. Furthermore, the inhabitants of the area to be bombed were to be warned in advance. Bombing was a last resort and not to be random or indiscriminate.[16] Yet no documents from Iraq before August 1924 show that the procedures outlined in the report were followed, and there is much evidence to the contrary. To Salmond, bombing was a 'merciful act' and would 'reduce casualties to both sides' in the longer term. In reality, the report was a sham and a post hoc effort to satisfy the consciences of politicians and officials at home, and to protect British officials in Iraq. Tanaka concludes, 'no fundamental changes actually occurred in the RAF's doctrine of strategic bombing before or after the *Note on the Method of Employment of the Air Arm in Iraq*'.[17] Similarly, we will see that US bombing practice in Afghanistan had not fundamentally changed by the time of writing (June 2009) despite the use of precision weapons and claims of elaborate targeting practices and rules of engagement resulting from international criticism of high civilian casualty rates.

Wedding Massacres in Afghanistan 2001–2009

Wedding massacres represent a particular subset of civilian casualties resulting from coalition and especially US air strikes in Afghanistan. They outline in sharp relief the characteristics of the air war against Afghan civilians. There are also continuities from the earlier period of bombing civilians in colonial contexts in the Middle East, Africa and Asia. Finally, they give the lie to the sinister euphemism of 'collateral damage'. Eight wedding massacres have been reported in Afghanistan, all in Pashtun villages. Nearly all cases have been covered by sections of the Western media, although the quality of the coverage is very uneven. Sometimes local journalists, with their greater knowledge, provide more complete reports. The eight wedding massacres that we know of are: 15 October 2001, in Mazar-e-Sharif, about which little is known but which resulted in five dead;[18] 29 December 2001, in Qalaye Niazi, two to four miles north of Gardez, Paktia province; 16 May 2002, in Bal Khel, Sabari district, thirty miles north-east of Khost, in which an AC-130 gunship fired on the village killing at least ten civilians;[19] 1 July 2002, in Kakarak and nearby villages, in the Deh Rawud district, Uruzgan province, which resulted in over sixty dead;[20] 27 May 2007, in Haji Nabu, Gereshk district, Helmand province in which 'up to 48 civilians' were killed when a coalition jet bombed a house where a wedding party was in progress;[21] 16 August 2007, in Nangar Khel/Sha Mardan, Wazi Khwa district, Paktika province, in which eight civilians were killed in a ground attack on a wedding party by Polish commandos using mortars and machine guns;[22] 6 July 2008, in Ka Chona/Khetai, Deh Bala district, Nangarhar province; and 3 November 2008, in the Wocha Bakhta/Wegh Bakhtu, Shah Wali Kot district, fifty miles north of Kandahar city, Kandahar province, in which thirty-six civilians celebrating a wedding were killed in an evening attack by ground troops, helicopters, and fixed wing aircraft.[23] Let me focus on two of these massacres.

1. 29 December 2001. Qalaye Niazi, two to four miles north of Gardez, Paktia province.

US aircraft mounted a pre-dawn air strike on a suspected Taliban/al-Qa'eda compound using a B-52 bomber, a fighter bomber and two helicopters (according to villagers), or two B-1B bombers and one B-52 (US Central Command). Paktia province, on the border with Pakistan, was the scene in previous weeks of numerous US actions against retreating Taliban and al-Qa'eda fighters. But survivor Janat Gul told Reuters that there were only civilians present when the attack took place. Gul was the only survivor from his family – twenty-four relatives were killed among the more than one hundred dead. A Reuters cameraman surveying the destruction and large craters saw 'scraps of flesh, pools of blood and clumps of what appeared to be human hair'. The journalist was shown a new grave where fifty of the victims had just been buried. According to villagers many of the dead could not be identified. In the aftermath of the air strike US officials 'hotly denied' that any civilians had died and said that surface to air missiles had been fired from the compound. According to Haji Saifullah Ahmadzia, head of the tribal council, an arms dump destroyed in the bombing had been seized from retreating Taliban six weeks earlier. He invited American personnel to come to see the destruction for themselves. A US spokesman said, 'You don't have a village launching surface-to-air missiles at aircraft. You have a known al Qaida-Taliban leadership compound.' No evidence has been provided that missiles were indeed fired at US planes from the village. Commander Dave Culler, spokesman at US Central Command, said 'follow-up reports said there was no collateral damage'. He told journalists, 'If there were civilian injuries, it is the fault of Taliban and Al-Qa'ida for living among innocent people not connected with their crimes'. Mr. Ahmadzia, however, believed that a rival tribe had given 'wrong information' to the US military with the aim of provoking an attack.[24]

Further details came out over the next few days, highlighting inconsistencies in the US version of events. A BBC team, including weapons expert David Holly, visited Qalaye Niazi and checked five destroyed buildings. In Holly's words, 'Two were ammunition dumps and three were clearly houses. The bombs fell exactly where they wanted to ... straight onto the buildings. There were no stray bombs – there was no cratering between the buildings. Civilians had died in those houses – to me that looked like poor intelligence. Somebody should have checked which ones were the ammunition dumps and which ones were housing families.'

According to Abdullah, a security head for 'a local warlord', about 120 people killed in the strike were buried in mass graves in the cemetery about a mile away.[25] *Guardian* journalist Rory Carroll found more disturbing evidence to dispute the continuing American denial of civilian casualties, including children's bloody shoes and skirts, bloodied school books, a woman's scalp, sweets in red wrappers, and wedding decorations. There was 'charred meat' stuck to the rubble of the houses. Villagers said it was not the remnants of Taliban or al-Qa'eda fighters, but the flesh of 'farmers, their wives and children, and wedding guests'. He also heard survivors explain what they believed had led to the catastrophe. The Americans had been duped into attacking Qalaye Niazi by a rival anti-Taliban warlord, Aghi Badshan Khan Zadran (also known as Pacha Khan Zadran), who had ambitions to gain power in Paktia and Paktika provinces to add them to Khost, his stronghold. He was known to some tribal elders to have made threats to call in US planes if they did not support him, and his men had been seen with US Special Forces.[26] If this was true, the US military did not bother to confirm his 'intelligence'. As for the Taliban arms dump in the village, an elder, Taj Mohammad, said that when the Taliban regime fell, they informed the new authorities about it but nothing was done. 'We left it. What else were we supposed to do with it?' It had been stored in two unfinished houses that, together with three inhabited houses, made up a small cluster some distance from the centre of the village. In the three houses lived ten families, growers of wheat, apples and grapes. At the time of the attack, an additional two dozen people were in the three occupied houses to celebrate a wedding. The attack came in two waves. The first destroyed the five buildings and everyone in them. The second came an hour later and hit villagers who were digging in the ruins and probably others who were fleeing. At the time of Carroll's investigation, only scraps of human flesh and the carcasses of sheep, dogs and a cow lay at the scene. The remains of the dead were extracted from the ruins two days after the attack with shovels and tractors and buried in eleven mass graves, and some remains were taken by visitors from Khost for burial elsewhere.[27]

The figures for the dead range from fifty-two, including ten women and twenty-five children (UN and the International Committee of the Red Cross), to 107, including women and children (Gardez hospital staff), to 120 (various estimates from villagers).[28]

2. *6 July 2008. Ka Chona/Khetai, Deh Bala district, Nangarhar province.*

('The two village names used in reports are unexplained.) An American fixed-wing aircraft bombed a party celebrating a double wedding. Many of the party were trapped in a narrow mountain pass on their way to the home of one of the grooms. In double weddings each family exchanges a bride and groom. In the first reports of the incident from the BBC and *The Times*, the US military denied that any of those killed were women and children and said that they were militants who had attacked a NATO base with mortars. Captain Christian Patterson told the AFP news agency that the US military had not received any reports of civilian casualties: 'It was not a wedding party', he said. 'There were no women or children present.' Another spokesman, Lieutenant Nathan Perry, said, 'This may just be normal, typical militant propaganda'. According to a US statement, 'Intelligence revealed a large group of militants operating in Deh Bala district. Coalition forces identified the militants in a mountainous region and used precision air strikes to kill them.' Deh Bala district governor, Haji Amisha Gul, told *The Times* that twenty-seven people had been buried with another ten wounded. 'The attack happened at 6.30AM. Just two of the dead are men, the rest are women and children. The bride is among the dead.' Among the injured survivors was Kerate, who said that about seventy people, mostly women and children, were following the custom of escorting the bride to meet her groom: 'We were bombed. I couldn't figure out what had happened and I went unconscious. When I woke up, I saw lots of people killed and injured.' The *Sydney Morning Herald* interviewed an Afghan man, Lal Wazir, who had helped to take some of the wounded to Jalalabad hospital. His story matched that of the district governor.[29]

At least two investigations probed the incident. By 11 July, an Afghan government team appointed by President Karzai found that forty-seven civilians were killed by the US air strike. All but two were women and children. Nine more were wounded and another ten were presumed dead, buried under rubble. The American investigation had not concluded by that date. A US spokesman, Lieutenant-Colonel Rumi Nielson-Green, told *The Times*: 'Any loss of civilian life is tragic and we go to great lengths to avoid civilian deaths. Certainly, I can say that no civilians were targeted.'[30]

A local member of parliament, Mirwais Yasini, who is also the deputy speaker of the country's lower house, told a BBC team that civilian casualties 'widened the gap' between the Afghan people, the government, and the international coalition.[31] This is no doubt why President Karzai flew by helicopter to Deh Bala to meet with relatives of the victims 'to share their grief' and spent two hours meeting with tribal elders, promising to send family heads of those who had lost relatives to Mecca for the haj, and gifts of land to those affected.[32]

The London based non-profit Institute for War and Peace Reporting (IWPR) also has journalists in Afghanistan, one of whom visited the site, and with their local expertise they were able to add to earlier accounts. The massacre occurred during the traditional *wara* procession, when a large party of mostly women and children escorts the bride to her husband's residence. The procession had left very early in the morning due to the extreme heat of the July sun. As they went, the journalists reported, they sang, 'in keeping with centuries-old wedding traditions'. One of the two grooms was fifteen-year-old Attiqullah, son of Lala Zareen. In the wake of the attack his bride, Ruhmina, lay dead, as did Lala Zareen's daughter. When interviewed, Lala Zareen's brother, Malek Zareen, 'paced back and forth in a small room at his home, tears streaming down his face. "We lost 15 members in our own family," he said. "Eight members of the bride's family were killed, and 22 other relatives were martyred. My nephew Attiqullah has lost his mind".' Attiqullah's wedding had been arranged quickly by his father after his own wife had died. A double wedding was the best idea because it would be cheaper to arrange. So Lala Zareen's daughter was exchanged for a bride for Attiqullah, Ruhmina, thus also ensuring that there would be a woman in the household to care for the men.[33]

A member of the Afghan government's own investigation team, Dr Borhanullah Shinwari, told the IWPR that they had visited the site and that all the people killed were civilians. He reflected the local demand for justice. 'The perpetrators should be dragged into court and judged, as a lesson to others. People's patience has gone. They can no longer tolerate this.' 'Give these to Hamed Karzai,' said one Nangarhar elder, pointing to a mound of bloodstained clothing and shoes belonging to the victims. 'Tell him, "These are gifts from the women who walked barefoot and hungry to the ballot box to vote for you, in spite of the dangers. And you sent them bombs as gifts, courtesy of your foreign friends".'[34]

The IWPR also interviewed American spokesman Lieutenant Perry by phone. He said that the Coalition military 'makes every effort to avoid civilian casualties, but were taking the allegations seriously'. 'We are conducting our own investigation', he said, but refused to withdraw previous statements that all the deaths at Khetai were of 'hostile combatants'.[35] The US military's findings have not been released.

In September an NBC producer visited Attiqullah and saw the graves. Attiqullah had recovered sufficiently to give his own version of events.

It was 6.30 in the morning and there were 300 of my relatives and friends gathered at my house waiting for the bride to arrive,' he said. Attiqullah, by now his eyes brimming with tears, was barely audible and wanted to appear strong in front of me. He was fighting hard not to lose control ... 'I was watching the cooks cut the meats, prepare the potatoes, and wash the rice,' he continued. 'This was all for me and I felt so happy and proud. I was day-dreaming of welcoming my bride, wondering how she would feel as she entered my house and also how I would feel. I was counting the minutes to her arrival.' 'Then there was a loud explosion on the top of the mountain,' Attiqullah, crying, explained... 'I saw balls of fire explode in the sky, the mountain seemed to be burning. I ran from the house and started climbing. I ran faster and faster. I could hear the cries of the children and women. And then the second explosion.' Attiqullah's house, a simple structure of mud, rock and wood, is built along the side of the mountain. It took him half an hour to run up the mountain, his uncle running with him. 'And then there was a third explosion,' he said. 'Oh my God!' Attiqullah was now sobbing uncontrollably. 'I saw my bride and my family members; I saw the pieces of their bodies scattered all over the place.[36]

When the *Guardian* asked about the incident in December 2008 the US military said they were not familiar with the details 'but would look into it'.[37]

Marriage and Weddings in Pashtun Culture

Central to Pashtun identity is the concept of *Pashtunwali*, a system of customary law and a code of honour. Membership in a Pashtun tribe is based on a genealogy that refers to ancient mythology. Within the tribe or clan, authority is not concentrated in one individual according to hereditary right, but is dispersed amongst males according to birth, status, and achievement.[38] Tribal society is thus decentralized with much cohesion relying on *Pashtunwali*, which rests on 'honor and hospitality, hostility and ambush', according to anthropologist Louis Dupree, who also describes it as 'a tough code for tough men, who of necessity live tough lives'.[39] This is no doubt true, but it leaves out the centrality of questions of gender and notions of responsibility in relation to sexual difference.[40] In rural areas marriage is typically endogamous and cousin or close marriages are favoured, thus the cohesion of the tribe is founded on both real and invented ancestral lines.[41] Weddings are the public, recognizable face of much that holds Pashtun society together.[42] Indeed, Nancy Tapper, an authority on gender and marriage among the Pashtun, writes that 'marriage ceremonies and the character of relations constructed through marriage were [in the early 1970s] the principal arena of practical politics', and, 'Among Durrani [western] Pashtuns ... the control of women's behavior and their exchange in marriage are perhaps the most important criteria used to define their ethnic identity'.[43] One might assume that through thirty years of civil war and the collapse of national institutions 'practical politics' at the local level has become even more central for survival.[44] In this context weddings are markers of a community and culture's insistence on survival. They reveal how in the most difficult of circumstances Afghans carry on with life, with the processes of protecting and reproducing their families and communities. While women and children represent the majority of those present on such occasions, even if segregated by gender, they do not in fact feature in US/NATO discourse on wedding massacres, nor literally – when a village is bombed or attacked by A-10 aircraft with their five barrelled cannon or by A-130 helicopter gunships.

Connections

The circumstances surrounding each of the above cases varies but there are also numerous commonalities. As in colonial bombing, most attacks occur at night or in the early morning. Mud walled structures are attacked with heavy weapons, sometimes 2,000 pound bombs.[45] Afghan village residential patterns make the carnage even worse for individual families. Groups of close agnates tend to live in adjacent houses – the decentralized nature of society tends to be expressed spatially so that distant relatives and non-relatives reside further away.[46] We see this reflected in the appalling losses suffered by families directly involved in the wedding ceremonies. Villages are turned into combat zones or even free fire zones. The result is heavy casualties, especially of women and children.

Ironically, US and NATO military forces are highly reliant on advanced technology, even if their intelligence capabilities often seem weak. No branch of military might over the last century has excited greater 'technological fanaticism' than airpower. This applies particularly to the USA where the 'fanatics' of air war during the Second World War dedicated themselves 'to assembling and perfecting their methods of destruction'.[47] Mark Selden takes this further and argues that 'technological fanaticism is inseparable from American nationalism and conceptions of a benevolent American-dominated global order'.[48] 'Precision warfare', which is central to concepts of a new Western way of war, and uncritically accepted by the mainstream media, is referred to as 'a triumph of branding' by Carl Conetta of Project Ploughshares.[49] A recent book from the perspective of the US military counsels caution over the promises of 'immaculate warfare', the dream of the technology fanatics, yet ultimately falls back on technological determinism. Its editor writes, 'Within ... limitations ... precision weapons do make it more possible to use force in accord with canons of justice'.[50] Yet the technological precedents, as we have seen, were to be found in colonial wars in Africa and Asia where conflict was racialized. Consider one reaction to the message sent by the pioneering aerial bombardment in Tripoli in 1911. An enthusiastic observer of the campaign wrote of the exhilaration that an 'unassailable' Italian pilot might feel: 'The empty earth beneath him, the empty sky above and he, the solitary man, sailing between them! A feeling of power seizes him. He was flying through space to assert the indisputable superiority of the white race. Within his reach he had the proof, seven high explosive bombs. To be able to sling them from the heavens themselves – that was convincing and irrefutable.'[51]

Were the attacks planned? If so, this is strong evidence for failure to protect Afghan civilians and gives the lie to any pretence of accidental or 'collateral damage'. There was in fact advanced preparation in most cases. Thus the overly cautious conclusions drawn by Human Rights Watch must be challenged. In their report 'Troops in Contact: Air Strikes and Civilian Deaths in Afghanistan', they write 'Whether civilian casualties result from aerial bombing in Afghanistan seems to depend more than anything else on whether the air strike was planned or was an unplanned strike in rapid response to an evolving military situation on the ground'.[52] The situations they describe point to binary categories of either carefully prepared attacks which use a 'pattern of life analysis' to ensure that no civilians are present based on 'eyes on the ground', reconnaissance, and visual confirmation; or evolving and unplanned engagements, typically in 'troops in contact' situations, when ground troops facing insurgents call in supporting air strikes, or when Special Operations Forces are faced with superior numbers of Taliban fighters.[53] What is missing here is an intermediate category of planned attacks where the careful avoidance of civilian casualties is just not evident. The air strike on Qalaye Niazi was planned well in advance. The Polish ground attack on Nangar Khel/Sha Mardan was planned at least several hours earlier. Let us not forget that a US statement on the massacre at Ka Chona/Khetai said that 'Coalition forces identified the militants in a mountainous region and used precision air strikes to kill them'. The attack took place at 6.30 am. This suggests at least some degree of planning. The night massacre of wedding celebrants at Kakarak near Deh Rawud in July 2002 was planned, if we are to accept a revised statement from the US military that it had 'intelligence' that Mullah Omar and Mullah Baradar were present in Deh Rawud/Kakarak. Based on the evidence, planned air strikes and attacks on villages have been absolutely lethal for Afghan civilians when large numbers of people gathered together for customary rituals and ceremonies. Allowing for the above analysis, the importance of the question of intent is vastly exaggerated.[54] Marc Herold, the leading expert on civilian casualties in Afghanistan, writes:

> What needs to be made very clear is that Afghan civilian casualties are not accidents or mistakes. They result from careful calculation by US commanders and military attorneys who decide upon the benefits of an air strike versus the costs in innocent civilian lives lost. These are calculated predicted deaths made all the worse when US/Nato air or ground assaults are carried out in the middle of the night when the typical Afghan family numbering six to seven members is asleep. Are we surprised that 72% of the identifiable

Afghan civilians killed by the US/Nato during the first eight months of 2008 are women and children?[55]

The refinements of precision technology have made little difference to Afghan civilians in the current conflict. The transfer of risk from coalition forces to civilians and contempt for Afghan lives have made sure of that. Indeed, there is a direct line between the 'humane bombing' of Iraq in the 1920s and the wedding massacres 'out of the blue' in today's Afghanistan.

Notes

1. Luke Harding, 'No US Apology over Wedding Bombing', 3 July 2002, www.guardian. co.uk/world/2002/jul/03/afghanistan.lukeharding; Saeed Ali Achakzai, 'It Was Like an Abattoir – Blood All Around', 4 July 2002, www.guardian.co.uk/world/2002/jul/04/ afghanistan; 'Afghan: U.S. Bomb Hits Wedding Party', http://archives.cnn.com/2002/ WORLD/asiapcf/central/07/01/afghanistan.bombing/; also Ahmed Rashid, *Descent into Chaos: The U.S. and the Disaster in Pakistan, Afghanistan, and Central Asia* (New York, 2009), 142.
2. Achakzai, 'It Was Like an Abattoir'.
3. Mark Levene, 'Introduction', to Mark Levene and Penny Roberts (eds), *The Massacre in History* (New York and Oxford, 1999), 9; Jacques Semelin, *Purify and Destroy: The Political Uses of Massacre and Genocide* (London, 2007), 323.
4. As at Mukaradeeb on 19 May 2004, and Falluja, 8 October 2004.
5. Semelin, *Purify and Destroy*, 323–24.
6. Martin Shaw, *The New Western Way of War: Risk-Transfer War and its Crisis in Iraq.* (Cambridge and Malden, Mass., 2005), 67.
7. Levene's approach to the question of technology and distance is inconsistent. See 'Introduction', 2–3, 6, 29–31.
8. Semelin, *Purify and Destroy*, 325.
9. Shaw, *New Western Way of War*, 86 (Shaw's emphasis).
10. Sven Lindqvist, *A History of Bombing* (London, 2002), §77, 78, 74, 85, 88, 102.
11. For this point see Stephen J. Rockel, '"Collateral Damage": A Comparative History', in Stephen J. Rockel and Rick Halpern (eds), *Inventing Collateral Damage: Civilian Casualties, War and Empire* (Toronto, 2009).
12. Lindqvist, *History of Bombing*, §102; Yuki Tanaka, 'British "Humane Bombing" in Iraq during the Interwar Era', in Yuki Tanaka and Marilyn B. Young (eds), *Bombing Civilians: A Twentieth Century History* (New York and London, 2009), 13–16.
13. Lindqvist, *History of Bombing*, §102, 112; Tanaka, 'British "Humane Bombing"', 16–29, for details.
14. Tanaka, 'British "Humane Bombing"', 20–21; Lindqvist, *History of Bombing*, §112.
15. Tanaka, 'British "Humane Bombing"', 21.
16. Tanaka, 'British "Humane Bombing"', 24–28.
17. Tanaka, 'British "Humane Bombing"', 28.
18. See Marc Herold's database, AfghanDailyCount, from 'A Dossier on Civilian Victims of United States' Aerial Bombing of Afghanistan: A Comprehensive Accounting' at: http://pubpages.unh.edu/~mwherold/.
19. www.iol.co.za/news/world/10-killed-as-us-bombs-afghan-wedding-1.86752; David Rohde, '1,000 British Marines Join Australians in Firefight', 18 May 2002, www. nytimes.com/2002/05/18/international/asia/18AFGH.html; 'US Denies Attacking Wedding', 18 May 2002, http://tvnz.co.nz/content/101808. The Bal Khel massacre is mentioned in the US Congressional Record-House for 23 July 2002.

20. Marc Herold documents the incident. See 'The Massacre at Kakarak', *Frontline*, 19, 16 (3–16 August 2002), www.hinduonnet.com/fline/fl1916/19160660.htm.

21. Tim Albone, Tahir Luddin and Michael Smith, 'Nato Airstrikes Anger Karzai', 24 June 2007, www.thetimesonline.co.uk/tol/news/world/middle_east/article1977591. ece. For more on the condemnation by Karzai as well as Afghan and international NGOs in mid-2007, see Aryn Baker, 'Backlash from Afghan Civilian Deaths', 23 June 2007, www.time.com/time/world/article/0,8599,1636551,00.html.

22. The massacre has been covered in Poland but virtually ignored in the English-language press. Some Polish media reports were posted in English. See 'Polish NATO Troops Charged with Murdering Afghan Civilians', 14 November 2007, http://afp. google.com/article/ALeqM5hhaO1uTvbV-7j-gFInwQqixZ2qZw; Nicholas Kulish, 'An Afghanistan War-Crimes Case Tests Poland's Commitment to Foreign Missions', 29 November 2007, www.nytimes.com/2007/11/29/world/europe/29poland.html; Zoltán Dujisin, 'Poland: Facing War Crimes in Afghanistan', 27 December 2007, http://ipsnews.net/news.asp?idnews=40611; Iwona Bojarczuk, 'What Happened at Nangar Khel Village?', 21 February 2008, www.krakowpost.com/article/1033; Dave Markland, 'Nangar Khel: NATO's Unknown Massacre', 18 May 2008, http://stopwarblog.blogspot.com/2008/05/nangar-khel-natos-unknown-massacre.html; Marcin Kacki, Marcin Górka and Adam Zadworny, 'Nangar Khel: A Reconstruction', 28 July 2008, http://wyborcza.pl/1,86871,5496838,Nangar_Khel___a_Reconstruction.html; Marcin Górka, 'Nangar Khel: Inspecting the Scene', 15 July 2008, http://wyborcza. pl/1,86871,5456788,Nangar_Khel__Inspecting_the_Scene.html.

23. Given space constraints this case will not be discussed here; however, media coverage in the immediate aftermath was extensive.

24. 'US Strikes Kill 100 Civilians', 1 January 2002, tvnz.co.nz/view/page/425822/74774; Rory Carroll, 'US Accused of Killing over 100 Villagers', 1 January 2002, www. guardian.co.uk/world/2002/jan/01/afghanistan.rorycarroll; Peter Foster, 'UA Bombs "Kill 107 Villagers"', 1 January 2002, www.telegraph.co.uk/news/worldnews/asia/ afghanistan/1380078/US-bombs-kill-107-villagers.html; Andrew Buncombe and Kim Sengupta, 'US Accused of Killing 100 Civilians in Afghan Bombing Raid', 1 January 2002, www.independent.co.uk/news/world/asia/us-accused-of-killing-100-civilians-in-afghan-bombing-raid-621643.html.

25. Richard Miron, 'Pressure Grows to Stop Afghan Bombing', 3 January 2002, http:// news.bbc.co.uk/2/hi/south_asia/1740727.stm.

26. Rory Carroll, 'Bloody Evidence of US Blunder', 7 January 2002, www.guardian. co.uk/world/2002/jan/07/afghanistan.rorycarroll. For more on Pacha Khan Zadran, warlords and intertribal fighting in south-east Afghanistan, see www.globalsecurity. org/military/world/afghanistan/zadran.htm.

27. Carroll, 'Bloody Evidence of US Blunder'. For civilian casualties in Afghanistan during the first months of the war, see Ian Traynor, 'Afghans Are Still Dying as Air Strikes Go On. But No One is Counting', 12 February 2002, www.guardian.co.uk/ world/2002/feb/12/afghanistan.iantraynor.

28. See notes 24–26.

29. 'Afghan Strike "Hit Wedding Party"', 6 July 2008, http://news.bbc.co.uk/2/hi/middle_ east/7492195.stm; Tom Coghlan, 'Afghan Inquiry into American Bombing of "Wedding Party"', 7 July 2008, www.timesonline.co.uk/tol/news/world/asia/article4281078. ece; 'Karzai Orders Probe into Deadly U.S. Strike', 6 July 2008, www.cnn.com/2008/ WORLD/asiapcf/07/06/afghan.attack/index.html; 'US Planes "Hit Afghan Wedding Party, Killing 27"', 7 July 2008, www.smh.com.au/news/world/us-planes-hit-afghan-wedding-party-killing-27/2008/07/07/1215282687896.html.

30. Tom Coghlan, 'Afghan Government Says 47 Civilians Killed When US Bombed Wedding Party', 11 July 2008, www.timesonline.co.uk/tol/news/world/asia/article4315724. ece; James Sturcke and agencies, 'US Air Strike Wiped Out Afghan Wedding Party, Inquiry Finds', 11 July 2008, www.guardian.co.uk/world/2008/jul/11/afghanistan.usa. *The Guardian* gives a different breakdown, saying that thirty-nine were women and children.

31. 'Afghan Survivors Tell of Wedding Bombing', 13 July 2008, http://news.bbc.co.uk/2/hi/south_asia/7504574.stm.
32. 'Afghan Leader Visits Site Where US-led Strikes Hit Wedding', 17 July 2008, http://afp.google.com/article/ALeqM5h4sfwKjDTSgaZpTIxeD3W6xQYhQA.
33. Ezatullah Zawab and Hafizullah Gardesh, 'Nangarhar Elders Demand Retribution for US Air Strike', 16 July 2008, www.iwpr.net/?p=arr&s=f&o=345743&apc_state=heniarre3f02e18e7eba48c779397f86384a332.
34. Zawab and Gardesh, 'Nangarhar Elders Demand Retribution'.
35. Zawab and Gardesh, 'Nangarhar Elders Demand Retribution'.
36. Iqbal Sapand, 'A Heartbroken Groom in Nangarhar', 3 September 2008, http://world-blog.msnbc.msn.com/archive/2008/09/03/1330613.aspx.
37. Clancy Chassay, 'I Was Still Holding My Grandson's Hand – The Rest Was Gone', 16 December 2008, www.guardian.co.uk/world/2008/dec/16/afghanistan-taliban-us-foreign-policy.
38. Ralph H. Magnus and Eden Naby, *Afghanistan: Mullah, Marx and Mujahid* (Boulder, 2002), 14–15.
39. Louis Dupree, *Afghanistan* (Princeton, 1973), 126–28.
40. Nancy Tapper, *Bartered Brides: Politics, Gender and Marriage in an Afghan Tribal Society* (Cambridge, 1991), 15–16.
41. Magnus and Naby, *Afghanistan*, 14.
42. For 'traditional' Afghan wedding practices see Dupree, *Afghanistan*, 197–205.
43. Tapper, *Bartered Brides*, 11, 25, 279, 284, and *passim*. There are regional variations where tribal cohesion and politics are not so closely linked. See Jeanne Berrenberg, 'Beyond Kinship Algebra: Values and the Riddle of Pashtun Marriage Structure', *Zeitschrift für Ethnologie*, 128, 3 (2003), 269–92.
44. Tapper recognizes historical change in Pashtun ideology and practice concerning male control over women, reproduction, and female labour, expressed through marriage. See *Bartered Brides*, 19.
45. For more on village architecture, see Dupree, *Afghanistan*, 132–42.
46. Tapper, *Bartered Brides*, 9.
47. Michael Sherry, quoted in Mark Selden, 'A Forgotten Holocaust: U.S. Bombing Strategy, The Destruction of Japanese Cities, and the American Way of War from the Pacific War to Iraq', in Tanaka and Young, *Bombing Civilians*, 86.
48. Selden, 'A Forgotten Holocaust', 87.
49. Carl Conetta, *Disappearing the Dead: Iraq, Afghanistan, and the Idea of a 'New Warfare'* (Cambridge, MA, 2004), 26; Shaw, *New Western Way of War*.
50. Stephen D. Wrage, 'The Ethics of Precision Air Power', in Wrage (ed.), *Immaculate Warfare: Participants Reflect on the Air Campaigns over Kosovo and Afghanistan* (Westport, Conn., 2003), 96. Despite the subtitle there is no analysis of the use of air power in Afghanistan.
51. Lindqvist, *History of Bombing*, §80.
52. 'Troops in Contact: Air strikes and Civilian Deaths in Afghanistan' (Human Rights Watch, September 2008), 29.
53. 'Troops in Contact', 29–31.
54. See the critical literature on the doctrine of double effect, for example, David Lefkowitz, 'Collateral Damage', in Larry May (ed.), *War: Essays in Political Philosophy* (Cambridge, 2008); Rockel, '"Collateral Damage": A Comparative History'.
55. Marc Herold, 'Truth as Collateral Damage', 22 October 2008, www.guardian.co.uk/commentisfree/2008/oct/22/afghanistan-nato. For further analysis of civilian casualties in Iraq and Afghanistan, see Conetta, *Disappearing the Dead*; Shaw, *New Western Way of War*; Thomas W. Smith, 'Protecting Civilians … or Soldiers? Humanitarian Law and the Economy of risk in Iraq', *International Studies Perspectives*, 9 (2008), 144–64; Rockel, '"Collateral Damage": A Comparative History'.

SELECT BIBLIOGRAPHY

Abramenko, Andrik. 'Alexander vor Mazagae und Aornus. Korrekturen zu den Berichten über das Massaker an den indischen Söldern', *Klio*, 76 (1994), 192–207.

Ageron, Charles-Robert. 'Le "Drame des harkis": Mémoire ou histoire?' *Vingtième siècle*, 68 (2000), 3–15.

Aleida, Martin. 'Dark Night', in Harry Aveling (ed. and trans.), *Gestapu: Indonesian Short Stories on the Abortive Communist Coup of 30th September 1965*. Honolulu: University of Hawaii, 1975, 83–96.

Alleg, Henri. *La Question*. Paris: Editions de Minuit, 1961.

Amiri, Linda. *Les fantômes du 17 octobre 1961*. Paris: Editions Mémoire-Génériques, 2002.

Anderson, Robert. *Fighting the Mill Creeks*. Chico: The Chico Record Press, 1909.

Appadurai, Arjun, 'Dead Certainty: Ethnic Violence in the Era of Globalization', *Public Culture*, 10 (1998), 255–47.

———. *Fear of Small Numbers: An Essay on the Geography of Anger*. Durham and London: Duke University Press, 2006.

Arendt, Hanna. *The Origins of Totalitarianism*. London: Allen & Unwin, 1967.

Aussaresses, Paul. *Services spéciaux, Algérie 1955–1957: Mon témoignage sur la torture*. Paris: Perrin, 2001.

Aveling, Harry (trans. and ed.). *Gestapu: Indonesian Short Stories on the Abortive Communist Coup of 30th September 1965*. Honolulu: University of Hawaii, 1975.

Barnard, Leo. 'The Battle of Cassinga, 4 May 1978: A Historical Reassessment Part 1: The Course of the Battle and Ensuing Controversy', *Journal for Contemporary History*, 31:3 (December 2006), 131–46.

———. 'The Battle of Cassinga, 4 May 1978: A Historical Reassessment Part 2: Interviews with two SADF soldiers', *Journal for Contemporary History*, 31:3 (December 2006), 147–60.

Bartov, Omer. *Murder in our Midst: the Holocaust, Industrial Killing, and Representation*. Oxford: Oxford University Press, 1996.

Baynham, Elizabeth. 'An Introduction to the *Metz Epitome:* its Traditions and Value', *Antichthon*, 29 (1995), 60–77.

Bell, David A. *The First Total War: Napoleon's Europe and the Birth of Warfare as We Know It*. Boston: Houghton Mifflin, 2007.

Benzoni, Elena. 'Les sacs des villes à l'époque des guerres d'Italie (1494–1530): les contemporains face au massacre', in David El Kenz (ed.), *Le massacre, objet d'histoire*. Paris: Gallimard, 2005, 157–70.

Bernard, Philippe. 'The Magistrates' Court of Paris Acknowledges the "Extreme Violence" of the Police Crackdown of 17 October 1961', in Richard J. Golsan (ed.), *Memory and Justice on Trial: The Papon Affair*. London: Routledge, 2000, 240–42.

———. 'An Interview with Benjamin Stora', in Richard J. Golsan (ed.), *Memory and Justice on Trial: the Papon Affair*. London: Routledge, 2000, 233–36.

Berrenberg, Jeanne. 'Beyond Kinship Algebra: Values and the Riddle of Pashtun Marriage Structure', *Zeitschrift für Ethnologie*, 128:3 (2003), 269–92.

Bingham, Caroline. *Beyond the Highland Line: Highland History and Culture*. London: Constable, 1991.

Blanning, T.C.W. 'Liberation or Occupation? Theory and Practice in the French Revolutionaries' Treatment of Civilians outside France', in Mark Grimsely and Clifford J. Rogers (eds), *Civilians in the Path of War*. Lincoln: University of Nebraska Press, 2002, 111–35.

Bossy, John. *The English Catholic Community, 1570–1850*. London: Darton, 1975.

Bosworth, A.B. *A Historical Commentary on Arrian's History of Alexander*. 2 vols. Oxford: Oxford University Press, 1980, 1995.

———. 'The Humanitarian Aspect of the Melian Dialogue', *Journal of Hellenic Studies*, 113 (1993), 30–44.

———. *Alexander and the East: The Tragedy of Triumph*. Oxford: Oxford University Press, 1996.

———. 'Introduction', in A.B. Bosworth and E.J. Baynham (eds), *Alexander the Great in Fact and Fiction*, Oxford: Oxford University Press, 2000, 1–22.

Bourdieu, Pierre. *Algeria 1960: the Disenchantment of the World, the Sense of Honour, the Kabyle House or the World Reversed*. Trans. Richard Nice. Cambridge: Cambridge University Press, 1979.

———. *Esquisses algériennes*. Paris: Seuil, 2008.

Boyce, James, 'Fantasy Island', in Robert Manne (ed.), *Whitewash: On Keith Windshuttle's Fabrication of Aboriginal History*. Melbourne: Black Inc. Agenda, 2003, 17–78.

Breytenbach, Jan. *Eagle Strike! The Story of the Controversial Airborne Assault on Cassinga 1978*. Sandton: Manie Grové Publishing, 2009.

Brody, Hugh. *The Other Side of Eden: Hunter-Gatherers, Farmers, and the Shaping of the World*. London: Faber and Faber, 2002.

Broome, Richard, 'The Statistics of Frontier Conflict', in Bain Attwood and S.G. Foster (eds), *Frontier Conflict: The Australian Experience*. Canberra: National Museum of Australia, 2003, 88–98.

———. *Aboriginal Victorians: A History Since 1800*. Crows Nest, NSW: Allen & Unwin, 2005.

Browning, Christopher R. *Ordinary Men: Reserve Police Battalion 101 and the Final Solution in Poland*. 2nd edn. New York: Harper Collins, 1998.

———. *Ordinary Men: The 101st Reserve Battalion of the German Police and the Final Solution in Poland*. New York: HarperPerennial, 1992.

Brunet, Jean-Paul, 'Police Violence in Paris, October 1961: Historical Sources, Methods and Conclusions', *The Historical Journal*, 51:1 (2008), 195–204.

Brunt, Peter. *Italian Manpower*. Oxford: Clarendon Press, 1971.

Burschel, Peter, 'Das Heilige und die Gewalt. Zur frühneuzeitlichen Deutung von Massakern', *Archiv für Kulturgeschichte*, 86:2 (2004), 341–59.

Butler, Judith, 'Ethical Ambivalences', in Marjorie Garber, Beatrice Hanssen and Rebecca L. Walkowitz (eds), *The Turn to Ethics*. New York: Routledge, 2000, 15–28.

———. *Precarious Life: The Powers of Mourning and Violence*. London: Verso, 2004.

Campbell, Alastair. *John Batman and the Aborigines*. Malmsbury: Kibble Books, 1987.

Cannon, Michael. *Who Killed the Koories?* Port Melbourne, Vic.: William Heinemann Australia, 1990.

Canny, Nicolas. *Kingdom and Colony. Ireland in the Atlantic World 1560–1800*. Baltimore: Johns Hopkins University Press, 1988.

————. 'Religion, Politics and the Irish Rising of 1641', in J. Devlin and R. Fanning (eds), *Religion and Rebellion*. Dublin: University College of Dublin Press, 1997, 40–70.

————. *Making Ireland British, 1580–1650*. Oxford: Oxford University Press, 2001.

————. 'Religion and Violence in Early Modern Ireland', in K. von Greyerz and K. Siebenhüner (eds), *Religion und Gewalt: Konflikte, Rituale, Deutungen (1500–1800)*. Göttingen: Vandenhoeck & Ruprecht, 2006, 175–94.

Canosa, Romano. *Graziani*. Milan: Mondadori, 2004.

Carlton, Charles. *Going to the Wars: The Experience of the British Civil Wars 1638–1651*, 2nd edn. London: Routledge, 1995.

Carney, Elizabeth, 'Alexander and Persian Women', *American Journal of Philology*, 117 (1996), 563–83.

Caygill, Howard, 'Levinas's Political Judgement: The *Esprit* Articles 1934–1983', *Radical Philosophy*, 104 (2000), 6–15.

Cayton, Andrew R.L. and Fredrika J. Teute (eds). *Contact Points: American Frontiers from the Mohawk Valley to the Mississippi, 1750–1830*. Chapel Hill: University of North Carolina Press, 1998.

Chacon, Richard J. and David H. Dye. 'Introduction to Human Trophy Taking: An Ancient and Widespread Practice', in Richard J. Chacon and David H. Dye (eds), *The Taking and Displaying of Human Body Parts as Trophies by Amerindians*. New York: Springer, 2007, 8–21.

Champion, Craige B. 'Romans as Barbaroi: Three Polybian Speeches and the Politics of Cultural Indeterminacy', *Classical Philology*, 95 (2000), 425–44.

Chanthou, Boua, 'Genocide of a Religious Group: Pol Pot and Cambodia's Buddhist Monks', in P. Timothy Bushnell, Vladimir Shlapentokh, Christopher K. Vanderpool, and Jeyaratnam Sundram (eds), *State-Organized Terror: The Case of Violent Internal Repression*. Boulder, Co: Westview Press, 1991, 227–40.

Chomsky, Noam and Edward S. Herman. *The Washington Connection and Third World Fascism*. Boston: South End Press, 1979.

Christie, Michael F. *Aborigines in Colonial Victoria, 1835–86*. Sydney: Sydney University Press, 1979.

Clark, Ian D. *Scars in the Landscape: A Register of Massacre Sites in Western Victoria, 1803–1859*. Canberra: Aboriginal Studies Press, 1995.

Coates, Peter. '"Unusually Cunning, Vicious and Treacherous": Extermination of the Wolf in United States History', in Mark Levene and Penny Roberts (eds), *The Massacre in History*. New York: Berghahn Books, 1999, 163–83.

Cohen, William, 'The Harkis: History and Memory', in Patricia M. Lorcin (ed.), *Algeria 1800–2000: Identity, Memory and Nostalgia*. Syracuse: Syracuse University Press, 2006, 164–80.

Collins, J.H., 'Caesar as a Political Propagandist', *Aufstieg und Niedergan der römishen Welt*, 1:1 (1972), 922–66.

Collinson, Patrick. *The Birthpangs of Protestant England: Religious and Cultural Change in the Sixteenth and Seventeenth Centuries*. London: Macmillan Press, 1988.

Conetta, Carl. *Disappearing the Dead: Iraq, Afghanistan, and the Idea of a 'New Warfare'*. Cambridge Mass.: Project on Defense Alternatives, 2004.

Connor, John. *The Australian Frontier Wars, 1788–1838*. Sydney: UNSW Press, 2002.

Conquest, Robert. *The Great Terror; Stalin's Purge of the Thirties*. New York: Macmillan, 1968.

Conway-Lanz, Sahr. *Collateral Damage: Americans, Noncombatant Immunity, and Atrocity after World War II*. New York: Routledge, 2006.

Cook, Sherburne. *The Population of California Indians, 1769–1970*. Berkeley: University of California Press, 1976.

Coster, Will, 'Massacres and Codes of Conduct in the English Civil War', in Mark Levene and Penny Roberts (eds), *The Massacre in History*. New York: Berghahn Books, 1999, 89–105.

Cribb, Robert (ed.). *The Indonesian Killings of 1965–1966: Studies from Java and Bali.* Clayton, Vic: Monash University, 1990.

——. 'Introduction: Problems in the Historiography of the Killings in Indonesia', in Robert Cribb (ed.), *The Indonesian Killings of 1965–1966: Studies from Java and Bali.* Clayton, Vic: Monash University, 1990, 1–44.

——. 'The Indonesian Massacres', in Samuel Totten, William S. Parsons and Israel W. Charney (eds), *Century of Genocide: Eyewitness Accounts and Critical Views.* New York: Garland, 1997, 233–60.

——. 'Genocide in Indonesia, 1965–1966', *Journal of Genocide Research,* 3 (2001), 219–39.

Critchett, Jan. *A Distant Field of Murder: Western District Frontiers 1835–1844.* Carlton, Vic.: Melbourne University Press, 1990.

Crouch, Harold. *The Army and Politics in Indonesia.* Ithaca: Cornell University Press, 1978.

Curthoys, Ann. 'Autobiography and Cultivating the Arts of the Female Self', in Jane Bennett and Michael J. Shapiro (eds), *The Politics of Moralizing.* New York: Routledge, 2002, 93–122.

——. 'Raphaël Lemkin's "Tasmania": An Introduction', *Patterns of Prejudice,* 39 (2005), 164–66.

—— and John Docker. 'Introduction – Genocide: Definitions, Questions, Settler-Colonies', *Aboriginal History,* 25 (2001), 5–11.

—— and John Docker. *Is History Fiction?* Ann Arbor: University of Michigan Press, 2005.

—— and John Docker. 'Defining Genocide', in Dan Stone (ed.), *The Historiography of Genocide.* London: Palgrave, 2008, 9–41.

Dao, Loan. 'What's Going On with the Oakland Museum's "California and the Vietnam Era" Exhibit?', *Amerasia Journal,* 31:2 (2005), 88–106.

Dawkins, Richard. *The God Delusion.* London: Bentham 2006.

De Grand, Alexander, 'Mussolini's Follies: Fascism in Its Imperial and Racist Phase 1935–1940', *Contemporary European History,* 13:2 (May 2004), 127–47.

Del Boca, Angelo (ed.). *Le guerre coloniali del fascismo.* Bari-Roma: Laterza, 1991.

——. *I gas di Mussolini.* Rome: Editori Riuniti, 1996.

——. *Italiani Brava Gente.* Vicenza: Neri Pozza, 2005.

Della Peruta, Franco. 'War and Society in Napoleonic Italy: The Armies of the Kingdom of Italy at Home and Abroad', in John Davis and Paul Ginsborg (eds), *Society and Politics in the Age of the Risorgimento. Essays in Honour of Denis Mack Smith.* Cambridge: Cambridge University Press, 1991.

Deutscher, Isaac. *The Non-Jewish Jew.* London: Oxford University Press, 1968.

Diamond, Jared. *The Rise and Fall of the Third Chimpanzee.* London: Vintage, 1992.

Docker, John. 'Are Settler-Colonies Inherently Genocidal? Re-reading Lemkin', in Dirk Moses (ed.), *Empire, Colony, Genocide: Conquest, Occupation, and Subaltern Resistance in World History.* New York: Berghahn, 2008, 81–101.

——. *The Origins of Violence: Religion, History and Genocide.* London: Pluto, 2008.

——. 'Sacredness and Uncaring for the Other: Levinas and Patrick White', in Makarand Paranjape (ed.), *Sacred Australia: Post-Secular Considerations.* Melbourne: Clouds of Magellan, 2009, 188–209.

Donagan, Barbara. *War in England 1642–1649.* Oxford: Oxford University Press, 2008.

Douglas, Mary. *Purity and Danger: An Analysis of Concepts of Pollution and Taboo.* London: Routledge and K. Paul, 1966.

Douthit, Nathan. *Uncertain Encounters: Indians and Whites at Peace and War in Southern Oregon, 1820s–1860s.* Corvallis: Oregon State University Press, 2002.

Dowd, Gregory Evans. *War Under Heaven: Pontiac, the Indian Nations & the British Empire.* Baltimore: Johns Hopkins University Press, 2002.

Drinnon, Richard. *Facing West: The Metaphysics of Indian-Hating and Empire-Building.* Minneapolis: University of Minnesota Press, 1980.

Dupree, Louis. *Afghanistan.* Princeton: Princeton University Press, 1973.

Eckstein, Arthur M. 'T. Quinctius Flamininus and the Campaign against Philip in 198
    B.C.', *Phoenix*, 30 (1976), 1119–42.
Edwards, David. 'A Haven of Popery: English Catholics Migration to Ireland in the
    Age of Plantations', in Alan Ford and John McCafferty (eds), *The Origins of
    Sectarianism in Early Modern Ireland*. Cambridge: Cambridge University Press,
    2005, 95–126.
Eggermont, Pierre Herman Leonard. 'Alexander's Campaign in Gandhara and Ptolemy's
    List of Indo-Scythian Towns', *Orientalis Lavaniensia Periodica*, 1 (1970), 63–124.
Ehrhardt, C. 'Xenophon and Diodorus at Aegospotami', *Phoenix*, 24 (1970), 225–28.
Einaudi, Jean-Luc. *La Bataille de Paris. 17 octobre 1961*. Paris: Seuil, 1991.
El Kenz, David (ed.). *Le massacre, objet d'histoire*. Paris: Gallimard, 2005.
Elbourne, Elizabeth. 'The Sin of the Settler: The 1835–36 Select Committee on Aborigines
    and Debates Over Virtue and Conquest in the Early Nineteenth-Century British
    White Settler Empire', *Journal of Colonialism and Colonial History*, 4:3 (2003),
    1–49.
Eley, Geoff. *Forging Democracy: The History of the Left in Europe 1850–2000*. New York:
    Oxford University Press, 2002.
Faivre, Maurice, 'L'histoire des Harkis', *Guerres Mondiales et Conflits Contemporains*, 51
    (2001), 55–63.
Feldman, Allen. *Formations of Violence: The Narrative of the Body and Political Terror in
    Northern Ireland*. Chicago: University of Chicago Press, 1991.
Fels, Marie Hansen. *Good Men and True: The Aboriginal Police of the Port Phillip District
    1837–1853*. Carlton, Vic.: Melbourne University Press, 1988.
Finaldi, Giuseppe. 'The Italian Ethiopian War', in Gordon Martel (ed.), *A Companion to
    International History 1900–2001*. London: Blackwells, 2007, 220–32.
———. *Mussolini and Italian Fascism*. London: Pearson, 2008.
Finley, Milton. *The Most Monstrous of Wars: The Napoleonic Guerrilla War in Southern
    Italy, 1806–1811*. Columbia, S.C.: University of South Carolina Press, 1994.
Forrest, Alan. *Napoleon's Men. The Soldiers of the Revolution and Empire*. London:
    Hambledon and London, 2002.
Fuoss, Kirk W. 'Lynching Performances, Theatres of Violence', *Text and Performance
    Quarterly*, 19 (1999), 1–27.
Gardner, Peter Dean. *Gippsland Massacres: The Destruction of the Kurnai Tribes 1800–
    1860*, 3rd edn. Ensay, Vic.: Ngarak, 2001.
Geertz, Clifford. *The Religion of Java*. London: The University of Chicago Press, 1960.
———. *The Social History of an Indonesian Town*. Cambridge, Mass.: Massachusetts
    Institute of Technology, 1965.
Geldenhuys, Jannie. *A General's Story: From an Era of War and Peace*. Johannesburg:
    Jonathan Ball, 1995.
Gellately, Robert and Ben Kiernan (eds). *The Specter of Genocide: Mass Murder in
    Historical Perspective*. New York: Cambridge University Press, 2003.
Gentile, Emilio. *Fascismo di pietra*. Bari-Rome: Laterza, 2007.
George, Edward. *The Cuban Intervention in Angola, 1965–1991: From Che Guevera to
    Cuito Cuanavale*. London: Cass, 2005.
Getty, J. Arch and Oleg V. Naumov. *The Road to Terror: Stalin and the Self-Destruction of
    the Bolsheviks, 1932–1939*. New Haven, Conn.: Yale University Press, 1999.
Gewald, Jan-Bart. 'Who Killed Clemens Kapuuo?' *Journal of Southern African Studies*,
    30 (2004), 559–76.
Gittings, John. 'The Indonesian Massacres, 1965–1966: Image and Reality', in Mark
    Levene and Penny Roberts (eds), *The Massacre in History*. New York: Berghahn
    Books, 1999, 247–62.
Gooch, John. *Mussolini and His Generals: The Armed Forces and Fascist Foreign Policy,
    1922–1940*. Cambridge: Cambridge University Press, 2007.
Goodall, Jane. *The Chimpanzees of Gombe: Patterns of Behavior*. Cambridge, Mass.:
    Harvard University Press, 1986.

Goukowsky, Paul. *Diodore de Sicile Bibliothèque Historique: Livre XVII*. Paris: Les Belles Lettres, 1976.

Greengrass, Mark. 'Hidden Transcripts: Secret Histories and Personal Testimonies of Religious Violence in the French War of Religion', in Mark Levene and Penny Roberts (eds), *The Massacre in History*. New York: Berghahn Books, 1999, 69–88.

Grossman, Dave. *On Killing: The Psychological Cost of Learning to Kill in War and Society*. New York: Bay Back Books, 1996.

Hamoumou, Mohand. *Et ils sont devenus harkis*. Paris: Fayard, 1993.

———— and Jean-Jacques Jordi. *Les harkis, une mémoire enfouie*. Paris: Editions Autrement, 1999.

Harold, Christine and Kevin Michael DeLuca. 'Behold the Corpse: Violent Images and the Case of Emmet Till', *Rhetoric & Public Affairs*, 8 (2005), 263–86.

Harris, Cole, 'How Did Colonialism Dispossess? Comments from an Edge of Empire', *Annals of the Association of American Geographers*, 94 (2004), 165–82.

Hautreux, François-Xavier, 'L'engagement des Harkis (1954–1962): Essai de périodisation', *Vingtième Siècle*, 90 (2006), 33–45.

Herbstein, Denis and John Evenson. *The Devils are Among Us: The War for Namibia*. London: Zed Books, 1989.

Heryanto, Ariel. *State Terrorism and Political Identity in Indonesia: Fatally Belonging*. New York: Routledge, 2006.

Heywood, Annemarie. *The Cassinga Event: An Investigation of the Records*. Windhoek: National Archives of Namibia, 1994.

Hibbard, Caroline. *Charles I and the Popish Plot*. Chapel Hill: University of North Carolina Press, 1983.

Hildebrand, George C. and Gareth Porter. *Cambodia: Starvation and Revolution*. New York: Monthly Review Press, 1976.

Hoig, Stan. *The Sand Creek Massacre*. Norman: University of Oklahoma Press, 1961.

Holt. Frank L. *Into the Land of Bones: Alexander the Great in Afghanistan*. Berkeley: University of California Press, 2005.

Hornblower, Simon. *A Commentary on Thucydides: Volume III*. Oxford: Oxford University Press, 2008.

House, Jim. 'Antiracist Memories: The Case of 17 October 1961 in Historical Perspective', *Modern and Contemporary France*, 9:3 (2001), 355–68.

Howard, Michael. 'Constraints on Warfare', in Michael Howard, George Andreopoulos and Mark Shulman (eds), *The Laws of War: Constraints on Warfare in the Western World*. New Haven: Yale University Press, 1994, 1–11.

Humphrey, Michael. *The Politics of Atrocity and Reconciliation. From Terror to Trauma*. London: Routledge, 2002.

Hunt, David. 'Images of the Viet Cong', in Robert M. Slabey (ed.), *The United States and Viet Nam from War to Peace: Papers from an Interdisciplinary Conference on Reconciliation*. Jefferson, NC: McFarland & Company, 1996, 51–63.

Jensen, Richard. 'Big Foot's Followers at Wounded Knee', *Nebraska History*, 71:4 (Winter 1990), 194–212.

Kagan, Donald. *The Fall of the Athenian Empire*. Ithaca: Cornell University Press, 1989.

Kagan, Kimberly. *Eye of Command*. Ann Arbor: University of Michigan Press, 2006.

Kantrowitz, Stephen David. *Ben Tillman & the Reconstruction of White Supremacy*. Chapel Hill: University of North Carolina Press, 2000.

Karr, Ronald Dale. '"Why Should You Be So Furious?": The Violence of the Pequot War', *Journal of American History*, 85 (1998), 876–909.

Kearney, Hugh. *Strafford in Ireland 1633–41: A Study in Absolutism*, 2nd edn. Cambridge: Cambridge University Press, 1989.

Kennedy, Paul and George Andreopoulos. 'The Laws of War: Some Concluding Reflections', in Michael Howard, George Andreopoulos and Mark Shulman (eds), *The Laws of War: Constraints on Warfare in the Western World*. New Haven: Yale University Press, 1994, 214–25.

Kiernan, Ben. *Blood and Soil: A World History of Genocide and Extermination from Sparta to Darfur*. Melbourne: Melbourne University Press, 2008.

Knox, MacGregor. *Common Destiny: Dictatorship, Foreign Policy, and War in Fascist Italy and Nazi Germany*. Cambridge: Cambridge University Press, 2000.

———. *Hitler's Italian Allies: Royal Armed Forces, Fascist Regime, and the War of 1940-1943*. Cambridge: Cambridge University Press, 2000.

Kobo, Joseph. *Waiting in the Wing*. Milton Keynes: Word Publishing, 1994.

Konishi, Shino. 'The Father Governor: The British Administration of Aboriginal People at Port Jackson, 1788–1792', in Matthew McCormack (ed.), *Public Men: Political Masculinities in Modern Britain*. London: Palgrave Macmillan, 2007, 54–72.

Labanca, Nicola. *Una guerra per l'impero. Memorie della campagna d'Etiopia, 1935-6*. Bologna: il Mulino, 2005.

Larina, A. *This I Cannot Forget: the Memoirs of Nikolai Bukharin's Widow*. New York: W.W. Norton & Co, 1993.

Le Huu Dan. *Tuyen Tap Su That / Accounts of the Truth*. Fremont, Calif.: Xuat Ban Publishing Co., 1998.

Le Sueur, James D. *Uncivil War: Intellectuals and Identity Politics during the Decolonization of Algeria*. Philadelphia: University of Pennsylvania Press, 2001.

Lee, Wayne E. *Crowds and Soldiers in Revolutionary North Carolina: The Culture of Violence in Riot and War*. Gainesville, FL: University Press of Florida, 2001.

Lefkowitz, David. 'Collateral Damage', in Larry May (ed.), *War: Essays in Political Philosophy*. Cambridge: Cambridge University Press, 2008, 145–64.

Lemkin, Raphaël. *Axis Rule in Occupied Europe*. New York: Columbia University Press, 1944.

Lepore, Jill. *The Name of War: King Philip's War and the Origins of American Identity*. New York: Knopf, 1998.

Levene, Mark and Penny Roberts (eds). *The Massacre in History*. New York: Berghahn, 1999.

Lindley, Keith. 'The Impact of the 1641 Rebellion upon England and Wales', *Irish Historical Studies*, 18:70 (1972), 143–76.

Lindqvist, Sven. *A History of Bombing*. London: Granta Books, 2002.

Love, Walter D. 'Civil War in Ireland: Appearances in Three Centuries of Historical Writing', *The Emory University Quarterly*, 22 (1966), 57–72.

McCormack, Jo. *Collective Memory: France and the Algerian War (1954–1962)*. New York: Lexington Books, 2007.

McKerral, Andrew. *Kintyre in the Seventeenth Century*. Edinburgh: Oliver and Boyd, 1948.

MacLean, Nancy. 'The Leo Frank Case Reconsidered: Gender and Sexual Politics in the Making of Reactionary Populism', in Jane Dailey, Glenda Elizabeth Gilmore, and Bryant Simon (eds), *Jumpin' Jim Crow: Southern Politics from Civil War to Civil Rights*. Princeton: Princeton University Press, 2000, 183–218.

MacMaster, Neil, Jim House and Bruno Poncharal. 'La Fédération française du FLN et l'organisation du 17 octobre 1961', *Vingtième Siècle*, 83 (2004), 145–60.

Madley, Benjamin. 'From Terror to Genocide: Britain's Tasmanian Penal Colony and Australia's History Wars', *Journal of British Studies*, 47:1 (January 2008), 77–106.

Magnus, Ralph H. and Eden Naby. *Afghanistan: Mullah, Marx and Mujahid*. Boulder, Co.: Westview Press, 2002.

Malan, Magnus. *My Life with the SA Defence Force*. Pretoria: Protea Book House, 2006.

Mallett, Robert. *Mussolini and the Origins of the Second World War, 1933–1940*. Basingstoke: Palgrave-Macmillan, 2003.

Mann, Michael. *The Dark Side of Democracy: Explaining Ethnic Cleansing*. Cambridge: Cambridge University Press, 2005.

Martin, Jean-Clément. *Révolution et contre-révolution en France de 1789 à 1995*. Rennes: Presses universitaires de Rennes, 1996.

———. *Violence et Révolution. Essai sur la naissance d'un mythe national*. Paris: Seuil,

2006.

Mayeux, I. 'Harki, entre totem et tabou: Désastres et trouvailles d'une histoire collective refoulée et traumatique', *Pratiques Psychologiques*, 13:4 (2007), 443–57.

Meiggs, R. *The Athenian Empire*. Oxford: Oxford University Press, 1972.

Melber, Henning. 'Namibia's Past in the Present: Colonial Genocide and Liberation Struggle', *South African Historical Journal*, 54 (2005), 91–111.

Melville, Henry. *The History of Van Diemen's Land, From the Year 1824 to 1835*. Sydney: Horwitz-Grahame, 1965.

Meyer, Jack A. 'Wellington and the Sack of Badajoz: A "Beastly Mutiny" or a Deliberate Policy?', *Proceedings of the Consortium on Revolutionary Europe, 1750–1850*, (1991), 251–57.

Milfull, John. 'Decolonising Europe? The Colonial Boomerang', *Australian Journal of Politics and History*, 54 (2008), 464–68.

Morrill, John. *The Nature of the English Revolution: Essays by John Morrill*. London, New York: Longman, 1993.

———. 'How Oliver Cromwell Thought', in John Morrow and Jonathon Scott (eds), *Liberty, Authority, Formality: Political Ideas and Culture, 1600–1900*. Exeter: Imprint Academic, 2008, 89–111.

Mortimer, Rex. *The Indonesian Communist Party and Land Reform, 1959–1965*. Clayton, Vic: Monash University, 1972.

Moses, A. Dirk. 'The Non-German German and the German German: Dilemmas of Identity after the Holocaust', *New German Critique*, 34 (2007), 45–94.

——— (ed.). *Genocide and Settler Society: Frontier Violence and Stolen Indigenous Children in Australian History*. New York: Berghahn Books, 2004.

——— (ed.). *Empire, Colony, Genocide: Conquest, Occupation, and Subaltern Resistance in World History*. New York: Berghahn, 2008.

——— and Dan Stone (eds). *Colonialism and Genocide*. London: Routledge, 2007.

Moyar, Mark. 'A Call to Arms', *Passport: The Newsletter of the Society for Historians of American Foreign Relations*, 38:3 (December 2007), 17–22.

Murray, Keith. *The Modocs and their War*. Norman: University of Oklahoma Press, 1959.

Muthu, Sankar. *Enlightenment against Empire*. Princeton: Princeton University Press, 2003.

Namhila, Ellen Ndeshi. *The Price of Freedom*. Windhoek: New Namibia Books, 1997.

Nangola, Mvula Ya and Tor Sellström. *Kassinga: A Story Untold*. Windhoek: Namibia Book Development Council, 1995.

Nérard, François-Xavier. 'La mémoire de Boutovo, massacres de masse des années trente en Russie soviétique', in Luc Buchet and Isabelle Seguy (eds), *Vers une anthropologie des catastrophes: Actes des 9e journées d'anthropologie de Valbonne*. Antibes: Editions Apdca, 2008, 143–59.

Ngo Vinh Long and Daniel C. Tsang. 'Vietnam Today', *Critical Asian Studies*, 34:3 (2002), 459–64.

Oliver, Kendrick. *The My Lai Massacre in American History and Memory*. Manchester: Manchester University Press, 2006.

Ostler, Jeffrey. *The Plains Sioux and U.S. Colonialism from Lewis and Clark to Wounded Knee*. Cambridge: Cambridge University Press, 2004.

Outram, Quentin. 'The Demographic Impact of Early Modern Warfare', *Social Science History*, 26:2 (2002), 245–72.

Palmer, Alison. *Colonial Genocide*. Adelaide: Crawford House, 2000.

Paperno, Irina. 'Exhuming the Bodies of Soviet Terror', *Representations*, 75 (2001), 89–118.

Péju, Marcel and Jacques Charby. *Les porteurs d'espoir*. Paris La Découverte, 2004.

Péju, Paulette. *Ratonnades à Paris* précédé de *Les Harkis à Paris*. Paris: La Découverte, 2000.

Penn, Nigel. *Forgotten Frontier: Colonist and Khoisan on the Capes Northern Frontier in the 18th Century*. Athens: Ohio University Press, 2005.

Perceval–Maxwell, M. *The Outbreak of the Irish Rebellion*. Dublin: Gill and Macmillan 1994.

Perlmutter, David. *Photojournalism and Foreign Policy: Icons of Outrage in International Crises*. Westport, Conn.: Praeger, 1998.

Phelps, Teresa. *Shattered Voices: Language, Violence and the Work of Truth Commissions*. Philadelphia: University of Pennsylvania Press, 2004.

Planche, Jean-Louis. *Sétif 1945, histoire d'un massacre annoncé*. Paris: Perrin, 2006.

Plomley, N.J.B. (ed.). *Weep in Silence: A History of the Flinders Island Aboriginal Settlement*. Hobart: Blubber Head Press, 1987.

———. *Jorgen Jorgenson and the Aborigines of Van Diemen's Land*. Hobart: Blubber Head Press, 1991.

Porter, D. Gareth. 'The 1968 "Hue Massacre"', *Indochina Chronicle*, 33 (24 June 1974), 2–13.

Posel, Deborah. 'Symbolizing Violence: State and Media Discourse in Television Coverage of Township Protest, 1985–7', in Noel Chabani Manganyi and Andre du Toit (eds), *Political Violence and the Struggle in South Africa*. Basingstoke: Macmillan, 1990, 154–71.

Powell, Anton. 'Julius Caesar and his Presentation of Massacre', in Anton Powell and Kathryn Welch (eds), *Julius Caesar as Artful Reporter: the War Commentaries as Political Instruments*. London: Duckworth with the Classical Press of Wales, 1988, 115–24.

Preston, David L. *The Texture of Contact: European and Indian Settler Communities on the Frontiers of Iroquoia, 1667–1783*. Lincoln, NE: University of Nebraska Press, 2009.

Pritchard, David. 'War and Democracy in Ancient Athens: A Preliminary Report', *Classicum*, 31:1 (2005), 16–25.

Pritchett, William Kendrick. *The Greek State at War: Part V*. Berkeley: University of California Press, 1991.

Rae-Ellis, Vivienne. *Black Robinson: Protector of the Aborigines*. Carlton, Vic.: Melbourne University Press, 1988.

Rambaud, Michel. *L'Art de la Déformation Historique dans les Commentaires de César*. Paris: Les Belles Lettres, 1953.

Rashid, Ahmed. *Descent into Chaos: The U.S. and the Disaster in Pakistan, Afghanistan, and Central Asia*. New York: Penguin Books, 2009.

Rees, Laurence. *Their Darkest Hour*. London: Ebury Press, 2008.

Renfrew, Colin and Malcolm Wagstaff (eds). *An Island Polity: The Archaeology of Exploration in Melos*. Cambridge: Cambridge University Press, 1982.

Reynolds, Henry. *The Other Side of the Frontier*. Ringwood, Vic.: Penguin, 1982.

———. *Fate of a Free People: A Radical Reexamination of the Tasmanian Wars*. Ringwood: Penguin Books, 1995.

Richards, Jonathan. 'The Native Police of Queensland', *History Compass*, 6:4 (May 2008), 1024–36.

Riggsby, Andrew M. *Caesar in Gaul and Rome*. Austin: University of Texas Press, 2006.

Roberts, Tony. *Frontier Justice: A History of the Gulf Country to 1900*. St. Lucia: University of Queensland Press, 2005.

Rochat, Giorgio. 'L'attentato a Graziani e la repressione italiana in Etiopia nel 1936–37', *Italia Contemporanea*, 118 (1975), 3–38.

Rochijat, Pipit. 'Am I PKI or Non-PKI?', trans. by Benedict Anderson, *Indonesia*, 40 (1985), 37–56.

Rockel, Stephen J. '"Collateral Damage": A Comparative History', in Stephen J. Rockel and Rick Halpern (eds), *Inventing Collateral Damage: Civilian Casualties, War and Empire*. Toronto: Between-the-Lines Press, 2009, 1–93.

——— and Rick Halpern (eds). *Inventing Collateral Damage: Civilian Casualties, War and Empire*. Toronto: Between-the-Lines Press, 2009.

Rodogno, Davide. *Fascism's European Empire: Italian Occupation During the Second World War*. Cambridge: Cambridge University Press, 2006.

Rose, Charles Brian. 'The Tombs of the Granicus River Valley', in Inci Delemen (ed.), *The Achaemenid Impact on Local Populations and Cultures in Anatolia*. Istanbul: Turkish Institute of Archaeology, 2007, 247–64.

Ross, James. *The Settler in Van Diemen's Land*. Melbourne: Marsh Walsh, 1975.

Rothenberg, Daniel. '"What We Have Seen Has Been Terrible". Public Presentational Torture and the Communicative Logic of State Terror', *Albany Law Review*, 67 (2003–2004), 465–99.

Rousselet, Kathy. 'Butovo: La création d'un lieu de pèlerinages sur une terre de massacres', *Politix*, 20 (2007), 55–78.

———. 'Les mémoires de la Grande Terreur: Butovo', in Marie-Claude Maurel and François Mayer (eds), *L'Europe et ses représentations du passé. Les tourments de la mémoire*. Paris: L'Harmattan, 2008, 131–45.

Rousso, Henry. *Le Syndrome de Vichy*. Paris: Seuil, 1987.

Roy, Ian. 'England turned Germany? The Aftermath of the Civil War in its European Context', *Transactions of the Royal Historical Society*, 28 (1978), 127–44.

Ruff, Julius R. *Violence in Early Modern Europe*. Cambridge: Cambridge University Press, 2001.

Ryan, Lyndall. *The Aboriginal Tasmanians*. Vancouver: University of British Columbia Press, 1981.

Sabin, Philip. 'Face of Roman Battle', *Journal of Roman Studies*, 90 (2000), 1–17.

Sadosky, Leonard. 'Rethinking the Gnadenhütten Massacre: The Contest for Power in the Public World of the Revolutionary Frontier', in David Curtis Skaggs and Larry L. Nelson (eds), *The Sixty Years' War for the Great Lakes, 1754–1814*, East Lansing: Michigan State University Press, 2001, 187–214.

Scarry, Elaine. *The Body in Pain: The Making and Unmaking of the World*. New York: Oxford University Press, 1985.

Schabas, W.A. *Genocide in International Law*. Cambridge: Cambridge University Press, 2000.

Schilling, Heinz. 'Die konfessionellen Glaubenskriege und die Formierung des frühmodernen Europa', in Peter Herrmann (ed.), *Glaubenskriege in Vergangenheit und Gegenwart*. Göttingen: Vandenhoeck and Ruprecht, 1996, 123–37.

Schivelbusch, Wolgang. *The Culture of Defeat: On National Trauma, Mourning, and Recovery*. London: Granta, 2004.

Selden, Mark. 'A Forgotten Holocaust: U.S. Bombing Strategy, the Destruction of Japanese Cities, and the American Way of War from the Pacific War to Iraq', in Yuki Tanaka and Marilyn B. Young (eds), *Bombing Civilians: A Twentieth Century History*. New York and London: New Press, 2009, 77–96.

Semelin, Jacques. 'In Consideration of Massacre', *Journal of Genocide Research*, 3:3 (2001), 377–89.

———. 'Towards a Vocabulary of Massacre and Genocide', *Journal of Genocide Studies*, 5:2 (2003), 193–210.

———. *Purify and Destroy: The Political Uses of Massacre and Genocide*. London: Hurst and Company, 2007.

Shagan, Ethan Howard. 'Constructing Discord: Ideology, Propaganda, and English Responses to the Irish Rebellion of 1641', *Journal of British Studies*, 36:1 (1997), 4–34.

Shaw, Martin. *The New Western Way of War: Risk-Transfer War and its Crisis in Iraq*. Cambridge, Mass.: Polity, 2005.

Simms, Hilary. 'Violence in County Armagh, 1641', in B. Mac Cuarta (ed.), *Ulster 1641: Aspects of the Rising*. Belfast: Queen's University of Belfast 1993, 123–38.

Slotkin, Richard. *Regeneration through Violence: The Mythology of the American Frontier, 1600–1860*. Middletown, CT: Wesleyan University Press, 1973.

Smith, Anthony D. *Chosen Peoples: Sacred Sources of National Identity*. Oxford: Oxford University Press, 2003.

Smith, Thomas W. 'Protecting Civilians ... or Soldiers? Humanitarian Law and the Economy of Risk in Iraq', *International Studies Perspectives*, 9 (2008), 144–64.

Spencer, Stephen. *Race and Ethnicity: Culture, Identity and Representation*. London and New York: Routledge, 2006.

Steele, Ian Kenneth. *Betrayals: Fort William Henry and the Massacre*. New York: Oxford University Press, 1990.

Steenkamp, Willem. *Borderstrike! South Africa into Angola*. 3rd edn. Durban: Just Done Publications, 2006.

Stone, Dan. *Constructing the Holocaust: A Study in Historiography*. London: Vallentine Mitchell, 2003.

—— (ed.). *History, Memory and Mass Atrocity: Essays on the Holocaust and Genocide*. London: Vallentine Mitchell, 2006.

—— (ed.). *The Historiography of Genocide*. London: Palgrave Macmillan, 2008.

Stora, Benjamin. *Le livre, mémoire de l'histoire: réflexions sur le livre et la guerre d'Algérie*. Paris: Préau des collines, 2005.

——. *La guerre des mémoires: la France face à son passé colonial (conversations with Thierry Leclère)*. La Tour d'Aigues: Aube, 2007.

Stoyle, Mark. *Soldiers and Strangers: An Ethnic History of the English Civil War*. New Haven: Yale University Press, 2005.

Stuart, George. *Bret Harte, Argonaut and Exile*. Boston: Houghton Mifflin Company, 1931.

Tal, Kali. *Worlds of Hurt: Reading the Literatures of Trauma*. Cambridge: Cambridge University Press, 1996.

Talbert, Richard J.A. (ed.). *Barrington Atlas of the Greek and Roman World*. Princeton: Princeton University Press, 2000.

Tanaka, Yuki. 'British "Humane Bombing" in Iraq during the Interwar Era', in Yuki Tanaka and Marilyn B. Young (eds), *Bombing Civilians: A Twentieth Century History*. New York and London: New Press, 2009, 8–29.

—— and Marilyn B. Young (eds). *Bombing Civilians: A Twentieth Century History*. New York and London: New Press, 2009.

Tapper, Nancy. *Bartered Brides: Politics, Gender and Marriage in an Afghan Tribal Society*. Cambridge: Cambridge University Press, 1991.

Taussig, Michael. 'Culture of Terror – Space of Death: Roger Casement's Putumayo Report and the Explanation of Torture', *Comparative Studies in Society and History*, 26 (1984), 467–97.

Tolney, Stewart E. and E.M. Beck. *A Festival of Violence: An Analysis of Southern Lynchings, 1882–1930*. Urbana: University of Illinois Press, 1995.

Trevelyan, George Macaulay. *England under the Stuarts*. London: Routledge, 2002.

Uekert, Brenda K. *Rivers of Blood: A Comparative Study of Government Massacres*. Westport, Conn.: Praeger, 1995.

Valat, Rémy. *Les Calots bleus, Histoire d'une police auxiliaire pendant la Guerre d'Algérie*. Paris: Ed. Michalon, 2007.

van Langenberg, Michael. 'Gestapu and State Power in Indonesia', in Robert Cribb (ed.), *The Indonesian Killings of 1965–1966: Studies from Java and Bali*. Clayton, Vic: Monash University, 1990, 45–62.

Vaughan, Alden. 'Frontier Banditti and the Indians: The Paxton Boys' Legacy', *Pennsylvania History*, 51:1 (1984), 1–29.

Vidal-Naquet, Pierre. *Torture dans la République*. Paris: Editions de Minuit, 1998.

——. 'Préface', in Paulette Péju, *Ratonnades à Paris précédé de Les Harkis à Paris*. Paris: La Découverte, 2000, 5–19.

Vigarello, Georges. *A History of Rape: Sexual Violence in France from the 16th to the 20th Century*. Malden, Mass.: Polity Press, 2001.

Walser, Gerold. *Bellum Helveticum*. Stuttgart: Franz Steiner Verlag, 1998.

Waswo, Richard. *The Founding Legend of Western Civilization: From Virgil to Vietnam*. Hanover: Wesleyan University Press, 1997.

Watts, N.H., trans. *Cicero, the Speeches*. Cambridge, Mass.: Harvard University Press, 1931.

Weaver, John C. *The Great Land Rush and the Making of the Modern World: 1650–1800*. Montreal: McGill-Queen's University Press, 2003.

Wees, H. Van. *Greek Warfare; Myths and Realities*. London: Duckworth Academic and Bristol Classical Press, 2004.

—— (ed.). *War and Violence in Ancient Greece*. London: Duckworth and the Classical Press of Wales, 2000.

Werth, Nicolas. 'Les "opérations de masse" de la "Grande Terreur" en URSS, 1937–1938', *Bulletin de l'IHTP*, 86 (2006), 6–167.

——. *L'ivrogne et la marchande de fleurs: autopsie d'un meurtre de masse*. Paris: Tallandier, 2009.

White, Richard. *The Middle Ground: Indians, Empires, and Republics in the Great Lakes Region, 1650–1815*. New York: Cambridge University Press, 1991.

Whitehead, David and P.H. Blyth. *Athenaeus Mechanicus, On Machines. Historia Einzelschriften 182*. Stuttgart: Franz Steiner, 2004.

Whitehead, Neil L. 'On the Poetics of Violence', in Neil L. Whitehead (ed.), *Violence*. Santa Fe, NM: School of American Research Press, 2004, 55–79.

Wieringa, Saskia E. 'Sexual Metaphors in the Change from Soekarno's Old Order to Soeharto's New Order in Indonesia', *Review of Indonesian and Malaysian Affairs*, 32 (1998), 143–78.

Windschuttle, Keith. *The Fabrication of Aboriginal History: Volume One, Van Diemen's Land, 1803–1847*. Sydney: Macleay Press, 2002.

Wirth, G. and O. von Hinüber. *Der Alexanderzug Indische Geschichichte*. Munich: Artemis Verlag, 1985.

Woell, Edward J. *Small-Town Martyrs and Murderers: Religious Revolution and Counterrevolution in Western France, 1774–1914*. Milwaukee, Wis.: Marquette University Press, 2006.

Wolfe, Patrick. 'Settler Colonialism and the Elimination of the Native', *Journal of Genocide Research*, 8:4 (2006), 387–409.

Wrage, Stephen D. 'The Ethics of Precision Air Power', in Stephen D. Wrage (ed.), *Immaculate Warfare: Participants Reflect on the Air Campaigns over Kosovo and Afghanistan*. Westport, Conn.: Praeger, 2003, 85–100.

Yardley, John and R. Develin. *Justin: Epitome of the Philippic History of Pompeius Trogus*. Atlanta: Scholars Press, 1994.

—— and Waldemar Waldemar. *Justin: Epitome of the Philippic History of Pompeius Trogus, vol. 1, Books 11–12*. Oxford: Oxford University Press, 1997.

Young, Kenneth R. 'Local and National Influences in the Violence of 1965', in Robert Cribb (ed.), *The Indonesian Killings of 1965–1966: Studies from Java and Bali*. Clayton, Vic: Monash University, 1990, 63–100.

Young, Marilyn B. *The Vietnam Wars, 1945–1990*. New York: HarperPerennial, 1991.

Zemon Davis, Natalie. 'The Rites of Violence: Religious Riot in Sixteenth–Century France', *Past and Present*, 59 (1973), 55–59.

Zukier, Henri. 'The Twisted Road to Genocide: On the Psychological Development of Evil during the Holocaust', *Social Research*, 61 (1994), 423–55.

NOTES ON CONTRIBUTORS

Gary Baines is an Associate Professor in the History Department, Rhodes University, South Africa. He has published extensively on the history of Port Elizabeth and is the author of *A History of New Brighton, Port Elizabeth, 1903–1953: The Detroit of the Union* (Lewiston, NY, 2002). He is currently researching South Africa's 'Border War' about which he has written a number of articles and an edited collection (with Peter Vale), *Beyond the Border War: New Perspectives on Southern Africa's Late Cold War Conflicts* (Pretoria, 2008).

Elizabeth Baynham is Senior Lecturer in the School of Humanities and Social Science, University of Newcastle, Australia. Her research interests include the history and historiography of Alexander the Great, especially the Roman sources, Quintus Curtius Rufus, Justin and the Metz Epitome. Her books include *Alexander the Great: The Unique History of Quintus Curtius* (Ann Arbor, 1998); and (with Brian Bosworth) *Alexander the Great in Fact and Fiction* (Oxford, 2000). She is currently working (with John Yardley) on a translation and commentary on the Metz Epitome for the Clarendon Ancient History series.

Jane Bellemore is a Senior Lecturer in Greek, Latin and Ancient History at the University of Newcastle, Australia. She has published widely on the historiography of the Late Roman Republic and Early Empire. Her articles have appeared in *Antichthon*, *Klio*, and the *Classical Quarterly*.

Brian Bosworth is Professor of Ancient History at Macquarie University, Professor Emeritus of Classics and Ancient History, University of Western Australia, and Conjoint Professor of Classics at the University of Newcastle, Australia. He is a leading researcher in Greek and Roman history and a world authority on the era of Alexander the Great and its historiography, especially Arrian. He has published seven books, including two distinguished commentaries on Arrian's history, *Conquest and Empire: the Reign of Alexander the Great* (Cambridge, 1988); *From Arrian to Alexander* (Oxford, 1988); *Alexander and the East* (Oxford, 1996); and *The Legacy of Alexander* (Oxford, 2002).

John Docker is an honorary professor in the Department of History at the University of Sydney. He is the author of *1492: The Poetics of Diaspora* (London, New York, 2001) and (with Ann Curthoys) *Is History Fiction?* (Sydney, 2005). He has written on genocide in relation to Raphael Lemkin, colonialism, and the Enlightenment, and published *The Origins of Violence: Religion, History and Genocide* (Sydney, 2008).

Philip Dwyer is Associate Professor in Modern European History at the University of Newcastle, Australia. He has published widely on the revolutionary and Napoleonic eras. He is the editor of *Napoleon and Europe* (London, 2001), and (with Alan Forrest) *Napoleon and His Empire: Europe 1804–1814* (London, 2007). His *Napoleon: The Path to Power, 1769–1799* (London, 2007 and New Hampshire, 2008), won the National Biography Award. He is currently working on the sequel.

Giuseppe Finaldi is Associate Professor of history at the University of Western Australia. He is the author of *Mussolini and Italian Fascism* (London, 2008) and *Italian National Identity in the Scramble for Africa* (Bern, 2009) and is currently writing a history of the Italian Empire.

Rob Harper is an Assistant Professor of History at the University of Wisconsin-Stevens Point. During 2009–2010, he was an Andrew W. Mellon Foundation/ACLS Recent Doctoral Recipients Fellow at the Institute for Research in the Humanities at the University of Wisconsin-Madison. His work has appeared in the *William and Mary Quarterly* and the *Journal for Genocide Research*. He is currently writing a book tentatively entitled *Politics Ungoverned: Coalition Building and Colonialism on a Revolutionary Frontier*.

Hélène Jaccomard is Professor in French Studies at the University of Western Australia. She researches in the theory and practice of contemporary autobiographies, testimonials, and fiction. Her interest in the Algerian War stems from her examination of the growing Franco-Maghrebine literature. She is the author of three articles on the Algerian War seen through the eyes of Mehdi Charef, Azouz Begag, Tahar ben Jelloun and Nini Bouraoui amongst others, which appeared in *Nottingham French Studies, Australian Journal of French Studies*, and *Essays in French Literature*.

Inga Jones is a postdoctoral research fellow at the University of Sussex. Her main research interests include religious, political and military developments in early modern Europe, and especially the effect religion had on the conduct of war during the seventeenth and eighteenth centuries. She is an associate editor of the *Minutes and Papers of the Westminster Assembly*, and is currently finalising *'A Sea of Blood?' A Comparative Study of Massacres during the Wars of the Three Kingdoms, 1641–53*.

Scott Laderman is Associate Professor of History at the University of Minnesota, Duluth. He is the author of *Tours of Vietnam: War, Travel Guides, and Memory* (Durham, NC, 2009). His work has appeared in several edited collections and in the *Pacific Historical Review*, the *Historical Journal of Film, Radio, and Television*, and a number of other publications. He is currently writing a book entitled *Empire in Waves: Surfing, Surf Culture, and U.S. Foreign Relations*.

Benjamin Madley is an Andrew W. Mellon Postdoctoral Fellow in the Department of History and the Native American Studies Program at Dartmouth College. He earned his Ph.D. from Yale University and his work has appeared in the *European History Quarterly*, the *Journal of Genocide Research*, the *Journal of British Studies*, and *The Western Historical Quarterly*. He is currently working on a book entitled *American Genocide: The California Indian Catastrophe, 1846–1873*.

Laurence W. Marvin is Professor of History at Berry College, Mt. Berry Georgia, and is a specialist in medieval warfare and crusade history. His articles have appeared in *The Journal of Medieval History, War in History, The Historian* and *Viator*. He is the author of *The Occitan War: A Military and Political History of the Albigensian Crusade, 1209–1218* (Cambridge, 2008).

François-Xavier Nérard is an Assistant Professor at the Université de Bourgogne, France. He is an associate member of the CERCEC (Centre for Research on Russia, the Caucasus and Eastern Europe) in Paris. He has published numerous articles on the history of Stalinist Russia and is the author of *Cinq pour cent de vérité* (Paris, 2004) on denunciations in the USSR during the 1930s. He is currently working on the memory of violence in the USSR, especially in the Leningrad region, and is editing a book on victims' sites of memory in Europe (sixteenth to twenty-first centuries).

Annie Pohlman is Program Leader for Southeast Asia at the Asia-Pacific Centre for the Responsibility to Protect. Based at the University of Queensland, it is a research and advocacy centre for the prevention of genocide and mass atrocities in the region. Her areas of publication include Indonesian history, genocide studies, torture, gendered experiences of violence, testimony, Southeast Asian history and politics, and the prevention of mass atrocities.

Stephen J. Rockel is an Associate Professor of History at the University of Toronto. He specializes in East African social history, and in colonial and postcolonial conflicts in Africa and Asia. His book, *Carriers of Culture: Labor on the Road in Nineteenth-Century East Africa* (Portsmouth, N.H., 2006), was awarded the Joel Gregory Prize. He recently edited (with Rick Halpern) *Inventing Collateral Damage: Civilian Casualties, War and Empire* (Toronto, 2009).

Lyndall Ryan is Conjoint Professor of History in the School of Humanities & Social Sciences at the University of Newcastle. Her classic text, *The Aboriginal Tasmanians,* first published in 1981, opened up the field of colonial frontier violence in Australia. Since then she has published widely on settler massacres on the Australian colonial frontier. She is also the author of *The Tasmanian Aborigines: A History since 1803* (Sydney, 2012).

Katrina Schlunke teaches cultural studies at the University of Technology, Sydney. She is the author of the monograph *Bluff Rock. Autobiography of a Massacre* (Fremantle, 2005), and numerous articles on Indigenous massacres and their memorials including 'More than Memory. Performing Place and Postcoloniality at the Myall Creek Massacre Memorial', in Gay McAuley (ed.), *Unstable Ground: Performance and the Politics of Place* (Brussels, 2006). She is currently working on a project looking at Captain Cook in the popular Australian imagination, as well as writing about the seen/unseen massacre in film. She co-edits the *Cultural Studies Review* and is Deputy Director of the Transforming Cultures Research Centre.

Blanca Tovías is a University of Sydney Postdoctoral Research Fellow. Her research interests include the history, ethnology, and literature of the First Nations of the Great Plains. She is one of two managing editors of the *Journal of Iberian and Latin American Research*. She has co-edited (with David Cahill) *New World, First Nations: Native Peoples of Mesoamerica and the Andes under Colonial Rule* (Brighton, 2006); and *Elites Indígenas en los Andes: Nobles, Caciques y Cabildantes bajo el Yugo Colonial* (Lima, 2003). She is the author of *Colonialism on the Prairies: Blackfoot Settlement and Cultural Transformation, 1870–1920* (Brighton, 2011).

Claudia Weber is a researcher at the Hamburg Institute for Social Research, Germany. She also teaches East European history at Leipzig University and University of Basel (Switzerland). She is the author of *Auf der Suche nach der Nation. Erinnerungskultur in Bulgarien 1878–1944* (Berlin and Münster, 2006) and has published several articles on war memory in the Balkans as well as on violence and Stalinism. She is currently writing a book on ideology and the communication of the Katyn Forest Massacre and Stalinist terror in Europe during the Cold War.

INDEX

CSSS

A

Aberdeen, Battle at 65–7, 68, 69
Aboriginal people
    Aboriginal Protectorate 95, 97, 104–5,
        107
    Aboriginal resistance model 97
    decimation in Victoria of 95, 107–8
    disease introduced by settlers,
        Aboriginal deaths from 97
    eradication in Victoria of 98, 101–2
    massacre sites in Victoria, Australia 94
    Tasmania, massacres against
        Aborigines in 112–13
    in Victoria, Broome's history of 95,
        96–7, 107
Abramenko, Andrik 35
Accuracy in Media 221
Ackland, Len 217
Ada, Queen of Caria 34
Addis Ababa massacre (February, 1937)
    245–9, 256
    acts of reprisal, call for cessation from
        Fascist party leader 248–9
    eyewitness accounts 247–8
    Fascist character of 246–7
    'squadism' in 247–8
Aegospotami, executions of prisoners at
    17–19, 20, 22, 23, 24n9
Aeneid (Virgil) 12
Afghanistan, wedding massacres and war
    in 271–82

advanced technology, coalition
    dependence on 280–82
*Air Arm in Iraq, Note on the Method
    of Employment of* (Iraq High
    Commissioner, 1924) 273
air strikes 272
bombing in imperial warfare 273
'collateral damage' 281
connections between bombing
    examples 280–82
Deh Rawud district, massacre of
    wedding guests (July, 2002) 271–2,
    281
genocide 272
The Guardian 276, 279, 282n1,
    283n24, 284n37
Human Rights Watch 281
indiscriminate nature of 'air policing'
    273–4
Institute of War and Peace Reporting
    (IWPR) 278–9
Iraq (1920s), experimental 'air
    policing' in 273–4
Ka Chona/Khetai, Deh Bala district,
    massacre of wedding guests (July,
    2008) 277–9, 281
marriage ceremonies, practical politics
    and 279–80
'merciful' nature of bombing 274
Pashtun culture, marriage and
    weddings in 279–80

War and Genocide

General Editors: Omer Bartov, Brown University; A. Dirk Moses, European University Institute, Florence, Italy/University of Sydney

There has been a growing interest in the study of war and genocide, not from a traditional military history perspective, but within the framework of social and cultural history. This series offers a forum for scholarly works that reflect these new approaches.

"The Berghahn series Studies on War and Genocide *has immeasurably enriched the English-language scholarship available to scholars and students of genocide and, in particular, the Holocaust."*—**Totalitarian Movements and Political Religions**